Transnationalism and the Asian American Heroine

Transnationalism and the Asian American Heroine

Essays on Literature, Film, Myth and Media

Edited by LAN DONG

McFarland & Company, Inc., Publishers
Jefferson, North Carolina, and London

Portions of Catherine Gomes' essay were published originally in *Reception: Texts, Readers, Audiences, History.* Vol. 1, fall 2008: 82–86, and are reprinted with permission.

LIBRARY OF CONGRESS CATALOGUING-IN-PUBLICATION DATA

Transnationalism and the Asian American heroine : essays on literature, film, myth and media / edited by Lan Dong.
    p.   cm.
Includes bibliographical references and index.

ISBN 978-0-7864-4632-2
softcover : 50# alkaline paper ∞

1. American fiction — Asian American authors — History and criticism.   2. American fiction — Women authors — History and criticism   3. Asian American women in literature.   4. Asian American women in motion pictures.   5. Asian American women — Intellectual life.   6. Transnationalism in literature.   7. Feminism in literature.   I. Dong, Lan, 1974–
PS153.A84T75   2010
813'.54093522 — dc22   2010037322

British Library cataloguing data are available

© 2010 Lan Dong. All rights reserved

No part of this book may be reproduced or transmitted in any form or by any means, electronic or mechanical, including photocopying or recording, or by any information storage and retrieval system, without permission in writing from the publisher.

Front and back cover illustration © 2010 Shutterstock

Manufactured in the United States of America

McFarland & Company, Inc., Publishers
  Box 611, Jefferson, North Carolina 28640
    www.mcfarlandpub.com

Acknowledgments

My gratitude goes to the College of Liberal Arts and Sciences at the University of Illinois–Springfield and my friends and colleagues who have supported me in various ways while this book took shape. Thanks to Nicole Overcash for her superb editorial assistance. I want to thank the contributors, whose scholarship on heroism, feminism, transnationalism, and Asian American literature and culture opened my eyes on many levels and whose locations on different continents represent the transnational scope of this collection.

Finally, yet importantly, I owe a debt of gratitude to my family who, as always, has been patient and supportive when I was "spirited away" by work.

I wish the reader the pleasure of discovery that I experienced while reading the articles gathered in this collection.

TABLE OF CONTENTS

Acknowledgments v

Introduction: Heroines of Transnational Asian America
   Lan Dong   1

Part I: Myth, History and Beyond

Of Princesses Pari and Fox Girls: Nora Okja Keller's Transnational Performance of Korean Histories and Myths
   Silvia Schultermandl   9

Water Birth: Domestic Violence and Monstrosity in Hiromi Goto's *The Kappa Child*
   Nancy Kang   26

Between Ruination and Reconciliation: Dragon Princesses, Cambodian American Heroines, and Loung Ung's *Lucky Child*
   Cathy J. Schlund-Vials   46

Part II: Battles, Rituals and Worship

From Female Self-Sacrifice to Korean Freedom Fighter: Yu Guan Soon in Theresa Cha's *Dictée*
   Karen An-hwei Lee   63

Merlinda Bobis: The Transnational Filipina Warrior Between the Postcolonial Exotic and the *Babaylan/Catalonan*
   Marie-Therese C. Sulit   82

Mulan Against Gwan Gung: Performing Myths on a Transnational Stage
   Lan Dong   103

Part III: Multination, Transnation and Communities

Re-Imagining Happily-Ever-After in Bharati Mukherjee's *Jasmine*
  Amy N. Nishimura   118

Adopting a Different Posture and Relocating One's Roots: The Trung Legend in Vietnamese American Narratives
  Tina Lynn Powell   134

The Nicole Subic Rape Case and the *Chingada* in the Philippine Imaginary
  Danicar Mariano   152

Part IV: (Un)Spoken Subjects, Cross-Cultural Heroines and Media

Lost in Translation: American Critical Audience and the Transnational Chinese Swordswoman
  Catherine Gomes   168

Phoolan Devi: The Primordial Tradition of the Bandit Queen
  J. Sunita Peacock   187

Translating Mother's Tongue(s) and Traveling Bodies: Palimpsest and Diaspora in Maxine Hong Kingston's *The Woman Warrior*
  Pei-Ju Wu   203

About the Contributors   221

Index   225

INTRODUCTION
Heroines of Transnational Asian America
Lan Dong

Critical discussions on the intersection between transnationalism and Asian American and Asian diaspora women inspired this collection. Beginning in the 1990s, scholars in Asian American and Asian diaspora studies have articulated the need to widen the traditional focus within national boundaries to a transnational framework as a result of globalization, "a process that denied the centrality of the nation-state" (Lee and Shibusawa vii). Since then, many scholars have embraced a transnational approach in Asian American and Asian diaspora studies (for example, Liu 137–40; Lee and Shibusawa vii; Daiya 265; Elliott 14–15). Collectively this project is an attempt to explore the connections between transnationalism and Asian American and Asian diaspora women and to discuss particular texts, characters, and thematic threads at the crossroads of Asian American studies and transnational feminism. As Nina Glick Schiller states, transnational refers to "political, economic, social and cultural processes that extend beyond the borders of a particular state, include actors that are not states, but are shaped by the policies and institutional practices of states" (96). Although the essays gathered here do not always agree on the use of transnationalism as a concept, all of them examine the possibilities and challenges in transnational Asian America, exploring how certain cultural products approach the issues of gender and sexuality central to feminist discourse and how they intersectionally engage with questions of nation-state, globalization, race, and ethnicity as part of transnational Asian American narratives.

Immigrants bring values, perspectives, and resources with them to a new land; in the process of their cultural adaptation, particular continuities and discontinuities, modifications and transformations of traditional practices, as well as the invention of new cultural practices may occur (Ng Intro ix). Transnational migration thus is "inextricably linked to the forces of global capitalism ... constantly across borders." Within this context Asians who migrated to the

United States maintain many "transnational practices" (Hu-Dehart Intro 9). Sau-ling C. Wong and Jeffrey J. Santa Ana's review essay not only provides an overview of representations of gender and sexuality in Asian American literature within the context of Asian American cultural criticism and history, but also renders the relationality of gender, race, and ethnicity. As they have stated, Asian Americanness, gender, and sexuality "cannot be considered independent of one another, nor can they be regarded as merely additive isolates" (Wong and Santa Ana 172). Some essays in this volume take up heretofore underrepresented texts or characters. Their marginality or absence is linked to the centrality and visibility of more dominant stories. Others attempt to recuperate influential works in Asian American and Asian diaspora studies that unsettle and challenge established epistemological boundaries and categories.

This book is structured according to themes that highlight the ways in which history, worship, community, and media representation are interlaced. The essays seek to interrogate the very meanings and implications of transnational Asian American women. The three essays in Part I, "Myth, History and Beyond," center on mythologized history and historicized myth reflected in the selected literary texts. Silvia Schultermandl takes on a transnational approach in looking at Nora Okja Keller's references to myths and shamanism in her fiction. She argues that in Keller's novels *Comfort Woman* (1997) and *Fox Girl* (2002), the transnational performance of Korean history and myth is entangled with the feminist nature of the powerful tradition of shamanism. Through the complexity and cultural hybridization of her characters, Keller inserts her politics of location as a biracial Hawaiian writer. In her essay, Schultermandl examines specifically how transnational appropriation, such as Keller's, demands from the reader sensitivity to the multiple locations of subjectivity from which Keller's writing derives. As Schultermandl's analysis indicates, Keller's fiction challenges the reader to trace the references of traditional myths among Korea, Hawai'i and the U.S. mainland, thus providing an example of "complex, dialogical national and transnational formulations of Asian American imaginations" (Lim et al 2). Arguing that myth as a symbolic gesture originates in Korean culture — yet reverberates in a global world in Keller's storytelling — Schultermandl opens up new areas of scholarly inquiry by questioning how events on the local level are shaped by global power structures. In this sense, her analysis of Keller's novels provides a "gendered understanding of globalization" (Freeman 1010).

Nancy Kang demonstrates how Japanese Canadian writer Hiromi Goto's novel *The Kappa Child* (2001) presents feminist meditation of the issues of immigrant survival, domestic violence, and female self-acceptance. Focusing on the unnamed narrator and her complex relationship with her father, Kang reconceptualizes our understanding of domestic abuse in Asian North American literature and communities. She argues that Goto's novel questions the notion of home being a safe space and re-inscribes the meaning of warrior on the localized, personal level. According to Kang, the narrator, as an androgynous figure and an anti-model-minority character, relays a path to warrior life, seeking both selfhood and womanhood. In a mixed genre combining elements of science fiction and ethnic *Bildungsroman*, *The Kappa Child* uses the myth of the genderless, alien-life river monster "kappa" as an anti-violence intervention as well as a coping mechanism for the narrator to deal with familial alienation. The mythic kappa's ambiguity mirrors the protagonist's non-conformity in her self-conscious development from victim to survivor and then to warrior woman. The narrator's evolutionary process highlights how transnationalism actually can trace back to the genesis of Asian American studies in the 1960s that sought to draw parallels between the struggles of minority groups in the West and their Third World counterparts (Ty and Goellnicht Intro 8). The myth of kappa, re-invented in Goto's novel, becomes a trope of transnational possibility of the narrator's Asian North American experience in a small prairie town.

Beginning her chapter with the stark contrast between the monumental Angkor Wat and the memorial site of Tuol Sleng Prison in Cambodia, Cathy J. Schlund-Vials positions Cambodian nationhood in the past as the political and structural foreground of Loung Ung's memoir, *Lucky Child: A Daughter of Cambodia Reunites with the Sister She Left Behind* (2005). Ung's book maps her journey from a displaced Cambodian child refugee to a Cambodian American grown-up. Schlund-Vials examines the destruction as well as creation in transnational Cambodian American literary production. Exploring how the narrator undergoes a process of post-genocidal recovery and reconciliation as she constructs a selfhood, Schlund-Vials shows how a transnational approach helps us rethink and reconsider Asian American narratives—such as Ung's—beyond national boundaries. Connecting Ung's narrative with the dragon princess who facilitates the creation of Cambodia, Schlund-Vials critically engages with the narrator's coming-of-age as a Cambodian American side by side with Cambodia's nation-building.

The three essays in Part II, "Battles, Rituals and Worship," share thematic concerns as they examine historical and ritual battles or worships in Asian American and Asian diaspora cultural productions. Karen An-hwei Lee provides a refreshing reading of Theresa Cha's canonical work *Dictée* (1982) that centers on the sixteen-year-old Korean Christian martyr Yu Guan Soon, leader of the 1919 Independence Movement against Japanese occupation. In her analysis, Lee uses the term "woman warrior" to refer to a historical, literary, or mythical female figure who performs male tasks or social roles for the purpose of avenging a family, village, nation, or an oppressed group. Her discussion of Cha's experimental work is contextualized with Walter Lew's work, evolving women's discourses in Korea, children's books, feminist funerals, and women's newspapers. Traditionally Yu Guan Soon's story is marginalized in Korean historical narratives either by oblivion or by over-emphasizing her female virtues of submission and self-sacrifice. Lee argues that while Yu Guan Soon's story embodies the revolutionary values of an oppressed people, the traditional nationalist rhetoric explicitly serves the ideologies of patriarchal systems. As Lee's essay indicates, contemporary revisions in Korea and America give her story a feminist spin and underscore her as pro-choice and pro-action, thus representing the potential for female agency. In particular, Cha's revision subverts the patriarchal framework of Korean national history, in which Yu Guan Soon's story is relegated to the margins or is told with a skewed focus on her torture and death. In restoring Yu Guan Soon's historical significance in her cross-genre representation, Cha highlights the courage, resistance, and empowerment of this young female freedom fighter.

In her study, Marie-Therese C. Sulit investigates the translational and transnational elements reflected in the works of Merlinda Bobis, a Filipina Australian writer. Addressing displacement and anxiety, the power of language, tensions between religiosity and spirituality, and the contemporary marketplace, Sulit examines Bobis' genre crossing in her works on the Spain/U.S./Philippines encounters that challenge the rhetoric of ethnic exoticism and the cultural other. Positioning the *babaylan/catalonan* in the Philippines' history informed by imperialism and colonialization, Sulit discusses its allegorical representation of the warrior, the teacher, the healer, and the visionary. Reading Bobis as a contemporary *babaylan/catalonan*, Sulit's essay reveals the material and symbolic meanings of Bobis' transnational position. It argues that the works by Bobis expose contradictions and complexities within the Philippines' colonial encounters and exemplify a model for a transnational consciousness.

Lan Dong's reading of David Henry Hwang's play, *FOB*, aims to unearth the implications of the ritualistic battles between two legendary figures—Fa Mu Lan and Gwan Gung—both of whom are influential in Asian American cultural production and community life. Through performing myth on stage, Hwang's play offers a close look at hybridity and multiplicity within one's identity. His work transplants Fa Mu Lan and Gwan Gung who originated from Chinese folklore, and then were re-invented in Chinese American mythology. The symbolic battles that he envisions give these characters a theatrical spin and invite the audience to contemplate gendered and politicized Chinese American identities within the context of transnational migration. The juxtaposition of realistic characters and their mythological persona demonstrates a "figurative distance" between American-born generations and immigrant newcomers. Dong argues that Hwang's play draws on the cross-cultural tradition as a reference point to call the audience's attention to racism, imperialism, gender politics, and the characters' fluid identities within a transnational context.

Amy N. Nishimura's essay leads Part III, "Multination, Transnation and Communities." Through a close reading of the signifiers embedded in Bharati Mukherjee's *Jasmine* (1989), Nishimura suggests an "enmeshed cultural pluralism" in the novel. These nuances, she argues, represent multinational cultural memory. The leading character, despite her exotic beauty, not only demonstrates cultural complexity in her constantly crossing the shifting, deconstructed and re-invented boundaries but also provides a venue for the author in which to insert observational reading and editorial commentaries. Engaging with such critics as Julia Kristeva and Shirley Geok-lin Lim, Nishimura's essay argues against a simplistic reading of *Jasmine* as a "happily-ever-after" narrative. Instead, it examines how Mukherjee's fictional construction highlights the multitude of points of view and a global intersection within American society.

Tina Lynn Powell's essay examines how the traditional legend of the Trung sisters has been relocated in Vietnamese American narratives. She defines transnationalism as a method beyond national borders and a mode of scholarship by which to interrogate identity formation among immigrants. As she shows in her analysis of the allusions to the Trung sisters' legend in three works—Le Ly Hayslip's *When Heaven and Earth Changed Places* (1989), Dao Strom's *Grass Roof, Tin Roof* (2003), and Lan Cao's *Monkey Bridge* (1997)—transnationalism is about cultural negotiations. The liberation leaders and sister queens, Trung Trac and Trung Nhi, are revered figures in Vietnamese culture and hold particular significance in Viet Nam's national history. Their story has embraced multiple variations in history, poetry, drama, and other forms. Their warrior womanhood fits the needs of forging a national identity against Chinese imperial authority in history, the French colonial rule in the early twentieth century, and then American occupation during the Vietnam War. On the one hand, these embodiments reveal Viet Nam's long history of women warriors, among whom the Trung sisters stand out as archetypes. Their legend has been retold with an emphasis on romantic love, ideal womanhood, patriotism and Confucian values like filial piety in Viet Nam. On the other hand, Hayslip's, Strom's and Cao's works represent the invocation of the Trung sisters' legend through which one can trace and narrate transnational Vietnamese American experiences.

Danicar Mariano's analysis bridges the controversial Nicole Subic rape case (that took place in the Philippines in 2005) with the trope of the *chingada* (meaning the passive woman who is "ripped open") that is rooted in Mexico and related to Spain's colonial rule. Examining such online discourses as blogs and Internet commentaries from Filipinos as well as Filipino Americans, Mariano discusses how the rape complainant Nicole has been viewed both as a nationalist heroine and a shameless whore. In her analysis, Mariano unpacks the fantasy behind the U.S.–Philippine colonial relationship and its gendered undertones. In addition, her essay scrutinizes the Nicole Subic rape case through the militarization, immigration, and sovereignty that afflicted the sexualized and feminized Philippine nation, and examines the image of the Filipina as a marker of the nation's morality and modernity.

Finally, Part IV, "(Un)Spoken Subjects, Cross-Cultural Heroines and Media," arises from the interest in approaching heroic women characters in media, history, and literature from a cross-cultural angle. Catherine Gomes' essay examines the dynamics between the transnational Chinese swordswoman and a critical American audience. Analyzing three recent martial arts films, *Crouching Tiger, Hidden Dragon* (2000), *Hero* (2002), and *House of Flying Daggers* (2004), along with their critical aftermath, Gomes discusses the complexity and fluidity of cultural representation that resulted in transnational media productions. She contextualizes the Chinese swordswoman within the history of Chinese martial arts films and their influence outside of China and Chinese-speaking regions. Looking at Hong Kong at differing historical crossroads, Gomes examines how cinematic representations of the swordswoman reflect the status quo of the society: from women's financial independence in the 1960s and 1970s, to police corruption and drug triads in the 1980s, and then to anxiety and uncertainty over the upcoming "return" to mainland China in the 1990s. Her analysis of American popular and critical film reviews of the Chinese swordswoman suggests that her character has been interpreted within a "fabricated structure" that tries to make sense of the physical strength of the gendered Asian woman.

Focusing on the multi-dimensional marginality of the Bandit Queen Phoolan Devi, due to her gender, age, and caste, J. Sunita Peacock's essay examines Devi's experience as it is portrayed in both her biography, *The Bandit Queen of India: An Indian Woman's Amazing Journey from Peasant to International Legend* (2006), and Shekar Kapoor's film, *The Bandit Queen* (1994). Through her study of Devi's life, Peacock questions three integral aspects of Indian society: caste, religion, and the Indian goddess. She argues that all these elements are inextricably intertwined with one another and affect women's social status in significant ways. Peacock examines how Devi symbolically embodies both the "beneficent" and the "destructive" sides of the Hindu goddess and how her female body becomes a metaphor for the history of pre- and post-colonial India. In discussing Devi's evolving identity from a peasant, low caste girl, to a bandit queen, to an inmate, and then to a government official, Peacock positions Devi's body as the symbolic site for colonial/postcolonial/patriarchal dialogues.

Using Maxine Hong Kingston's canonical work *The Woman Warrior: Memoirs of a Girlhood among Ghosts* (1976) as a case study, Pei-Ju Wu explores the complexity of language and body. Adopting Inderpal Grewal, Caren Kaplan, Rey Chow, and Chandra Talpade Mohanty's studies on transnational feminism as a theoretical framework, Wu's chapter examines Kingston's reconstruction of the matrilineal text/body in *The Woman Warrior*. She argues that the narrator Maxine is a cultural translator who attempts to capture her family history. As Rocío G. Davis and Sämi Ludwig have pointed out, "Asian American literature offers a very rich field of investigation because in it we comprehend transcultural literary phenomena beyond geographic, national, ethnic, and even linguistic boundaries" (Intro 9). The hyphenated plurality of Maxine's cultural position as a Chinese American indicates maternal bodies in the past as the sources of her-selves. The imaginative apparatus, with which Kingston tells and retells her family stories, reinvents the narrations of her textual body. Looking at the reworking of Maxine's stories, Wu guides the reader to discover how maternal bodies have been deleted from family history, obligated to put on male garments, relinquished professional aspiration as a medical doctor, turned delirious, or seen merely as a reproductive machine for producing Han descendants.

Now that Asian American literature has gained momentum outside the United States, particularly in Asia and Europe (Wong 2004, 29),[1] it is important to move beyond national boundaries. "Paying more attention to the story beyond U.S. borders forces us to rethink established narratives about the Asian American experience" (Lee and Shibusawa xii). Collectively these contributors' readings call for critical attention to transnational Asian American and Asian diaspora women. The critical engagement presented in this book echoes the awareness of "creative and intellectual pluralism" within Asian American and Asian diaspora studies (Davis and Ludwig Intro 18). The interdisciplinary approaches of the contributors—whose remarkable thematic spectra and critical insights reflect their particular training and research in different cultures and cross-cultural contexts—display refreshing perspectives in Asian American literary studies and transnational feminism from four continents. Through unraveling what Thomas Holt has called the "narratives of contradiction and incoherence" (7), these essays together offer a new perspective on multivalent reconstructionalist productions that extends beyond any national literature or culture.

Notes

1. In 1995 Sau-ling Wong already discussed the implications and complexities of a denationalized and transnational Asian American identity. Some of the examples indicating the internationalization of Asian American literary studies are included in Wong's more recent essay, "When Asian American Literature Leaves 'Home'" (29–30).

Bibliography

Daiya, Kavita. "Provincializing America: Engaging Postcolonial Critique and Asian American Studies in a Transnational Mode." *South Asian Review* 26.2 (2005): 265–75, 304.

Davis, Rocío G. and Sämi Ludwig, eds. *Asian American Literature in the International Context: Readings on Fiction, Poetry, and Performance*. Müster, Hamburg, and London: Lit Verlag, 2002.

Elliott, Emory. "Diversity in the United States and Abroad: What does It Mean When American Studies is Transnational?" *American Quarterly* 59.1 (2007): 1–22.

Freeman, Carla. "Is Local: Global as Feminine: Masculine? Rethinking the Gender of Globalization." *Signs* 26.4 (2001): 1007–37.

Holt, Thomas C. *The Problem of Race in the 21st Century*. Cambridge, MA: Harvard University Press, 2002.

Hu-DeHart, Evelyn, ed. *Across the Pacific: Asian Americans and Globalization*. Philadelphia, PA: Temple University Press, 1999.

Lee, Erika and Naoko Shibasawa. "Guest Editors' Introduction: What Is Transnational Asian American History? Recent Trends and Challenges." *Journal of Asian American Studies* 8.3 (2005): vii–xvii.

Lim, Shirley Geok-Lin, John Blair Gamber, Stephen Hong Sohn, and Gina Valentino, eds. *Transnational Asian American Literature: Sites and Transits*. Philadelphia, PA: Temple University Press, 2006.

Liu, Haiming. "Transnational Historiography: Chinese American Studies Reconsidered." *Journal of the History of Ideas* 65.1 (2004): 135–53.

Ng, Franklin, ed. *Adaptation, Acculturation, and Transnational Ties among Asian Americans*. New York and London: Garland Publishing, 1998.

Schiller, Nina Glick. "Transmigrants and Nation-States: Something Old and Something New in the U.S. Immigrant Experience." *The Handbook of International Migration: The American Experience*. Eds. Charles Hirschman, Philip Kasinitz, and Josh DeWind. New York: Russell Sage Foundation, 94–119.

Ty, Eleanor and Donald C. Goelinicht, eds. *Asian North American Identities beyond the Hyphen*. Bloomington and Indianapolis: Indiana University Press, 2004.

Wong, Sau-ling C. and Jeffrey J. Santa Ana. "Review Essay: Gender and Sexuality in Asian American Literature." *Signs: Journal of Women in Culture and Society* 25.1 (1999): 171–226.

Wong, Sau-ling C. "Denationalization Reconsidered: Asian American Cultural Criticism at a Theoretical Crossroads." *Amerasia Journal* 21.1&2 (1995): 1–27.

———. "When Asian American Literature Leaves 'Home': On Internationalizing Asian American Literary Studies." *Crossing Oceans: Reconfiguring American Literary Studies in the Pacific Rim*. Eds. Noelle Brada-Williams and Karen Chow. Hong Kong: Hong Kong University Press, 2004. 29–40.

Part I:
Myth, History and Beyond

OF PRINCESSES PARI AND FOX GIRLS
Nora Okja Keller's Transnational Performance of Korean Histories and Myths

Silvia Schultermandl

In a 2003 *MELUS* interview with Young-Oak Lee, Nora Okja Keller argues about the use of myths and references to shamanism in her fiction: "I had a long interest in Korean shamanism. It's a powerful and fascinating tradition, and I'm drawn to its feminist nature—the fact that the majority of shamans, and the most prominent shamans, are women. It's a tradition that allows women an unconventional voice in traditional society" (151). Strong female characters, although they are not necessarily shamans,[1] are indeed prevalent in Keller's fiction. But their prominent presence does not merely represent Keller's interest in exploring forms of subversive female agency. The particular cultural contexts in which these strong female characters act are equally important. In the same *MELUS* interview, Keller acknowledges that the mythologies she incorporates into her novels, *Comfort Woman* (1997) and *Fox Girl* (2002), very much reflect her own politics of location as a Hawaiian writer who appropriates her Korean heritage through the act of storytelling. Korea-born and Hawai'i raised, Keller considers her use of myths, like the fortunetellers she met in Hawai'i, as "mixtures of many things and many cultures" (Young-Oak Lee 152).

Keller's own cultural location as a Hawaiian writer of Korean heritage indeed influences her writing. In the above-mentioned *MELUS* interview, Keller attributes such a syncretism in her transnational rendition of Korean myths to her own hybrid identity: "I am a mixture of many things, so I cannot say, 'Oh, this part is Korean, this part is American, this part is from Hawaii.' It's all woven together, so I couldn't pick it apart" (Young-Oak Lee 146). Similarly, in an interview with Terry Hong, Keller offers the following description of the influence that being *hapa* has on her writing: "It's not something I really think about when I write, but all those things—being *hapa*, being a Korean American woman, being 'local' in Hawai'i—all that gets filtered through my work. I try to leave those identity labels behind and work just on the story, but when I go back, I can see how *hapa* characters come out in *Fox Girl*."

Like the female protagonists in her novels, Keller undertakes both physical and imaginary journeys that span the distance between Korea and Hawai'i. Keller likens her acts of writing to a journey into another world, one that is different from the one she usually inhabits. In her interview with Terry Hong, Keller describes how her "dual life" informs her routine as a writer. She specifies:

> My waking life, which is my real life, is centered around my family — my two daughters, who are 8 and 2, the mother-daughter things we do, arts and crafts, piano lessons, school pageants. Then there's my other life, my writing life, which usually takes place in the dark of night when the kids are sleeping. It really is as if I enter another world: I go to another place, inside of myself, and it is a dark place.

Keller thus appropriates two different metaphors to describe her cultural location as a writer: first her status as a *hapa* woman, and second, her life as a working parent. Both circumstances of her life and the duality, even multiplicity they evoke, make it very clear that Keller does not seek to label herself as "just one thing" but relishes in the complexity of her subjectivity.

This awareness of the dynamics of cultural hybridization and their representation through myths and stories positions the female protagonists in her novels — whether they identify as shamans or whether their actions cohere with other mythical and fantastical elements in the narratives — at the core of contemporary discussions in transnational studies. Keller uses a transnational appropriation of Korean history and myths in her fiction. In *Fox Girl* she incorporates the fable of Fox Girl into the story about a young sex worker on a U.S. military camp town in Korea. In *Comfort Woman* she adopts the myth of Princess Pari as a means to express the emotional and cultural negotiations of a young Korean American woman and to remember her mother's submission into sexual servitude in a Japanese military camp in Korea. In both cases, the mythological figures bear importance for the protagonists' gender consciousness, but they do so not in relation to traditional Korean social norms but by underscoring the power structures that emerge from the personal encounters between the Korean protagonists and their experiences of globalization, such as through immigration and transnational sex work.

Keller's depiction of traditional myths and shamanism in her fiction displays a keen awareness of the various ways in which traditional stories of a particular national community can be appropriated in a transnational context. This awareness of the transnational context in which she writes about Korean historical and social realities characterizes Keller's fiction in two ways. First, by acknowledging the hybrid nature of the myths she employs, Keller performs "literary gestures" that emphasize the narrative construction of the myths more than their potential claims to cultural authenticity.[2] Second, these fantastical elements that the use of myths and shamanism bring to the stories reposition the historical elements that Keller incorporates in her fiction. Since her novels are heavily invested in historical research about Korean women's experiences of Japanese colonialism and American militarism respectively, her use of myths is not only a means of incorporating Korean cultural history into her writing, but also addresses prevalent issues in contemporary Korean society, including the very legacies that stem from the historical experiences of colonialism and militarism. As such, Keller's use of Korean traditions does not provide an essentialist understanding of myths as a genre or that of "Korea" as a pure and nationalistic concept. Instead, Keller's fictional construction (such as through narrative technique, plot sequencing, and framing) of these myths is a means of negotiating the cultural encounters that her Korean protagonists have. Hence, both modes and contexts of representation in Keller's fiction challenge the reader to trace the transnational transference of these myths between Korea, Hawai'i, and the U.S. mainland, and thus position Keller's work at the center of recent Asian American critique.

Myths as Cultural Narratives

In Keller's novels, both of which adopt the genre of the *Bildungsroman*,[3] myth has a distinct function. Throughout *Fox Girl*, the legend of the mythical figure of Fox Girl mirrors the living conditions of Hyun Jin, a teenage prostitute in an American military town in Korea. For her father and her step-mother, her involvement with the flourishing sex industry in her village constitutes an act of dishonor towards her parents, her ancestors, and her country. In contrast, for her friend Sookie's mother Duk Hee, who is Hyun Jin's birthmother, as the novel reveals towards the end, the mythical Fox Girl is a role model in subversive survival tactics, perhaps the same tactics that the sex workers employ with the American soldiers who promise them security, marriage, and a new life in the U.S. Like Fox Girl, Duk Hee leads a life as an outcast within her own community: while her relationship with the American GIs who date her provides her with a greater supply of food and other American goods, she is shunned by the villagers. During the time when she suffers from a sexually transmitted disease contracted from one of the GIs, her confinement to the so-called Monkey House also signifies the degree to which she can be temporarily alienated from the sexual industry of the military complex. Her position as an outsider, however, also enables her to reshape concepts of womanhood within the transnational encounter between GIs and Korean women. Sung-Ae Lee proposes that typically female schemata of Korean patriarchy include the following: "submissive," "beautiful," "obedient," and "self-effacing." In contrast, male schemata include "authoritarian," "strong," "transgressive," and "initiating" (Sung-Ae Lee 135). In her life as a sex worker, Duk Hee adopts both schemata and thus deconstructs the normality that underlies them. She is thus a modern incarnation of the legendary figure of Fox Girl, who, in several different versions of the Korean folktale, cleverly operates within her community by transgressing the community's moral codes. Furthermore, by teaching Sookie and Hyun Jin how to best survive the sexual military industry and possibly to use it to their own advantage, Duk Hee impersonates the very life lessons that might be deduced from the legend of Fox Girl. Both Fox Girl and Duk Hee, through their agency and the messages that they communicate through their acts, represent alternative models of femininity that disrupt patriarchy.

In *Comfort Woman*, Keller's use of myth introduces the complex relationship between Beccah and her mother Akiko,[4] who is haunted by the memory of her life in a military brothel in Korea. The novel starts with Beccah's memory of her mother's transition from a "normal" behavior to one that Beccah cannot make sense of: Beccah does not refer to these times as abnormal, nor does she seem to have a mode of relating to such times.

> During such times, the body of my mother would float through our one-bedroom apartment, slamming into walls and bookshelves and bumping into the corners of the coffee table and the television. If I could catch her, I would try to clean her cuts with *Cambison* ointment, dab the bruises with vinegar to stop the swelling. But most times I just left her food and water and hid in my bedroom, where I listened to long stretches of thumping accentuated by occasional shouts to a spirit named Induk [Keller 1997, 4].

These two examples from *Fox Girl* and *Comfort Woman* communicate different ways of reading myth: in *Fox Girl*, myth is indicative of a variety of meanings that storytelling in general and myth in particular carry with themselves. The figure of Fox Girl suggests that there are multiple ways of reading a person's behavior, just like there are multiple ways of reading a story. That this poses a challenge to the reader becomes evident from Beccah's confrontation with the limits of her own imagination. Because the mythical world that is part of her mother's life is foreign to her, Beccah metaphorically shuts herself off into a room in which this mythical world is unlikely to touch her. The potential unrelatability of myth and the multiple perspectives of a story refute essentialist readings of the above passages.

These two different ways of reading myth in Keller's fiction bear particular significance for Asian American studies and transnational studies. Reading myth, with a full understanding of what myth as a generic convention is able to achieve, can liberate Asian American literature from the demands of some readers, in particular the very common demand that Asian American literature must present to the reader a level of insight into Asian culture. Keller herself has never explicitly commented on her use of Korean folktales and their "authenticity." Perhaps because she readily acknowledges the multiple cultural influences on her writing, critics have not tried to hold her accountable for the accuracy of her knowledge of Korean folktales, legends, and myths. In contrast, Maxine Hong Kingston has received extremely avid criticism for the creative freedom she applied in her literary appropriations of Chinese legendary figures in her writing, even despite the fact that "Kingston has never made any claims, explicit or implicit, to historical veracity" (Wong 1988, 7). Much of Kingston's artistic expressionism has been discredited as unfamiliarity with or misrepresentation of Chinese culture. Kingston's deconstructionist and feminist revisioning of the tale about a Chinese American woman's aunt in China counters the strict distinction between "real" and "fake" Asian Americans (cf. Chin) and the sexism that Asian American nationalist critics of the 1970s purported. While it is true that Kingston upset many Chinese American readers and critics by her seemingly inaccurate use of details about Chinese mythology and history, to read her text only for its historical accuracy discredits its "artistic vision" and denies the author the creative freedom with which she embellishes her stories, as Kingston protests in her essay "Cultural Mis-readings by American Reviewers" (63).

The criticism that Kingston received for her appropriation of Chinese legends makes apparent the extent to which readers' expectations towards a text determine whether the author's literary strategies are successful. At the same time, it is also indicative of the cultural stereotypes that many Asian American authors are up against. What Keller's and Kingston's work demands from the reader is a sensitivity to the multiple locations of subjectivity from which their writing emerges without having to claim one label over another. Keller and Kingston offer two examples of Asian American texts that depict "the complex, dialogical national and transnational formulations of Asian American imaginations" that some scholars identify as a driving force in much of contemporary Asian American literature (Lim et al. 2). Keller and Kingston exemplify that Asian American literature "can no longer be viewed as merely a minor ethnic province of a domestic American canon" (Lim et al. 22). In this light, Asian American literature does not simply offer "'windows' into the presumed alterity of other cultures" (Amireh and Majaj 2), as the expectation towards Kingston's inclusion of Chinese legends suggests; it underscores the

> diasporic, mobile, transmigratory nature of Asian American experience, a history characterized by disparate migratory threads, unsettled and unsettling histories churned by multiple and different Asian ethnic immigrant groups each with a different language and cultural stock, different value and belief systems, and different notions of literary aesthetics, albeit most largely mediated through the English language [Lim et al. 1].

By integrating myth and legendary stories into their own writing, Keller and Kingston inadvertently force the reader to explore to which extent s/he can still understand what their stories entail, both in terms of content as well as literary strategies. In other words, the conscious use of myth in their writing cleverly puts the readers' readiness to accept the stories to the test.

The readiness to understand a text, especially one that lies outside of one's own cultural imaginary, is a central issue in Keller's and Kingston's embedding of the relating of myth into complicated mother-daughter relationships. While the distance that results from the lack of understanding with which American-born daughters meet their Asian-born mothers has become a well-established trope in Asian American literature,[5] in Keller's fiction the use of myth adds particular relevance to the daughter's quest to make sense of her mother's stories. In *Comfort Woman*, for instance, Beccah's ongoing conflict with her mother makes it difficult for her to empathize with her mother's life story and the ways in which she expresses her trauma, grief, and memory. Throughout the novel, Beccah thus actively develops strategies with which to approach her mother's stories, her mother's past, and her mother's eccentric behavior. These practices of finding strategies with which to approach the cultural narratives of her family heritage are also in place for the book's reading audience, who might experience a similar degree of alienation towards the mothers' stories (cf. Schultermandl 2009; 2009). And while I do not mean to argue that protagonists like Beccah become an ideological place-holder for an entire American reading audience,[6] I see the same reading mechanisms at play in the daughters' investigations of the cultural narratives that run in their families as those that characterize the communication of myths in general.

Myth, like every literary text, only "works" if the reading audience can understand it. According to Paul Ricoeur, "[t]he meeting between text and reader is a meeting between the whole of the text's claims, the horizon which it opens onto, the possibilities which it displays, and another horizon, the reader's horizon of expectations" (492). This horizon of expectations can be contained by readers' expectations towards generic conventions (cf. Beebee) as well as towards their own assumptions about cultural and material realities of specific ethnic communities in the U.S. (cf. Partridge). Both, the expectations towards the text and related questions about the text's very nature — such as whether it is true "or just a story" (Kingston 1989, 15) — become especially evident in readers' responses to myths. Such is Beccah's feeling in *Comfort Woman* when she comments on the nature of her mother's stories: "I grew cautious of my mother's stories, never knowing what to count on or what to discount. They sounded good — most of the stories she told me included the phrase: 'It was a hard time but a happy time'" (32). In line with Ricouer's assertions about the interactions between text and reader, Beccah experiences this meeting between text and reader in her assessment of her mother's story and of the context in which the storytelling occurred. By evaluating, even judging, the validity of her mother's stories, Beccah consciously engages with the text and investigates to which extent the stories meet her "horizon of expectations." Her verdict, "[t]hey sounded good," indicates her approval of the stories and their claims, a successful meeting between reader and text, as it were. But while this verdict offers a positive example of a successful meeting between reader and text, many other examples in Keller's fiction underscore the potential misunderstandings and the resulting confusion for the reader i.e. the recipient of the story. Hyun Jin's reaction to the version of Fox Girl's legend that Duk Hee tells her is indicative of a much different relationship between reader and text. When Hyun Jin explains "I never heard that ending before" (Keller 2002, 27), she indicates that she does not fully accept the version of the legend. Her reaction is particularly important for Keller's use of myth because, as Sung-Ae Lee proposes, it "may alert readers to the possibility of other narrative patterns" (142). This frees Keller's use of myth from possible claims to authenticity and emphasizes the literary and performative nature of the text. It furthermore underscores the "invisible contract" that the reader has with the text, a contract which conditions the reader to look for established narrative patterns. Keller's use of myth, however, asks readers to think beyond such patterns, and by implication, read her texts with a fresh perspective.

Keller's protagonists find themselves ensnared in a process of filtering out meaningful messages from the legends that they grow up with.[7] And in so doing, they encounter what Roland Barthes defines in "Myth Today" as the dual nature of myth: "myth is a system of communication ... a message.... Myth is not defined by the object of its message, but by the way in which it utters this message: there are formal limits to myth, there are no 'substantial' ones" (109). Barthes's assertion that myth has both formal and contextual elements points to the literary performances that shape myth and determine to what degree the reader recognizes these stories as myths in the first place. What an investigation of myth in Keller's fiction therefore refutes is a reading that singles out the strictly Korean or the strictly American literary traditions that may emanate from her work. In the same vein, the question of the extent to which her use of myth is "authentic" becomes equally irrelevant as the question of whether she writes with the intention of explaining Korean myths to an American audience. These questions have been raised in relation to Asian American authors and their literary productions in the past, and much of contemporary scholarship in Asian American studies has offered approaches that successfully debunk such notions (see, for instance, Lowe; Kang; Chuh).

Instead, Keller's use of myth underscores the literary, or more precisely, fictional character of her work by forcing the reader to read more closely and perhaps more carefully towards cultural misreading and misappropriation. In this sense, myth functions as a symbolic gesture of the transnational nature of the kind of storytelling that Keller depicts and deploys. In *Comfort Woman*, for instance, Keller's use of two distinct narrative voices epitomizes the complex relationship between Akiko and her daughter Beccah and the cultural misunderstandings that overshadow their daily interactions (see also Schultermandl 2007; 2009). But the myth of Princess Pari is more than just a contemporary appropriation of a traditional Korean legend; it also provides a commentary on the act of storytelling itself and on the representation of social and material realities through fiction. Indeed, the myth of Princess Pari is not only an allegory on the act of storytelling itself, but it also sheds light on the transnational reception of the legacies of the surviving comfort women and their demands for redress. This so called "comfort woman debate" not only offers an allegory for Korean nationalist feminism, but it also signifies Asian American and American involvement in the comfort woman debate and thus in its transnational character (see Thiesmeyer; Thoma). Similarly, the myth of Fox Girl is an allegory on transnational sexual labor in a global era.

Both Keller's novels, as the following sections of this chapter will show, deal with sexual exploitation and commodification of Korean women (cf. Madsen). However, both depict female characters who cleverly subvert and thus survive the power structures that oppress them. Their subversive strategies become emblematic through the transnational rendition of traditional myths that Keller's novels present.

Myth in *Comfort Woman*

The degree to which the different cultural traditions of Hawai'i, Korea, and continental U.S. are at play in the literary representations of myth in Keller's fiction becomes tangible in her debut novel, *Comfort Woman*. The book centers on the theme of cultural encounters between an American-born daughter, Beccah, and her Korean-born mother, Akiko. Through a poly-vocal narrative, Keller's novel sketches the difference between Beccah's and Akiko's cultural identities. The novel starts with Beccah's realization upon Akiko's death that she hardly knew her mother. The challenge is to "start imagining her life" (26), a challenge whose complexity becomes apparent from Beccah's inability to write her mother's obituary in the form that she usually produces as a writer for the local newspaper. Her mother's shamanic rituals constitute a cultural gap in Beccah's ability to relate to her mother's past; Akiko's silence about her past also distances the two women from each other. But when Beccah listens to the tape recording her mother left for her in which Akiko remembers the many women who were killed in the camps, it becomes clear to Beccah that this uncovering of a hidden past of her family history, and by extension, of Korean history at large, is part of the legacy she inherited from her mother.

This involves her need to negotiate the stories her mother did and did not tell her. Keller indicates Beccah's filial piety by using the myth of Princess Pari as a recurring theme in indicating a daughter's responsibility toward her family. As a young girl, Beccah learns about Princess Pari's clever ways of distracting Saja, the Death Messenger, with offerings of food and thus enables her parents to flee "back through the gates of hell, through the earth, through the skies, and into Lotus Paradise, where they were reborn as angels" (49). In one of the novel's earlier chapters, Beccah remembers this story at a point when she is grappling with her mother's death. Through a flashback moment in the narrative, she relives both the comfort she felt when she was nestled in her mother's lap while hearing the story and the anxiety she felt even then about whether she, too, would be able to express her love for her family in such a profound way. Singing along with her mother the song that led Princess Pari to her parents, Beccah asserts "The river song. I'll never forget it, okay, Mom? You sing that song, and no matter what, I'll find you, okay? I'll be like Princess Pari, and I'll rescue you" (50). Years later, however, Beccah realizes that she failed to keep that promise to her mother and thus ends that same chapter with the following words: "When the time came, when she needed me, I had failed to rescue her. No Princess Pari, I could not swim to the far shores of death to pull my mother back to life; I could not even put my feet in the water" (51).

The fact that Beccah fails to do justice to her mother's memory, thus failing to be the Princess Pari that she promised to become one day, resonates with Akiko's desire to speak about the many deaths of her fellow "comfort women" in the Japanese military camps. Speaking out maintains a special function in the resistance to the colonial and sexual oppression that the women endured in the military camps. As Akiko's narratives of her life in the military camp illustrate, the demand to keep quiet, forced into servitude and silence by the soldiers, emphasizes the power of language and self-narration. When one of the women defends herself by shouting, "I am Korea, I am a woman, I am alive. I am seventeen, I have a family just like you do, I am a daughter, I am a sister" (20), she exemplifies to what degree speaking out is not only a subversive act, but also a survival strategy. Akiko's chapters in the novel have a similar function. Inspired by the testimony of Keum-ja Hwang, a comfort camp survivor whose lecture Keller heard in 1993, Akiko's narratives of the atrocities she has experienced depicts a missing chapter in Korean history on the one hand and personalizes the fate of a "comfort woman" by depicting the individual circumstances that led to her confinement in the military camp on the other hand.[8] Akiko's narratives are a means with which to reconstitute agency, thus countering the denial that pushed the demands for redress articulated by the former sex slaves into oblivion. And because these narratives are entangled with the narrative of her Hawaiian daughter Beccah, they also create visibility of such injustices in an American, and by extension an international, context.

Given the importance of storytelling as a strategy of resistance and survival, it is crucial for Beccah to be able to relate to and narrate her mother's life. At first, this seems unfeasible, but towards the end of the novel Beccah does find a way to connect with her mother's legacy. Like in Princess Pari's legend, a song prepares Beccah for her performance as an active agent of her mother's memory, an act that intensifies and reshapes her relationship with her mother: "I performed the actions of my mother, caring for the spirits of the house, in order to feel my mother once again. I wanted to be able to feel her next to me, to sense her spirit—for if there really are such things, I knew they would come to me, feeling my need for her, in death as she rarely did in life" (169). The "song" that inspired Beccah to perform this ritual to commemorate her mother's life is her mother's voice recorded on tape as she performs a *chesa*, a commemorative ritual to honor those women who came before her, including the spirit of Induk, another former sex slave.

In this context, the legend of Princess Pari becomes the overarching theme for female solidarity: united in song and a sense of responsibility toward each other, Beccah, Akiko, and the legendary Princess Pari carry out their acts of resistance against multiple forms of oppression.[9] Because all three female figures are up against specific constraints that the societies in which they live place upon them, their acts of defiance mark their successful emancipation from these constraints. Through these acts of defiance, their lives also become relevant sources of personalized history.

Myth in *Fox Girl*

Like *Comfort Woman*, Keller's second novel, *Fox Girl*, also presents a complex cultural encounter. The legendary figure that lends the novel its name offers cues about how to read the global interaction that Keller's novel sketches. *Fox Girl* is set in an American military town in Korea during the Korean-American War. The sex industry in this military town is both a main source of income for the local population and a place in which the effects of globalization (through warfare) become visible. The novel follows Hyun Jin, a teenage prostitute, through these glocal interactions: her initiation into sex work, her conflict with her family, her search for her birthmother, and finally, her adoption of her sister Sookie's daughter and their immigration to the U.S. All occur on a specific local level but are shaped by global power structures. In the midst of this *bildungsromanesque* development is the question about the degree to which Hyun Jin can still act as a free agent within the militarized and exploitative conditions of America Town. Keller provides a possible answer to this question in her use of the legend of Fox Girl as an indication of how to read the figure of Hyun Jin.

The book's title itself characterizes subversive power and agency as a means of survival and justice. The title alludes to the fable about a girl who disguises herself as a fox and then kills all but one of a hundred schoolboys. While Hyun Jin, who first hears this story from her father, grew up considering Fox Girl an evil creature, she later learns that Fox Girl did not kill out of spite but in order to regain what rightfully belongs to her: the jewel of knowledge. In the father's version of the fable, Fox Girl is a malicious creature who kills innocent boys and her disguise is indicative of her evil character. Hyun Jin hears an entirely different version of the Fox Girl fable from Duk Hee, Sookie's mother who, as it turns out towards the end of the novel, is Hyun Jin's birthmother. In Duk Hee's version, Fox Girl once owned the jewel of knowledge, which was "hidden under her tongue" (26) and got stolen by a schoolboy when she allowed him to kiss her and get a taste of knowledge. From Duk Hee's version of the story,

Hyun Jin learns that Fox Girl uses her power of disguise to reclaim what she rightfully owns. She thus understands that Fox Girl is not a malicious, bloodthirsty monster but a disenfranchised creature who seeks to restore her agency. Duk Hee's version of the fable emphasizes much more the wrongs that have been done to the girl than her allegedly bad character.

Given the fact that there are two very different lessons implied in the telling of the fable of Fox Girl, Keller accords special importance to an exploration of Hyun Jin's own appropriation of the myth. This appropriation is an ongoing process, just as much as Hyun Jin's participation in and awareness of her personal role in the sexual industry is concerned. At the beginning of the novel, Hyun Jin's remark that "I don't want to be a fox girl.... They are evil creatures" (26) seems to conjure up the lesson that her father implied by drawing on the fable of Fox Girl in order to instill in Hyun Jin proper family values and morals. As a young woman, the image that Hyun Jin is supposed to get from the fable of Fox Girl is that "murder," which in the fable is a metaphor for female disobedience and perhaps for female agency as well, is undesirable in a woman; when Fox Girl is described as an evil creature, this seems to be a commentary on her un-feminine behavior. Such is also the implication when Hyun Jin's stepmother calls her a "fox girl" who is "[e]ating up her own family" (122).

In contrast, when Duk Hee contests in reply to Hyun Jin's assertion of the evil character of Fox Girl that "[i]t depends on who tells the story" (122), she inadvertently raises issues about the constructedness of moralistic concepts such as good and evil, right and wrong. By emphasizing that stories are always constructed with a particular message implied, Duk Hee diverts our focus of interest away from the controversial figure of Fox Girl and onto the narrator of the fable: different narrators appropriate Fox Girl as an iconic figure that exemplifies a particular, but always a context-specific, message. Hyun Jin's father's use of the Fox Girl story seems to teach his daughter about traditional gender roles. The Fox Girl in his version becomes an evil creature because she is proactive and seeks justice, two qualities that are at odds with the image of the passive, docile woman within traditional patriarchal societies. In contrast, Duk Hee's version refuses to stigmatize Fox Girl; instead, she is represented as a human figure who, in the face of hardship and injustice, uses a clever disguise to regain power and identity.

In particular, Duk Hee's emphasis on the girl's use of disguise characterizes female agency as intricately linked to subversion. This also pertains to the issue of sexual labor, the two being linked through Duk Hee's choice to tell the Fox Girl fable as she teaches the two girls about make-up, the form of disguise available to them. When Hyun Jin realizes that the heavy make-up Sookie wears resembles "an ageless mask, cool and deadly, capable of swallowing the jewel of a man's soul" (27), she understands that in order to survive the military town, she must use the same clever disguise as Fox Girl did. This clever disguise appears in the novel at a crucial point in Hyun Jin's development: her decision to immigrate to the U.S. Her motivation to do so is her recently accepted responsibility for Sookie's baby daughter, Myu Myu. In order to earn enough money for herself and Myu Myu, Hyun Jin adopts the role of the "Hunni Girl," the "freak — who would do anything" in her life as a sex worker (192). As a successful business strategy, Hyun Jin performs sexual services to a degree or in a fashion that the other sex workers reject. By so doing, she adopts a persona through which she attracts more attention from the soldiers who visit the porn shops and strip clubs, which she might not receive otherwise given the pronounced birthmark on her face. While the birthmark marks her as an outsider, as "ugly," as one of "The Butt Twins" (3), her adopted role as the "Hunni Girl" marks her financial success within the sex industry of the military town.

And it is this strategic disguise that eventually enables Hyun Jin's access to the U.S. Because she has acquired the status of a prominent sex worker in America Town, she draws the attention of a Hawai'i based sex-club owner who seeks to hire new girls for her club. In the context of transnational sexual labor, the fable of Fox Girl also opens up an interesting reading of Hyun Jin's and Sookie's escape to the U.S. As they did in America Town, they need to adopt the roles attributed to them through the unequal division of power between the first and the third world.[10] Shedding light on the lengths to which Hyun Jin is willing to pursue her own American Dream adds further complexity to Keller's use of myth in her work. The myth of the American Dream, as Hyun Jin has come to know it while she was living in America Town, comprises an overtly optimistic ending to a complicated and, at times, depressing fate of a young woman. Although Hyun Jin realizes that working in Hawai'i is no different from working in America Town, the novel seems to suggest towards the end that although jobless and stranded in Hawai'i as an illegal immigrant, Hyun Jin's life has taken a turn for the better.

Myth and the American Dream

For Keller's protagonists, this appropriation of the American Dream can only succeed in the transnational context of their personal genealogies: Keller's renditions of the myths of Princess Pari and Fox Girl are strategic moments within her construction of the complex and fascinating cultural encounters in which the borders between American and Korean culture become blurred. The same blurring of boundaries occurs on the level of Keller's integration of myth into the "real" story of Beccah's and Hyun Jin's lives: while the myths that they grow up with and that ultimately shape their personalities originate in Korean culture, the ways in which they reverberate within the young women's lives also encompass their experiences in a global world. For instance, Beccah's acceptance of her role as dutiful daughter who carries on her mother' battle for visibility for the victims of the sexual oppression in the Japanese comfort camps emerges only after she is able to piece together her own oppression as an immigrant woman in Hawai'i. It is true that Hawai'i in Keller's fiction is characterized by a considerable degree of cultural diversity, but Beccah undergoes a great deal of stigmatization as a young girl because of her mother's "crazy" behavior, which is indicative of her status as an outsider. In this sense, even in moments in the novel when Beccah does not feel that she is linked to her mother's past life in Korea, her mother's immigration to the U.S. as a missionary's wife suggests a continuous victimization. As such, Keller's novel evokes what Carla Freeman has defined as a "gendered understanding of globalization" (1010). Freeman asserts that in the context of global mobility, "producers, consumers, and bystanders of globalization are not generic bodies or invisible practitioners of labor and desire but are situated within social and economic processes and cultural meanings that are central to globalization itself" (1010). In this sense, transnational sex workers in Keller's novel are not merely providers of gendered services; they are also consumers of the gendered roles available to them in a system founded on exploitation and inequality. This idea, the notion that transnational sex workers are consumers of the gendered roles available to them in the unequal distribution of labor within the New Economy, is only partly satisfactory in dealing with questions of agency for sex workers. But it is precisely this new definition of production and consumption that seems to be at play in Keller's treatment of sexual labor in general and Hyun Jin's appropriation of the American Dream. Similarly, the American Dream to which Hyun Jin has access is one that continues to manifest the same power relationships between American men and Asian immigrant women. When Hyun Jin maintains, "though I was three thousand miles away from Korea, I was still trapped in America Town" (269), she does so with an understanding of the transnational entanglements that lead up to the sexual industry she participates in.

The legacy of military and sexual oppression of Korean women is a story within the mythologies of the American Dream that is not very often heard. Keller's novels, which generated abundant interest both in the comfort woman debate and in the transnational sex industry in American military camps overseas, write into American culture those events that are often marginalized within the literary and social imaginary of American history. The marginalization of such narratives also raises issues about the validity and the authenticity of the stories and their tellers, as the denial by Japanese Prime Minister Shinzo Abe of the occurrence of sexual servitude during World War II exemplifies (cf. Onishi). What the surviving comfort women experienced due to Abe's dismissal of their claims is not only a further silencing of their claims but a nullification of their past. And perhaps because such stories are difficult to understand, they themselves operate with not so dissimilar dimensions as does mythology. Like the legends about Princess Pari and Fox Girl, these stories depend on the acceptance by the listener and reader for various purposes, including the historical, literary, and political dimensions of these stories.

Notes

1. Shamanism in Keller's work has been discussed mostly in relation to Akiko, one of the protagonists in *Comfort Woman*. Akiko's struggle to deal with the traumatic experiences in the military camp where she was subdued into sexual slavery at the age of twelve, her difficult transition into Hawaiian society after her immigration, and her complex and confusing relationship with her daughter Beccah raise important issues about the symbolic meaning Keller might have assigned to Akiko's shamanism. In *Double Agency: Acts of Impersonation in Asian American Literature and Culture* (2005), an insightful study of the acts of impersonations that Asian American cultural productions have performed to communicate, re-vision, and negotiate on their own terms Asian American identities, Tina Chen considers the many potential enactments that Akiko's shamanism might signify:

> Is she a woman so traumatized by her past that she becomes a victim to a manipulative scheme to exploit the hopes of others, a scheme dependent upon her friend and manager's exploitation of her own mental instability? Is she perhaps more of a sham than a shaman, putting on the false face of ecstatic trance in order to support herself and her daughter? Or is she truly able to communicate with spirits, ancestral and otherwise, in an effort to resolve both her personal suffering and the suffering of the community in which she lives? [117].

2. In *Literary Gestures: The Aesthetic in Asian American Writing* (2006), Rocío G. Davis and Sue-Im Lee caution against the practice of reading Asian American literature primarily for depictions of gender, ethnicity, and cultural details at the expense of engaging the texts' literary and performative qualities. Too much attention to the social and material realities of the Asian American communities represented in Asian American literature not only underestimates the texts' aesthetic qualities, but also connotes a degree of Orientalism that accredits ethnic American literature an ethnographic rather than a literary quality (see also Kim). For a more general discussion on literary aestheticism and multi-ethnic textual politics, see Elliott et al.

3. Samina Najmi offers an analysis of Keller's "decolonization" of the genre of the *Bildungsroman* in her novel *Comfort Woman*. I would argue that this re-appropriation of the traditional genre of *Bildungsroman* coupled with war narratives in order to, as Najmi's discussion proposes, "interrupt dominant feminist and nationalist discourses" (210), also applies to *Fox Girl*.

4. Akiko is actually the name that the Japanese soldiers gave her when she was forced into sexual servitude in the camps. Her real name is Soon Hyo, but throughout the novel, neither the reader nor Beccah herself knows her Korean name. Only in one of the last chapters does Beccah discover a letter that addresses her mother by this name, the same letter that discloses her mother's past life in Korea.

5. For a comprehensive discussion of mother-daughter conflicts as symbolical representations of the cultural clashes that result from a lack of understanding between Western audiences and non–Western cultural capital, see Schultermandl's study *Transnational Matrilineage: Mother-Daughter Conflicts in Asian American Literature* (2009).

6. Sau-ling C. Wong has used the term "sugar sisterhood" in discussing Amy Tan's portrayal of daughters who are so close in ideology to the presumed white-middle class audience of Tan's fiction that the success of her novels about Chinese American mother-daughter relationships seems to rest solely on Tan's tailoring of her storylines to well-established literary patterns in feminist literature. For details on this discussion, see Wong 1995.

7. Strictly speaking, myth and legend are two different concepts: unlike myths, legends are more deeply rooted in cultural traditions, as are folktales and all stories that

are less concerned with the supernatural than myths are. Several scholars have proposed readings of Keller's fiction that analyze the stories embedded within the plot as folktales, legends, or simply as stories. Reading them as myths, as I do in this chapter, highlights the fictionality of the stories on the one hand and the implied contract between reader and text on the other.

8. That Akiko was basically sold into sexual slavery by her own family so that they could afford to pay for her sister's dowry is a detail in the character and plot development that is equally shocking and illuminating about the complex social realities. It complicates the question to what extent Korean women participated "willingly" in the military sex industry.

9. Jong Kun Lee has made a similar point in an excellent comparison between the original myth and Keller's rendition of it (432–35).

10. Deborah Madsen points out that "Keller suggests that the U.S. provides the model for the sex industry in South Korea — 'American Town' in South Korea is indistinguishable from Hawai'i in terms of the sex clubs, street prostitution, and porn shops" (80). While I agree with the ideological similarities between America Town and the sexual industry of South Korean Women in the U.S., I believe that Keller's novel makes a crucial distinction in its depiction of Hyun Jin as a transnational sexual worker from her experience as a prostitute in South Korea. At least women have a public life outside of sex work in Korea, whereas in the U.S. we see Hyun Jin only in terms of her life as a sex worker who needs to provide for her daughter.

Bibliography

Amireh, Amal, and Lisa Suhair Majaj. "Introduction." *Going Global: The Reception of Third World Women Writers*. Eds. Amal Amireh and Lisa Suhair Majaj. London: Garland, 2000. 1–20.

Barthes, Roland. "Myth Today." *Mythologies*. Trans. Annette Lavers. New York: Hill and Wang, 1972. 109–59.

Beebee, Thomas O. *The Ideology of Genre: A Comparative Study of Generic Instability*. University Park, PA: Pennsylvania State University Press, 1994.

Chen, Tina. *Double Agency: Acts of Impersonation in Asian American Literature and Culture*. Stanford, CA: Stanford University Press, 2005.

Chin, Frank, Jeffrey Paul Chan, Lawson Fusao Inada, and Shawn Hsu Wong. "Preface." *Aiiieeeee!: An Anthology of Asian-American Writers*. Eds. Frank Chin, Jeffrey Paul Chan, Lawson Fusao Inada, and Shawn Hsu Wong. Washington, DC: Howard University Press, 1974. vii–xvi.

Chuh, Kandice. *Imagine Otherwise: On Asian American Critique*. Durham and London: Duke University Press, 2003.

Davis, Rocío G., and Sue-Im Lee, eds. *Literary Gestures: The Aesthetic in Asian American Writing*. Philadelphia, PA: Temple University Press, 2006.

Elliott, Emory, Louis Freitas Caton, and Jeffrey Rhyne, eds. *Aesthetics in a Multicultural Age*. New York and Oxford: Oxford University Press, 2002.

Freeman, Carla. "Is Local: Global as Feminine: Masculine? Rethinking the Gender of Globalization." *Signs* 26.4 (2001): 1007–37.

Hong, Terry. "The Dual Lives of Nora Ojka Keller." *AsianWeek* 4–10 April 2002. 15 Dec. 2009 <http://apa.si.edu/Curriculum%20Guide-Final/norakellerbio.htm>.

Kang, Laura Hjun Yi. *Compositional Subjects: Enfiguring Asian/American Women*. Durham and London: Duke University Press, 2002.

Keller, Nora Okja. *Comfort Woman*. New York: Penguin, 1997.
_____. *Fox Girl*. New York: Penguin, 2002.
Kim, Elaine H. "Defining Asian American Realities through Literature." *The Nature and Contexts of Minority Literature*. Eds. Abdul JanMohammed and David Lloyd. New York and Oxford: Oxford University Press, 1990. 146–70.
Kingston, Maxine Hong. "Cultural Mis-readings by American Reviewers." *Asian and American Writers in Dialogue: New Cultural Identities*. Ed. Guy Amirthanayagam. London: Macmillian, 1982. 55–65.
_____. *The Woman Warrior: Memoirs of a Girlhood Among Ghosts*. New York: Vintage, 1989.
Lee, Jong Kun. "Princess Pari in Nora Okja Keller's *Comfort Woman*." *Positions: East Asian Cultures Critique* 12.2 (2004): 431–56.
Lee, Sung-Ae. "Re-visioning Gendered Folktales in Novels by Mia Yun and Nora Okja Keller." *Asian Ethnology* 68.1 (2009): 131–50.
Lee, Young-Oak. "Nora Okja Keller and the Silenced Woman: An Interview." *MELUS* 28.4 (2003): 145–65.
Lim, Shirley Geok-lin, John Blair Gamber, Stephen Hong Sohn, and Gina Valentino, eds. *Transnational Asian American Literature: Sites and Transits*. Philadelphia, PA: Temple University Press, 2006.
Lowe, Lisa. *Immigrant Acts: On Asian American Cultural Politics*. Durham and London: Duke University Press, 1996.
Madsen, Deborah L. "Nora Okja Keller: Telling Trauma in the Transnational Military-(Sex)industrial Complex." *Interactions* 15.2 (2006): 75–84.
Najmi, Samina. "Decolonizing the Bildungsroman: Narratives of War and Womanhood in Nora Okja Keller's *Comfort Woman*." *Form and Transformation in Asian American Literature*. Eds. Zhou Xiaojing and Samina Najmi. Seattle, WA: University of Washington Press, 2005. 209–30.
Onishi, Norimitsu. "Denial Reopens Wounds of Japan's Ex-Sex Slaves." *The New York Times* 8 March 2007. 7 May 2009 <http://www.nytimes.com/2007/03/08/world/asia/08japan.html?scp=19&sq=comfort%20women&st=cse>.
Partridge, Jeffrey F.L. *Beyond Literary Chinatown*. Seattle, WA: University of Washington Press, 2007.
Ricoeur, Paul. *Reflection and Imagination: A Ricoeur Reader*. Ed. Mario J. Valdés. Toronto: University of Toronto Press, 1991.
Schultermandl, Silvia. "Hooked on the American Dream? Transnational Sexual Labor in Nora Okja Keller's *Fox Girl*." *Feminist Studies in English Literature* 15.2 (2007): 159–84.
_____. "Teaching Kingston's 'No Name Woman' as a Primer for Reading Multi-Ethnic American Literature." *Exploring Spaces: Practices and Perspectives*. Eds. Dorothea Steiner and Sabine Danner. American Studies in Austria. Ser. 8. Münster: LIT Verlag, 2009. 53–73.
_____. *Transnational Matrilineage: Mother-Daughter Relationships in Asian American Literature*. Contributions to Transnational Feminism. Ser. 1. Münster: LIT Verlag, 2009.
_____. "Writing Rape, Trauma, and Transnationality onto the Female Body: Matrilineal Em-body-ment in Nora Okja Keller's *Comfort Woman*." *Meridians: feminism, race, transnationalism* 7.2 (2007): 71–100.
Thiesmeyer, Lynn. "U.S. Comfort Women and the Silence of the American Other." *Hitting Critical Mass* 3.2 (1996): 47–67.
Thoma, Pamela. "Cultural Autobiography, Testimonial, and Asian American Transnational Feminist Coalition in the 'Comfort Women of World War II' Conference." *Frontiers* 21.1–2 (2000): 29–54.

Wong, Sau-ling C. "Necessity and Extravagance in Maxine Hong Kingston's *The Woman Warrior*: Art and the Ethnic Experience." *MELUS* 15 (1988): 3–26.
_____. "'Sugar Sisterhood': Situating the Amy Tan Phenomenon." *The Ethnic Canon: Histories, Institutions, and Interventions.* Ed. David Palumbo-Liu. Minneapolis, MN: University of Minnesota Press, 1995. 174–210.

WATER BIRTH
Domestic Violence and Monstrosity in Hiromi Goto's The Kappa Child

Nancy Kang

The Kappa Child, published in 2001 by Japanese Canadian writer Hiromi Goto, splices together the genres of science fiction and ethnic *Bildungsroman*. The resulting double helix is a quirky feminist meditation on the traumas of immigrant survival, domestic abuse, and the intricacies of an Othered woman's search for self-acceptance and reciprocal love. Even though the unnamed narrator emerges as a warrior figure, she begins deeply conflicted about her family, hyper-conscious of her perceived failures as a daughter, and troubled by childhood trauma. The path to warrior life involves claiming both space and freedom for expressions of alternative selfhood. For Goto's narrator, the primary issue involves reconfiguring personal expectations about family life, particularly the role of her father as traditional patriarch deserving of filial loyalty and love despite years of committing physical and psychological abuse.

Critical responses to *The Kappa Child* have avoided deep engagement with this subject. This hesitancy reflects the onto-epistemological double bind that domestic abuse poses; it is socially tabooed and yet remains a persistently open secret in many Asian North American communities, whether in fiction or in the lived experience of survivors and witnesses. Selections from the Asian American canon feature family violence but often fail to pose any active or sustained ideological challenge. For instance, *The Fifth Chinese Daughter* (1950) has Jade Snow Wong's father loom "large and menacing" with a punishment for the minor disobedience of the children having arrived at home late, despite his having been informed of the inconvenience ahead of time by one of the older daughters. The autobiographer recalls, "Swiftly the switch cut the air and whistled sharply just before it landed across the back of Jade Snow's bare calves" (Wong 66). Instead of objecting to the whipping, Jade Snow's mother makes the stipulation that her husband not beat the children on their heads, lest their intellects be affected (Wong 67). While some adults might express concerns about possible physical or emotional trauma incurred from such arbitrary shows of force, Mrs. Wong focuses on future academic achievement instead. She not only exemplifies skewed priorities, but also reaffirms the stereotype of the education-obsessed Asian parent. Similarly, Ko, an internment camp survivor in Jeanne Wakatsuki Houston and James Houston's *Farewell to Manzanar* (1973), uses "sheer noise and fierce display" as he brandishes a cane against his wife. His daughter Jeanne reflects, "Inside my own helplessness I cowered, sure he was going to kill her or hurt her very badly, and the way Mama lay there I believed she was actually ready to be beaten to death" (Houston and Houston 59). These incidents suggest that more often than not, tight-knit, usually less-assimilated immigrant families balk at having their private matters enter any public forum that may invite censure, outside interference, and an embarrassing loss of face. Bound by these pressures, Goto's protagonist must mobilize against excesses of patriarchal authority, risking her irreproachable status as her "father's daughter" in order to achieve a semblance of peace and mental stability. The abusive father, I argue, is thus the most powerful and complex adversary in this woman warrior's journey.

The Kappa Child's narrator emerges in a decidedly contemporary moment. Instead of having a white-collar profession as might be expected of stereotypical Asian immigrant children, she is a proud "collector of abandoned shopping carts" (Goto 1). A recluse with a penchant for luxurious sleepwear (which she unblinkingly dons in public), she is an androgynous figure with a deeply ambivalent relationship with her father.[1] Unnamed and the product of rural farming communities of the Canadian West, she nevertheless emerges as a portal into a world where pregnancy is neither ascertained by medical diagnostics nor remains localized in the womb. This warrior woman's development is essentially homeopathic: only through the intervention of the kappa, a green, alien-like "river monster" from Japan does the self-perceived human monster become powerful, validated, even desirable (Goto 180).[2] This paradox underscores the lack of emotional support and self-actualizing potential in the narrator's human environment, especially in her immediate family.

Although many readers may associate the term "warrior" with the heavily masculinized discourse of epic — namely the grandiose and ancient conflicts between nations, tribes, abstract cosmic forces, or simply, great men — this reinscription of the archetype focuses more on localized, personal struggle.[3] Unlike times of war when male violence tends to be aligned or equated with heroism, this instance narrows nation down to its more immediate corollary, the family. It asks when — if ever — violence between intimates is acceptable. Unlike the popular woman warrior of the Chinese classical text "Ballad of Fa Mu Lan," Goto's narrator does not engage in battle *in lieu* of her father but rather struggles *against* him, as does her symbolically potent family of women: three sisters and mother, Okasan. Through recourse to Japanese folklore, the hermeneutics of sexual and racial alterity, and an awareness of the overall tragic-comic sensibility required for living with a less-than-perfect family, *The Kappa Child* re-charts the notion of *safe space*. It deconstructs the presumption that the home is devoid of danger and that Asian immigrant parents can be defined in a uniform way, such as being staunchly supportive and unequivocally sacrificial. It also seeks alternatives to the suffering silences of the battered child. As Wendy Pearson observes, the novel is centrally "about families, both the ones you're born into and the ones you make for yourself." The safer, more secure family is not one devoid of fathers, but devoid of absolutist fathers (or husbands) who fail to respect and understand the women who share their lives. What King-Kok Cheung has observed about Kingston's woman warrior applies to Goto's narrator: "[Amid discouraging realities] she can only forge a viable and expansive identity by refashioning patriarchal myths and invoking imaginative possibilities" (164). Such possibility propels the narrator outside of her family in search of alternative kinships.

Trans-America, Asian Style

In "Heterogeneity, Hybridity, Multiplicity: Marking Asian American Differences," Lisa Lowe underscores the parallels between literal and conceptual mobility: "[W]e might conceive of the making and practice of Asian American culture as nomadic, unsettled, taking place in the travel between cultural sites and in the multivocality of heterogeneous and conflicting positions" (39). Because Asian America is ever "in process," it will "continue to try borders and revise interiors" (Palumbo-Liu 393). This evolutionary process underscores how transnationalism is not as new as many believe; it actually hearkens back to the genesis of Asian American studies in the 1960s which sought to draw parallels between the struggles of minority groups in the West and their Third World counterparts (Ty and Goellnicht Intro 8). Thus, what is "resolutely national" is complemented by the "insistently transnational, [which comprises] migrancy, global diaspora, flexible citizenship and neo-colonial relations between decolonized homelands and the U.S." (Schueller 170).

In contemporary transnational discourses, profound tensions exist between the need for family cohesion and the desire for personal autonomy, the feminist imperative to contest and dismantle patriarchy, and the struggle to diminish social inequalities arising between an Asian-descent minority and a non–Asian majority (Cheung 168).[4] This discussion of *The Kappa Child* offers insight into the emotional dynamics of transnational Asian families, focusing on the North American diaspora and how migration and settlement (in this case, from Japan to the rural prairies of Alberta, Canada) influence an immigrant family's adherence to traditional child-parent relations. The text compels readers to evaluate the adaptations made by the second generation, with their parents often assumed to be strict and espousing such Confucian values as obedience, politeness, deference to tradition, loyalty, discipline, and conformity. Many of these beliefs have been passed down through generations but with varying degrees of fidelity. The hierarchy that places the father at the head of the family is often accepted as a given as well as a right. Goto questions this assumption by having an intensely flawed patriarch and a troublingly subservient wife and children. Since transnationalism's ethos positions subjects "between worlds" in a spatio-cultural, geo-political arena that brings together "countries of origin and adopted homelands" (Berson ix), this dynamic is certain to foment new creative sensibilities applicable to real-life situations. Those values identifying ideal domesticity, intergenerational roadblocks, and hierarchical gender roles converge in Goto's novel.

Although a comprehensive exploration of family life in the text would require more space than can be accommodated here, existing Asian American critical apparatus is useful for placing this Japanese Canadian novel in a North American context. This interchange is possible because of the historical parallels between Canada and the U.S. (among them, hopeful immigrant sojourners forced into bachelor societies, the formation of ethnic enclaves, racist exclusion laws, regional polarities, and assimilation-related clashes). Yet Asian and Asian American Studies do not have the same institutional history in Canada as they do in the United States. While borrowing and overlap of discourses remains intellectually fortifying, a discrete Canadian aesthetics also demands both attention and definition.[5] As Eleanor Ty and Donald C. Goellnicht assert, "Asian North American" is a term that can be deployed as a bridge once there is an awareness of "both the national differences between the U.S. and Canada and the significant heterogeneity within the purview of the term" (2). While identifying along national lines may be the first impulse for citizens of either country, transnationalism reminds us that Asian America is neither fixed nor unitary; nor is it ever divorced completely from a global, postcolonial perspective.[6]

This scope and breadth demonstrate why the myth of the kappa, neither indigenous to Canada nor to North America, informs Goto's entire novel; it is a trope of transnational possibility, of Asian experience embodied in the supernatural, mythic, and hyper-real — but re-vivified in the local and almost anti-cosmopolitan environment of a small, arid prairie town. King-Kok Cheung reiterates how the nationalistic inclination to "claim America" through cultural nationalism has been replaced by an interest in forging stronger bonds with Asia. The critical impulse shifts from "being concerned primarily with social history and communal responsibility to being caught in the quandaries and possibilities of postmodernism and multiculturalism" (Cheung 1). These latter terms do not mean interpreting the national as regressive and the transnational as progressive[7]; rather, the imperative is to learn more about the history of imperialism and other resistance movements, attempting to understand their enduring relevance on both sides of the border (Schueller 171). Transnationalism also makes room for personal readings of nationhood, as when Goto's narrator, following her family from coastal British Columbia to landlocked Alberta, smells a Japanese cucumber in a greasy-spoon diner. It provokes a startling reaction: "My head spun dizzy with a flash of memories not mine. An unknown ache twisted my heart. Tears filled my eyes and longing rose, not from my stomach, but from the belly of my soul" (Goto 146).

As with this intimation of a foreign yet familiar place, transnational warrior women confront experiences that defy narrow definitions. Transnationalism establishes, dismantles, and mediates boundaries between non-majority cultures, targeting such concerns as the divergent interests of immigrant versus native-born, and the threat of hegemony by better-established ethnic groups over smaller, less acknowledged ones. The expression of the transnational can be intensely localized and personal, even to the extent of emerging at the cellular level; or, it can be as it is in Goto's work where the "trans" implies a movement across, not just spatially but through more abstract categories like ontological spheres, cultural orientations, and metaphysical planes. Some readers may be reminded of the concept of the "new *mestiza*" whereby theorist Gloria Anzaldúa leavened the idea of national consciousness by combining gender, race, sexuality, and geography. She argued that "*la mestiza* is a product of the transfer of the cultural and spiritual values of one group to another" (Anzaldúa 78), a mixture that renders her ethnic and lesbian body a mythic, sentient, political yet undeniably personal medium. Judith Raiskin explains, "While this [*mestiza*] synthesis does undermine the dualities of colonialism, racism, and sexism, for Anzaldúa the utopian vision is not a synthesis providing unity or stasis. Rather, it embodies a continual confrontation of difference" (163).

From There to Here: Myth as Anti–Violence Intervention

Physically, the Japanese kappa is an "aquatic, frog-like creature with webbed hands and feet, a small turtle-like shell, beaked mouth, and a bowl-shaped head" (Goto 277). It is the bowl's water that actually confers the supernatural powers, not the kappa's seemingly grotesque body. Also, because its habitat rests "in the borders between natural and human environments," the kappa is an overall hybrid, inhabiting multiple spaces and yet avoiding the stigma associated with typical monsters and aliens as threatening interlopers in the human world (Goto 277). In the hours between dusk and dawn, this water spirit has been spotted most frequently in Japan, with occasional appearances in other Asian countries, but none in North America — the author notes — until now (277). This pan–Asianness finds complements later in the text as the *Japanese* immigrant narrator half-copulates, half-wrestles with a kappa after a *Chinese* wedding banquet, only to eventually pursue a relationship with a

Korean Canadian grocer. The kappa's presence acts (not unlike water) as a solvent, bringing together disparate ethnicities and dissolving the assumption that myths are the imaginative jurisdiction of children. Also, that the kappa myths sprang from the tongues of the protagonist's Issei (first-generation) parents renders the prairie town to which the family moves "glocal," or simultaneously global and local. This observation finds greater credence when we consider how the kappa has the capacity to drown children and livestock as much as it can help humans through such practices as setting bones and alleviating drought. Goto explains that those who come in contact with the kappa usually meet one of two opposite fates: healing or death (Bouchard 3). The protagonist's father, teller of kappa stories but batterer of his own children, possesses the same power to create as well as destroy. Here in North America, he is beset with continually fallow fields, and it is the self-esteem and sanity of his family that require the living water that he will not — rather than cannot — give. The kappa steps in, but less as a surrogate than as an embodiment of hope, healing, and an expanded worldview.

Through an ironical and deliberately non–Christian recasting of the Immaculate Conception, Goto's narrator discovers that she is pregnant with — and by — a kappa. Her ravenous appetite for Japanese cucumbers, a favorite meal of these tricksters, juxtaposed with her barely-suppressed sexual attraction to her best friends (the lesbian couple, Midori and Genevieve), generates phallic humor while adding to a semiotics of sexual indeterminism. Much of the story, from the narrator's sexuality to the mechanisms of the kappa child's conception, remains unclear. The hermeneutics are appropriately fluid, as water is the kappa's *sine qua non* and imperative for human survival as well. The kappa child was conceived in a moonlight-drenched sumo wrestling match with a kappa "Stranger," a "retro-dressed person of questionable gender and racial origin" (Goto 121). For all of its strangeness, the encounter, like the protagonist herself, is contradictory and idiosyncratic. Instead of being a fight where one player wins, the struggle is mutually pleasurable, a sort of orgasmic *lucha libre*. The kappa, whether as childhood myth or embodied presence, reconfigures the limits of the possible and the real. Indeed, the narrator's voice is intermingled with that of the kappa child's, an *in utero/ex utero* duet that catalyzes the woman warrior's belated growing-up process. Indirectly, the kappa's presence offers an alternative to violence and self-diminution through the formation of alternative, ostensibly "post-familial" kinship bonds. Because intimacy, comfort, and acceptance are not givens as far as her particular family is concerned, they must be sought out in spaces well beyond the bonds of blood and early childhood experience.

Like her amphibious seducer, the narrator is steeped in ambiguity; her childhood friend Gerald Nakamura Coming Singer asks, "You a boy or a girl?" to which she retorts, "You Blood or Japanese?" (168). Prior to meeting this biracial neighbor, she saw Native and Asian Canadian identities as fixed and immiscible; their combination, initially at least, was "incomprehensible" (188). Recalling her childhood obsession with the *Little House on the Prairie* series, she realizes First Nations peoples were unproblematically construed as enemies by the author, Laura Ingalls Wilder, the intertextual foil to the narrator's own frontier-dwelling, four-daughter family. Noticing in a loaded way that her father Hideo "could pass for an Indian" (43), Goto's protagonist realizes that fathers do not always merit or give unconditional love, just as so-called Indians may not inhabit "teepees on the prairies...[but rather] live next door on a chicken farm" (188). The narrator lives in an environment where supposed enemies become friends and those who are supposed to guide and protect (namely the father) end up morphing into "the enemy" (230). Yet this is no Manichean allegory of good versus evil; she admits that her father is "a bastard all right, but a poor and generous one" (173). In a skillful intertextual twist, the narrator actually encounters the ghost of an abused Laura — now more truly a foil because of shared trauma — in a television set, with "starving face, lips cracked with malnutrition" (252). The young girl tells her that the much-loved autobiography of pioneer life depicted childhood "all wrong" (253). It is the narrator, survivor and witness, who can actually testify to the less-than-idyllic truth about families fractured by domestic abuse (253). Thus, instead of blaming the enemy from without, she looks within the safe space of the family home. She then starts to ask questions no one is bold enough to ask: "Did Laura's pa hit the ma?" (43). These questions illuminate the fault-lines running across family, chronology, and race. The implied violence within the home galvanizes the contemporary woman warrior to come to terms with her past as less of a formula and more of a process.

The narrator and her sisters lead adult lives that are "impenetrable to each other" (183) although as children, they shared a tenuous solidarity in "never knowing when the [next] blow would fall. Or on whom" (233). She is particularly haunted by the image of Okasan's face being struck by a "swinging arc of arm": "Smack. A hand-shaped stain on my mother's cheek, the color of pain and humiliation" (70). Instead of lashing out against their father, the daughters fold their feelings inward in what many readers may construe as a paralyzing passivity. It is the force of the fantastic, the kappa, who intervenes in this domestic war zone, albeit at a remove of years and not as a typical savior figure. As a response to the gendered and racial hierarchy of the strong Asian father and submissive Asian mother, the kappa emerges as genderless and non-parental. It does not, as with many sidekicks in children's stories, serve as a mentor, comrade, or even friend; here, it is a one-night stand, the briefest of lovers. Sometimes the nature of its antics (among them, peeping at or fondling women, as well as sucking entrails out of the anuses of people who offend it) are gender-ambiguous and even "queer." The kappa's mythic and ontological ambiguities mirror the non-conformity of Goto's androgynous protagonist. It reminds the reader of the "Ballad of Fa Mu Lan" which features gender crossing as its central motif. One stanza of that poem reads: "The he rabbit tucks his feet under to sit/The she rabbit dims her shiny eyes/The two rabbits running side by side./Who can see which is the he and which the she?" (lines 58–62 qtd. in Chin 138). What occurs here is the conflation of male and female into indistinguishable complementariness, not unlike the traditional Chinese synergy of the *yin/yang*. The kappa, alongside the narrator, suggests a generative site between such traditional binaries as male/female, native/transplanted Asian, and myth/reality. The text is not, however, a conventional meditation on liminality, or the threshold state between one state of being and another,[8] because the kappa child is a part of and yet *apart from* its presumptive human parent. The kappa and the hybrid child, although it never manifests directly, serve as a vehicle for re-evaluating the discourse of the monstrous as well as establishing a heroics of resistant — as opposed to submissive — filiality.

Gods and Monsters

King-Kok Cheung reminds us that an alternative ethics governs Asian male violence: "Unfortunately, the ability to perform violent acts implied with the concepts of warrior and epic hero is still all too often mistaken for manly courage; and men who have been historically subjugated are all the more tempted to adopt a militant stance to manifest their masculinity" (167). For men of Asian descent, the challenge is the need to rehabilitate their flawed public image instituted by racist stereotyping, as well as assert their validity in an environment that is perhaps exclusionary of non-whites in the first place. If they repudiate the feminine as part of the emasculation that was accorded to them culturally (through menial labor in sectors like cleaning and cooking), they myopically buy into the equation of "woman equals degrading." Asserting masculinity need not be aggressive, sexist, and patriarchal. In his reading of Carlos Bulosan's memoir *America Is in the Heart* (1946), E. San Juan, Jr. casts the figure of the Asian immigrant in a surprisingly gender-ambiguous light. Bulosan finds himself Othered as a Filipino and as a non-citizen alien. After surviving such torments as being viciously beaten and having his testicles crushed, he brings forth a new version of himself through an "inward process of self-awareness, a mode of internalization, more precisely self-gestation or parthenogenesis" conveyed through tropes of containment, pregnancy, and birth (San Juan 260). Beyond forced bachelorhood and second-class citizenry that Asian American men in particular have had to contend with since their arrival on the continent, there is a connection between birth (delivery) and the more metaphysical abstraction of *deliverance* from a previous position or state of self, even when there is no literal child to be had. The feminine association is positive and enriching rather than embarrassing and disempowering.

For Goto's narrator, this process of gestation and birth is a metaphor for consolidating and "let[ting] go" of a lifetime of concentrated, hitherto unexamined experiences of abuse (245). The kappa child is what compels the consolidation of these feelings: "My childhood spills into my adult life despite all my attempts at otherwise and the saturation of the past with the present is an ongoing story" (215). She confesses, "[T]he longer I'm pregnant, the more my thoughts are pulled to my childhood. Long gone and unvisited for good reason. I thought I had earned the right to forget" (233). In essence, the presence of the kappa child catalyzes her adult process of growing up; she must now start cataloguing her emotional archive and "cleaning house," as it were. Although her maturity emerges belatedly, it occurs on her own terms. The analysis of *The Kappa Child* presented in this chapter acknowledges the rich potential for transnational and feminist readings, but has a focus that is more centripetal than centrifugal, bringing us back to the family as the core of self-formation (or in abusive scenarios, de-formation). Distancing herself from the family—especially the father—is a way of drawing closer to the narrator's self. Also, while monsters and warriors appear to be ontological opposites, Goto's objective is to free us from even that assumption; wars need not be fought on a grandiose scale, and the personal agonies of a self-conscious woman of color—both monster and warrior simultaneously in the arena of her mind—are definitely worth examining. The author explains, "I wanted a central character that would be seen as malformed and unbeautiful, kind of like Richard III—almost troll-like—but still a hero" (Bouchard 1).

Monstrosity also morphs from a primarily physical modality to a moral one; as Goto theorizes, "It's this idea that you can have all these challenging, twisted things in your family that can cause psychological malformation. The question is then how do you move beyond that and enable yourself?" (Bouchard 1). Just as genes are passed down from parents, so too are traumas; the former may be non-negotiable, but the latter are not. Although the kappa stories and the traditional Confucian family are derived from Asian culture, they manifest not in any uniformly positive or negative way (for instance, as a great leap forward toward assimilation or backward to reclaim an imagined past); rather, we learn the imperative of living for ourselves with the inheritances we have been dealt rather than merely accepting them without the sense of agency or self-respect to refuse.

When Father Doesn't Know Best: Violence and Family Hierarchy

The Confucian model of the family still dominates the public perception of Asian North American life. This is even more the case if the parents are first-generation immigrants like those in *The Kappa Child*. Chinese American journalist Helen Zia explains the typical approach to family order in her immigrant household: "[T]he father, as patriarch, is the master of the universe. In our household it was understood that no one should ever disobey, contradict, or argue with the patriarch who, in the Confucian hierarchy, is a stand-in for God. My mother, and of course the children, were expected to obey God absolutely" (11). A strong hand is one way by which the Confucian father might ensure compliance in his children. Obviously, not every nuclear family's patriarch, whether Asian immigrant or not, uses violence in his domestic realm; what goes un(der)-examined is less the existence of patriarchal power and more the abuse of it. Goto's narrator, like Zia, takes a position toward her father that is fundamentally ambivalent; while these young women strive to be filial, they simultaneously crave the respect merited by full-grown, autonomous adults. Each daughter must save face (that is, preserve the family honor, lest the abuse become public) but grapple with the priority of saving her own life. Goto's narrator admits, "It isn't like I feel an overwhelming surge of affection whenever I think of our father, but, I don't know, an emotion I can't name stays small and silent in the depths of my heart. I can't cut off my feelings from him, my monster, my hero" (245).

The unnamable feeling that she "can't cut off" is filial duty, or the intertwined sense of biological connection, emotional obligation, and customary respect that exists between Asian North American parents and their children. Like Shakespeare's Prospero who must claim Caliban's darkness as his own, the narrator must negotiate her way through her paternal conflicts, burdened with the decision of privileging either her status as obedient daughter or as a person with the moral courage to extricate herself from the toxic household. The oxymoronic "my monster, my hero" captures the divided sensibility of the speaker who considers her own person to be monstrous. This is perhaps a complex sublimation of violent feelings for her father onto herself. She begins the narrative with a powerfully distorted self-image, considering hers a "monstrous gaze" (49) that accompanies "turtle shoulders" (10)[9], "unsightly toenails" (11), a "pumpkin expanse" of head (16), "colossal teeth" (21), a "square body" (24), an "exploding excuse for hair" (69), "ugly lips" (121), "bratwurst fingers" (142) and "bratwurst toes" (184). By this description, she is a freak, a collage of animal, vegetable, human, and non-human parts; in short, a monster. Perhaps her fragmentation is a parody of the blazon technique that early sonneteers used to praise the physicality of the poetic subject, breaking the beloved down into a collection of much-lauded body parts. She may be depicting the abused body, an accumulation of hurts that lacks unity, coherence, and veers toward caricature, hyperbole, and the grotesque. She also calls herself an "ugly pregnant Asian" (14) and "a short ugly Asian with a bad attitude" (84). The ugliness here is less a function of racist stereotyping than a result of her *personally* accumulated shortcomings. Her announcement, "I am not a beautiful Asian" (51) implies that not all Asians are categorically ugly. She does, however, acknowledge that being Asian adds to her sense of displacement in a racially homogenous environment. As she lacks a belief in her own dignity and human worth, even a minor childhood squabble floods her with self-hatred; she asks, "How can I face [her friend Gerald] again when I was a monster myself?" (261). Perhaps the saving grace is that if her father can exist as a combination of hero and monster, surely she can benefit from the same deconstructive momentum. The movement, in this case, would be her transformation from monster to hero.

The fear of familial and community ostracism in close-knit ethnic communities is not an exclusively Asian diasporic concern, but it does resonate with many tradition-bound, image-conscious Asian immigrant families. As Leslie Chang explains about her Chinese American childhood, there is a contrast between the private, protective stance of the family and its use of public exposure as a form of internal policing: "Whenever I failed at something, I felt that everyone knew. My problems had already been discussed at dinner tables throughout the community, passed around on the lazy Susan like a dish of stinky tofu. I know this because my own family did the same, and I leapt in, as eager as the next to winnow out the weak" (67). Goto's narrator explains from the perspective of a ten-year-old why her mother could not leave the abusive household: "[S]he couldn't save herself, let alone her children, and that was that. Going to white outsiders wasn't an option for an Asian immigrant family like us. If you ditched the family, there was absolutely nothing left" (199). Shame is a central deterrent in traditional as well as contemporary Asian diasporic families; in ancient Japanese culture, for instance, we recall the *sepukku*, or ritual suicide, as a way of retrieving lost honor or maintaining a heroic stance. Beyond cleansing a personal wrong, this sacrifice often rectified the image of a nation, state, or another such major collective, making the personal act a simultaneously symbolic and public-minded one. By that taken, a family member's daily life would ideally demonstrate praiseworthy and honorable choices; these, in turn, would bring respect to the entire group. We know from the examples above, however, that immense pressures accompany such an expectation, and that assuming all members will conform to an often abstract standard of stellar behavior may result in isolation, self-hatred, and ultimate estrangement. Thus, while the narrator's family defers to the father for leadership, his love remains conditional and fringed with doubt and fear. Listening to kappa stories becomes a reward rather than an easy expression of affection: "We waited. Would he tell us? Were we good enough?" (46). During the children's formative years, the isolation of the farming town exacerbated this problem, as the daughters and their mother had few opportunities for community support and alliance-building, especially with other women. Using icy irony, the narrator muses about whether the daughters owed Okasan anything: "And if we stick around, our mother might get it into her head that her children ought to notice her and give her the love she always wanted but could never receive. Ha! That's a laugh. We can't even love ourselves" (31).

In *Women in the Trees: U.S. Women's Short Stories about Battering and*

Resistance, Susan Koppelman stresses that it is as important to parse through the responses of women to brutality as it is to unpack the motivations of the abusers (xix).[10] Goto's narrator recalls what would have been the worst-case scenario: "Dad finally beat up Okasan so bad she has to be hospitalized. Battered, bleeding, no one there to save her. Okasan finally killed him. A knife" (206). Okasan's imagined actions are both desperate and cathartic, ridding the family of the immediate source of the violence and exonerating the perpetrator in the name of self-defense. At the same time, this would have been a pyrrhic victory. Since he was the fulcrum of family life, Hideo's erasure would have been as traumatic as the mother's possible mental response to the killing (insanity). Okasan does attack her husband with a knife, but while sleepwalking. She wounds him superficially by cutting his Achilles tendon, rendering him crippled but far from dead. A similar belated attack comes from the reserved youngest daughter, Mice; this episode, involving an axe rather than a knife, forces the father to acknowledge his history of violence and even inquire as to whether the narrator has "come to kill" him when she arrives at the abandoned farmhouse (259). Whether with knife, axe, or sharpened tongue, the gesture of cutting the flesh parallels—and foreshadows—the severing of family ties. Homeopathically, this is a gesture which also presages the narrator's healing process.

In the climactic confrontation with Hideo, she deploys both fists and words, demanding an apology for the abject fear and rejection that enshrouded their collective lives: "I'd use my bare hands. I'd slap you stupid until you cried, then I'd start punching you, slowly, all over, then I'd finish you off with kicks until every bone of your body was shattered" (259). This threat is particularly poignant because earlier, she describes her mother as "so boneless she might fall to pieces if anyone touched her" (127). Kappas are healers, we recall, skilled at reattaching severed limbs and setting broken ones (75). Her own experiences include being hit so hard while digging for water that the shovel drops from her hands (199). Hideo's defensive tactic is to appeal to his daughter's sense of filial obligation, using guilt to ensure her continued compliance. She realizes the incommensurability of being an obedient daughter while hungering to break the cycle of acquiescence and soul-crushing retreat: "Dad looks up and stares into my eyes. 'You are my child,' he says slowly. 'I'm not like you,' I manage. Shake my head in refusal" (259). This is a necessary yet painful repudiation of what she always wanted from him: acknowledgement and honest communication. Later, more confident perhaps because of her kappa pregnancy, she even dares to laugh at his physical discomfort after Okasan's attack. He is a pathetic figure at this point, addicted to nasal spray to counteract dryness, a snow-haired man living alone in a house whose "face is dark" (256). His daughter's laughter emphasizes the tragic-comic sensibility that has been developing in her ever since she discovered the alien pregnancy. The kappa child kicks up a rippling mirth that explodes out of her mouth: "I try to stop myself, but I can't, I laugh until my eyes water" (261).

Addressing violence with ironical laughter acts to "expose abusers for what they are: cowardly bullies, animated clichés, buffoons choosing to indulge in tantrums" (Koppelman xxiii). The capacity to laugh in the face of death subverts the idea of perpetual victimhood without trivializing the reality of the violence and its potentially life-threatening consequences. Although "American literature is not riddled with criminals who get away with crime," there are numerous stories of heroes who vanquish beasts, do away with sin, and rectify evil, often through murder (Koppelman xxii). These heroes tend to be male, although a female version can most plausibly exist; able to kill her abuser without guilt, she "reinforces the idea not of criminals but of cultural heroes" (Koppelman xxiii). Goto's narrator cannot, however, perform the role of vanquishing hero without emotionally wavering between the "good daughter" ideal and the survivor energized by anger: "My god. I was beating up an old man. My hands shake and I bite my lip. No, I won't start crying in front of him now" (260). Her compassion for his age and sex is a function of hitherto unquestioned patriarchy and her adherence to a cultural background that reveres elders and parents alike. It is a given, too, that parricide is unnatural, even more so for subjects who grew up dogmatically believing that one's parents know best. Unlike Fa Mu Lan's narrative in which the daughter fights *in place* of her father, Goto's warrior woman fights the very man that she is supposed to protect. On the farm years earlier, when he assaults her—a child—for incubating fresh eggs in their sweltering car, she recalls, "The tears were pouring but my mouth would never cry." Having been slapped so many times, she observes, "My face was dead, so nothing mattered" (179). Her restraint now, in direct contrast to his historical *lack* of restraint, establishes her moral superiority.

Killing the abuse does not necessitate killing the abuser, at least literally. When she chooses to retreat, it is a graceful exit, not a reluctant, cowardly one. The woman warrior acknowledges her heroic position in the confrontation by alluding to one of the oldest monster-vanquisher pairings in Western culture: "And if Grendel was aged-frail by the time Beowulf caught him, would the hero have shown compassion?" (261). This Anglo-Saxon saga illuminates how the act of revenge has its own repercussions. Being mature means understanding that some choices we make will inflict pain on others; what remains pivotal are the degree and the motivations for doing so. In this Asian North American context, we understand children cannot always be the models of obedience that their parents (if highly traditional) demand, nor should their parents expect it. Another difficult realization is that there are more ways to assess lived experience than assigning blame. In one instance, the narrator imagines her sister PG "in the belly of a library, searching archives for the lost secret spells of forgiveness" (171). Slither, the eldest girl who "always got hit" (198), encourages the narrator to receive counseling: "If you don't let the hatred go, he continues to oppress your life, just like if you were still living in his house" (266). As for Okasan's choice to cross borders with Janice Nakamura, a Nisei (second-generation) neighbor, Slither advises, "We don't need to understand. Can't you give her the space to act in her own self-interest? For once in her life she manages to imagine a better life for herself.... We should be celebrating in her honor" (267). The narrator cannot completely repudiate her father without undermining his formative role in her life, nor can she deny that there were "good times too," as when he was "all smiling and looking happy" (193). What's more, she would not have known about the existence of the kappa if not for her parents' stories.

She remains cognizant of his challenges as an immigrant of color without letting them cloud the dimensions of personal responsibility for his abuse: "Dad dreamt a futile dream but one he never gave up. Is that respectable? Maybe it was the ultimate challenge, the last immigrant frontier: to do the impossible in a hostile land" (192). Beyond the hurdles posed by visible minority status, he remains culpable: "Maybe he was just an asshole and couldn't admit he was wrong. Either way, the results are the same for the rest of us now. We drag around the baggage of our lives together" (192). Jules, an older Asian Canadian male who touches her life briefly, poses as a surrogate father. He explains: "Many people don't even think. They enact their lives without understanding the consequences of their choices" (187). As Hideo retreats from his daughter's attack, he argues lamely that he "did what [he] had to do" (260). This reasoning is not only clichéd, but also attempts to absolve him of all responsibility. His final injunction, "You're grown up. You do what you want" (260), frees his child from filial obligation but cannot adequately compensate for the years she and her sisters had to "gauge the buttons of [their] father's anger" (226). She recognizes the ultimate irony of her position, and the cost of letting go of the past: "I want to have the last word. Tonight. I want the last word. But there is nothing to say" (261). What has happened is the balance of power between father-god and subservient daughter-supplicant has shifted; it is a complete upheaval of the Confucian familial hierarchy. The conversation needs to continue within for the sake of her mental health. "A child isn't born bitter," she reflects. "Knowing that being grown up was no swell place to be means that you are grown up enough to notice. And you can't go back from there. You have to forge another route, draw your own map" (13). She has won her freedom without the sweetness of victory.

The Stranger Self: Refracted Imagery of Monstrosity and the Way Forward

Although conventionally Japanese, the first name Hideo is mildly reminiscent of the English word "hideous." This coincidence propels the semiotic of monstrosity well beyond its typical meanings: physical deformity and psychological or moral degeneracy. Hideo is central to the warrior's journey because he — not the alien kappa — is the epicenter of emotional conflict, making what we assume to be a safe space (the home) dangerous and indeed, even haunted.

Like his daughter, he participates in the discourse of the monstrous in a way that is again saturated with contradictions. This is important because like him, the narrator embodies the unexpected and the *Unheimlich*. Disjuncture and surprise, primary modalities of fantasy, are part of an overall paradigm for interpreting why the kappa (and kappa child) can be counted as symbols of transnational Asian feminist liberation. As Maxine Hong Kingston's warrior persona explains, "I learned to make my mind large, as the universe is large, so that there is room for paradoxes" (35).

In "Asian American Realities through Literature," Elaine H. Kim asserts, "One of the main points of *The Woman Warrior* is that a marginal person indeed derives power and vision from living with paradoxes" (200). Even Frank Chin, acerbic critic of Kingston's text, acknowledges that warrior life should not be an exclusively male domain: "In Confucianism, all of us — men and women — are born soldiers. The soldier is the universal individual. No matter what you do for a living...you are a fighter. Life is war" (138). Wars, however, need not be violent. While Kingston's autobiographical novel invites "feminist critiques ... [of] the severely restrictive roles imposed on women, social evils such as rape, footbinding, ostracism, and murderous violence" (Lim 276), the scope is transnational and premised on long-entrenched beliefs transplanted from the ancestral homeland to America on the wings of imagination. *The Kappa Child* asks us to theorize how such restrictions manifest into newer, more complex versions of feminine identity where the nation-as-family is less important than the dynamics of the individual family itself. For instance, during Easter, nervous fumbling by one daughter leads to a minor accident at the dinner table. Mice's filial act of serving her father some turkey results in the bird slipping comically into his lap. Hideo's immediate reaction, a raised fist, is part of a "pattern so ingrained he can't stop" (27). The phrasing implies, erroneously, that violence springs from an innate source rather than a learned one. The pattern would not be "ingrained" without his consent. The daughters watch how his actions ultimately negate the painstaking labors of their mother, but there are the rumblings of resistance:

> Then, we all stand. Slither, me, PG, and even Mice. We all stand, around the table, silent. And we are not small. Dad can see that we are grown. We aren't little children and he can't strike us anymore. His eyes scorch our faces, muscles in his jaw clenched into teeth, blood shooting into his forehead, our silent protest to his face. Rage frustrated, he turned to the table itself. Grabs two fistfuls of tablecloth and pulls. Turkey carcass, stewed cabbage rolls, buns, sashimi, sekihan, potato salad, peas and carrots. The hours of work Okasan has spent, wasted on the floor [27].

Easter is a celebration of the ascension of Christ, who, with the Father and Holy Ghost, forms the Christian trinity. The breakdown of the family under the tyranny of a (human) patriarch neutralizes the sacred power of the occasion and questions the appropriateness of the father-god. By mentioning that she and her sisters had "non–Christian prayers" (115), the narrator disengages herself from that religion's paradigm of the omnipotent Father, supplanting it with a decentralized belief system more accommodating of diverse spiritualities (among them, folk deities, pantheism, and the occult). This, in turn, is a model with which to understand human and more-than-human existence as collaborative rather than competitive. She explains, "[M]aybe, when humans are gone, our myths will come alive, wander over the remnants of our uncivilization. Kappa, water dragons, yama-uba, oni. Selkie, golem, lorelei, xuan wu. The creatures we carry will be born from our demise and the world will dream a new existence" (223). This apocalyptic, multicultural vision implies that an older, homogenous, and rigidly patriarchal order should be supplanted by a less hierarchical, more fluid, democratized perspective. It does not have to be woman-centered, but it certainly includes women. That is precisely why the kappa child is conceived during a millennial moment, the last visible lunar eclipse of the twentieth century, with a Stranger of indeterminate race, sex, and species. By mentioning the feminine symbol of the moon, eclipses (often viewed as portents of cataclysmic events in non–Christian societies), and an elderly lady's unprovoked attack of her "heathen soul" (9), the narrator posits alternative spiritualities as a liberation from the absolutism of both the God-as-Father and father-as-god.

Gently but cataclysmically, *The Kappa Child* places in stark relief the real pain of familial alienation. The narrator's pregnancy, which she initially mocks as "abnormal" (12), mediates her shift in self-consciousness from victim to survivor to warrior woman. Because of this event, she cannot live as she did before. As Lisa Harris observes, "[O]nly after the narrator's 'alien' pregnancy is resolved, does the narrator overcome its [her] feeling of being 'alien' in the family, and accept loved ones into its [her] life" (par. 19).[11] What Goto calls the "unmanifested creature-child" is a synecdoche for the nascent self (142). After all, the creature does not remain in the womb, traveling throughout the body and signaling its presence in such places as her armpit, buttocks, and even left ear (148, 183, 218). It also presages something more — self-confidence — that only she can produce and maintain, albeit with the emotional midwifery of helpful friends and even seductive (S)trangers. This pregnancy is truly "pro-creation," advocating the construction of a positive, productive, and rehabilitated sense of self in the wake of abuse by intimates. Since motherhood requires a powerful investment of mental and physical energy, the woman warrior must accept the heroic imperative of taking care of another in order to nurture a new version of the self. In turn, it is telling that once the narrator begins to appreciate herself, she lets others — namely a potential lover — into her life. Over the process of gestation (sliding from literal to metaphorical over the course of the text), she realizes that it is "[h]ard to know what to believe and what not to believe in this world," but her capacity to "become tolerant of incredible stories" is a consummate act of self-reflection and self-love (116).

Notes

1. Lisa Harris uses the pronoun "it" to describe this narrator as a means of "prevent[ing] recourse to the gendered baggage that Goto so carefully dismantles" (21). I am using the feminine pronoun "she" because the protagonist mentions gynecological tests, menstruation and pregnancy, typically female experiences. Also, I acknowledge the intertextual imperative of her family having four daughters to parallel the family of Laura Ingalls. The problem with the pronoun "it" is its association with the less-than human, such as animals; while fetuses are often referred to in this pre-gendered, neutral way, there are other connotations that Goto would likely wish to avoid, among them the dehumanization of Othered people, including lesbians and gays. Harris' use of "it," however, does resonate with Margaret Ezell's observation of feminist thinkers "who refuse to accept a single definition of 'woman' or of 'female expression," [and] ask us to listen for a multiplicity of voices, to be aware constantly of the fluidity and sheer abundance of possibilities attached to the search for 'difference' when it is not defined as being rigidly dichotomized or competitively hierarchical" (17).

2. Goto also deploys kappas in her young adult novel *The Water of Possibility* (2002). Contemporary Japanese writers well known to Western readers like Ryunosuke Akutagawa (author of *Rashomon*) have used the folk character; see his *Kappa* (1926).

3. Western readers tend to associate warrior lifestyles with a Eurocentric tradition, including ancient Greek and Roman fighters in Homeric tributes, the loyalty of an Anglo-Saxon thane under the *comitatus* system, and the romantic questing of knights in medieval allegory. Beyond figures like the Amazonian queen Hippolyta or St. Joan of Arc, women warriors—especially Asian ones—are more foreign. Asian heroines like Fa Mu Lan are undoubtedly women warriors, but what is concurrently needed is a spectrum of heroism that goes beyond the martial; for instance, the character Sim Ch'ŏng of the tragic Korean opera *Sim Ch'ŏng Jŏn* arguably demonstrates the same heroism as Mu Lan, offering up her body in exchange for her blind father's sight. As Korean American filmmaker Kyung-Ja Lee explains, "you can only sing in that kind of opera if you cough up blood. You cry so much that you end up with a deep, choked-up voice" (167). Speaking through blood and pain is an act that testifies to a child's filial devotion.

4. For discussions of Asian transnationalism in literature, see Lee (1999); see also Lim et al (2006). Lim et al (1999) is not Americocentric, focusing on gender roles in Southeast, East, and Pacific Asia.

5. See Goellnicht.

6. For caveats about terminology like "hybridity," "plural identities," and "border crossing," which may compromise the specificities of Asian American experience, see Koshy. For a broad discussion of the nexus between cultural transformation and the transfer of goods, services, and people, see Lowe. See Espiritu on Asian American panethnicity.

7. See Ong for a discussion of travel, capitalism, and flexible citizenship.

8. Liminality is now an interdisciplinary term, but anthropologist Victor Turner defined liminal entities as "neither here nor there; they are betwixt and between the positions assigned and arrayed by law, custom, convention, and ceremonial" (1969: 95). Cf. Turner's "Variations."

9. This metaphor is ambiguous because turtles in Native North American mythology are positive symbols. Certain creation myths (for example, the Iroquois creation story) have the world being formed on the turtle's back. As Lakota Mary Crow Dog recalls, a turtle woman is "a strong, self-reliant person, because a turtle stands for strength, resolution, and long life.... A turtle is a strength of mind, a communication with the thunder" (24). In Chinese culture, turtles signify longevity and good luck.

10. Although many texts meditate on the effect of battery on women's lives, see especially the feminist perspectives in Bair and Cayleff; Herman; Walker; and NiCarthy.

11. While Wendy Pearson insists that the text is not a novel aimed at depicting the rigors of immigrant life, *The Kappa Child* does target and magnify the sensations of Otherness that many non-white immigrants (and other members of minority groups) encounter. Okasan eventually leaves her husband to roam America in search of alien-abduction survivors from non–European backgrounds. The term "alien," after all, applies to extraterrestrials as well as strangers, outsiders, and non-citizens, especially in a social climate like the present when national belonging is so much at the forefront of political and legal discourse. These terms coincide with the deeply-rooted historical assumption that Asian-descent individuals are not "really" Americans or Canadians but rather, to quote the title of Ronald Tataki's eponymous book, "strangers from a different shore."

Bibliography

Akutagawa, Ryunosuke. *Kappa*. 1927. Trans. Geoffery Bownas. London: Peter Owen-Publishers, 2006.
Anzaldúa, Gloria. *Borderlands/La Frontera: The New Mestiza*. San Francisco, CA: Spinsters/Aunt Lute, 1987.
Bair, Barbara, and Susan E. Cayleff, eds. *Wings of Gauze: Women of Color and the Experience of Health and Illness*. Detroit, MI: Wayne State University Press, 1993.
Berson, Misha, ed. *Between Worlds: Contemporary Asian American Plays*. New York: Theatre Communications Group, 1990.
Bouchard, Gilbert. "Little Magic on the Prairie: Writer Hiromi Goto Brings a Creature of Japanese Myth into a Transformative Story of a Child Growing Up in Alberta." *Globe and Mail* 27 Nov. 2001. R3.
Chang, Leslie. *Beyond the Narrow Gate: The Journey of Four Chinese Women from the Middle Kingdom to Middle America*. New York: Plume-Penguin, 1999.
Cheung, King-Kok, ed. *An Interethnic Companion to Asian American Literature*. New York and Cambridge: Cambridge University Press, 1997.
_____. "The Woman Warrior versus The Chinaman Pacific: Must a Chinese American Critic Choose between Feminism and Heroism?" *A Companion to Asian American Studies*. Ed. Kent A. Ono. Malden, MA: Blackwell, 2005. 157–74.
Chin, Frank. "Come all Ye Asian American Writers of the Real and the Fake." Ono 133–56.
Crow Dog, Mary, and Richard Erdoes. *Lakota Woman*. New York: Grove, 1990.
Espiritu, Yen Le. *Asian American Panethnicity: Bridging Institutions and Identities*. Philadelphia, PA: Temple University Press, 1982.
Ezell, Margaret J. M. *Writing Women's Literary History*. Baltimore, MD: Johns Hopkins University Press, 1993.
Goellnicht, Donald C. "A Long Labor: The Protracted Birth of Asian Canadian Literature." *Essays on Canadian Writing* 72 (2000): 1–41.
Goto, Hiromi. *The Kappa Child*. Calgary, AB: Red Deer Press, 2001.
_____. *The Water of Possibility*. Regina: Coteau Books, 2002.
Harris, Lisa. "Eating and Reading Hiromi Goto." *Cuizine: The Journal of Canadian Food Cultures* 1.1 (2008): par. 1–29. *Erudite: Promoting and Disseminating Research Database*. 2 Feb. 2009 <http://www.erudit.org/revue/cuizine/2008/v1/n1/019372ar.html>.
Herman, Judith Lewis. *Trauma and Recovery*. New York: HarperCollins, 1992.
Houston, Jeanne Wakatsuki, and James D. Houston. *Farewell to Manzanar*. New York: Houghton Mifflin, 1973.

Kim, Elaine H. "Asian American Realities Through Literature." Ono 197–214.
Kingston, Maxine Hong. *The Woman Warrior: Memoirs of a Girlhood among Ghosts.* New York: Vintage, 1977.
Koppelman, Susan. "Introduction." *Women in the Trees: U.S. Women's Short Stories About Battering and Resistance, 1829–2000.* Ed. Koppelman. New York: Feminist Press of City University of New York, 2004. xvii–xxxi.
Koshy, Susan. "The Fiction of Asian American Literature." *Asian American Studies: A Reader.* Eds. Jean Yu-Wen Shen Wu and Min Song. New Brunswick, NJ: Rutgers University Press, 2000. 467–95.
Lee, Kyung-Ja. "A Humble Messenger." *East to America: Korean American Life Stories.* Eds. Elaine H. Kim and Eui-Young Yu. New York: The New Press, 1996. 164–73.
Lee, Rachel C. *The Americas of Asian American Literature: Gendered Fictions of Nation and Transnation.* Princeton, NJ: Princeton University Press, 1999.
Lim, Shirley Geok-lin. "'Growing with Stories': Chinese American Identities, Textual Identities (Maxine Hong Kingston)." *Teaching American Ethnic Literatures.* Eds. John R. Maitino and David R. Peck. Albuquerque, NM: University of New Mexico Press, 1996. 273–91.
Lim, Shirley Geok-lin, Larry E. Smith, and Wimal Dissanayake, eds. *Transnational Asia Pacific: Gender, Culture, and the Public Sphere.* Urbana, IL: University of Illinois Press, 1999.
Lim, Shirley Geok-lin, Gina Valentino, John Gamber, and Stephen Sohn, eds. *Transnational Asian American Literature: Sites and Transits.* Philadelphia, PA: Temple University Press, 2006.
Lowe, Lisa. "Heterogeneity, Hybridity, Multiplicity: Marking Asian American Differences." *Diaspora* 1.1 (1991): 24–44.
_____. *Immigrant Acts: On Asian American Cultural Politics.* Durham and London: Duke University Press, 1996.
NiCarthy, Ginny. *Getting Free: A Handbook for Women in Abusive Relationships.* 2nd ed. Seattle, WA: Seal Press, 1986.
Ong, Aihwa. *Flexible Citizenship: The Cultural Logistics of Transnationality.* Durham and London: Duke University Press, 1999.
Palumbo-Liu, David. *Asian/American: Historical Crossings of a Racial Frontier.* Stanford, CA: Stanford University Press, 1999.
Pearson, Wendy. "Saturating the Present with the Past: Hiromi Goto's *The Kappa Child*." Rev. of *The Kappa Child. Strange Horizons.* 6 Jan. 2003. 1 Mar. 2009 <http:www.strangehorizons.com/2003/20030106/kappa_child.shtml>.
Raiskin, Judith. "Inverts and Hybrids: Lesbian Rewritings of Sexual and Racial Identities." *The Lesbian Postmodern.* Ed. Laura Doan. New York: Columbia University Press, 1994. 156–72.
San Juan, Jr., E. "Searching for the Heart of 'America' (Carlos Bulosan)." Maitino and Peck 259–72.
Schueller, Malini Johar. "Claiming Postcolonial America: The Hybrid Asian-American Performances of Tseng Kwong Chi." Ty and Goellnicht 170–85.
Turner, Victor. *The Ritual Process: Structure and Anti-Structure.* Chicago, IL: Aldine, 1969.
_____. "Variations of the Theme of Liminality." *Secular Ritual.* Eds. Sally Falk Moore and Barbara Myerhoff. Assen, Netherlands: Van Gorcum, 1977. 36–52.
Ty, Eleanor, and Donald C. Goellnicht, eds. *Asian North American Identities: Beyond the Hyphen.* Bloomington, IN: Indiana University Press, 2004.
Walker, Lenore E. *Terrifying Love: Why Battered Women Kill and How Society Responds.* New York: Harper and Row, 1989.

Wong, Jade Snow. *Fifth Chinese Daughter*. 1950. Seattle, WA: University of Washington Press, 2002.
Wong, Sau-ling C. "Denationalization Reconsidered: Asian American Cultural Criticism at a Theoretical Crossroads." *Amerasia Journal* 21.1–2 (1995): 1–27.
Zia, Helen. *Asian American Dreams: The Emergence of an American People*. New York: Farrar, Straus and Giroux, 2000.

BETWEEN RUINATION AND RECONCILIATION
Dragon Princesses, Cambodian American Heroines, and Loung Ung's Lucky Child
Cathy J. Schlund-Vials

> Cambodia has a legend that originates with the marriage of a foreigner and a dragon princess, or nagi, whose father was the king of a waterlogged country. According to one version of the myth, a Brahmin named Kaundinya, armed with a magical bow, appeared one day off the shore of Cambodia. The dragon princess paddled out to meet him. Kaundinya shot an arrow into her boat, frightening the princess into marrying him. Before the marriage, Kaundinya gave her clothes to wear, and in exchange her father, the dragon king, [according to French archeologist Louis Finot] "enlarged the possessions of his son-in-law by drinking up the water that covered the country. He later built them a capital, and changed the name of the country to 'Kambuja.'" — David Chandler, A History of Cambodia (18)[1]

Youk Chhang, Director of the Documentation Center of Cambodia, provocatively notes, "Cambodia is known to the world for two things—Angkor Wat and the 'killing fields.' Some believe one came from God and the other from hell" ("Genocide site in Cambodia Draws Tourists.").[2] To be sure, the religious majesty of Angkor Wat — the largest standing temple in the world — operates in conspicuous contrast to Tuol Sleng Prison (S-21), Cambodia's most well-known Khmer Rouge genocide museum.[3] Even with this seeming discrepancy, the "city of temple" (Angkor Wat's meaning in Sanskrit) and the "hill of poisonous trees" (the Khmer translation of "Tuol Sleng") produce an interrelated view of Cambodian nationhood vis-à-vis built ruins and ruination. In particular, within Cambodia's multi-million dollar tourist economy, the architectural remains of Angkor Wat (a *de facto* religious ruin) monumentalize the Classical Khmer period in the twelfth and thirteenth centuries (*Sir Banister Fletcher's History of Architecture* 794). Alternatively, Tuol Sleng Prison, an equally significant tourist site, memorializes the twentieth-century loss of 1.7 million Cambodians (25% of the extant population) during the ruinous Khmer Rouge "killing fields" era from 1975 to 1979.[4]

If Angkor Wat (as a built monument) demonstrates the glory of a bygone age, Tuol Sleng Prison structurally bears witness to the more recent genocidal past. The Vietnamese invasion of the country in 1979 led to the large-scale political dissolution of Democratic Kampuchea. Soon after, the Khmer Rouge prison was converted from torture detention center to genocide museum. Under the curatorial supervision of Vietnamese General Mai Lam, Tuol Sleng was intended to provoke—through the material presentation of Khmer Rouge atrocities emblematized in photographs, paintings, blood-stained floors, victim skulls, and instruments of torture—Cambodian loyalty to the Vietnamese-occupied People's Republic of Kampuchea (1979–1993). Since its politicized inception, the museum continues to function as an increasingly indispensable site of memory, memorializing the genocidal realities of "Pol Pot time" for Cambodian and non–Cambodian visitors alike.

Almost thirty years have passed since the deposal of the Khmer Rouge. After decade-long debates over jurisprudence, governance, and funding, the U.N/Cambodian Khmer Rouge Tribunal (or Extraordinary Chambers in the Courts of Cambodia—ECCC) has only recently begun trying five former Khmer Rouge officials for crimes against humanity and war crimes. Indeed, obstructionist political machinations previously impeded the tribunal's commencement, prompting critics and human rights activists alike to wonder if justice will ever come to Cambodia. All the same, Tuol Sleng figures keenly in tribunal news principally because the first individual facing trial is S-21's notorious prison warden, Kaing Guev Eak (also known as Duch). Under Duch's directorship, fewer than twenty out of an estimated 14,000 to 17,000 prisoners detained (including men, women, and children) survived their imprisonment.[5] To date, Duch is the only high ranking Khmer Rouge officer to face the tribunal and his sentencing is scheduled to take place in spring 2010. Of those indicted for crimes against humanity, war crimes, and crimes against the state including Ieng Sary, Ieng Thirith, Nuon Chea, and Khieu Samphan, only one—Duch—has publicly confessed.[6]

Within this strikingly unreconciled juridical milieu, the purposeful juxtaposition of Angkor Wat and Tuol Sleng Prison devastatingly reinforces Cambodia's ruination a propos recent state-authorized mass violence. The stark contrast between monument and memorial highlights a Cambodian and Cambodian American fixation on the pre-genocide past. As historian David Chandler avers, "In the twenty-first century, Cambodia is a country that has been scarred by its recent past and identifies itself closely with distant periods. It is the only country in the world that boasts a ruin on its national flag" (11). Angkor Wat's ruined visage is therefore tragically apt for a nation necessarily preoccupied by its history. Concomitantly, in the contested light of contemporary Cambodian juridical politics, Tuol Sleng seems equally and catastrophically appropriate.

Consequently, Youk Chhang's abovementioned bifurcated casting of Cambodia through "heaven" and "hell" draws attention to the means by which the nation's history (and juridical body politic) circulates within a larger narrative economy. Situated within the nation's booming tourist industry, inclusive of religious and "atrocity" voyeurism, Angkor Wat and Tuol Sleng incontrovertibly come together as distinctively historic Cambodian destination points.[7] Despite differences of form, historicity, and structure, Angkor Wat and Tuol Sleng collectively constitute a complex, interconnected spatiality that converges almost seamlessly upon two separate moments of nation-state ruination.[8] In the case of Tuol Sleng, fundamental to this ruination legacy is the ever-thorny and heretofore unanswered question of reconciliation — wherein the inimical is formally acknowledged and formerly situated — for Cambodian victims, bystanders, and perpetrators.[9]

What is more, Chhang's binaried pronouncement of past Cambodian nationhood, coupled with the monument/memorial dichotomy of Angkor Wat and Tuol Sleng, politically and structurally foreground Cambodian American Loung Ung's memoir, *Lucky Child: A Daughter of Cambodia Reunites with the Sister She Left Behind* (2005). Positioned amid calls for justice, claims of trauma, and genocidal narratives of ruin, Ung's *Lucky Child* dialogically promulgates a multivalent reconstructionist literary project. Focused on narrative reconciliation through transnational articulation, familial reunification, and metaphoric nation-building, *Lucky Child* is for these reasons interstitially located between memorialization and monumentalization. Accordingly, Ung's "sisterly" story vacillates between memories of loss and transnational stories of survival in the United States and Cambodia.

Illustratively consistent with the author's larger political project — to contemplate the genocide and its aftermath from the vantage point of a Cambodian American — *Lucky Child* thematically echoes the author's contemporaneous assertion in a April 17, 2005 *New York Times* op-ed. The book was published on the thirtieth anniversary of the Khmer Rouge takeover of Phnom Penh, which signaled the start of the Democratic Kampuchean regime. Ung reflects, "...when my thoughts turn from the genocide to its survivors, I am immensely proud. Our people have been waiting twenty-six years for justice, but we have stayed strong, resilient, and hopeful.... My Cambodia today is beautiful, even as it continues to recover from the killing fields" (2009). This sense of "recovery" is manifest in *Lucky Child*'s dedication, which is directed "to the Khmer people — for theirs are not only the voices of war, but testimonies of love, family, beauty, humor, strength, and courage." Drawing on Ung's multifaceted articulation of "recovery," this chapter attaches the contrasting dimensions of "destruction" to "creation" within the space of transnational Cambodian American literary production. Insofar contemporary Cambodian, and by extension

Cambodian American, selfhood is constructed through profound moments of loss, Cambodian American author Loung Ung's assertion of "recovery," suggestive of reconstruction and restoration, produces a reading of (imagined) reconciliation.

In this sense, Ung's verbalization of "recovery" addresses human rights scholar Martha Minow's provocative question about "facing the past" after genocide: "After mass atrocity, what can and should be faced about the past?" (118). Within this "aftermath" context of post-genocide reconciliation and reunification, the title of Ung's memoir becomes more historically legible. Inclusive of "reuniting" and "left-behindedness," Ung's designation makes clear the central thematic aim of the memoir: to document the author's journey from unsettled refugee to reconciled Cambodian American.

If, as anthropologist John Marston convincingly argues, the Khmer Rouge deliberately utilized metaphors of construction via public celebrations of the nascent Democratic Kampuchean nation-state, then Ung's focus on Cambodia's original creation myth suggests a retrospective resistive act (114).[10] Set after the Killing Fields era, during Cambodia's post–Democratic Kampuchean transition period, Ung implicitly accesses Cambodia's foundational myth to heroic nation-building effect. Concurrently, the memoir begins in 1980, which coincides with the Congressional passage of the Refugee Act. Particularly relevant to Southeast Asians, this act enabled the entrance of 150,000 Cambodian refugees into the United States. Hence, *Lucky Child* accesses a post–Khmer Rouge, post–1980 Refugee Act transnational imaginary. Whereas Loung Ung's debut memoir, *First They Killed My Father: A Daughter of Cambodia Remembers* (2000), describes "life under the Khmer Rouge," *Lucky Child* is principally concerned with "life after the Khmer Rouge" (1980–2003).

As Ung declares, "*Lucky Child* begins where *First They Killed My Father* left off and follows both my life in America and Chou's life in Cambodia" (2005, xiv). Extending the building metaphor, Ung's pronouncement of "beginning" makes available an analysis of Ung's genocide memoir *First They Killed My Father* as a foundation text. Correspondingly, *Lucky Child* is at the level of narrative, plot, characterization, and history, very much erected on Ung's first memoir, which recounts through a predominantly first-person child narrator the obliteration of Cambodian life. If *First They Killed My Father* testifies to the destruction of Cambodian selfhood by the totalitarian Khmer Rouge, then *Lucky Child*'s sister story speaks to the creation of a post–Democratic Kampuchean citizenship within Cambodia. Simultaneously, Ung's autobiographical story of growing up after the Khmer Rouge in the United States opens up, to varying degrees, possibilities of diasporic belonging for the Cambodian refugee-turned-Cambodian American.

In addition, the construction project that ultimately dominates *Lucky Child* strategically employs a traditional Cambodian past to engender a story of "recovery." In this regard, Ung's account of her sister Chou's experiences in a

Vietnamese-occupied Cambodia functions alongside her own American coming-of-age story as a U.S. refugee in Vermont. Metaphorically fixed to each other, both stories rely on the direct and indirect use of the "Cambodian princess" (nagi) figure.[11] As evident in David Chandler's recapitulation of Cambodia's creation myth, as shown in the opening epigraph, the dragon princess operates as a legendary national heroine whose filial affiliation facilitates the dragon king's creation of Cambodia. Equally, this nationalistic legend, concentrated on the marriage between Khmer (the dragon princess) and Indian (the Brahmin), produces an original Cambodian selfhood predicated on politicized transnational current of culture and bodies. Within *Lucky Child*'s narrative fabric, Ung tactically revises this creation myth to speak to a post–Democratic Kampuchea era wherein "dragon princesses" once again are needed for nation-building.

Specifically, the heroism of Cambodian and American women who resist the Khmer Rouge directive to forget depends on the metaphoric marriage of the foreign (refugee) with the domestic. Following suit, it is the Cambodian American Loung Ung who weaves together a transnational story of two sisters whose disparate experiences in the United States and Cambodia connect to a larger narrative of a post–Democratic Kampuchean Cambodia. As a former national-turned-foreigner, Ung is both a "Cambodian princess" and foreign prince, whose memoir recuperates or "recovers" a heretofore submerged Cambodian history. Moreover, the reconciliation between past and present forms an analogous heroism in Cambodia. This epic frame encapsulates women like Ung's sister, who defy the previous regime by maintaining traditional Khmer rites and cultural practices. Complicating a coherent reading of Cambodia through a "princess" schema is the question of sovereignty. In particular, for a Cambodia under Vietnamese occupation, unstable political circumstances, glaringly apparent in the United Nation's recognition of the Khmer Rouge as a legitimate authority until 1991 and made worse by an obliterated infrastructure, obscure the existence of a legible sovereign figure or the dragon king.

In spite of the masculinist underpinnings of the foundational myth, Ung privileges the role of women in the making of Cambodian American selfhood and remaking of Cambodian nationhood. After all, *Lucky Child* features two female protagonists or two "princesses." The myth that undergirds the memoir's narrative structure is clearly at play in Ung's fairy tale-like introduction to her sister's story, which commences "across the ocean in the tropical land of Cambodia" (2005, 14). Fundamental to the manufacture of citizenship and nation is a seemingly anachronistic anti–Khmer Rouge resistance, especially when contrasted with the post–Democratic Kampuchean temporality of the memoir. Whereas Loung Ung bears witness to the Khmer Rouge past, which contradicts the Democratic Kampuchean directive to forget, Chou otherwise makes visible a transition-riddled Cambodian present still haunted by the Khmer Rouge.

Expressly, though the Khmer Rouge regime was ostensibly ousted in 1979, within the memoir Cambodia is still characterized by disruption and violence. As Ung narrates, her sister "is careful to step only on well-used paths.... For as beautiful as the countryside is, Chou knows that beneath the wildflowers, green grass, red dirt, and the wetlands are mines, grenades, bombs, and other tangible remnants of war awaiting her every step" (2005, 130). Juxtaposing "wildflowers, green grass, red dirt, and the wetlands" with "mines, grenades, [and] bombs," Ung underscores "tangible" and intangible "remnants of war" that, notwithstanding the Vietnamese occupation, highlight the persistence of the Khmer Rouge. Historically, from 1979 to 1989, the Khmer Rouge was still recognized by the United Nations as the legitimate governing body in Cambodia.[12] Most revealing is the past and present lack of prosecution concerning leaders of the regime — including "Brother Number One," Pol Pot, who died of natural causes in 1998.[13] Inadvertently, the comparative distinction between "natural" and "man-made" (for instance, wildflowers versus grenades) hearkens back to Chhang's national portrayal of "heaven" and "hell."

Alternatively, Ung must traverse dominant post–Vietnam War-era U.S. ethno-racial frameworks which threaten to undermine the author's assimilative assertions. Midway through *Lucky Child*, Ung confesses, "Since the movie *Platoon* came out, I have been beseeched with requests for 'a good time.' And though I have no plans — not now or ever — to see war movies, many stupid boys somehow see me in them." Ung then acknowledges, "I guess because I'm Asian and speak English badly, I must remind them of the Vietnamese prostitutes in these films" (2005, 135). Outwardly innocuous, the boys' collective characterization of Ung vis-à-vis a sexualized Southeast Asian female subjectivity betrays a more significant Cold War politics. For that reason, the 1969–1973 U.S. bombings of the Cambodian countryside, i.e. the so-called B-52 Menu attacks, were indicative of a more expansive Vietnam War effort, and fomented the destabilization of Cambodia's government. In turn, this destabilization and ensuing civil war significantly engendered the rise of the Khmer Rouge who from the outset promised peace. Divergently, Ung's gender identity — stereotypically reified through alleged promiscuity — is racially marked. Like Chou, Ung must intimately contend with military actualities, which in the United States take mass media form and produce racial stereotypes.

Returning to genre, Ung's *Lucky Child* as identifiable *Bildungsroman* brings to light the author's literary attentiveness to individual and national reconstruction and rehabilitation. Ung's coming-of-age narrative analogizes nascent nation-building (or rather nation-rebuilding) efforts in Cambodia and assimilationist self-construction in the United States. Geographically set in Cambodia and the United States, Ung's divided memoir takes on diasporic dimensions. *Lucky Child*'s polygeographic character is immediately observable in the author's opening contention that *Lucky Child* "brings us back to the caring people who went out of their way to extend a helping hand. Whether it was a kind word spoken to me as a child [in the United States] or a morsel of food that sustained Chou for one more day [in Cambodia]" (xiv). The absence of clear nation-state signifiers in Ung's original multisited reading of "kindness" instantiates—principally through omission—a transnational reading produced through the divided juxtaposition of Cambodian and U.S. settings.

Within *Lucky Child*'s narrative space, geopolitical boundaries are even more blurred in relation to the unbounded transnational flow of traumatic memory. Such currents of trauma end on two distinct nation-state points. Even so, such recollections temporally and geographically materialize through equivalent temporalities and locales (the Killing Fields era in Cambodia). Demonstratively, Ung divulges that "in the quiet recesses of my mind, the Khmer Rouge lurks and hovers in dark alleys, waiting for me at the bend of every corner. No matter how far I run, I cannot escape the dread that they have followed me to America" (2005, 27). With specific mention to her "mind," Cambodian American Ung psychologically configures and concretizes the trauma of the Killing Fields era through the personification of a perceived Khmer Rouge threat. In the face of geographic and historic distance, such a threat persists "no matter how far one runs." Analogously, Cambodian Chou "sees ghosts roaming around the villages.... She knows she cannot allow herself to think too much about death; such a path will lead her to wonder about how Pa, Ma, and Geak [her younger sister] died" (Ung 2005, 130).

Even with memory coherences, *Lucky Child* is chiefly invested in two "coming-of-age" stories at the level of plot and characterization. For author/protagonist Ung, this *Bildungsroman* narrative is exposed through multiple acts of U.S. acculturation, evident through descriptions of dress, the acquisition of American slang, and American teenage angst. As Ung becomes more and more assimilated, she ceases, by her own declaration, to be "a proper Cambodian girl" (2005, 100). In contrast, as Chou enters adolescent and young womanhood, she increasingly embodies (and for the most part embraces) a decidedly more traditional Cambodian female subject position. Assuming the initial role as a sisterly caretaker, Chou marries, becoming a dutiful wife and devoted mother. Foreshadowing her sister's marital and maternal proclivities, Ung relates that Chou "dreams of someday having children and a family of her own to love and care for" (2005, 134). Quite the opposite, Ung rejects Khmer family frames and is, by her own admittance, "boy crazy" (2005, 138). Taken together, if Ung and Chou are indeed "dragon princesses," then they reflect two paradoxical modes of idealized selfhood. For Ung, an adolescent desire to date gestures toward her Americanization. This Americanized sensibility in turn cements her Cambodian American-ness. On the contrary, Chou's marriage aspirations attest to an adherence to a traditional Khmer gender role, which concretizes her Cambodian-ness, according to *Lucky Child*'s logics.

Be that as it may, in the face of "American desire," Ung's primary "coming of age" conflict in the memoir is on the whole assimilative. This assimilationist tension appears in particular chapter titles, which address through oppositional means the Cambodian American protagonist's alienation. Such titles include "Minnie Mouse and Gunfire," "Hungry, Hungry Hippos," "Totally Awesome U.S.A.," and "Sweet Sixteen." The use of American popular culture designations in comparison to narratives of traumatic alienation function as subversive signifiers via Ung's at times elusive Americanization journey.

For example, in the opening chapter, "Welcome to America," Ung recounts her reaction to a Disney-themed bedspread. Ung writes, "tracing my finger over the mouse's large round ears and the duck's protruding fat beak, I smile and think what fun it would be to belong to such a family." The defamiliarization of Disney icons echoes Ung's alienation with regard to her new home. This alienation is reiterated later, with Ung's assertion, "'I'm home!' I tell myself, but the world remains strange to me" (2005, 11). Despite the use of "welcome" in the chapter title, Ung's account makes visible an oppositional reaction. In turn, Ung's declaration of "home" is undermined with the assertion of "strangeness," which makes plain her refugee estrangement.

If Ung's refugee status is reiterated through such U.S. encounters, Chou's Cambodian citizenship is confirmed through her adherence to traditional frames. Like the original "dragon princess," Chou marries and reproduces (literally and figuratively) the nation. The headings attributed to Chou's narrative are rooted in traditional Khmer culture, exemplified by titles such as "Betrothed" and "Peasant Princess" (connected to the Khmer practice of arranged marriages and marriage ceremony). Certainly, the description of Chou on her wedding day—wherein she resembles "the golden goddess Apsara"—hearkens back to the "dragon princess" characterization and calls to mind the female goddess figures featured on the bas-reliefs of Angkor Wat (Ung 2005, 170). This reading is substantiated at the start of the wedding scene, wherein Chou is told by the "wedding dresser" that she will turn Ung's sister "into a beautiful princess" (2005, 170). A pre–Democratic Kampuchean Buddhist sensibility materializes in titles such as "Restless Spirit" and "Living Their Last Wind," which draw on Theravada Buddhist spiritual understandings of the self. Indeed, as the dominant religion in both pre- and post–Khmer Rouge Cambodia, Theravada Buddhism speaks to two separate moments of national cultural identity. Alternatively, as one of the two main strands in Buddhist practice (along with Mahayana Buddhism), such religious allusions indirectly allow for a potentially more universal, expansive reading of contemporary Cambodia.

The direct allusions to tradition and religion in these chapters accrete more significant meaning given Khmer Rouge policy, which attempted to obliterate past Cambodian practices to facilitate a cultural return to "year zero." The insertion of specific dates in chapter headings (e.g. "June 10, 1980") potently and unapologetically resists this Khmer Rouge directive. The titles and foci of Chou's chapters are likewise embedded in a contemporary Cambodian political landscape shaped by familial reunification, ongoing tension, war, and chaos: "Amah's Reunion," "War in Peace," and "A Child Is Lost." Interestingly, Ung renders her narrative portions using a first person point of view, whereas Chou's narrative is told through a third person omniscient perspective.

The dissimilarity via points of view produces a tangible sisterly distance within *Lucky Child*'s literary imaginary. Geographic distance and spatial remoteness are reinforced by the three sections of the memoir. Part one is entitled, "Worlds Apart," and temporally centers on a period from June to December in 1980. The second section (1983–1986) is named "Divided We Stand." The third section — marked by multiple returns to Cambodia (1989–1995)—is aptly titled "Reconnecting in Cambodia." *Lucky Child* concludes with an epilogue, which is set in 2003.

Taken together, the chapter and section titles—replete with Cambodian and American allusions—adhere to one another through initial separation (apartness) and divisiveness. The articulation of "reconnection" in the final section collapses the geopolitical imaginaries of the United States and Cambodia. Ung rejects a bicultural characterization in favor of a more porous transnational portrayal, making visible diasporic dimensions within the text. Ung eschews a divisive articulation in favor of a collective categorization. As anthropologists May Ebhiara, Carol Mortland, and Judy Ledgerwoods maintain, such a diasporic subject position forces one to

> abandon a view of Khmer refugees as biculturals, people who come from one culture and now live in a second, and exchange it for a perspective that sees war, flight, camp life, and resettlement as a series of distinctive cultural experiences that have far-reaching impact on refugees. "Being Khmer" is a particular and cultural orientation set within a particular context shared only by other Cambodians [19].

Haunted by memories of the Killing Fields era yet focused on a Cambodian and Cambodian American present, Ung's *Lucky Child* is a text circumscribed by ruin, embedded in ruination, and committed to reconciliation. Concurrently, Ung's titular insistence that she is still a "daughter of Cambodia" despite her location in the United States at the outset confirms her membership into a larger Cambodian imaginary that exists in the shadow of large-scale, state-authorized loss.

For Loung Ung, the autobiographical protagonist, the failure of easy assimilation into the U.S. body politic — in part because of her traumatic past — makes dramatically less stable the memoir's dominant U.S. "melting pot" characterizations even with the early admission that she was able to experience "living the American dream" (2005, xiii). And in the face of early authorial claims of "recovery," reconciliation, and reunification, Ung's journey from Cambodian refugee to Cambodian American is nonetheless marked by repeated declarations of "anger and revenge" that are eventually — though not immediately — replaced within the narrative by assertions of reconciliation and acceptance. For instance, as Ung struggles to learn and speak English, she relates: "Sometimes I wish I had a T-shirt that reads 'I don't speak like you. I'm from another country. We don't speak English there. So stop being rude!' But no such t-shirt exists. And I don't want to explain how I started school as a ten-year-old in the second grade because then I will have to tell them about Cambodia and the Khmer Rouge" (2005, 101). Militating against facile linguistic assimilation, Ung's desire for another communicative mode, through writing, foreshadows her literary projects in *First They Killed My Father* and *Lucky Child*, which effectively transmit the legacy of "Cambodia and the Khmer Rouge." At the same time, Ung's refusal to explain her status is at first predicated on the contradictory traumatic desire to not vocalize the genocidal past.

For Chou, at stake is how the Khmer Rouge period continues to impact Cambodian life more than a decade after war, famine, and genocide. Juxtaposing her "American dream life" with her sister's Cambodian reality, Ung relates that her own experiences with wealth occur in stark contrast to her sister's life "in a squalid village with no electricity or running water" (2005, xiii). What is more, in a text focused partially on familial reunification, it is the fifteen years of separation (from 1980 to 1995) that haunts Ung, transforming into an "obsession that has taken me back to Cambodia over twenty times" (2005, xii). From the outset, this return is "imagined" through the articulation of Chou's experiences in Cambodia alongside Ung's navigation of the U.S. cultural landscape. However, by the memoir's conclusion, this return to Cambodia — replete with descriptions of reunion and reunification — is through plot actualized and explored.

Chou's narrative takes a markedly different path. *Lucky Child* maps her journey from a displaced Cambodian refugee in a Thai refugee camp to a full-fledged Cambodian citizen. In this sense, Chou's story of return engages an alternative migration tale, which in turn foregrounds a post–Democratic selfhood cartography. Interestingly, Chou's story — despite Cambodian-centric registers — in the end resembles an American "rags to riches" narrative and model minority characterization. Ung's declaration that Chou has, in effect, succeeded in the face of overwhelming odds, inclusive of genocide, post–Khmer Rouge instability, and continued political destabilization, depends on a sisterly success made possible by patience, perseverance, and hard work. As Ung narrates, as Chou prepares to move into a new home, she "stares back at her hut. She sees her adolescence spent collecting water, chopping wood, preparing meals, and braving Khmer Rouge attacks. By the time the truck reaches the bend in the road, Chou smiles at the memories of her life, their survival, and the births of her children" (Ung 2005, 239). Even so, Chou's reflection on "the memories of her life" does not represent a wholesale acceptance of her Cambodian reality, which requires her to "brave Khmer Rouge attacks." Such raids leave Chou "anxious, paranoid, fretful, and unable to sleep," making visible political instability and the persistence of the Khmer Rouge.

Indeed, Chou must resort to transnational flows of capital, from the United States in the form of her now Americanized brother Meng, as a means of humanitarian escape (Ung 2005, 240). It is through capitalistic currents that Chou is able to escape life in a "squalid village." In *Lucky Child*'s concluding moments, Chou "falls asleep in a new house" (244). This solution in some ways foregrounds a limitation within a text that struggles to memorialize the past and monumentalize the present. Though a de facto "Cambodian princess," Chou still lacks the economic capital to rebuild and must instead depend on a former national-turned-foreigner (Meng) for viability and, to an extent, survivorability. In this regard, *Lucky Child* privileges a capitalistic mode for socioeconomic possibility alongside a model minoritization of persevering Cambodian selfhood.[14]

Returning to a U.S. context, Ung's narrative of life in the United States is constantly interrupted by memories of Democratic Kampuchea. This conflation is apparent in the third chapter, the aforementioned "Minnie Mouse and Gunfire." The Ung family sponsors have invited Ung, her brother, and her sister-in-law to a Fourth of July picnic, which culminates in a firework display. The sounds of the fireworks force Ung into a realm that is "outside of time and space and in a world where Cambodia and American collide, with me stuck somewhere in the middle." Ung continues:

> A baby screams as the soldiers reach into the bomb shelter and pull out a woman. Her clothes are black and dirty and her face is muddy. She clutches the baby to her breast, and begs for mercy, taking me back to the death of Ma and Geak [Ung's younger sister]. All of a sudden, my world goes red and I am back in America, disoriented and terrified.... "One ... Two ... Three," I breathe as pictures of Cambodia and America are superimposed one on top of the other ... [2005, 31].

For those familiar with Ung's first memoir, *First They Killed My Father*, the above scene occurs at the end of the text, during the period of the Vietnamese invasion in 1979. Ung confirms this connection with a brief recapitulation of her friend Pithy's death, which figures keenly in this section of the first memoir. Nonetheless, Ung's description is filled with allusions to life under the Khmer Rouge — the "black" dress of the woman, the mention of soldiers, the emphasis on the color "red"— that in turn highlight the actualities of Democratic Kampuchea, which forced its citizens to dress in black pajama-like clothing and live under harsh military rule. The mention of "red" in the passage suggests not only a bodily understanding of loss (the millions dead) but also reminds the reader of the Khmer Rouge ("red" Cambodians).

As Ung narrates this scene, memories of Cambodia overwhelm the protagonist despite her location in the United States. This characterization of transnational memory is repeated through the course of the memoir. For Ung, the transnational flow of traumatic memory produces feelings of undesirability and ambiguity. On the one hand, memory preoccupies the narrative structure of *Lucky Child* for it accesses state-authorized mass violence and large-scale human loss. On the other hand, Ung as protagonist becomes a conflicted transnational subject. Unable to fully forget the past, Ung nevertheless struggles to Americanize.

The obstructionist nature of genocide memory and Khmer Rouge remembrance is most discernible in a chapter entitled, "The Killing Fields in My Living Room." The issue of "home," which in this instance occurs within a domestic Vermont imaginary, is literally invaded by a cinematic reminder of the Cambodian genocide. Ung writes:

> The commercial begins with a group of helicopters flying into view like a swarm of dragonflies, then cuts to scenes of bombs dropping onto Cambodia, and the Khmer Rouge soldiers storming into Phnom Penh. On the screen, as the soldiers raise their guns and fists to the sky in victory, Haing Ngor, the actor playing Dith Pran, stands alone in a flooded rice field. Dressed in a wet black tattered shirt and pants that cling to his thin frame, his face contorts as he realizes he has stepped into one of Cambodia's many mass graves.... From somewhere in my brain, the smell of putrid flesh leaps off the television and fills my nostril ... [2005, 124].

Akin to the Fourth of July incident, Ung remembers moments of violence—in this case, such acts involve her mother Ma and her little sister Geak. This recollection of suffering is reinforced by a subsequent mass media description of the Ethiopian famine, which features televised reportage of starving children. Despite the geographic specificity of each instant—the living room in the United States, the cinematic treatment of Democratic Kampuchea, and the news report on Ethiopia—the impulse to memorialize the past and the country of origin through the revelation of loss conflicts with Ung's desire that "the Lord Buddha will keep the war away and out of my head" (2005, 126).

Similarly, chapters focused on Chou make visible the impact of the Khmer Rouge regime and civil war on contemporary life. What follows "The Killing Fields in my Living Room" is the previously mentioned "Living Their Last Wind," wherein the narrative shifts to Chou's experiences in Cambodia. The chapter is filled with three scenes of Cambodian landmine deaths, and the title refers to the final moments before death. Like Ung, Chou remembers her mother's and sister's deaths under the Democratic Kampuchean regime. The emphasis on torment within the chapter can also be read respective of Buddhist thought, which maintains that suffering is necessary for human world transcendence. The Cambodian villages become doubly haunted spaces. Alongside the deaths of almost two million Cambodians is the ongoing loss of human life after the deposal of the regime. Therefore, "Living Their Last Wind" memorializes the Killing Fields era and its aftermath.

Comparable to Ung's narrative, Chou's story is rooted in memories of the past that are inextricably attached to an involuntary genocidal remembrance. In sum, the two narratives highlight the traumatic terrain that locates both Cambodian and Cambodian American subjects. More significant, the absence of facile resolution afforded to both characters—which takes the form of "forced memory"—becomes one of the central conflicts in a text that in many ways attempts to foment transnational reconciliation. In addition, the inclusion of Chou's narrative within the fabric of the memoir operates as another site of negotiation for Ung as Cambodian American subject. As Ung imagines Cambodia through Chou's narrative, she in effect attempts to bring the Khmer Rouge past into accordance with a Cambodian present. This reconciliation structurally occurs in a memoir divided between autobiography and ethnography. As Ung's story collides into Chou's story, *Lucky Child* engenders a transnational historiographic rendering experiences and recollections.

Furthermore, to reconcile suggests the reestablishment of a close relationship, a resolution of conflict, and embodies the notion of acceptance. Within the literary imaginary of *Lucky Child*, Ung endeavors to not only "reunite with the sister she left behind," as the full title reminds the reader, but lay to rest a host of mixed feelings about the country of origin and her experiences in the country of settlement. These mixed feelings circumscribe Ung's refugee status, embedded in a reality of forced relocation. Though the full title of the memoir suggests a consistent desire to "reunite" with her Cambodian sister, the majority of Ung's narrative is spent reconciling this desire with a stronger impulse to forget the past, and it is only in the concluding chapters of the memoir that Ung returns to Cambodia. Chou's narrative is also framed according to a discourse of reconciliation, in which the "sister left behind" must contend with life in a nation forever changed as a result of genocide and war. Thus, what emerges is a narrative of two "heroines of Cambodia" who negotiate connective histories of displacement and dislocation.

Such narratives of displacement and dislocation are eventually supplanted by declarations of reaffirmation and reclamation. This particular reconciliation occurs in the final chapter of the memoir entitled, "Ma's Daughters," which once again emphasizes the familial frame of the text. The year is 1995, and Ung has graduated from college. Ung admits that "when [she] think[s] about being back in Cambodia, [she] is filled with fear" but decides to go with her brother Meng despite her anxiety (2005, 249). Her initial return to Cambodia is marred by her American sensibility with regard to clothing. Dressed in "comfortable, practical, loose-fitting black pants, brown T-shirt, and black Teva sandals," Ung resembles in raiment a Khmer Rouge cadre (2005, 251). The awkwardness of this incident quickly shifts to Chou's excitement over the reunification with her sister. The two return to their family home in Phnom Penh, which serves as the ultimate setting for reconciliation within the memoir. The tension between being American and being Cambodian is reconciled in this final moment as Ung states, "I understand then that though America may be my home for the moment, Cambodia will always be my heart and my soul." Ung imagines her dead father in this instance, and tells him that she is "not afraid anymore" (2005, 255).

The epilogue that follows reconfirms this declaration, for Ung is back in

Cambodia visiting her sister. And it is in this final scene that the shift from memorial to monument is most apparent. The memoir concludes with a scene from a family reunion that occurs in 1998 in Bat Deng, Cambodia. The reunion celebrates the over "five hundred relatives and friends old and new" and commemorates family members lost in the genocide. Ung avers, "even though I'd witnessed the worst of man's inhumanity to man, in my family and my life experiences I'd also seen the very best of man's humanity to man" (2005, 264). Ung declares her wholesale commitment to memory with the pronouncement that she will always remember those lost, and *Lucky Child* ends with a scene wherein she and her sister Chou pray together. The reunification is therefore made complete within the literary imaginary of the text.

Concomitantly, by the memoir's conclusion, Loung Ung offers an alternative negotiation of Cambodian/Cambodian American selfhood that ultimately moves away from the dominant victimhood narrative of ruination and toward reconstruction as a viable channel to nation-state reconciliation. In so doing, *Lucky Child* memorializes the Killing Fields era, directly speaks to the refugee experience, and monumentalizes Cambodian/American survivability. Correspondingly, *Lucky Child*—focused on sisterly frames and narratives—becomes a literary monument to the role of women in forging a post–Democratic Kampuchean selfhood. Such selfhood is constructed through memory of the past and reunification. The revelation of past trauma, at least within the memoir's structure, makes possible a heretofore underexplored literary route to reconciliation. With its implicit focus on two types of "Cambodian dragon-princesses," Loung Ung's *Lucky Child* is to an extent a story about heroism and heroines.

The bilateral memorialization/monumentalization that occurs in the memoir speaks to what Youk Chhang would later propose as a reconciliation structure. In accordance with the annual International Women's Day celebrations, on March 8, 2008, Youk Chhang, Director of the Documentation Center of Cambodia, proposed the building of a statue to commemorate the achievements of Cambodian women. In an article entitled, "Heroines of Cambodia," Chhang professed:

> All female survivors of Democratic Kampuchea are heroines of Cambodia. Seventy percent of the survivors of the Khmer Rouge regime in 1979, women have been a central force in the reconstruction of the nation. They reshaped the nation's economy during the tumultuous decades of the 1980s and 1990s, when civil war with the Khmer Rouge ensued.... Furthermore, it was through their unwavering efforts that Cambodian culture, education, and traditions, which nearly vanished at the hands of the Khmer Rouge, were reinstituted in the social fabric of daily life. Under these difficult circumstances, the women of Cambodia demonstrated great strength and resilience [*Searching for the Truth* 6].[15]

The figure, standing twenty-five feet high, would feature a woman holding a young child. Averring that the statue would operate as a memorial and a monument to Cambodian women, Chhang highlights a gendered correlation between female bodies and Cambodian nationalism. Chhang ascribes to women a form of heroism constructed on the assumption of cultural and economic recuperative roles during and after the Democratic Kampuchean regime. Divided into seven parts, the bottom third of the statue would be "buried beneath the soil, representing the millions who died in the genocide." The remaining four parts, "located above ground, [would] symboliz[e] the millions who survived" (*Searching for the Truth* 6).

The plans for the statue potently underscore, through the delineation of distinct parts, the seven million who lived in Cambodia at the time of the Khmer Rouge takeover. Based on a visual vocabulary that combines loss and reclamation, Chhang's mother and child statue monumentalizes reproduction of affective forms of Cambodian citizenship via the gendered body. Facing west, which, according to Buddhist belief, is the "direction of death," Chhang concluded that the statue would "evoke sorrow and compassion, not anger and revenge" and remind viewers of "who we are and where we came from" (*Searching for the Truth* 6). The statue's westward gaze — in the "direction of death"— geographically gestures toward the United States and metaphorically directs attention to Cambodian American refugee bodies.

Unintentionally, Chhang's statue proposal encapsulates the task facing Cambodian American refugee writers whose memoirs commemorate loss and monumentalize survival from the West and within the "direction of death." What is more, the "evocation of sorrow and compassion, not anger and revenge," intimately connects to Loung Ung's reconstructionist project, which tries to negotiate the genocidal past alongside unreconciled justice claims in the present. Hence, in form and function, Ung's memoir literarily enacts comparable collapses between memorialization and monumentalization by means of familial affiliation, dragon princesses, and transnational citizenships.

Notes

1. Quoted in David Chandler's *A History of Cambodia*. According to Chandler's footnote on page 250, see Louis Finot, "Sur quelques traditions indochinoises," *Bulletin de la Commision Archéologique de l'Indochine* (1911): 20–37.

2. According to the Documentation Center of Cambodia's website, "Since its inception, the Documentation Center of Cambodia (DC–Cam) has been at the forefront of documenting the myriad crimes and atrocities of the Khmer Rouge era. DC–Cam was founded after the U.S. Congress passed the Cambodian Genocide Justice Act in April 1994, which was signed into law by President Clinton. That legislation established the Office of Cambodian Genocide Investigations in the U.S. State Department's Bureau of East Asian and Pacific Affairs in July 1994, which was charged with investigating the atrocities of the Khmer Rouge period (1975–1979)."

3. Prior to 1974, Tuol Sleng was a Cambodian high school.

4. To expand, both Angkor Wat and Tuol Sleng represent distinct nodes in Cambodian

history wherein foreign influences play a major role. Originally a Hindu temple, Angkor Wat became a Buddhist religious center during the thirteenth century. The Indian influence on the temple — discernible in Vishnu-themed bas-reliefs and its galleried temple structure — architecturally coexists with a column of Buddha statues, consistent with the temple's Theravada Buddhist conversion. Tuol Sleng's roles as a genocide museum further confirms the Vietnamese 1979 victory in Democratic Kampuchea and makes visible some of the stakes involved in Cambodia's post-genocide nationhood.

5. If Tuol Sleng's Duch embodies the Khmer Rouge, then it follows that S-21 becomes an unquestionable architectural metonym for Democratic Kampuchea. Correspondingly, on February 27, 2008 (roughly a year before the official start of the tribunal in March 2009), Duch was asked by trial administrators to reenact alleged crimes on museum grounds to symbolically and publicly foment the reconciliation process. On the one hand, the reenactment request and subsequent performance matched the tourist-centric spectacularization of Tuol Sleng as a legible site of unimaginable human loss. Insofar Tuol Sleng as a genocide museum commemorates victims of the Khmer Rouge regime, Duch's performance also carries the possibility of producing closure through the performed acknowledgement — or reenactment — of crimes against humanity. On the other hand, such horrific exhibition palpably coheres to a prosecutorial agenda fixed to Tuol Sleng's blood and bloodied history.

6. Complicating calls for justice are the ages of Khmer Rouge perpetrators and Cambodian victims. The majority of defendants and witnesses are in their early seventies. It is unclear whether most of those indicted and those who will provide testimony will survive the hybrid U.N./Khmer Rouge Tribunal, which has been delayed and impeded by claims of corruption, lack of funding, and defense attorney brinksmanship. And, there is the very issue of embodied memory. In Cambodia, where more than 65% of the population was born after the Angka era, Pol Pot time has largely been forgotten. The absence of genocide education in public school curricula partially explains the results of a University of California at Berkeley Survey, in which four out of five Cambodians rated their knowledge of the period as "poor" or "very poor."

7. At the same time, the Khmer Rouge Tribunal for the most part dominates all news about the nation in international mass media outlets.

8. Though Angkor Wat ostensibly celebrates a high point in Khmer architecture, the colonization of Cambodia since the sixteenth century (by the Thai, the Vietnamese, and the French) retrospectively underscores the post-thirteenth-century dissolution of a sovereign nation-state. Accordingly, Angkor Wat is both monument and memorial, a multivalent structure that encompasses a sovereign Khmer past and globalized Cambodian present. For Cambodian Americans living in the United States, Angkor Wat becomes a potent symbol of pre–Democratic Kampuchean nationhood, an observation confirmed by the constant mention of the monument in contemporary Cambodian American autobiography focused on life "under the Khmer Rouge."

9. Concomitantly, Khmer Rouge Tribunal reportage — focused on atrocity accounts and emotional outbursts — particularizes and scripts an affective Democratic Kampuchean legacy of ruination (e.g. in stories of victims who testify about trauma and confessional perpetrators).

10. According to John Marston, in Khmer Rouge proverbs, foundations and building metaphors were deployed to engender a body politic in a state of construction, where "people were told to build themselves" (114).

11. Incidentally, the author's first name — "Loung" — is directly linked to "dragon" at the level of translation. In her debut memoir, Ung relates, "When I was small, much younger than I am now, Pa told me that in a certain Chinese dialect my name, 'Loung,' translates into 'dragon'" (Ung 2000, 10).

12. One reason why the Khmer Rouge occupied such a prominent role in the U.N. was because of U.S. support for the regime following the Vietnamese invasion. This support was built on an extended anti–Vietnam foreign policy that continued after the conclusion of the Vietnam Conflict.

13. Pol Pot was, following the Vietnamese invasion, convicted of crimes of genocide by the People's Republic of Kampuchea. This conviction held little political weight, and Pol Pot was not imprisoned nor punished. Indeed, it was not until 1997 that Pol Pot would be tried again (as part of a Khmer Rouge show trial). After that trial, the former Brother Number One was sentenced to house arrest.

14. Moreover, Ung's position as a Sino-Cambodian American who positions herself as a "daughter of Cambodia" was a source of controversy with the publication of *First They Killed My Father* among 1.5 generation Cambodian American readers who pushed questions of narrative and racial authenticity.

15. Soon after Chhang's proposal, the Cambodian Red Cross stated on March 19, 2008 that it would be unable to fund the statue due to cost. See Veasna.

Bibliography

Chandler, David. *A History of Cambodia*. 4th ed. Boulder, CO: Westview Press, 2008.

Chhang, Youk. "Heroines of Cambodia." *Searching for the Truth* (Magazine of the Documentation Center of Cambodia). Special English Edition, First Quarter 2008. 6. Documentation Center of Cambodia. "History." 1 September 2009 <http://www.dccam.org/Abouts/History/Histories.htm>.

Ebihara, May M., Carol A. Mortaland, and Judy Ledgerwood, eds. *Cambodian Culture Since 1975: Homeland and Exile*. Ithaca, NY: Cornell University Press, 1994.

"Genocide site in Cambodia Draws Tourists." 14 August 2006. *USA Today*. 5 May 2009 <http://www.usatoday.com/travel/destinations/2006-08-14-cambodia-genocide-tourism_x.htm>.

Marston, John. "Metaphors of the Khmer Rouge." *Cambodian Culture Since 1975: Homeland and Exile*. Eds. Ebihara, Mortaland, and Ledgerwood. Ithaca, NY: Cornell University Press, 1994. 105–18.

Minow, Martha. *Between Vengeance and Forgiveness: Facing History after Vengeance and Mass Violence*. Boston, MA: Beacon Press, 1998.

Sir Banister Fletcher's A History of Architecture (Twentieth Edition). London: Architectural Press, 1996. 794.

Ung, Loung. "A Birthday Wrapped in Cambodian History." 17 Apr. 2005. *New York Times*. 1 Sept. 2009 <http://www.nytimes.com/2005/04/17/opinion/17ung.html>.

_____. *First They Killed My Father: A Daughter of Cambodia Remembers*. New York: HarpersCollins, 2000.

_____. *Lucky Child: A Daughter of Cambodia Reunites with the Sister She Left Behind*. New York: HarpersCollins, 2005.

Veasna, Mean. "Red Cross Declines Funding Women's Statue." 19 March 2008. *VOA News*. 9 July 2008 <http://www.voanews.com/Khmer/archive/2008-03/080319>.

PART II: BATTLES, RITUALS AND WORSHIP

FROM FEMALE SELF-SACRIFICE TO KOREAN FREEDOM FIGHTER
Yu Guan Soon in Theresa Cha's Dictée

Karen An-hwei Lee

At the age of sixteen, Korean Christian martyr Yu Guan Soon (1903–1920) led the March First Independence Movement against the Japanese occupation in 1919. Lighting torch signals on the hills and marching to forty villages on foot, Yu Guan Soon organized the first mass demonstration for Korean nationalism. Tragically, both her parents were murdered by the Japanese military police during the riots. Yu Guan Soon herself was captured, stabbed in the chest, interrogated, and imprisoned, where she was eventually murdered by torture. Japanese officials delivered her dismembered body to the Methodist missionary school she attended before her arrest. Today, her remains are interred at the entrance of her birth village in Yongdu-ri, Byeongcheon-myeon. A memorial beacon is lit annually on Mount Maebong where she launched the independence movement.

While Yu Guan Soon's story of courageous freedom-fighting is told in some Korean children's books,[1] traditional historical narratives typically marginalize Yu Guan Soon's story in two ways: failing to mention her at all or with minimal acknowledgment, if any, patronizing her role in Korean independence by extolling stereotypical feminine virtues of submission and self-sacrifice.[2] Consequently, in a pattern of elisions and contradictions, her story is either effaced or relegated to marginal status in the official narrative of Korean nationalism. Yu is also eclipsed by comparisons to Joan of Arc, a French historical figure widely known in a Western hegemonic context.[3]

With a renewal of interest in Yu Guan Soon's story in Korea and abroad, contemporary revisions of Yu represent her story and subjectivity in a woman-centered light, emphasizing female agency through empowered verbal and visual descriptions of her will to resist not only colonial oppression but also marginalization within the Korean nationalist insurgency due to her age and gender. For the purposes of this analysis, the term "woman warrior" is used to refer to a female figure — historical, literary, or mythical — who performs male tasks or social roles with the aim of avenging a family, village, nation, or a group of people oppressed by war, poverty, or colonial rule. While women warriors may embody the revolutionary values of an oppressed people, the nationalist spirit present in traditional stories about Yu Guan Soon and Fa Mulan, for example, explicitly serve the ideologies of patriarchal systems. However, as the stories are transposed from Asia to Asian America in a transnational context, the woman warrior's outstanding execution of traditionally male tasks—fighting in wars, marching to villages, or igniting political protests— is interpreted or re-visioned not to affirm patriarchal nationalist values, but rather, to represent the potential for female agency.[4] Likewise, Korean children's storybooks like *Ahn Chang-ho, Yu Gwan-sun* (2007), published by the Academy of Korean Studies with the intent of reaching a global English-speaking readership, exhibit Yu's transformation as such.

In narrative revisions by Theresa Cha and Kim Haewon, for instance, Yu Guan Soon forcefully resists Japanese soldiers who arrest, imprison, and torture her along with other compatriots. Far from the submissive schoolgirl portrayed in traditional historical narratives, this young woman is resourceful, self-disciplined, compassionate yet physically aggressive and expresses powerful emotions ranging from anger to great sorrow. The representation of her initial survival of Japanese torture thus changes from that of female self-sacrifice in Confucian tradition to that of a historical figure constructing power, resistance, and female agency. Yu's Christian faith may also be interpreted as a source of divine inspiration, political revolution, and female empowerment rather than a doctrinal belief system dictating female self-erasure, devaluation, and self-destruction. Thus Yu's spiritual altruism, bolstered by her strong political convictions, is one of individual choice and pro-action, ultimately galvanizing the Korean political resistance.

In examining the details and imagery inhabiting the revisions of Yu's story, I introduce the concept of the "feminist funeral" to position her martyrdom within a narrative context that values the role of women in shaping their own collective memories as well as nationalist histories. Rather than assigning a woman's death to the margins of historical erasure or amnesia, a feminist funeral performs a cultural resurrection to commemorate the achievements in a woman's life. Furthermore, according to the Korean alternative newspaper, *The Women's News,* Korean women were not allowed to participate in social rituals of death, which were traditionally reserved for male privilege until recently.[5] A feminist funeral therefore consists of an actual public ceremony in a physical setting with media press in both print and on-line forums, providing women with local and global opportunities to voice their ideas, share grievances, and participate in a social privilege traditionally denied to them. It is a chance to promote political awareness about social equity for women in a community setting. Similarly, as textual feminist funeral, the memory of Yu is exhumed and re-memorialized in narrative portrayals of female empowerment on both Korean and American soils, inviting the reader's participation in constructing revised memories. To this end, this chapter examines representations of Yu Guan Soon in Theresa Cha and Walter Lew's works.

Significantly, Yu Guan Soon's transposition to American soil in Theresa Cha's *Dictée* (1982) and Walter Lew's 1992 *Excerpts from: ΔIKTH / DIKTE, for DICTEE (1982)* exhibits variants of woman warrior transformations where Yu is resurrected as an avenging historical female figure in a transnational context, echoing redemptive themes of resistance, atonement, and empowerment. These American revisionist phenomena parallel emerging representations in Korean women's writings. International transplantations of Yu's story from geographic "Eastern" to "Western" soil, at least from the special locus of Yu's historical moment, challenge geography-based binary assumptions that the West is feminist and progressive yet the East is antiquated, exotic, and patriarchal. Woman-centered discourse and political activism evolved in America and in Korea, although the roots are traced to different time periods.[6] It should be noted that while evolving Korean women's discourse reshapes Yu's story through children's books, feminist funerals, and women's newspapers, tourist publications of Yu's birth village and place of imprisonment still refer to the patriarchal Confucian values of filial piety and female submission. For instance, "Bequests and Remains of Loyalty and Filial Piety" appears on the "Historical Site of Patriot Yu Gwan-sun." Moreover, although Yu Guan Soon's transposition to American soil increases her visibility as a Korean political leader, her role in Korean independence is still little known among Americans with sparse mention in women's studies and historical scholarship. For these reasons, this is a particularly fruitful moment to re-exhume Yu Guan Soon in critical considerations of Asian women warriors within transnational contexts.

In her astute historical analysis of Yu Guan Soon's role in *Dictée*, Elaine Kim points out that Cha's representations of Yu emphasize her female agency rather than self-sacrificial submission and therefore have "an ambivalent relationship" to the traditional nationalist narrative (16). This ambivalence is lucidly apparent at the beginning of *Dictée*, when Yu appears as the central figure in CLIO HISTORY, the first of nine sections named after Greek muses. Kim observes how Cha retrieves and revises Yu's story from "official Korean History:" whereas traditional historical narratives "emphasize the details of Yu's torture and death" for the ultimate good of a patriarchal society "while encouraging Korean nationalism," Cha's innovative version highlights Yu's strong leadership skills, her resistance to dismissive attitude from independence movement activists because of her age and gender, and finally her "courageous 'backtalk'" to the Japanese soldiers (16). Kim contextualizes the significance of Cha's choice in the patriarchal framework of Korean nationalist history where Yu is typically marginalized as a single young woman whose heroism, patronized as self-sacrificial feminine submission, escapes confinement to Confucian female roles of motherhood or marriage, namely, the "official feminine ideal" embodied by famous maternal figure Shinsaim-dang (mother of a Confucian scholar) and female military strategist Pak-ssi Pu-in who brought "fame and honor to her husband" (15–16). Cha's choice of Yu Guan Soon herself as a historical Korean figure, therefore, already contains an element of subversion in its ambivalent relationship to the patriarchal framework of "official Korean History," which this chapter will further explicate in Cha's representation.

An austere portrait of Yu Guan Soon, cropped from the photograph of nine missionary school classmates adorning the back cover of *Dictée*, introduces CLIO HISTORY with the announcement of Yu's birth, her death, and that "she is born of one mother and one father" (Cha 25), followed by the classical Korean ideographs for "female" and "male" on facing pages. With these binary verbal-visual juxtapositions, Cha sets the stage for what Kim characterizes as the ambivalent relationship Yu already embodies in relation to official Korean nationalist history. In CLIO HISTORY'S short initial biography, Yu's parents are mentioned in a signature generic or symbolic sense, although Yu is presented as an individual who is defined by the traditional familial role of a female in terms of her marital status or her motherhood. As a sixteen-year-old woman, Yu's status is socially ambivalent, if not invisible within a patriarchal society. She is neither a wife nor a mother but an unwed daughter — and female minor; her value in a male-dominated world of Korean nationalism arises from her willingness to sacrifice herself to the point of enduring severe torture and to surrender her life for the greater social good, as was expected of loyal women. Following the calligraphic "female" and "male" ideographs, however, Cha's text immediately reveals the author's revisionist stance in portraying Yu: "She makes complete her duration. As others have made complete theirs: rendered incessant, obsessive myth, rendered immortal their acts without the leisure to examine whether the parts false the parts real according to History's revision" (Cha 28).

Assuming that "she" refers to Yu Guan Soon, I suggest Cha resurrects Yu not only by mentioning the universal facts of her historical existence ("she is born of one mother and one father") but also by highlighting the notion that historical narrative, too, is a sequence of propaganda-related representations (created by "others") or "obsessive myth" that deifies its figures in form of interchangeable archetypes: "History records the biography of her short and intensely-lived existence. Actions prescribed separate her path from the others. The identity of such a path is exchangeable with any other heroine in history, their names, dates, actions which require not definition in their devotion to generosity and self-sacrifice" (Cha 30). It is part of Cha's textual undertaking, then, to exhume the past's forgotten or ambiguous remnants in the form of official documents, historical writings by Western scholars and "others," and archival photographs pieced together in CLIO HISTORY — "to examine whether the parts false the parts real according to History's revision" (Cha 28). Interspersed with her innovative version of Yu's story, these critical elements dispose of the traditional feminine virtues of "generosity and self-sacrifice" dictated by filial piety and patriotism (Cha 30).

That Cha's poetic experiments on dictation in *Dictée* function as figurative postcolonial critiques of power and subjectivity, positioning Cha at the linguistic interstices of various identities, is often elucidated in literary scholarship. Lisa Lowe comments on the model of dictation as it correlates to the Althusserian concept of interpellation and "bad subjects" who resist conforming to the oppressive colonial state (54). In other words, Cha's textual repetitions, omissions, and disrupted uses of dictation illustrate such resistance by spotlighting "the connections and conflicts between historically differentiated sites of subjectivity" (Lowe 54). As a Korean American woman, Cha locates herself in a Western hegemonic context as a (post)colonial subject whose body is a political, textual, and physical battlefield of cultures, histories, and tongues: American, Korean, French Catholic, young, and female, to name a few diverse social categories. Additionally, this intricate matrix is complicated by contradictory yet intersecting binaries, since Cha is "Western" with "Eastern" heritage as a Korean Catholic American fluent in French, English, and Korean. Indeed, she is a woman who is not easily sifted into neat labels, similar to Yu Guan Soon's ambivalent relationship to Korean nationalism.

Trinh Minh-ha describes this experience of multiple identities within a woman — wherein cultural heritages may be repressed or in conflict while others are hidden or concealed by assimilation into dominant cultures— as a series of boundary-crossing *redepartures*, especially concerning the polyglot nature of tongues: "When identity is doubled, tripled, multiplied across time (generations) and space (cultures), when differences keep on blooming within despite the rejections from without, she dares— by necessity. She dares to mix; she dares to cross the borders to introduce into language (verbal, visual, musical) everything monologism has repressed" (14). In selecting her representation of Yu as a prominent figure in *Dictée,* Cha aligns herself with a revolutionary freedom fighter who is young, female, outspoken, aggressive, and Korean; Yu is resurrected as a key historical leader who is further juxtaposed with other people linked to Cha's redepartures: Joan of Arc, Thérèse de Lisieux, and a male Korean patriot Ahn Joon Kun, also a Catholic convert. Likewise, Cha attended a Catholic school and learned French; two are women as Cha is a woman, and one shares a Korean heritage with Cha. Not coincidentally, too, all three were Christian martyrs and two were nationalists, as was Yu Guan Soon.

Consequently, Cha marks her identity crossings as a Catholic Korean American woman in a vexed historical site of what Trinh calls "struggles of borders" (14): Cha identifies with Yu Guan Soon as a woman warrior who exhibits traditionally masculine traits such as physical aggression and forceful "backtalk" in addition to her fiery religious convictions and decisive political actions. Not only does Cha embody different national histories in Western and

Asian contexts, but she also speaks multiple tongues and symbolically endures — as a female (post)colonial subject — various bodily afflictions in her identifications within a quartet of nationalist martyrs. A woman who already exists in an ambivalent relationship to Western cultural hegemony and Korean nationalist values is reconstructed as a battlefield of ideologies. Rhapsodically described in poetic asyndeton as "child revolutionary child patriot woman soldier deliverer of nation," Yu is similarly depicted through contradictions (child/woman) simultaneously embracing and transcending multiple social categories (Cha 37). Roles traditionally identified with males, such as "patriot" and "soldier," are juxtaposed with "woman" to create new associations: "patriot woman" and "woman soldier," culminating in "deliverer of nation" (Cha 37). In a woman's battlefield space where "struggles of borders" simultaneously fragment, battle, embrace, and transcend social categories, the duration mentioned at the beginning of CLIO HISTORY returns as "the completion of one existence. One martyrdom. For the history of one nation. Of one people" (Cha 37). In effect, Yu Guan Soon's dismembered female body — implicit in Cha's text — subtly genders Korea as female rather male, resonating with an earlier mention of Queen Min's assassination. By identifying Korean nationalism with a woman warrior figure, Yu Guan Soon, Cha recalibrates the various historical fragments in CLIO HISTORY as a (post)colonial female revisionist mosaic (Cha 30).

A woman's body as a battlefield, whether in martyrological or secular representations, may be interpreted with polar meanings, either as the product of female self-sacrifice or female freedom-fighting. While the role of torture is central to Christian hagiographies, underscoring martyrological identification with Christ's sufferings, crucifixion, and divine empowerment through a bodily resurrection, it is treated quite differently in official Korean historical accounts of Yu Guan Soon's life and Cha's woman warrior revision. The former accounts emphasize torture to demonstrate Yu's feminine willingness to obliterate herself for a greater patriarchal-identified good, whereas *Dicteé* constructs female power in Yu's resistance to psychologically and physically destructive goals of torture: isolation, indoctrination, and dehumanization. Consequently, the injustices are at least twofold in her death: the murder is an act of violation, as well as its role in the brutal coercion of a belief system upon an entire society. As Lucy Grig observes, hagiographic portrayals of violence inflicted upon martyrs may be seen as "playing a central role in constructing the power of the martyr, and that of his or her church" (1). Similarly, in her analysis of torture and early Christian martyrs, Maureen Tilley applies theories by psychologist Peter Suedfeld (a torture expert) and literary critic Elaine Scarry (*The Body in Pain*) to highlight how the physical nature of torture is also ideology-based, or that "torture attempts to control people who hold as true a vision of reality contrary to that of the torturers" (468). Cha describes Yu Guan Soon as surviving a chest stabbing after her arrest and resisting an interrogation, to which Yu surrenders no information. Yu uses her corporeal body and aggressive voice to resist the torturers' attempts to subjugate and dehumanize her. In light of Tilley's interpretations, Cha reconfigures Yu's body as a battleground consisting not only of Trinh's "struggles of borders" but also a turf war between the autonomous individual versus colonial state possession: "By remapping the 'normal' connections where physical pain brings psychic disintegration, the martyrs provided the torturers not with a well-known battle-ground but with an unfamiliar jungle" (Tilley 467). In Cha's subversive texts, Yu's reclaimed historical body is transformed into a site of physical and ideological resistance, a textual, ideological, and corporeal territory or "unfamiliar jungle" where psychic disintegration and bodily dismemberment articulate power by fragmenting the colonizer's version of reality. Yu symbolically resists colonial occupation through the indestructible integrity of an individual voice that withholds information, proclaims her beliefs, and protests the colonial occupation under extreme physical and psychological duress.

Lisa Lowe characterizes this painful site of political strife, embodied by Yu Guan Soon, as one of "corporeal division" where the body is both a material and symbolic anatomy, one that "bears the traces of colonial disfiguring and mutilation" (47). For instance, Cha's verbal-visual representations of textual and anatomical tongues are disrupted "as both organ and language" so the relations between physical and linguistic colonial violence underscore the pain endured by tortured subjects. The fragmentary language in Cha's text is therefore "uttered in resistance to the imposed competency in the colonizer's language" while it also exhibits a decoupling effect as words are detached from their meanings in a play of signifiers (Lowe 47): "*Truth embraces with it all other abstentions other than itself. Outside Time. Outside Space. Parallels other durations, oblivious to the deliberate brilliance of its own time, mortal, deliberate marking. Oblivious to itself. But to sing. To sing to. Very softly*" (Cha 28; italics in the original). This decoupling effect may also be compared to the psychological phenomenon of "hysterical fugue" referenced in Tilley's essay, an "altered state of consciousness in which language about realities and the realities represented are decoupled" (472). During this episode, the martyr experiences psychological detachment—in the sheer strength of her religious convictions, her mental reality is also preserved through physical abstention—as she disowns the body's modulation through severe pain into its own instrument of torture, a phenomenon caused, ironically, by the body's "complicit" transmission of agony. Indeed, "the links between emotions and their normal objects are also severed" and can include "changes in self-identity focusing on the body, such as disowning pain" (Tilley 473). The concept of hysterical fugue is another way to interpret the fragmentary linguistic effects of Cha's text, subverting the colonial narrative of physical violence, torture, and psychic disintegration as the critical collage empowers Yu Guan Soon with voice, visibility, and agency. A female subject's battlefields of corporeal and linguistic territories are decoupled from pain inflicted by violence and reconfigured as victory. Paired with

Dictée's postcolonial critique of imperialism, this reading of CLIO HISTORY as a hysterical fugue illustrates the transformative power of Cha's new representation of Yu as a woman warrior.

In her analysis of the psychological nature of torture and its relationship to subjectivity, *The Body in Pain*, Elaine Scarry suggests that martyrs who already practice asceticism are enabled to reconfigure the meaning of pain through their identification with Christ, preserving the integrity of their personal voices and convictions without psychic disintegration (qtd. in Tilley 470). Even death yields the potential of victory, since conceptual surrender to torture occurs only when "the victim is finally pushed beyond the ability to maintain contact with or articulate her own body, for she is pushed to a pre-lingual state where only the scream that she *cannot* control marks her existence. At this point the torturer has won and can control any articulation of the body in pain" (Tilley 470; italic in the original). Death, then, signals the final resistance to indoctrination: Yu's vocal intransigence to the very end and the remnants of her dismembered body are signs communicating the success of this martyr's individual fortitude, galvanizing the national spirit. The manner of Yu's death provides inspiration for the independence movement and demonstrates the failure of colonial torturers to "force that body, mind, and voice to participate in a new construction of reality" (Tilley 470). Not coincidentally, the word "duration" introduced at the beginning of CLIO HISTORY further conveys, beyond a sense of time continuum or existence, a special connotation in martyrological discourse, namely, the "duration" of torture.

Tilley describes martyrs who prepared for possible encounters with torture by practicing asceticism, such as food and water deprivation: "They even mimicked the duration and the sporadic nature of the starvation they would undergo" (471). Relationships between this mimicry of duration — implied in the reading of torture and resistance through Cha's revision of Yu's story, her ambiguous use of the word "duration," and its broken link to dictation as a model for interpellation — illustrate how dictation and mimicry, in and of themselves, exhibit what Lowe characterizes as an inherent failure of colonial power to interpellate subjects: "Like Cha's notion of dictation, interpellation is inherently contradictory; the function of interpellation — the sublation of differences in the reproduction of generic subjects as equivalent units of abstract labor — attests to a contradiction between an always recognized ground of differences and capitalism's demand for formally identical subjects" (Lowe 55). Allied with a heterogeneous quartet of religious and nationalist martyrs, Cha's female subject resists ideological subjugation, ultimately offering up her body as a battlefield interred in a textual feminist funeral that revives, memorializes, and resurrects her as a woman warrior rather than victim of self-sacrifice.

This concept of "duration" and its rich valences as time continuum, historical preservation, survival, and even the discourse of torture has further implications for myth's discursive functions in CLIO HISTORY. *Dictée*'s verbal-visual poetics are magnified in Walter Lew's critical collage response, *Excerpts from: ΔΙΚΤΗ / DIKTE, for DICTEE (1982)*, which harvests Cha's original sources and archival materials to pay homage to Cha after her death. In a sense, Lew's *Excerpts* performs an eloquent feminist funeral in tribute to Cha, Yu Guan Soon, and other female historical figures, mirrored in its photographic montages of sarcophagi, photocopied archival texts, and diverse images reminiscent of the poetic re-assemblages in *Dictée*. The section on Yu, in particular, is a multilayered critical collage featuring a fractured Korean-language children's book. Excerpted pages depicting ink-drawn images of a submissive and self-sacrificing schoolgirl Yu are interspersed with French subtitle references to Greek mythology, specifically, the death of Persephone and her attendant mystic Eleusinian rituals. Implicit in this critical design is the discursive nature of nationalism as a mythic construction of history and its heroes. Thus Lew's critiques of official Korean nationalist representations of Yu Guan Soon, harmonizing verbally and visually with Cha's work, elucidate the mythic deification of Yu to echo Cha's introduction to CLIO HISTORY concerning "obsessive myth, rendered immortal their acts without the leisure to examine whether the parts false the parts real according to History's revision" (Cha 28). By underscoring myth and ritual as systems of cultural signs with arbitrarily assigned meanings, Lew's critical play of signifiers detaches historical words and images from their original contexts. For instance, his placement of French captions describing the Eleusianian rituals under storybook pictures of Yu depicted in submissive postures and devotional expressions highlight the mythic tropes of female sacrifice in a political nationalist context, and further as potentially systemized forms of cultural obsession with female death. In the action of exposing these tropes, however, Lew also demonstrates the potential for revision and resurrection, obliquely referenced in "le ritual d'évocation" (Lew 59).

With Yu's head bowed in prayer, a hand resting over her heart, the traditional storybook version excerpted in Lew's work depicts a rosy-cheeked schoolgirl with a single braid down her back, wearing a traditional Korean *hanbok* as she attends her Methodist missionary school. Appearing much younger than sixteen and quite different in features from an actual photograph taken at that age, Yu's obedience and devotional attitudes are captured in her body language and Lew's excerpted English translations of the original Korean text, highlighting Yu's quietness, the soft voices of her classmates, silent prayers, and wistful expressions: "Kwan-sun had six especially close comrades. Whenever there was a free moment, they would gather in a quiet place and ever so softly talk among themselves.... Just as Kwan-sun had done, each now clasped her hands together, and, head bowed, prayed in silence" (Lew 41). The ellipses here mark intentional textual elisions in Lew's work, included pages later as this arrangement: "Kwan-sun had six especially close comrades. Whenever there was a free moment, they would gather in a quiet place and softly talk among themselves. 'Our country could become free, too, couldn't it?' Kwan-sun said to them" (Lew 53). In this poetic play of verbal-visual elisions, decoupage, and juxtapositions, Lew's *Excerpts* creates gaps and fissures in mythic-historical narratives which intersect, collide, and disrupt one another's discursive frameworks, yielding potential for new productions of meaning in subversive rituals.

Underpinning Lew's critical collage is its eloquent polyphonic counterpoint to *Dictée*, wherein female Greek archetypes, French saints, Korean martyrs, both Christian and secular ideologies are embodied by women who are dead yet revived, young and revolutionary, empowered to be victoriously sacrificial rather than self-obliterating. In addition to dismantling these cultural binarisms, Lew's critical collage illuminates the omnipresent yet contradictory disintegrations of these metanarratives through fragmentations, montages, and the intersections of multiple redepartures. By introducing captioned rituals involved with the Eleusinian mysteries, Lew's work reveals hidden contradictions in the Persephone myth as it relates, to some extent, to female martyrological discourse: a dead woman who is destroyed or dwelling in Hades yet whose presence is a catalyst for creativity and fecundity; whose body is death yet whose spirit is alive in memory; who is young, kidnapped and violated yet pure. In these conflicting binaries, femaleness is simultaneously equivalent to death (winter) and renewal (spring). A closer examination of the Eleusinian mysteries suggests, in juxtaposition to the storybook excerpts on Yu Guan Soon from *Uri nara choun nara:Yu Kwan-sun nuna wa samil undong* and Im In-su's *Yu Kwan-sun*, suggest how the recitation of master narratives is in itself a form of ritualistic observance, one perpetrating female archetypes limited to roles as mother, daughter, wife, saint, slave, or harlot.[7]

Echoing the choreography of French saints and Greek muses in *Dictée*, Lew's use of French texts refer to the place of Persephone's capture near Eleusis, where she was picking flowers one day when Hades abducted her. Yu Guan Soon, then, is aligned with Persephone to illustrate and disassemble mythic female parallels. French captions and images of the Eleusianian rituals are affixed to the Korean storybook's illustrations, referring to "le ritual d'évocation" underneath a picture of Yu Guan Soon bowing her head in silent prayer, "le depart des Enfers" or entrance to Hades on the former picture of Yu rotated upside-down, and "les symboles de l'abondance et de la vitesse des cultures" to the sky above Yu as she raises the Korean flag in the march for independence. In these collages, the mythical qualities of nationalist history's spiritual and heroic archetypes are disrupted, reassembled, and transformed within the context of postcolonial women's discourse, presenting the schoolgirl version of Yu as a cultural myth of inherent contradictions.

While mourned as death or absence, the female nationalist hero is also construed as a "goddess" of sorts, undergoing a mythic deification as her story is shaped and recounted as a symbolic vehicle for a society's epic values. In Yu Guan Soon's case, the Confucian feminine ideals of loyalty, selflessness, virtue, and submission are extolled. Accompanied by a classmate, Yu's deferential visit to the missionary teacher — to whom, as a proper schoolgirl, Yu bows respectfully — is captioned from Bérard's text as "les prêtres conduisent les mystes devant les deux déesses," or the priests lead the initiates before the two goddesses. Further captions referring to the Eleusinian mysteries continue under the storybook depiction of Yu preparing for the independence march, culminating in an ink-drawn scene of bloodshed when Japanese soldiers fire upon Korean protestors: "le coffret mystérique dans la barque infernale," or the mystical casket in the infernal boat, followed by a historical photograph of a weeping Korean girl, five or six years old, carrying a baby on her back, to all appearances two children abandoned to weather the elements alone on a desolate plain, "apocalyptique et eschatologie" (Lew 70). The text reminds us, however, that neither cultural narratives nor historical photographs are transparencies to elusive realities: *"The cloud of dust and smoke that is always over Eleusis/appears in a strangely transfigured light"* (Lew 75; italics in the original). Historical memory remains partly erased, partly reconstituted and reconfigured in a cycle of mythic self-perpetration and revision.

Returning to the concept of the feminist funeral as it relates to the intersections of postcolonial, hagiographic, and martyrological discourses in these representations of Yu Guan Soon, I suggest that Lew's *Excerpts* resurrects Cha to mourn her untimely and violent death, figuratively "canonizing" her memory much as Cha resurrects to mourn, re-narrate, and memorialize Yu. In a sense, Lew's work mirrors a series of feminist funerals as the photographs of open graves or stone sarcophagi appearing towards the end of the book signify, on various levels, the rituals of death in burial, oblivion, exhumation, and resurrection (93, 113). The concept of the feminist funeral has special significance in a Korean context, since women were traditionally excluded from participation in funerals. Indeed, collectively mourning and memorializing a resurrected historical female figure holds powerful cultural meaning for global women in transnational contexts. Yu Guan Soon and Theresa Cha, then, are construed as archetypal Persephones who descend underground to the realm of oblivion yet return in a renewal of life in Lew's critical collage. Lew opens a burial ground of historical amnesia to exhume then properly bury while resurrecting these women in revisionist memory, paying homage to in the style of Cha's signature poetic fragments in *Dictée*: *"did not die:/was/robbed of her death"* (Lew 91; italics in the original). His epilogue quotes Cha herself as he reflects upon his Paris visit to one of four memorials to Joan of Arc: "She says to herself she does not account for the sake of history./Simulated pasts resurrected in memoriam" (Lew 105).

Resisting simplified notions of "old world" or "Oriental" patriarchal nationalism and "new world" American feminism, the story of Yu Guan Soon has also been reclaimed in a progressive spirit published to Korean and English-speaking readerships. In a transnational context, the woman warrior revision appears on both American and Korean soils. Through various Korean media, including a women's print and on-line newspaper and an English-language children's storybook intended for Western audiences, Yu is represented as an intrepid young woman with a warrior heart rather than a submissive spirit. Although an examination of Korean tourism materials pertaining to Yu suggests otherwise—female self-sacrifice and filial piety in form of loyalty and duty to her country are stressed in tributes to Yu's birth, death, and place of imprisonment—*The Women's News,* a weekly English-language Korean newspaper with a readership of 98,000 and branches in eleven provinces, raises awareness of women's issues in light of Yu's nationalist activism. *The Women's News* collaborates with the House for Working Women under the Korean Ministry of Labor (scheduled to move to the Ministry of Women's Affairs), an education center for women providing professional and educational opportunities with career advising, a job agency, and a counseling center (*Women's News* par. 5). As part of its goals, it also aims to revive forgotten women in Korean history (*Women's News* par. 1), and advocates changing the tradition of "hoju" or paternal lineage, which subordinates a woman to her spouse's family in terms of the order of inheritance of the hoju title (*Women's News* par. 4). Working to change gender discrimination and increase opportunities for women's education and professional advancement, *The Women's News* makes references to the concept of the "feminist funeral" to imbue women's deaths with social significance, resurrect progressive ideals in women's lives today, and memorialize Korean historical women for posterity.

This intent is described in Choi Lee Bu-ja's article, "Women's Solidarity Shown through 'Feminist Funeral,' Women resurrected through sisterly love," which appeared in a 2002 edition of *The Women's News.* Choi reports on the "feminist funeral" in tribute to fourteen sex workers who perished in a fire in the red light district of Gunsan (Kunsan): "Until now, women were rarely allowed to fully participate in the social ritual of death, the natural conclusion of life. They were relegated to the role of grieving guests standing behind the men who took charge of the funeral. But now, women can be in charge, ensuring that a fellow woman's death moves beyond a personal incident to take on social, historical importance" (Choi par. 3). Participation in these social rites creates an opportunity to build Korean women's solidarity through shared common ground and community proaction. Choi further clarifies the distinctions between the traditional nationalist attitude towards a female martyr and the real need for progressive action behalf women who are victims of life-threatening and even fatal attacks: "Many women of social significance ... have died in the past, but their deaths sparked nationalistic antagonism against Japanese or American atrocities rather than indignation against the violation of women's rights" (Choi par. 2). A woman's experience of torture resulting in death (i.e. murder) is subsequently transformed from homage paid to her self-sacrifice ("she died for our nation") to a narration where, beyond emphasizing the woman's strength and fortitude, woman's death increases awareness of social inequities, abuses, and violations of rights ("this injustice should never have happened"), potentially leading to pro-action.

In discussing Yu Guan Soon's leadership in Korean national history, *The Women's News* publishes a photograph of Seodaemun Prison History Hall, which showcases a replica of the women's jail where Yu was imprisoned and tortured after her capture: "Four solitary cells, each less than 1 peyong (appx. 3.3m square) have ceilings so low that one cannot stand straight inside the cell. These cells, named 'Yu Gwan Sun Cave,' is the very place where the famous martyr Yu Gwan Sun died from unspeakable torture and cruel punishment" (*Women's News* par. 3). Although some feminist renditions of Yu's experiences intentionally downplay the role of torture to contrast their narrative representations against the official nationalist versions extolling her self-sacrificial martyrdom, this particular article, like *Dictée*, stresses the details of the painful deprivations and physical abuses Yu endured in solitary confinement lest history's palimpsest give her an anonymous funeral. The article further commented that journalistic writings contemporary to Yu actually recorded female nationalists' activities in great detail, both at home and abroad, yet are virtually lost or buried in archives: "Vivid records of the women's struggle are mostly written by foreigners, and the women-led 'Long Live Korean Independence' Movement was reported in much greater detail in the newspapers back then than in the historical records of the March First Movement we read today" (*Women's News* par. 5). Facing the threat of historical amnesia, *The Women's News* ends with a rallying cry to historic revival: "83 years ago, it was rare to see women in the streets, and all that was demanded of them was 'chastity' and 'obedience.' Let us go back in time to see how these faceless Korean women fought for freedom and justice. Let us revive their history and bring it back to our times" (*Women's News* par. 6).

Of course, *The Women's News* is not the only Korean publication that reclaims Yu Guan Soon in a new light. A Korean children's book, *Ahn Changho, Yu Gwan-sun* by Kim Haewon and Kim Jongmin, originally published by "The Center for Information on Korean Culture" at the Academy of Korean Studies, with an English translation made possibly by the permission of Woongjin Thinkbig, Inc., targets both Korean-speaking and English-speaking global audiences. The book's mission statement states three curricular and public relations goals: "'Supporting Korean Studies overseas,' 'Improving National Image through Revising Fallacies in Textbooks,' and 'Developing Introductory Materials on Korea for Foreigners.'" Also stated is the intent to globalize Korean culture and transmit "accurate information about Korea to the world." To this end, its narration of Yu Guan Soon's story (romanized as "Yu Gwansun" in this text) provides a version of Yu as a female national martyr in a revisionist vein. Demonstrating willful determination, Yu shouts loudly for Korean independence, captures and preserves the signs and symbols of Korean nationalism (a flag), and persuades a village elder to permit her to help lead the independence movement: "People were amazed that a young girl would walk a long distance to let people know of the march" (Haewon 22). Her physical actions are equally aggressive as she clenches her hands, throws a chair at the judge in the court of law, and hurls sharp retorts at Japanese soldiers. Her body language, in the words, is far from submissive or stereotypically feminine. Additionally, the narrative emphasizes her youthfulness to show how she resourcefully turns her age to a point of advantage: "'I will go and tell the people. I can easily travel around because I am young. They do not think I would cause trouble,' said Yu Gwansun breaking the silence" (Haewon 21). Neither is Yu discouraged when adults try to dissuade her from leading the movement due to her age and gender.

In effect, Yu's social marginalization due to her female gender, adolescence, and petite stature are identified with Korea's fiery colonial resistance — "a tiny country" with a great national spirit, so to speak — but this feminized embodiment, as a comparison, does not resort to patronizing Yu's social position as a single female minor, either, as in earlier "schoolgirl" portrayals of Yu. As a young woman, Yu is depicted as shouting with "a small but powerful voice" as she distributes Korean flags and enlists adults to join the movement (Haewon 24). In response to the imperial judge's sarcastic remark, "'Do you really think that a tiny country like Korean can become independent,' " Yu throws a chair across the room (Haewon 28). In this heated exchange of words and objects, imperial aggression is met by Yu's "backtalk," her quick physical reflexes, and occasional silence — her choice to withhold information. Hence not only Yu's body but the resonant echo of her voice is a politically charged battlefield of colonial resistance where the actions of one individual symbolize the courage of a nation. These representations of a petite female nationalist using her voice, her physique, and intellect to express strong convictions and apply her resourcefulness towards igniting a revolution also work against traditional stereotypes of Korean women. Yu is neither wife nor mother — neither one who is primarily concerned with fulfilling obligations to her parents when she is unmarried — nor one who serves the husband's family after marriage. Moreover, the historical photographs and earth-tone watercolors depicting Yu with a furrowed brow, deep frown, and decisive actions stand in stark contrast to the soft ink-drawn portrayals of a dutiful schoolgirl Yu in *Uri nara choun nara: Yu Kwan-sun nuna wa samil undong* and Im In-su's *Yu Kwan-sun,* one who obediently lays down her life for the good of her nation.

This text's descriptions of torture either mute or completely omit significant details (chest-stabbing, severe prison deprivations and living conditions, solitary confinement, and murder by dismemberment) perhaps with the intent of tailoring the material for a young readership. While torture is mentioned frequently in a general sense, certain omissions are noticeable for readers already familiar with traditional or revisionist nationalist versions. The chest-stabbing mentioned in *Dictée* is omitted, for instance. Rather, Yu's painful experiences are generalized to beatings from Japanese soldiers and feet "full of blisters and bruises" from walking village to village (Haewon 22). Imprisonment is mentioned, and a photograph of Seodaemun prison appears at the beginning of the story, but her death by dismemberment is excluded: "Yu Gwansun was tortured so badly that she could no longer stand on her own.... Yu Gwansun grew weaker and weaker from the torture" (Haewon 30). In spite of these omissions about the details of torture, this children's book "woman warrior" version of Yu is also resolute and altruistic, as in the other versions—not in a self-obliterating sense, but rather, in her steadfast determination to lead the independence movement and to show solidarity with other women—by sharing her meager prison food with mothers with infants, for instance (Haewon 30). Her altruism, however, is also mixed with youthful rebellion reminiscent of contemporary adolescence rather than Confucian ideals of female self-sacrifice. In a rather untraditional fashion, Yu disobeys her mother's wish for her to stay at home instead of leading the independence movement: "Mother, I can't waste any time. I have to tell everyone about our plans" (Haewon 22). Yet while this book's portrayal of Yu resists traditional stereotypes of Korean women in general, the mental and physical abuses described might raise little sense of outrage directed explicitly at the injustices Yu endured as violations of women's rights, which are clearly articulated in *The Women's News*.

The black-and-white photograph of Yu Guan Soon introducing *Ahn Chang-ho, Yu Gwan-sun* shows a young woman with austere features, a bold expression quite different from the delicate rosy-cheeked illustrations in *Uri nara choun nara: Yu Kwan-sun nuna wa samil undong* and *Yu Kwan-sun*. Although photographs and images are no more transparent realities than words—both operate as cultural vehicles for representations—the historical photographs appearing in this book do lend a convincing sense of an archival verisimilitude. Interpreted in context of Yu's woman warrior story, these historical documents are visual testimonies implying "this is real" and "these events actually occurred." The photographs in this children's book and *The Women's News* article on Yu Guan Soon are memory traces re-signified in a "woman warrior" spirit in contrast to the cyber-tourism sites which pour accolades upon Yu's selflessness, loyalty, and sacrifice. The marks on her body, as narrated in martyrological discourse, symbolize a scarred battlefield of ideologies in conflict over the land and its denizens. Patriotism, personal fortitude, and altruism highlight a woman warrior's leadership in a moment of Korean nationalist insurgency. In sharp contrast to gender stereotypes of Korean women, portrayals of Yu Guan Soon in *The Women's News* and the children's book by the Academy of Korean Studies indicate a transformative strain of the woman warrior story in Korean writings, paralleling representations of Yu Guan Soon in experimental image-text collages by authors of Korean American backgrounds, Cha and Lew. This woman warrior trope, then, may be a sign of a simultaneously evolving transnational trend in contexts of global feminism, evident in Asia as well as Asian America.

The implications of similar strains in the transformation of Yu Guan Soon from obedient schoolgirl to woman warrior—and from Asia to Asian America, or vice versa — in transnational contexts further contest the Orientalist binarism of "Confucian parental governance" versus "Western masculinist capitalism." This stereotype is a distortion based not only on geographical division and cultural differences but also on economic (capitalist) changes in contemporary societies, an issue examined by Jongwoo Han and L. H. M. Ling's "Authoritarianism in the Hypermasculinized State: Hybridity, Patriarchy, and Capitalism in Korea" (Han and Ling 56). Hence what is considered ideologically and technologically progressive is falsely associated with a masculinized "West" (modern), while the "East" is feminized as Oriental, exotic, or regressive (antiquated). Yu Guan Soon's simultaneous emergence as a woman warrior in Korean and Korean American texts, then, reflects feminist ideologies actively dismantling racist and sexist constructions in both societies, countering assumptions underlying both halves of the false binarism. Indeed, Mikyung Chin in "Reflections on Women's Empowerment through Local Representation in South Korea" points out that in contemporary Korean society, "feminism is no longer an unfamiliar word" (Chin 295), notably after the Korean women's movement of the nineties, as further discussed in Seungsook Moon's "Civil Society and the Women's Movement in Korea" (Moon 496).

All this is not to say, however, that Confucian or patriarchal ideals are extinct, as evidenced by conservative backlashes to the Korean women's movement described in Chin's essay, which articulates a continuing need for more political representation by women in local and national governing bodies. At minimum, the revisionist construction of a female nationalist figure to embody a society's epic values, advanced simultaneously by women's political activism reflected in various representations of Yu Guan Soon in Asia and America, evokes a developing transnational phenomenon wherein women's shared interests in turn inspire group mobilization and shape collective identities. Raka Ray and Anna Korteweg describe exactly this collective phenemonon in "Women's Movements in the Third World: Identity, Mobilization, and Autonomy" (53). Ray and Korteweg's comparative approach emphasizes the study of micro-cooperation among various women's groups, presenting local perspectives in developing countries rather than global or macro-level analyses. Examining these micro-level cooperations may reveal how a specific political regime's attitudes toward gender subordination may inadvertently create political spaces for women to organize, sparking "the articulation of a feminist consciousness" (Ray and Korteweg 54). I would further add, in our literary considerations of Yu, it would be imprecise to assume the rise of women's movements in these nations is solely a macro-level effect of Western ideologies shaping women's concerns in a global (capitalist) hegemonic context. Rather, the specific historical phenomenon of the Korean independence movement is noted in tandem with contemporary rises of gender consciousness in both Asian and Asian American societies.

In comparing Yu Guan Soon's transformation from a self-sacrificing girl to a young woman warrior in critical collages, women's newspapers, and children's books, one may readily observe how the experimental representations are far more aesthetically fractured than the journalistic or traditional storytelling narrative forms. Beyond the formal innovations of works by Cha and Lew, however, Korean diasporic writers are also exhuming and revising a buried and distorted past, reclaiming ancestral women's voices and their pivotal roles in history. Cha is further navigating the intersections of multiple identities in a hyphenated space of migrating "from Asia to Asian America" as a part of a Korean American woman's experiences. Ultimately, regardless of aesthetic, both the American collages and Korean texts depict the female body as a battlefield, a physical and discursive site of power struggles, whether in poetic or prose descriptions of visible wounds, "backtalk," or silence. Consequently, the violation of a woman's rights ceases to take secondary consideration as an injustice. Rather, she is no longer invisible or existing merely as a "field of discursive power" in the "colonial legacy of the appropriation of women's bodies and their reduction to the site of the power struggle between male nationalist elites and colonial administrators" (Moon 486). In other words, she is indeed corporeal in all senses of the word — her body is real, not immaterial — with a distinctly audible voice of her own.

The concepts of invisibility and a woman's body as a "field of discursive power," as related to abusive practices against women, arise significantly in Lata Mani's *Contentious Traditions: The Debate on Sati in Colonial India*. Focusing her study on self-immolation or ritual widow-suicide in colonial Indian society, Mani emphasizes how women whose rights were violated by the practice were entirely absent in the discursive power struggle between British colonial powers and Indian nationalists. While the British condemned the practice as "barbaric" to justify their imperial conquests, the Indian nationalists validated sati as a key component of their cultural identity. (qtd. in Moon 486) Therefore, Mani characterizes the widow's body as simultaneously invisible and a "field of discursive power." Similarly, with Tilley's reading of a martyr's body as a comparable "battlefield," our Korean and Korean American texts on Yu Guan Soon mark this very presence of the female body as visible — no longer obliterated — and an embattled site reclaimed for a feminist funeral involving the participation of women in a ritual traditionally reserved for men. Furthermore, the reading of wounds inscribed upon a woman's body, once interpreted as a signs of self-sacrifice for the greater good of a nation rather than cries for social justice for herself and her sisters, are brought to light only after historical amnesia and social marginalization nearly erased the initial evidence. Fractured collages such as Cha's *Dicteé* and Lew's *Excerpts* aesthetically and politically reflect the critical work, in a sense, of female bodies inscribed, scarred, and mutilated by such abuses forcing readers, like spectators, to bear witness not only to the invisible woman but to participate in the revision of historical memories, indeed, by virtue of bearing witness.

Notes

1. Examples of children's books are the Korean-language *Uri nara choun nara:Yu Kwan-sun nuna wa samil undong* (1968), Im In-su's *Yu Kwan-sun* (n.d.), and the English-language *Ahn Chang-ho, Yu Gwan-sun* (2007) written by Kim Haewon and published by the Academy of Korean Studies.

2. Traditional historical narratives of Korean history include ones authored by Yi (Lee) Gwangsu of the Gradualist Developmental Movement, the Radical People (Minjung) Movement of Sin Ch'aeho, and An Hosang's "One People Principle." For more context on Yu Guan Soon's marginal status in the master narratives of Korean history, please refer to Elaine Kim's discussion of "official Korean history" (16, 19).

3. Sample references of Yu Guan Soon as "Korea's Joan of Arc" appear in on-line circulars such as *Asahi Shimbun Weekly*, *Chingusai Newsletter*, and the Korean Global Television network's companion website, *Arirang*.

4. For a related discussion on women warriors, see Edwards whose article examines the narratives of two Chinese historical women warriors including the famous late Ming Dynasty Mulan "woman warrior" featured in the 1976 Asian American autobiographical novel by Maxine Hong Kingston, *The Woman Warrior: Memoirs of a Girlhood among Ghosts*. Although these women warriors are tasked with upholding patriarchal codes, they culturally represent what Edwards calls "disruptive potential" or subversion: "These symbols of female strength, performing exemplary deeds, served to support women who felt constrained by prescriptions of femininity. The revolutionary changes to women's social circumstances that developed within the Republican movement were indeed promoted by invocations of Hua Mulan and Qin Liangyu as models for emulation" (254). Interestingly, this potential for advancing gender equity is actually embedded within the patriarchal nationalist narratives themselves when a woman warrior's multiple discursive functions are considered in their specific historical contexts. Mulan's story (originally a ballad, later lengthened into a fiction narrative during the Ming Dynasty) lead to a few progressive social reforms described above (Edwards 225). However, this disruptive potential is in turn counteracted or "neutralized by the literary redactors of her tale" who explicitly affirm patriarchal values (Edwards 254). The complexities of these conflicting discourses yield, to say in the least, multi-faceted readings of the texts.

5. The first Korean "feminist funeral" took place on February 8, 2002 to commemorate fourteen sex workers who died in the red light district Gunsan (Kunsan) fire on January 29. According to journalist Choi Lee Bu-ja of *The Women's News*, the funeral was conducted at the accident site where victims were trapped without proper access to exits when the fire broke out. (par. 1) On the same day of the funeral, the Korean Women's Association United (KWAU) marched in a procession past the Seoul Metropolitan Police Agency. Choi notes such funerals are new public opportunities to protest violations of women's civil rights previously overshadowed by patriarchal nationalism: "Many women of social significance such as ex-comfort women grandmas and Gijichon women (hostesses patronized by American soldiers in Korea) have died in the past, but their deaths sparked nationalistic antagonism against Japanese or American atrocities rather than indignation against the violation of women's rights. When Poet Go Jeong Hee, known for putting her feminist ideas into action, died in 1991, her funeral was a 'National Literary Funeral,' much to the chagrin of women activists. Perhaps that is why so many women are showing an interest in this unprecedented 'Feminist Funeral'" (par. 2).

6. Seungsook Moon's 2002 article in *Journal of Asian Studies*, "Carving Out Space: Civil Society and the Women's Movement in South Korea," identifies the rise of Korean feminism with the 1987 launch of the Korean Women's Association United (KWAU), a joint venture of twenty-one feminist organizations. Moon contextualizes this historical

event within the post-authoritarian growth of civil society after the restoration of electoral democracy: "The growing complexity of the women's movement can be observed in its changing relationship to the democratizing state.... Founded as an oppositional group outside the state [in 1987], the KWAU registered with the state as an incorporated body in 1995" (Moon 490). In contrast to the fairly contemporary rise of Korean women's movements in the late Eighties, American women's activist programs for equity outcomes—organizations participating in democratic progressive reforms—are traceable to the early industrial laborers (women mill workers, seamstresses in sweat shops), educational and health reforms, and suffragettes, to name several historic examples.

7. Lew excerpts the texts and images for the Eleusinian mysteries from Claude Bérard's "Apocalypses Eleusiniennes" in Claude Kappler et al.'s *Apocalypses et Voyages dans l'Audelà* (1987), Karl Kerényi's *Eleusis: Archetypal Image of Mother and Daughter* translated by Ralph Mannheim, and George Emmanuel Mylonas' *The Hymn to Demeter and her Sanctuary at Eleusis*.

Bibliography

Cha, Theresa Hak Kyung. *Dictée*. Berkeley, CA: Third Woman Press, 1995.
Chin, Mikyung. "Reflections on Women's Empowerment through Local Representation in South Korea." *Asian Survey* 44.2 (2004): 295–315.
Choi Lee Bu-ja. "Women's Solidarity Shown through 'Feminist Funeral:' Women Resurrected through Sisterly Love." Trans. Cho Eung-joo. *The Women's News*. 2002. 1 March 2009 <http://www.womennews.co.kr>.
Edwards, Louise. "Women Warriors and Amazons of the Mid Qing Texts *Jinghua Yuan* and *Honglou Meng*." *Modern Asian Studies* 29.2 (1995): 225–55.
Grig, Lucy. "Torture and Truth in Late Antique Martyrology." *Early Medieval Europe* 11.4 (2002): 321–36.
Haewon, Kim. *Ahn Chang-ho, Yu Gwan-sun*. Geyonggi-do, South Korea: The Academy of Korean Studies, 2007.
Han, Jongwoo and L. H. M. Ling. "Authoritarianism in the Hypermasculinized State: Hybridity, Patriarchy, and Capitalism in Korea." *International Studies Quarterly* 42.1 (1998): 53–78.
Kim, Elaine. "Poised on the In-between: A Korean American's Reflections on Theresa Hak Kyung Cha's *Dictée*." *Writing Self, Writing Nation*. Eds. Elaine Kim and Norma Alarcón. Berkeley, CA: Third Woman Press, 1994. 3–30.
Lew, Walter. *Excerpts from: ΔIKTH / DIKTE, for DICTEE (1982)*. Seoul, South Korea: Yeul Eum Publishing Co., 1992.
Lowe, Lisa. "Unfaithful to the Original: The Subject of *Dictée*." *Writing Self, Writing Nation*. Berkeley, CA: Third Woman Press, 1994. Eds. Kim and Alarcón. 35–69.
Mani, Lata. *Contentious Traditions: The Debate on Sati in Colonial India*. Berkeley, CA: University of California Press, 1998.
Moon, Seungsook. "Carving Out Space—Civil Society and the Women's Movement in Korea." *Journal of Asian Studies* 61.2 (2002): 473–500.
Ray, Raka and Anna C. Korteweg. "Women's Movements in the Third World: Identity, Mobilization, and Autonomy." *Annual Review of Sociology* 25 (1999): 45–71.
Tilley, Maureen A. "The Ascetic Body and the (Un)Making of the World of the Martyr." *Journal of the American Academy of Religion* 59.3 (1991): 467–79.
Trinh, T. Minh-ha. *When the Moon Waxes Red: Representation, Gender, and Cultural Politics*. London and New York: Routledge, 1991.

MERLINDA BOBIS
The Transnational Filipina Warrior Between the Postcolonial Exotic and the Babaylan/Catalonan
Marie-Therese C. Sulit

Are postcolonial writers persuaded to represent their respective cultures, and to translate those cultures for an unfamiliar metropolitan readership? To what extent does the value ascribed to them and attributed to their writing depend on their capacity to operate, not just as representers of culture, but as bona fide cultural representatives? And is this representativeness a function of their inscription in the margins, of the mainstream demand for an "authentic," but readily translatable marginal voice? — Graham Huggan, The Postcolonial Exotic: Marketing the Margins [26]

This essay meditates on the role of the female ethnic writer through an analysis of Merlinda Bobis and her oeuvre of work, which brings the reader to the Philippines' pre-colonial time through the reconfiguration of the woman shaman — the *babaylan/catalonan*. Her work also offers insights into the country's colonial and postcolonial times. Through the translational and transnational elements of Bobis' literary and cultural productions, the reader can begin to "imagine community," to use Benedict Anderson's words. In the Guest Editors' "Introduction" to the October 2005 issue of the *Journal of Asian American Studies*, Erika Lee and Naoko Shibusawa define "transnational" in reference to the "political, economic, social and cultural processes that extend beyond the borders of a particular state, include actors that are not states, but are shaped by the policies and institutional practices of states" (viii). This useful definition enhances the ways in which Bobis' writings bring to foreground the management of her visibility in the contemporary, albeit transnational, marketplace — a location that displaces an emphasis on the U.S. nation state and instead further highlights the distinction between East and West.[1] Her translational and transnational situations and her position as a female ethnic writer function allegorically, thus highlighting the demands on so-called ethnic and minority women writers in their search for publishing venues and negotiations of the varied responses to their works. The literary marketplace acts as a site to shift the Philippines from *no place* to a *new* place, a position grounded in the transnational elements of Bobis herself as a female ethnic writer and the topics and themes within her works.

Merlinda Bobis, a Filipina Australian author (born and raised in the Philippines, relocated to Australia for her doctorate, and now resides and teaches in Australia), crosses genres as well as pivotal time periods in the Spain–United States–Philippines encounters. In her works, Bobis predominantly focuses on tensions within Philippine cultures and peoples as a means of exploring the neocolonial/postcolonial aftereffects of the colonial encounters with Spain and the United States. However, perhaps more provocative than her literary glosses of this history, which this chapter discusses below, Bobis' work raises the issue of the ambivalence regarding her status as a writer. This chapter suggests that the transnational nature of her writing augments this ambivalence. Her short story collection *The Kissing* (2001), published by Aunt Lute Press in the United States, was published by Spinifex Press as *The White Turtle* (1999) in Australia. The change in titles demonstrates the marketing decisions that shift the thematic focus from folklore and parable to romance, thus framing the Western reception of this author (its inherent translatable nature and transnational quality) as a transition from indigenous folk tale to transnational romance.[2]

In contrast to the romance and courtship theme of "The Kissing," the short story "The White Turtle" offers an alternative frame to explore the tensions between Bobis' position as author and the various responses from her audience as captured by the elements of and events in this story. In "The White Turtle," Bobis locates the story at a writers' festival in Australia that features Salvacion Ibarra (also known as Lola Basyon), "the seventy-year-old chanter from the Philippines" brought to this reading by an Australian anthropologist "who had fallen in love with her chant about the white turtle," a creation/anti-creation myth from the village of Iraya in the Bikol region (2001, 35, 37). Carrying the dreams of the dead children in Iraya, the white turtle buries the dreams in the sea where they grow into coral; as the turtle continues its task, its shell becomes more white (Bobis 2001, 37). These images underwrite Lola Basyon's excitement and sense of displacement, which begins this short story: "With no book or even paper to cling to, she [a storyteller and chanter] hid her hands under the folds of her *tapis* [skirt].... How in the world would they see the white turtle if I can only conjure it only in my dialect? Ay, *Dios ko* [My God], this is very difficult indeed" (Bobis 2001, 35). Thus, Bobis traces the responsibility of the storyteller to share their tales, extending a sense of cultural literacy without betraying either the sending or the receiving country's cultures.

On the one hand, this is a whimsical, if not impossible, wish as the opening epigraph of the short story reads, "I'll dream you a turtle tonight;/cradle on her back/bone-white./I'll dream you a turtle tonight," a chant performed atypically with harmonies produced in her throat, to which the audience members respond eagerly (Bobis 2001, 34). On the other hand, the fundamental hope for cultural translation and communication hinges on intelligibility, a complicated process mediated not only by the anthropologist but the fellow presenters as well who rely on the written word; in fact, one writer silently critiques her performance by believing that she belongs in a "multicultural or indigenous arts event, definitely not for a writers' festival" (Bobis 2001, 38). Bobis furthers the notion of collaboration as Lola Basyon relies on the work of an Australian anthropologist to extend her work to Western audiences. Their collaboration creates a new story about the cultural consumption of this audience, one that Bobis qualifies by showing that Lola Basyon cannot communicate with her audience at the reception since the anthropologist leaves her side to continue his own conversations with the audience and raise publicity for his own work. In so doing, Bobis characterizes the reception of Basyon's work by this diverse audience as cynical even antagonistic (a couple of her fellow presenters), genuine and sympathetic (female and younger audience members), even mercenary (a journalist insistent on taking her picture and "putting her arm around the waist of her greatest discovery") (2001, 42).

As Basyon's nervous excitement at the reception of her reading turns to comfort, aided by champagne and an easy conversation with a child, her most sympathetic and genuine audience member, she once again chants the story of the white turtle to ease the commotion. In this reading, she conjures the white turtle whose reception is likewise met with wonder, fear, and confusion as it too adds its harmonies to hers. Basyon's responsibility here relates the story without claiming ownership over it, since "the story that she chanted was written only on its back, never really hers. Only lent to her in a moment of music" and brings together this ephemeral community though this community's responses likewise indicate fracture as well (Bobis 2001, 48). The theme of ownership, even captivity, strangely closes this story: "Gloved hands steadying the creature, the police wondered about the unnameable emotion that stirred in their wrists, a strange, warm ripple of sorts. They lifted it with utmost tenderness as if it were a holy, precious thing. It was as large as the table, but oh so light" (Bobis 2001, 48). Perhaps the police represent a form of institutional control and power that can be subverted through storytelling as Bobis' prose in this particular short story shows this transcendent power of language, as the tale itself and its reception by audience members significantly hold precedence over the storyteller herself.

Similar to the connections and disconnections that the fictional Lola Basyon experiences at the writers' festival in Australia, Bobis admits to the sense of displacement and anxiety that initially shaped her experiences as a Filipina on the Australian landscape. In her essay "Border Lover," Bobis writes of the cultural encounter between Eastern and Western when she began working on her doctorate in creative writing:

> So for a long time, I felt that I was trying too hard to serenade my Australian audience, while worrying about how my Philippine audience would respond.... I was so cold during my first year in Australia. Cold, lonely, desperate. I went

there to write an epic poem, the "*Kantada ng Babing Mandirang Daragang Magayon*" (in Pilipino and English), for my doctorate. But for a whole year I was rendered dumbstruck by the cold. I tried to find assurance in my old poems. I sent them to Australian journals, wanting to be heard by this new audience, but I was rejected all the time; I could have papered the walls with rejection slips. My poems did not work for the Australian sensibility. I lost confidence. I could not write for a whole year and was ready to abort the epic [124].

Akin to the more marketable promise of changing the name of her short story collection from "The White Turtle" to "The Kissing," Bobis iterates a romance/courtship theme for her position as a Filipina writer to an Australian audience. Like Lola Basyon's collaboration with the Australian anthropologist, which produces a new chant, and translation of the chant, Bobis also underscores the "new timbre" of her voice from the Philippines to Australia though "this new audience"—"the Australian sensibility"— repeatedly rejected her work, particularly her poetry (2003, 124).

However, when her doctorate project, the epic poem *Kantada ng Babing Mandirang Daragang Magayon*, was written and performed, Bobis notes that her poetry "does not sit well with the Australian sensibility — unless [she] perform[s] it," a method that reveals the double-bind in which she finds herself as an "artist on the border":

> You might say I have pandered to my foreign audience. Because I realized that they would not accept me in printed form, I tried to find another way to reach them through something more easily recognizable: the body. I put my body on the line. There are two sides to this approach. One: I was the dancing native woman in full ethnic regalia, abetting the West's love for the exotic. On the other hand, yes, I was the dancing native, but dancing to a text that questioned how they looked at me [2003, 125].[3]

Realizing and arguably reclaiming her authorship through the vehicle of her body, Bobis portrays an awareness of the expectations of her Australian audience. However, she also resists and even goes beyond those expectations through the medium of her language (a "minor literature," to draw on Deleuze and Guattari), thus claiming her writing as a means to correct those expectations and perceptions of her as a transnational body.

In noting the West's "love for the exotic," Bobis' reflections remind the reader of Graham Huggan's definition of the "exotic." Huggan distinguishes between the erroneous belief in "the inherent quality" of exoticism and its guiding principle as "a particular mode of aesthetic perception" imposed on objects and people:

> one which renders people, objects and places strange even as it domesticates them, and which effectively manufactures otherness even as it claims to surrender to its immanent mystery. The exoticist production of otherness is dialectical and contingent; at various times and in different places, it may serve conflicting ideological interests.... Exoticism, in this context, might be described as a kind of semiotic circuit that oscillates between the opposite poles of strangeness and familiarity. Within this circuit, the strange and the familiar, as well as the rela-

tion between them, may be recoded to serve different, even contradictory, political needs and ends [13].

The dynamics of "The White Turtle" clearly depict the mode of rendering something strange into something familiar via the mediation of the Australian anthropologist. Despite his sympathetic identification with the chanter and especially the story of the white turtle, the anthropologist still circulates this story to the Australian audience of the writers' festival for their critical and uncritical reception, thus reflecting "conflicting ideological interests" and "different, even contradictory, political needs and ends" (Huggan 13). Bobis and her fictional surrogate, Lola Basyon, typify Huggan's notion of "the postcolonial exotic" as that which "occupies a site of discursive conflict between a local assemblage of more or less related oppositional practices and a global apparatus of assimilative institutional/commercial codes" (28). In order to clarify the connection between "oppositional practices" and "assimilative institutional/commercial codes," Huggan's tracks the tension between postcolonialism, which "posits itself as anti-colonial ... and works toward the dissolution of imperial epistemologies and institutional structures" and postcoloniality, which "is more closely tied to the global market ... and capitalises both on the widespread circulation of ideas about cultural otherness and the worldwide trafficking of culturally 'othered' artifacts and goods" (28).[4] Huggan isolates the ways in which the literatures of postcoloniality and postcolonialism convey "forms of *material* struggle," forms that apply to "the *symbolic* power" of these works, one that one can also attribute to its transnational quality, crossing East to West (28).

The discussions about the different marketing strategies of two different independent presses on opposite ends of the Pacific Ocean—though according to Bobis both are independent and Western presses—and the dilemma that Bobis finds herself as writer, which she dramatizes in "The White Turtle," suggest a hunger for authorship. This particular hunger shows how Bobis' works with postcoloniality and postcolonialism as outlined by Huggan. Huggan offers cautionary words regarding the continuities "between older forms of imperial exoticist representations and some of their more recent, allegedly postcolonial counterparts ... the *aesthetics of decontextualisation* and *commodity fetishism*" (16; italics in the original). These continuities are illustrated in "The White Turtle," when Lola Basyon and her chant are aesthetically decontextualized by the Australian audience. Bobis questions the process of commodity fetishism as Lola Basyon's fellow panelists sell and publicize their works in dispassionate and detached ways. Yet Bobis also resists the demonization of this process of cultural translation in her sympathetic characterization of the Australian anthropologist, who in spite of his flaws, still comes across as sympathetic.[5] Bobis' depiction of the attempts within the story to commodify the cultural translation of Lola Basyon's chant, of course, finds its external parallel in the two marketing strategies of the two presses, Spinifex and Aunt Lute.

Bobis, as a writer, complicates the binaries between what is Filipina and what is postcolonial literature because of her focus on the modern and contemporary state of the Philippines via the United States. She thus calls into question the binary of West versus East, as this dichotomy collapses in her works because of her as well as her characters' positionality. Huggan emphasizes the process of translation, via Gayatri Spivak, as one of dispersal rather than containment: "Translators must be alert to the shifting sands, the rhetoricity, of language; if they are not, then they risk merely adding another block to the 'neocolonialist construction of the non–West'" (25). Even though Bobis portrays the neocolonial effects of both Spain and the United States in the Philippines, she sees this as "strategic exoticism," one that works with the transnational position of the writer.

> Exoticism, after all, remains an at best unstable system of containment: its assimilation of their other to the same can never be definitive or exhaustive, since the "collision between ego's culture and alien cultures" ... is continually refashioned, and the effects that collision produces may unsettle as much as reassure, dislodge authority as much as reconfirm it.... "Strategic exoticism" is an option, then, but as we shall see, it is not necessarily a way out of the dilemma [Haggan 32].

Bobis, thus, illustrates the ways in which she "exercise[s] agency over [her] work" by demystifying the process of exoticism, and its material and symbolic trappings (Haggan 30). Reading Bobis as a contemporary *babaylan/catalonan* enables this process of demystification to occur, and in so doing, the material and symbolic trappings of her transnational position are revealed.

Tension between Religiosity and Spirituality, Politics of Gender and Language

One of the aspects of the Philippines' colonial history reflected in Bobis' writing is the role of Catholicism and the ways in which its internal contradictions shaped and continue to shape the subjectivities of the Filipinos. Bobis' use of the language of the body engages the distinction between the religious and the spiritual. Her surrogate storytellers evoke and invoke the trope of the *babaylan* (Bisayan) or the *catalonan* (Tagalog)—the shaman (men who dressed in women's garb) and predominantly women or sha(wo)men. These little-known figures speak to the movement from the spiritual and matrilineal to the religious and patriarchal. Through the sha(wo)men, a reversion back to the spiritual and matrilineal may be envisioned as a means to address the troubles of Eastern and Western fundamentalism and to examine the power of language in its creative use and propagandistic misuse.

Akin to the myth of the white turtle that Lola Basyon and Bobis share with us, Sr. Mary Mananzan discusses an alternative creation myth specific to the Philippines that posits the equality between man and woman inherent both in the imagery and the language of the myth:

> It is interesting to note that in the primitive tagalog alphabet, the word *god* is made up of three consonants: *Ba-Tha-La*. The first consonant is the first syllable of the word *babae* (woman), which symbolizes generation. The third consonant is the first syllable of *lalaki* (man), which symbolizes potency. They are joined by the middle consonant an inspired H, which means light or spirit. The word god therefore means the union of man and woman in light. And when one reads the word backwards, it reads *LaHatBa* meaning total generation, total creator (*todo creador*). In other words, the concept of god among the ancient Tagalogs was more closely linked with woman. When linked with both the concepts of man and woman, there is nuance of union, of mutuality, and not of subordination [148–49].

Interestingly, the concept of the God embodies both the masculine and feminine ideals and it emphasizes more of the feminine ideal.[6] This feminine ideal finds its human correlative in the *babaylan/catalonan* figures who acted as centers of the community for guidance and direction, wisdom, and health through language and action.

Carolyn Brewer has offered an understanding of the these matrilineal figures, deploying poststructural and postmodern theories of language as she reads the narratives by the Spanish conquistadores and church officials, their characterizations of these figures, and their methods for systematically co-opting, torturing, and exterminating them from the late-sixteenth to the late-seventeenth century. In the following excerpt, Brewer describes the spirituality that existed prior to the entrance of Spain and its use of Catholicism as its principal instrument of imperialism and colonialism:

> In what is now the Philippine Archipelago, before the arrival of Catholicism, a form of shamanistic Animism was the spiritual substratum or bedrock upon which the communities relied. Shamanism is typified by the ability of an adept to enter into an altered state of consciousness in order to heal the sick, communicate with the spirits of the dead and perform other supernatural feats. In sixteenth and seventeenth-century Philippines, the adepts were in the main women or men who dressed as women, whereas throughout the rest of the world where shamanism is practiced, usually the adepts were men [xvii].

Arguably, the most striking element of this description lies not in the purported "supernatural feats" of these figures, but rather, the prominence of the feminine, as Brewer writes, "throughout the rest of the world" wherein the shaman were believed to be (perhaps erroneously) only men. In a perhaps nostalgic or romantic gesture, Nick Carbó tracks women's writing in the Philippines to these figures:

> The tradition of women's writing in the Philippines can be traced back to the pre–Hispanic era of the archipelago when, in certain communities, priestess-poets called *babaylan* (Bisayan) and *catalonan* (Tagalog) held saw in the spiritual and ritualistic lives of the people. These women provided healing, wisdom, and direction for the inhabitants of their *barangays* (towns) with morality stories, myths, poems, prayers, and chants.... During the subsequent three hundred years of Spanish colonization under the Catholic Church, these priestess-poets gradually lost their positions of privilege, and much of that early oral tradition has been erased [vii–viii].

For over three hundred years, Spain and Catholicism sought to eradicate the opposition that these figures enacted and represented. Their methods of eradication, as Carbó suggests, occurred through language and action. Brewer illustrates these methods: the elimination of any opposition by torture and death; the use of community members, particularly young boys, to spy and report on the *babaylan/catalonan*; the utilization of the Catholic mass as a means to transform their messages to the community; and, the appropriation of the oral and written history of Philippines through the imposition of Spain's "masculinist, orientalist reconstruction of indigenous, non–Christianised peoples" via the conquistadores and church officials (30, xxiv). Those reconstructions not only marginalize and misrepresent these figures but they also demonize them, thus imposing a Judeo-Christian mythology onto the indigenous myths (Brewer xxiv, 41). In so doing, Spain introduced Christian images and messages, particularly of the "good" and "bad" Christian woman that the Filipinos internalized (Brewer 58). For those women, not tortured or killed, two modes of survival become known: a retreat to the lowland areas that has left very little archival but plenty of anecdotal evidence and adaptation or assimilation into the Catholic Church. Filipino communities then witnessed the transition from *baylanism* to *beaterismo*, in which nuns founded the orders, particularly the Poor Clare sisters, the sister order of the Franciscans (Brewer 191–92).[7] With the loss of privilege and the erasure of the oral and written tradition of the *babaylan/catalonan*, the Spanish ironically set the stage for transferring the controlling power over the colony to the United States in the late-nineteenth century.[8]

In order to distinguish themselves from the colonization processes of Spain, the United States promise the Filipinos access to education, hitherto denied to them by the Spanish as a means of sustaining institutional power. Carbó writes:

> The arrival of another colonizer, the United States, to the Philippines in 1898 brought a new language which the natives used to express themselves. 1902 to 1940 marks the period in which Philippines literature in English begins to "emerge" from the shackles of American colonization. During this period of literary "apprenticeship" (in English — as noted above, Filipinas already had well-established literary traditions in native dialects as well as in Spanish) several Filipina women took the front stage in the development of English as a Philippine literary tradition [ix–x].

The evocation and invocation of the *babaylan/catalonan* by Carbó suggests a possible re-emergence of the erased oral and written traditions of the indigenous peoples, particularly women. By underscoring the notion of an established Philippine literary tradition in other dialects and languages besides, and even before, English, he substantiates the historicity and continuity of this literary tradition amidst these particular colonial encounters in the Philippines, and thus, in the translational and transnational natures of these literary works. Significantly, he also argues for the subversive potential of writing in the languages of the colonizers, Spanish and English — a point that revises Renato Constantino's notion of "the miseducation of the Filipino."⁹

Sha(wo)manism as Exoticism: The Troubling Contradictions

Like Carbó, Huggan points out the pivotal role of English in regards to narratives of the colonial encounter. "English is," he writes, "the language of this critical industry [postcolonialism]," and as such, it is "a discourse of *translation*" (Haggan 4). Bobis herself echoes these sentiments in her essay "Border Lover," wherever she is via three particular languages, as a means of returning home, in a figurative sense, as she also crosses genres as a mode of crossing borders:¹⁰

> How does one negotiate through the border: from Bikol to Pilipino, to English, and then back? From poetry to drama then to the short story, then to the novel? And how does the writer cross over to the realm of performance? Further, how does the writer-performer move from the stage to radio and then to film? I have worked with all these areas. I have been crossing borders all the time.... No language can be imposed on me, because each language, by affinity, is actually mine. By a long shot then, English, like Pilipino and all other languages, is a hybrid of the first prehistoric cry which was fine-tuned in a specific cultural setting. So English is mine; I cannot be colonized by it. This shifting of perception is nothing new. It is echoed by many postcolonial arguments that have been around for a while. But there is nothing like living an argument, the body owning it, in order to save itself [119, 126–27].

Similar to Carbó, Bobis empties the English language of its hierarchical power, a rhetorical move that not only claims its hybrid nature as a language but also claims power in simply utilizing it. Her use of the English language functions as a means for translating events and situations in contemporary Philippine culture while also highlighting the transnational nature of these things throughout her oeuvre. However, Huggan points out a key caveat in regards to the processes of translation and cultural artifacts, such as narratives, commodity fetishism, or that which exchange a physical absence for a spiritual presence. This rhetoric thus iterates the inherent tendency to exoticize cultural "Others," and in so doing, the language of spirituality and religiosity of those cultural "Others" potentially reiterates a similar process of exoticization (Huggan 18).¹¹ Huggan further comments on three aspects of commodity fetishism, defined as the process of mystifying the circumstances of commodity production and consumption, that enable cultural artifacts and the artists that create them to, in his words, "acquire an almost talismanic status": "mystification (or leveling-out) of historical experience; imagined access to the cultural other through the process of consumption; reification of people and places into exchangeable aesthetic objects" (19). Thus, the exoticism of Filipina women as characters in literature as depicted by Filipina authors may be further enhanced by the frameworks of religiosity and spirituality, which may then enact another form of exoticism.

The trope of the *babaylan/catalonan* crosses borders from the landscape of the Philippines throughout the diaspora, just as Carbó locates it within the borders of the United States. Huggan's earlier discussion warns against the conversion of this trope from the *babaylan/catalonan* into the postcolonial exotic. In a similar move, San Juan Jr. cautions Filipinos in the United States about two specific pitfalls in attempting to understand "their own historical trajectory": "the nostalgic essentializing nativism that surfaces in the fetishism of folks festivals and other commodified cultural products that accompany tourist spectacles and official rituals" and "self-denial by mimicry, the anxiety of not becoming truly 'Americanized,' that is, defined by white-supremacist norms" (14–15). San Juan Jr. shows a severe skepticism of a "hybrid 'postcolonial' (translational and/or transnational) performativity with all its self-ingratiating exoticism and aura of originality" on the grounds that it perpetuates "atomistic individualism" (15).[12] Thus, the only means for avoiding these potential pitfalls is "to connect folklore and other cultural practices to the conflicted lives" of the Filipino peoples represented (San Juan Jr. 15).

By doing so (mis)representations and (mis)perceptions carry the potential to expose Western biases, stereotypes, and expectations and to offer a means to comprehend its translational and transnational characters. These forms carry the potential to demystify the processes that thus create and sustain such things, particularly of Eastern and Southeast Asian, particularly Filipina, artifacts, which function as "the site[s] of fixity and fantasy" (Bhabha 81).[13] Josephine Lee applies Bhabha's theory to the stereotype-as-fetish in order to explain how Philip Kan Gotanda's *Yankee Dawg You Die* and David Henry Hwang's *M. Butterfly* reveal the contradictory and internal logic that structures the stereotype, thus identifying the ways to suspend that logic (30). Furthermore, she addresses the "peculiar anxiety that arises from situations of contact," a notion that Bobis also brings to light in describing the drawbacks that she encounters as a Filipina artist depicting the predicaments and plights of mostly Filipina characters (95). These representations thus parallel the actual experiences of Filipinas in the New World Order as "servants of globalization" (to borrow Rhacel Salazar Parreñas evocative term). Bobis' works present modes of demystification and decolonization that challenge any analyses which simply present her writing a mere reflection of the processes of exoticism and commodity fetishism.

The Evocation and Invocation of the *Babaylan/Catalonan*

The evocation and invocation of the *babaylan/catalonan* found in Bobis' writing speak to two particular elements of this contemporary moment: a rhetoric of fundamental religious orthodoxy — both Western and Eastern — that authorizes violence or the separation of the spiritual or religious and the secular. This separation stems from modernity, with its rhetoric of progress, which then leads to formations of Otherness in imperial and colonial projects. More specifically, the aftereffects of modernity and globalization in relation to the Philippines–United States encounter, as Sr. Mary Mananzan's *Challenges to the Inner Room* and Leny Mendoza Strobel's *A Book of Her Own* (2004) have discussed, manifest themselves in the sex and entertainment industry, the mail-order bride industry, and the labor contract industry. Furthermore, as Strobel observes, there are eight million overseas Filipino workers; "poverty has pushed 600,000 Filipina women towards prostitution;" and "80% of Filipinos today fall below the poverty line, which is $124 a month" (102–03). Interestingly, Strobel also notes that "[s]ome fundamentalist religious groups sanctify the plight of the overseas workers by calling it the will of God, as a way for Filipinos to be used of God in evangelizing the rest of the world — whether by taking care of other people's children, cleaning other people's homes, cleaning hotel rooms, as entertainment workers in Japan, as mail order brides in Australia and Europe, or as sweatshop workers in Taiwan or Saipan," a calling, if you will, with which many Filipinas willingly comply (103). Thus, the evocation and invocation of the trope of the *babaylan/catalonan* is an allegorical necessity because the archetypes that this trope represents — the warrior, the teacher, the healer, and the visionary — taps into a spirituality that, according to Strobel, went underground to re-emerge and avail itself as a means for Filipinas to challenge the various forms of oppression.[14] The evocation and invocation of this trope underwrites the translational and transnational characterizations of Bobis' characters and their situations especially the female storyteller.

Using the languages of the Philippine diaspora, Bobis' works return to the earlier discussion about the hunger for authorship that frames this chapter. The performativity that infuses all of Bobis' work from the oral and the written to the visual encourages readers, listeners, and viewers to engage with the history of the Philippines — a history informed by the violence of imperialism and the colonial encounters with Spain and the United States. As an artist and a contemporary *babaylan/catalonan*, Bobis guides the reader through moments of discomfort, so as to move beyond exoticism and commodity fetishism:

> Orality in relation to memory means you have to speak the place aloud, so you remember it. You have to hear it, taste its syllables, roll them around the tongue in tactile play and, as eating is intimately bound with smell, breathe in those odors as well; only then can you see the place. The body knows, and it remembers. My writing is grounded in the body.... I am more interested in "sensing-knowing," in which the sensation comes with a little epiphany [2003, 131–32].

By grounding her writing in the body, as this quotation shows, Bobis fuses spirit with matter, thus suturing the split between the mind and the body. Moreover, her intention lies in moving her audience beyond the "libidinal," as she herself notes, to the revelatory—"the 'sensing-knowing,' in which the sensation comes with a little epiphany."

One of her performance pieces, "Rita's Lullaby," tracks the life of a thirteen-year-old sex worker, Rita: "I can buy the world with silver. /I can bribe the world with it. /I can beg the world with it" (Bobis 2003, 129). More particularly, she details Rita's sexual transaction, a blow job: "[M]y throat hurts/ from too much blowing. /My throat grows a lemon from too much blowing, /too sour from too much blowing" (2003, 129). Bobis' focus on the throat brings her audience back, as she holds, to the title of the piece, a lullaby, thereby displacing a song of comfort with feelings of discomfort that lead audience members to question the dynamics of poverty that impel a child to prostitution. In dealing with the medium of the radio, Bobis utilizes an approach similar to her approach to poetry and prose: "I must hear the image, hear the story.... At this point, I cross the border from poetry and theater, and move onto prose.... We are now moving into new-old territory" (2003, 131). Bridging these different forms through her methodology potentially gives Bobis access to her audience members, in her own words, forming an intimacy, a sense of conspiracy, with them (2003, 130). And as she remarks, "We invoke, thus evoke, a particular reality through language," a reality that demarcates a mode of decolonization that sutures mind with body (2003, 133).

These comments by Bobis resonate with Gilles Deleuze and Félix Guattari's notion of the deterritorialization that constitutes a "minor literature."[15] They focus on the body, particularly the mouth, as a means of juxtaposing writing with hunger rather than consumption, a desire perhaps that marks the necessity in representing reality. Deleuze and Guattari write:

> Rich and poor, each language always implies a deterritorialization of the mouth, the tongue, and the teeth. The mouth, tongue, and teeth find their primitive territoriality in food. In giving themselves over to the articulation of sounds, the mouth, tongue, and teeth deterritorialize. Thus, there is a certain disjunction between eating and speaking, and even more, despite all appearances, between eating and writing. Undoubtedly, one can write while eating more easily than one can speak while eating, but writing goes further in transforming words into things capable of competing with food. Disjunction between content and expression. To speak, and above all to write, is to fast [62].

In contrast to Deleuze and Guattari's application of deterritorialization, which concentrates on the alienation of the bourgeois individual as a response to modes of modernization, examining deterritorialization in the works of Bobis engages with the diasporic and transnational nature of her language and the use of the body as a means of connection with her audience. She crosses genres, refuses clichés and proverbs, and instead opts for the conversions of myths and folkloric stories in order to show the continuities and discontinuities of past and present colonial encounters.

Bobis' poem *Cantata of the Warrior Woman Daragang Magayon* (1998) showcases how she used performance, the body and the word, to create a sense of home in her state of displacement on the Australian landscape. Akin to her reliance on the senses to guide her language in "Rita's Lullaby" and her poetry, Bobis uses the body in the form to dance to connect spirit with matter. In her essay, "Border Lover," she muses:

> Some of the lines in *Daragang Magayon* in fact grew from verbalizing my actual dance figures. Literally, it was an act of "word-ing the body." Dance is, after all, a case of publishing in space. The moment of movement, if seen from a writerly perspective, is also the instance of publication. As I said, the very first lines of my epic poem came from that little survival exercise: dancing. The body and the word began collaborating. And the push and pull between these two art forms (writing and dance) became the new dance, poetry in performance which was what the epic poem eventually came to be [125].

"Word-ing the body," to use Bobis' words, allows for her to revise the myth of a beautiful but passive princess "Daragang Magayon" (literally "Beautiful Maiden," which iterates and reiterates her place as a commodified and fetishized object), "traded as war booty" by her father, the king of a tribe, to the warlord, Datu Pagtuga, into a warrior daughter.

In the traditional myth, Mount Mayon, a volcano in Bobis' home province in the Bikol region in the south of Luzon, the most northern island of the Philippines, holds the body of the princess. In this alternate version, the volcano emerges as a grave marker not only of the princess but also of the whole tribe as a casualty of war: a figurative rendering of the repetition of the neo-colonial mindset in the Philippines. The warrior princess disavows a fixed position as princess and as warrior, and instead,

> [S]he carves a new space where she will be not only a plodding follower of existing signs, but a creator of signs which are always fluid. Thus she remains in transition and always multiple. *Daragang Magayon* becoming the warrior woman is about crossing the border; as she crosses, she creates her own signs. Signs lead us to the issue of labels, stereotypes and, of course, names. I engaged the issue of naming, un-naming and namelessness in the epic.... She becomes "The Nameless One Who is All Names." Perhaps the border, where names and signs collapse, is after all a blissful state of namelessness. Or perhaps a state where we are constantly re-naming ourselves [Bobis 2003, 127].

Interestingly, the "state of namelessness," highlighted by Bobis, points towards a postcolonial, utopian moment wherein "names and signs collapse," even as she also emphasizes the neo-colonial predicament of naming and re-naming that reflects the history of the Philippines as war booty. Like Daragang Magayon, Spain claims the Philippines and it exchanges hands from Spain to the United States— all of which highlight the transnational colonial history of the Philippines embodied in Daragang Magayon.

Like Benjamin who outlines "The Task of the Translator," Bobis acknowledges the impossibility of seeking the recovery of the original story, accentuating instead the process of translation as a means for bridging the languages. Furthermore, she refuses to deploy a rhetoric of facile hybridity in her methodology for crossing genres and modes of being. Instead, she concentrates on the significance of representing the elements of the colonial and neo-colonial encounters as a means to redirect and recreate modes of access for herself and her audience into the very elements that destroyed the original story. In order to do so, she establishes, over and again, the continuity between the past and the present as she affirms the connection between mind and body. In "The Border Lover," Bobis repudiates the use of the heart to convey that connection and the difficulty in sustaining it. Rather, she chooses to locate it in the breastbone, the "human wishbone," as she writes: "I had to find another body part that is more supple, that could withstand the push and pull of colliding landscapes, that would resist rupture. The wishbone" (2003, 118). Moreover, she underscores the resiliency that also shapes and informs her work as a "border lover":

> Resilience is not so much about not breaking, as we do succumb to collapse once in a while. Resilience is more about the wish to not break. When the migrant artist buffeted by the winds of a new art form/voice by an audience who finds her sensibility too alien thus not worth engagement, to save herself, she rests on what seems like the tenuous comfort of a wish. Much like the little tendon between these two bones. So I find comfort in a bone. But even the bone, pliant as it is, is not invulnerable [Bobis 2003, 120].

Bobis tests limits, revises old forms, and invents new forms as a means of addressing her audience members with material that broaches the unfamiliar. Yes, she potentially exoticizes and fetishes that unfamiliar territory through her body and her history, but as Bobis decidedly claims: "I must throw them a bridge. I must teach them the language with which to read me" (2003, 135).

Conclusion

The consideration of Bobis as a contemporary *babaylan/catalonan* suggests that literature can function not only as a means of imposing a spiritual discourse onto the mainstream consciousness, but also in a more holistic way. The insidious nature of religion as the main instrument of imperial and colonial endeavors calls attention to the dynamics that historically separated spiritual and secular discourses. If liberal and modern ideology presents a clear division between the religious and the secular within institutions and structures of power in civil society, the suturing of the sacred and the secular via the works of Bobis believes everything to be sacred. Within this conceptual framework, the translational and transnational elements of her work provide a basis that is more productive and useful for contemporary times.

The encounter between the Philippines and Spain and between the Philippines and the United States show how a transnational spiritual discourse might counter religious didacticism. In "Remarks to the Methodist Delegation" dated November 21, 1899, President William McKinley writes about praying to the "Almighty God for light and guidance," or rather, specific justifications and rationales for the Philippines, which "had dropped into [their] laps" (Shirmer and Shalom 22). The last reason illustrates a profound irony: "there was nothing left for us to do but to take them all, and to educate the Filipinos, and uplift and civilize and Christianize them, and by God's grace do the very best we could by them as our fellow-men for whom Christ also died" (Shirmer and Shalom 22–23). If Spain already Christianized the Filipinos, then why did the United States simply reiterate, and then repeat, this task? The works by Bobis thus expose this and other contradictions about the colonial encounter and also reveal what she refers to as "a shared vulnerability," albeit it a drastically uneven one (Bobis 1999, 58).

This sense of "a shared vulnerability" has yet to permeate the institutions and structures that continue to dictate an uneven and unequal, simply impoverished, state of affairs in the Philippines, with its economy barely afloat thanks to the annual remittances of overseas Filipino workers to the World Bank and International Monetary Fund. These remittances famously prompted former President Cory Aquino to declare these workers as "modern day heroes" in spite of the fact that "fifteen families in the Philippines own 55% of the firms, and 330 family-owned conglomerates own 216 of the top 1000 firms in the country" in which Aquino's family holds its own position among them (Strobel 101).[16] The efforts of local community groups and non-governmental organization increasingly pose challenging to the elite-based politics that govern the civil society in the Philippines in the areas of the environment, human- and constitutional rights, and fair labor laws and practices.[17] Strobel significantly argues that these groups and organizations in the Philippines now serve as models for the civil societies throughout Asia. This point presents a compelling inversion of the perceived historical purposes of the Philippines in Asia as the only predominantly Christian and democratic nation-state throughout Asia and as such, the doorway to convert and exploit the rest of Asia.

However, one particular avenue of grassroots organizing in the Philippines that suggests a healthier alliance is an Asian feminist theology that works *in tandem with* U.S. feminism of the 80s. According to Sr. Mary Mananzan, the "Asian Women's Consultation" took place in 1985 in Manila after the founding and development of the Women's Commission of the Ecumenical Association of Third World Theologians, which addresses the violence against women within the context of all forms of institutionalized religion, and Gabriel, an organization specifically devoted to the predicaments and plights of the Filipinas throughout the world (189). By noting the various forms of oppression that cross East and West and North and South — namely violence in the home and exploitation in the economy, sex and work industry — a feminist movement that also creates a conceptual space for the spiritual inevitably addresses the influence of institutionalized religion as historically and predominantly patriarchal (Mananzan 94).

The focus of these organizations, which melds the spiritual and the secular, covers themes of personal and communal empowerment to transformative modes of thought that confront dualistic and absolutist forms (Mananzan 97–98).[18] Sr. Mary Mananzan charts a methodology for Asian Feminist Theology that aligns itself in the manner of literary interpretation because of its emphasis on the processes of contextualization and formulation of alternative readings, translations, interpretations, and languages of the traditional sacred narratives. Especially important are the forms of religious and cultural critiques that emerge as a result of these interpretive readings in conjunction with the "recovery of the authentic value of women's experience" en route to alternative visions for interaction and exchange (Mananzan 112–13).[19] Their use of the word "authentic" speaks to the value of actual and lived experience rather than the intellectual discussions about essentialism or fundamentalism regarding cultural identity as such. Such a movement thus operates as a mode of decolonization for the everyday experiences that women experience on personal, social, and cultural levels.

The shift from the religiosity of the Judeo-Christian tradition and the materiality of the secularism into an ontological mode of being that integrates the sacred with the secular certainly bears on the twentieth-century analogy of the Philippines as the "Lost Eden."[20] The works of Bobis, at the onset of the twenty-first century, sketch a path to revise and reclaim our notion of Eden. The aesthetics and politics of her work represent and update the oral tradition of the pre-colonial and colonial eras of the Philippines as well as translate the neocolonial/postcolonial trappings of a transnational print culture. Interrogating the dynamics that create and reinforce "the postcolonial exotic," through her evocation and invocation of the *babaylan/catalonan* allows Bobis to also explore the role of the intellectual, the use of indigenous cultures to gain access into the exotic and the spiritual, and the dynamics of the marketplace. These questions also gesture towards the consumption of Asian philosophies and popular cultural artifacts, which Bobis also challenges through her diasporic narratives framed by transnational exchanges.

This sense of "a shared vulnerability" also finds it literary parallel in Bobis' short story, "Border Lover" which also thematically glosses her poem, "Border Lover." In both, the colonial encounter between East and West reiterates itself in the system of higher education as the female narrator, a young scholar, chooses to leave the Philippines for a university in Australia, cheekily depicted as the multicultural land of Oz (Bobis 2003, 119). Though quite hesitant to conflate autobiography with fiction, Bobis nevertheless admits, in her essay "Border Lover," that her Mama Ola, her maternal grandmother, a "formidable matriarch" to whom she dedicates all of her works, represents " all the grandmothers, the wise women and the shamans in [her] stories" (121). And as such, the grandmother, in this story, compels the narrator to reflect on the effects of her lessons "there in the White Land" as she writes her "*tisis* (thesis)" and learns about "Kristeva's semiotic" and "*piminism* (feminism)" that inform her writing even as she also writes about her grandmother's "banana heart," which translates into "fancy squiggles on paper" (Bobis 2003, 120, 121, 124). True to form, Bobis metonymically correlates word with flesh (her gloss on Holy Communion) although she observes: "This inevitable trick of art gives us so little time to stay with the flesh. How quickly we are distanced" (2003, 121). Thus, her evocation and invocation of the *babaylan/catalonan* gives her a means to close this distance and find Eden, so to speak. This search for "home," as Strobel indicates, for women writers of the Philippine diaspora, is a revolutionary task for women located throughout the diaspora, a movement both involuntary and voluntary (153, 152, 150).

In a similar vein to the process of decolonization as implicit in works of literature from the Philippine diaspora, Cornel West describes the process of demystification, or "demystificatory criticism" as "prophetic criticism" (31). With its focus on "the central role of human agency [be it the critic, artist, constituency and audience]," the new cultural politics of difference "tries to keep track of the complex dynamics of institutional and other related power structures in order to disclose options and alternatives for transformative praxis" (West 31). West leaves open the conceptual and creative possibilities for the study of literature through its "representational strategies" as "creative responses" to material conditions and circumstances (31). Furthermore, West also characterizes the new cultural politics as "partisan, partial, engaged and crisis-centered, yet always keeps open a skeptical eye to avoid dogmatic traps, premature closures, formulaic formulations or rigid conclusions. In addition to social structural analyses, moral and political judgments, and sheer critical consciousness, there indeed is evaluation" (31). Even though West grounds his thoughts in a more secular discourse, its parallels to Mananzan's "Methodology for Asian Feminist Theology" accentuate the ways in which works of literature likewise hold pedagogical value as a means for assessment for contemporary culture, particularly regarding the transnational literary and cultural productions of the Philippines.

Thus, the works of Bobis bridges a secular with a sacred discourse located in the body through her trope of the border lover. This discourse exemplifies a pedagogy that not only glosses the history of the Philippines but also offers a model for a transnational consciousness. In so doing, Bobis grounds herself in the poignant flexible movements of the body as a means towards a methodology that dis-/re-places confusion with consciousness:

> In my practice, constantly besieged by this ache that is not quite in my heart, I have been passing from one mode of representation to another. Between these two bones, pushing and pulling each other as if in a dance, I am the border lover constantly in transition. And if I am in transition, I am more supple; I do not

break. I now understand that my forays into various disciplines, genres and languages are not a survival technique for the migrant artist — a technique which is not just of the word, but of the body. One great gift from being a border lover, especially when I get lost in this dance of transitions, is this — the body suddenly forgets absolute cultural contexts and conceptual frameworks. Perhaps this is a state that will save us from cultural, religious or ideological fixations, which leads to war and terrorism. I value culture but I detest cultural chauvinism from whatever side of the border. I believe in celebrating difference, but at the same time repudiate the preciousness and the tyranny of difference [2003, 128].

For the works of women writers of the Philippine diaspora and particularly those by Merlinda Bobis, the allegorical nature of writing functions as a means to read and understand confusing and traumatic contemporary events, especially those initiated by the United States with its history of violence as an empire, its perpetuation of this ongoing "War on Terrorism," and its support of neoconservative right-wing governments.[21]

Notes

1. In her book, *Imagining the Nation in Four Philippine Novels*, Maria Teresa Martinez-Sicat chooses novels about the Philippines' wars against Spain and the United States, a small fraction of time in the late nineteenth and early twentieth-centuries. Though the novels are both historical and contemporary, her focus on the ways in which these colonial wars also galvanized the Filipino peoples to forge a more cohesive national identity is quite astute even though I believe that she could have periodized these novels in more detail because of their disparate publication dates. As a side-note, Martinez-Sicat also briefly discusses the reasons why the novel as historical and contemporary is a challenging literary form with which to write because of the material lack of printing presses and access to them in the Philippines (19).
2. The opening short story, "An Earnest Parable" introduces the power of the story over the storyteller as a tongue passes from one home to the next in a multicultural neighborhood in Australia, where Bobis now resides. Another story, "Border Lover" muses on the cultural mediations that a writer and storyteller faces from the family and the academy as a granddaughter visits her grandmother who cooks her favorite Filipino dishes but cannot understand the terminology of her granddaughter anymore, a terminology about which she jokes and mimics and yet implies a certain level of distance that both experience as a result of the granddaughter's relocation to Australia.
3. Bobis also discusses her cross-genres forms, resultant of diasporic consciousness between Australia and the Philippines, as possessing a subversive element to traditional genres: "Yes, I have lost my first language, even as I gained a new form. And now I have even given up on my poetry, because it does not sit well with the Australian sensibility — unless I perform it." (2003, 125).
4. Huggans further illuminates the distinction between postcolonialism and postcoloniality (6).
5. Referencing Walter Benjamin's "The Task of the Translator," Huggan further observes: "What is at work here is a process, commodified of course, of cultural translation through which the marginalized other can be apprehended and described in familiar terms." (24).

6. These observations emphasize a heterosexual paradigm, which Brewer's work further complicates this paradigm by positing the transgender nature of the *babaylan/catalonan* figure poststructural and postmodern criticism.

7. For a poststructural reading of the *babaylan/catalonan* in the Philippines, see Cruz.

8. During the Spanish-American War from 1896 to 1898, Spain ceded its control of the Philippines (as well as Puerto Rico and Cuba) to the United States for $20 million. However, control of the Philippines is certainly a moot point since there was a strong resistance movement against Spain and the United States via the first general, and ultimately the first president, of the Philippine Republic, Emilio Aguinaldo.

9. Audre Lorde argues that the master's tools cannot dismantle the master's house because the dynamic sustains the hegemony of the master and structures the subjectivity of and denies the autonomy of the servant/slave.

10. Gloria Anzaldúa also comments on the language of marginal cultures, particularly Chicano Spanish as a border tongue in her seminal essay, "How to Tame a Wild Tongue."

11. There are parallels between my invocation of the indigenous Filipina spirituality as spectacle with African American churches and American Indian rituals and dynamics of exoticism and tourism.

12. San Juan Jr. further advocates against the subsumption of Filipino American subjectivity into an Asian American panethnicity because it "violates the integrity of the Filipino people's tradition of revolutionary struggle for autonomy, our outstanding contribution to humankind's narrative of the struggle for freedom from the violence of Othering and all modes of oppression" (15).

13. See Bhabha's remarks on the stereotype and its dynamics as fetish that betrays the anxiety of white supremacy in his essay, "The Other Question: Difference, Discrimination and the Discourse of Colonialism."

14. In 2005, the bi-ennial conference of the Filipino American Women's Network 2005 theme resurrected the trope of the *Babaylan*, which indicates a growing movement in the Filipino American community, in particular, of evoking and invoking this trope, and Delia Aquilar's presented astute thoughts on qualifying the uncritical usage of this particular trope.

15. For this usefulness, as opposed to its limitations, see Deleuze, Gilles and Félix Guattari.

16. See Benedict Anderson's important essay on the cacique democracy, a term that updates the pre-modern term oligarchy and adapts to the dynastic structures that govern the Philippines.

17. A doctoral candidate, L. Joyce Mariano, in the Department of American Studies at the University of Minnesota, Twin Cities, explores the cultural ideologies undergirding a cross-section of transnational organizations (e.g. corporate and diasporic philanthropic agencies, environmental justice agencies, Filipino American community organizations) between the United States and the Philippines in her dissertation, "Homeland Developments: Filipino Americans and the Politics of Giving."

18. Please see John Shelby Spong's *A New Christianity for a New World: Why Traditional Faith Is Dying and How a New Faith Is Being Born*. Mananzan's work is more ecumenical, moving beyond Catholicism and Christianity, as a whole, but Spong's ideas clearly imagine, though in a narrower vein, an emergent Christianity from the fundamental Christianity that has become more mainstream in recent years.

19. These ideas are as per an informal conversation with Mananzan, at the 2005 conference for the Filipina American Women's Network.

20. The women writers of the Philippines diaspora, such as Jessica Hagedorn, Ninotchka Rosca, and Linda Ty-Casper, offered critiques of the Marcos Regime through

their works of literature, a time during which all sectors of Philippine society took part: the military, the church, and the public.

21. Even with the change in administration in the United States, and with the election of President Barack Obama, the task of gauging the War on Terrorism and the role of the Philippines is still ongoing. Merlinda Bobis' first novel, *The Solemn Lantern Maker* (2009), explores the effects of the global War on Terror through the everyday lives of those who live in Manila.

Bibliography

Anderson, Benedict. "Cacique Democracy and the Philippines: Origins and Dreams." *New Left Review* I.169 (1988): 3–31.
Anzaldúa, Gloria. "How to Tame a Wild Tongue." *Out There: Marginalization and Contemporary Cultures*. Eds. Russell Ferguson, Martha Gever, Trinh T. Minh-ha, and Cornel West. New York: The New Museum of Contemporary Art and MIT Press, 1990. 203–11.
Bhabha, Homi K. "The Other Question: Difference, Discrimination and the Discourse of Colonialism." Ferguson, Gever, Trinh, and West 71–87.
Bobis, Merlinda. "The Border Lover." *Not Home, But Here: Writing from the Filipino Diaspora*. Ed. Luisa A. Igloria. Manila: Anvil, 2003. 118–37.
_____. *The Kissing: A Collection of Short Stories*. San Francisco, CA: Aunt Lute Press, 2001.
_____. "Promenade." *Summer Was a Fast Train Without Terminals*. Australia: Spinifex Press, 1999. 45–66.
Brewer, Carolyn. *Shamanism, Catholicism and Gender Relations in Colonial Philippines, 1521–1685*. Burlington, VT and England: Ashgate Publishing, 2004.
Carbó, Nick. "Introduction: The Other Half of the Sky." *Babaylan: An Anthology of Filipina and Filipina American Writers*. Eds. Nick Carbó and Eileen Tabios. San Francisco, CA: Aunt Lute Books, 2000.
Cruz, Reginald D. "Con el Sudor de su Rostro: Incipient Religious Communities for Women Established in Colonial Philippines until 1750 as Spaces of Co-optation and Defiance." *Religious Life Asia: Re-visioning Women in the Church* (October–December 2000): 46–85.
Deleuze, Gilles, and Félix Guattari. "What Is a Minor Literature?" *Out There: Marginalization and Contemporary Culture*. Ferguson, Gever, Minh-ha, and West 59–69.
Ferguson, Russell, Martha Gever, Trinh T. Minh-ha, and Cornel West. *Out There: Marginalization and Contemporary Culture*. New York: New Museum of Contemporary Art and MIT Press, 1990.
Huggan, Graham. *The Postcolonial Exotic: Marketing the Margins*. London and New York: Routledge, 2001.
Lee, Erika, and Naoko Shibusawa. "Guest Editor's Introduction: What Is Transnational Asian American History? Recent Trends and Challenges." *Journal of Asian American Studies* 8:3 (2005). vii–xvii.
Lee, Josephine. *Performing Asian America: Race and Ethnicity on the Contemporary Stage*. Philadelphia, PA: Temple University Press, 1997.
Mananzan, Sr. Mary John. *Challenges to the Inner Room: Selected Essays and Speeches on Women*. Manila: The Institute of Women's Studies, St. Scholastica's College, 1998.
Martinez-Sicat, Maria Teresa. *Imagining the Nation in Four Philippine Novels*. Quezon City: University of the Philippines Press, 1994.

San Juan, E., Jr. *After Postcolonialism: Remapping Philippines — United States Confrontations.* Lanham, Boulder, New York, and Oxford: Rowman and Littlefield Publishers, 2000.

Shirmer, Daniel B., and Stephen Rosskamm Shalom, eds. *The Philippines Reader: A History of Colonialism, Neocolonialism, Dictatorship, and Resistance.* Boston, MA: South End Press, 1987.

Spong, John Shelby. *A New Christianity for a New World: Why Traditional Faith Is Dying and How a New Faith Is Being Born.* San Francisco, CA: Harper San Francisco, 2001.

Stobel, Leny Mendoza. *A Book of Her Own: Words and Images to Honor the Babaylan.* San Francisco, CA: T'Boli Publishing and Distribution, 2005.

West, Cornel. "The New Cultural Politics of Difference." *Out There: Marginalization and Contemporary Cultures.* Ferguson, Gever, Trinh, and West 19–36.

MULAN AGAINST GWAN GUNG
Performing Myths on a Transnational Stage
Lan Dong

> Chinamen are made, not born, my dear. Out of junk-imports, lies, railroad scrap iron, dirty jokes, broken bottles, cigar smoke, Cosquilla Indian blood, wino spit, and lots of milk of amnesia. — Tam Lum from Frank Chin, The Chickencoop Chinaman

> The Woman Warrior went to the mirror, which had stayed unbroken, and let her gown come loose and drop to the ground. She turned and studied the ideographs that had long ago been carved into the flesh of her young back.... — Grace from David Henry Hwang, FOB

A recipient of the prominent fellowships from the Rockefeller Foundation, the Guggenheim Foundation, the New York State Council, and the National Endowment for the Arts and winner of a number of prestigious awards including Tony and Obie, David Henry Hwang is undoubtedly one of the most recognized and influential Asian American playwrights. For general readers and audiences, Hwang is probably best known for his provocative and controversial work *M. Butterfly*. This play, through its portrayal of the relationship between French diplomat Rene Gallimard and Chinese opera actor and spy Song Liling, addresses the complex interaction of love, betrayal, racism, sexism, and imperialism.[1] *M. Butterfly* has been honored with the Tony, Drama Desk, Outer Critics Circle, and John Gassner Awards. Due to its commercial success as well as its popular reception and critical acclaim, many believe that this play has made a significant breakthrough into the mainstream and "finally placed Asian American theatre on the United States theatrical map" (Lei).

As a "deconstructive text" informed by multiplicity and fragmentation, *M. Butterfly* questions the notion of the single unified identity and the fixity of interpretation within the context of transnational migration; yet it is by no means the playwright's first attempt to call attention to the interacting axes of gendered, racialized, and politicized construction of subjectivity when tangled up with transnationalism (Chen 1994, 132, 133). This critical agenda did not begin with *M. Butterfly*; rather this line of questioning began at the beginning of Hwang's play writing career in the late 1970s with his debut play, *FOB*. Yet there are distinctions: while Hwang's *M. Butterfly* deals with international politics and unmasks imperialism and its process of degradation and colonization (Kang 26), *FOB* offers a close look at hybridity and multiplicity within one's identity.[2]

In order to explore the question of identity within a cross-cultural context in *FOB*, Hwang transplants two figures who are well-known both in Chinese folk stories and in Chinese American literary tradition: Fa Mu Lan and Gwan Gung.[3] In writing his play with these specific cultural references to previously published works by Chinese American writers, he has made a conscious attempt to "validate the existence of a previous Asian American literary tradition" (Hwang 1989–1990, 16). Combining elements of realism, mythology, and fantasy, *FOB* depicts the tension and conflict between American-born Chinese and immigrant newcomers from China, and in the process this surrealistic drama dismantles "the realist character paradigm" in favor of more theatricalized representations of Chinese American identity (Jew 2006, 190). The symbolic battles performed by the actors on stage provide a platform for the characters as well as the viewers from which to contemplate gendered and politicized identities in transnational migration.

This chapter examines Hwang's theatrical exploration and development of two mythological characters: Fa Mu Lan, from Maxine Hong Kingston's book *The Woman Warrior: Memoirs of a Girlhood among Ghosts* (1976), and Kwan Gung, the god of the writers, warriors, and prostitutes from Frank Chin's play *Gee, Pop* (1976) (Hwang 1989–1990, 16).[4] It will investigate how, in drawing on the cross-cultural tradition as a reference point, Hwang uses mythology created by Kingston and Chin to review Chinese American history to call the audience's attention to racism, imperialism, gender politics, and the characters' fluid identities within a transnational context.

It is important to first provide a context for Hwang's creation of *FOB*. He wrote this play when he was a senior at Stanford University. Its first production was mounted in Stanford's Okada House dormitory. Directed by the playwright and produced by Nancy Takahashi for the Stanford Asian American Theatre Project, the performance took place on March 2, 1979. When *FOB* was accepted for production at the esteemed National Playwrights Conference at O'Neil Theater Center in Connecticut in 1979, Hwang was a twenty-two-year-old graduate fresh out of college. Director Robert Alan Ackerman introduced Hwang's play to producer Joseph Papp who then staged it at the New York Shakespeare Festival Public Theater from June 8th through July 13th, 1980. Papp's production, directed by Mako, won an Obie Award for the Best New American Play of the 1980–1981 Season, the 1980 Drama-Logue Playwriting Award, and the 1981 U.S.-Asia Institute Award. In 1982, *FOB* premiered in Singapore (Ester Kim

127; Savran 122). The New York-based Pan Asian Repertory Theater then staged another production of the play in the company's 1989–1990 season, directed by Hwang himself. In a way, *FOB* marked the beginning of Hwang's recognition as an emerging playwright.

Hwang once told an interviewer that *FOB* may be his favorite play simply because he wrote it so much out of instinct, before acquiring any of the so-called tools of playwriting (Savran 123). Compared with some of his subsequent work, its lack of pretension indicates the playwright's "nascent talent and social concern" (Gussow). One of the earliest plays to deconstruct "the turbulent processes through which Asian American identities are created" (Jew 2006, 196), *FOB* constitutes the first part of Hwang's dramatic trilogy reflecting the Chinese American experience.[5] It is important to note that Hwang was born and raised in an immigrant family in California. His father, Henry Yuan Hwang, was a banker who was born in Shanghai, moved to Taiwan, and then immigrated to the United States. His mother, Dorothy Huang Hwang, was a pianist and music teacher who grew up in a Chinese family in the Philippines before moving to the United States. The experiences of Chinese immigrants and their offspring in the United States and their bi- or multi-cultural background remain a wellspring of inspiration for Hwang's creative works, although throughout his playwriting career he has explored other subject matter and portrayed characters from additional cultural backgrounds as well. This chapter addresses three interrelated aspects in *FOB*: how the play presents utterly opposing characters who ironically share much more in common than they realize, thus challenging any fixed understanding of ethnic identity and revealing the complexity of racism; how the work reflects Chinese American history and prompts further contemplation through the interactions among characters in contemporary life, mythical fantasy, and performative battles; and how it ties all the dramatic elements together around the central theme of the "fluidity of identity" within the context of immigration and transnationality.[6]

The notion of fluid identity functions as the pivotal theme of *FOB*. Set in the backroom of a small Chinese restaurant in Torrance, California in 1978, this two-act play features three characters all in their early twenties: Dale who was born in the United States to Chinese immigrant parents and grew up striving to be all American; his cousin Grace who moved from Taiwan to the United States when she was ten, had her share of struggles to "fit in," and is currently attending college at the University of California at Los Angeles while working part time in her father's restaurant; and finally Steve who comes from a wealthy manufacturer's family in Hong Kong and recently arrived in California. These three characters form oppositional pairs onstage that act out realistic conflicts as well as ritual battles: FOB (an acronym for "fresh off the boat," represented by Steve) versus ABC (an acronym for "American born Chinese," embodied by Dale) as well as Fa Mu Lan (impersonated by Grace) versus Gwan Gung (Steve's mythological persona). Through these duos, the play offers the audience a view of "an internecine Chinese American conflict" (Moy 127). The title of the play, "FOB" is in fact historically a derogatory term for immigrant newcomers. The character Dale's monologue that serves as the prologue to open the play introduces the definition of FOB as well as its connotations, thus setting the stage for the play to explore what it means to have a bicultural heritage in America and how racism and prejudice can take different shapes and penetrate people's everyday lives without them being aware. Upon his entrance onto the stage, Dale gives a lecture to the audience aided by a blackboard:

> F-O-B. Fresh Off the Boat. FOB. What words can you think of that characterize the FOB? Clumsy, ugly, greasy FOB. Loud, stupid, four-eyed FOB. Big feet. Horny.... Someone you wouldn't want your sister to marry. If you are a sister, someone you wouldn't want to marry. That assumes we're talking about boy FOBs, of course. But girl FOBs aren't really as ... FOBish. Boy FOBs are the worst, the ... pits. They are the sworn enemies of all ABC — oh, that's "American Born Chinese"— of all ABC girls. Before an ABC girl will be seen on Friday night with a boy FOB in Westwood, she would rather burn off her face [Hwang 1983, 13].

Through Dale's extreme but not unique assimilationist attitude, the play presses the viewer to contemplate how racism can be internalized within the Chinese American community — a question examined throughout the play.[7] By referring to immigrant newcomers as "clumsy," "ugly," "greasy," "loud," "stupid," "four-eyed," and "horny" FOBs, Dale not only clearly indicates his contempt for immigrants who recently arrived onshore, but also points to the significance of gender since his hostile attitude is particularly toward "boy FOBs." Labeling FOBs as the "sworn enemies" of American-born Chinese up front through the character of Dale, the play then subtly unfolds the inevitable connections among the three characters. Using such a structure, Hwang's play points to the complexity within Dale's disdain and portrays his character paradoxically as both a victim as well as a perpetrator of racism.

As Dale articulates in the play, growing up as a son of immigrant parents, he was haunted by the "yellow ghosts" and therefore had to work particularly hard to be himself and to "not be a Chinese, a yellow, a slant, a gook. To be just a human being, like everyone else" (Hwang 1983, 35). Here both "human being" and "everyone else" are exclusive concepts. Dale's American birth may have given him the legal rights of a United States citizen, but it does not automatically ensure his American-ness in social life. He has to undergo a conscious process to shun Chinese heritage, to differentiate himself from his immigrant parents, and to make himself American. To him, normality and Chinese-ness are mutually exclusive. Now that he is "making it in American" and is "much better," Dale is proud of his transformation. To some degree, his effort to reject Chinese-ness can be viewed as an attempt to avoid being victimized by racism. Nonetheless, his absolute contempt of the FOBs ironically reveals an internalization of racism that is dramatically performed through his encounter with Steve. Their verbal, visual, as well as gestural differences set Dale and Steve's characters in a contrastive frame on stage. Dale is dressed preppie, drives an X-1/9, and acts "all American" while Steve wears a stylish summer outfit, has a Cadillac Fleetwood limousine with a private driver, and carries himself FOBishly. Although never appearing in his interaction with Grace, Steve begins to speak English with a Chinese accent during his first encounter with Dale. His FOBish English poses a contrast to Dale's impeccable American English.

Dale and Steve's duality thus reflects how Chinese Americans, as Tina Chen has conceptualized, are double agents "who work both to establish their own claims to a U.S. American identity and to critique the American institutions that have designated them as 'aliens' whose incorporation into the body politic is thus always already suspect" (2005, xix). In order to demonstrate a "figurative distance" between American born generations and immigrants, *FOB* calls not only for a careful investigation of the separation between "immigration" and "hyphenation," but also for an examination of the problems of naming and exclusion in Asian American theater and criticism.[8]

As Karen Shimakawa has proposed, Asian American theatre artists have been trying to show and tell us "how performance may be pressed into the service of, or may serve as a counterdiscourse to, those dominant narratives of national belonging and national exclusion" (163). The first theatrical representations of Asian Americans were created under the political climate of anti–Chinese xenophobia in late nineteenth century which culminated in the Chinese Exclusion Act of 1882. Bret Harte and Mark Twain's 1876 play, *Ah Sin*, for instance, portrays a servant character as a typecast of the stereotypical China man.[9] Early twentieth-century Asian American plays by and large feature the struggles of first generation immigrants along with nostalgia and racial discrimination. Racial stereotypes and exertions in theater are counterposed by Asian American playwrights in a variety of ways, one of which is through "a reconextualization that forces the audience to visualize in a double register that refuses the fixity" (Chen 2005, 61). The body doubles that Dale and Steve personify not only represent selves caught between worlds, but also embody the site of ideological contests over the very nature of that self (Lee 1997, 168). In his lecture to the FOBish Steve, Dale brings up the problematic dichotomy of "you" versus "us": "*You're* gonna decide *you* like *us*.... *You're* gonna decide to become an American. Yeah, don't deny it — it happens to the best of *us*. *You* can't hold out — *you're* no different. *You* won't even know it's coming before it has *you*. Before *you're* trying real hard to be just like the rest of *us*" (Hwang 1983, 29–30; italics added). All the mockery and insulting comments that Dale throws at Steve ironically are bounced back by the newcomer's rhetorical question in response: "such as your parents?" If Steve is "no different," so is Dale. Adding Dale's parents breaks the FOB versus ABC binary, thus making the distinction between "you" and "us" blurry. The character Dale to some extent represents the playwright's interest in "the degree to which we all may have been affected by certain prejudices in the society without having realized it, and to what degree we had incorporated that into our persons by the time we'd reached our early twenties" (qtd. in Ross).

Through his college-aged characters, Hwang casts light on the collective history of Chinese Americans and the transnational journeys of immigrants. The playwright articulates: "In my context, creating a mythology, creating a past for myself, involved going into Chinese history and Chinese-American history" (qtd. in Ross). Besides embodying a FOB in the late 1970s, Steve also impersonates Chinese immigrants of different generations who made the transpacific journey to the "Gold Mountain," played a crucial role in building the transcontinental railroad and developing California's agriculture, as well as contributed to the development of America in meaningful ways.[10] In present time, Steve comes from a wealthy family in Hong Kong whose journey to America is accompanied by abundant cash and luxury in everyday life. Yet his monologue in Act I, Scene I quickly brings the audience back to the beginning of the twentieth century:

> I come here five times—I raise lifetime fortune five times. Five times, I first come here, you say to me I am illegal, you return me on boat to fathers and uncles with no gold, no treasure, no fortune, no rice. I only want to come to America— come to "Mountain of Gold." And I hate Mountain and I hate America and I hate you! *(Pause.)* But this year you call 1914—very bad for China [Hwang 1983, 25; parentheses and italics in the original].

Through Steve's narration, the play introduces the transnational journeys of multiple generations and refers to the myth of the "Gold Mountain" in Chinese American history:

> The white ghosts came into the harbor today. They promised that they would bring us to America, and that in America we would never want for anything.... They told of a land [that is] a worker's paradise. A land of gold, a mountain of wealth, a land in which a man can make his fortune and grow without wrinkles into an old age.... All we need to do is sign a worker's contract. Yes, I am going to America [Hwang 1983, 38].

It is because of such promises and hopes that many Chinese made their way to America or "Mei Guo" (a Chinese term referring to the United States and literally meaning "beautiful country"), finding themselves becoming "strangers from a different shore" while their dreams were smashed in the reality.[11]

A similar example appears in the same scene in which Steve's speech makes a specific reference to the "paper son" in Chinese American immigration history:

> This is fifth time I come here. I tell you both my parents, I tell you their parents, I tell you their parents' parents and who was adopted great-granduncle. I tell you how many beggars in home town and name of their blind dogs. I tell you number of steps from my front door to temple, to well, to governor house, to fields, to whorehouse, to fifth cousin inn, to eighth neighbor toilet—you ask only: What for am I in whorehouse? I tell north, south, northeast, southwest, west, east, north-northeast, south-southwest, east-eastsouth—Why will you not let me enter in America? [Hwang 1983, 24–25].

Similar to some other Chinese American writers, Hwang represents here the onstage experiences and struggles of "paper sons."[12] Steve's monologue dramatically reflects the excruciating interrogation process that "paper sons" had to face as they hoped to pass the multiple rounds of questioning and earn an entry to the "Gold Mountain." Incorporating historical information in its imaginative and fantastic plots, Hwang's work indicates that Orientalism colors not only American policy but also people's mental frameworks. Steven's impersonation of early generations of Chinese immigrants entails at least two kinds of reading. For the audience who is familiar with Chinese American history, his speech provides enough hints for them to establish a connection between history and reality and to piece together the context. For those who have little knowledge on this subject matter, the play poses a challenge and at the same time intrigues them enough to want to learn more about these historical references and their implications.

Through such impersonation onstage, "the past inserts itself as a lesson taught to audiences;" "history is performed as ever present as a link with the past, allowing the Asian American spectator a sense of intimacy with an imagined community that bridges the ruptures of time and space" (Lee 1997, 148). Through the voice of Steve, Hwang's play reveals the condition of "a splintered and multiplicitous Asian American identity, one that is ruptured by the process of historical immigration" (Jew 2006, 199–200). In other words, the play reflects the complexity and multiplicity of the Chinese American identity through projecting all these elements onto one character.

Influenced by Sam Shepard, Hwang also experiments in *FOB* with non-realistic narrative structure as well as non-realistic character development, allowing his dramatic figures to serve as "the motivating forces behind the structural innovation."[13] The play combines "everyday settings and naturalistic dialogue with fantastic events or nonrealistic behavior" (Chu 476). Its satirical, fantastic, and highly theatrical imagination and methods help establish a model that Hwang uses in his other plays: the utilization of complex acts of narration and dramatization as well as the development of a central idea or paradigm in multiple layers. "Within these layers, Hwang often blends historical facts, familiar and unfamiliar cultural references, elements of pure fantasy, and dialogue that appears to represent ordinary speech, but is in fact funnier, faster paced, or more complex" (Chu 476). The following dialogue between Dale and Steve in Act II is an example of such a blend of "slice-of-life realism and yearning spiritualism-scattershot anger" (Gerard 44+), in which the characters seem to occupy different spaces:

Steve. I am GWAN GUNG!
Dale. What...?
Steve. I HAVE COME TO THIS LAND TO STUDY!
Dale. Grace...

Steve. TO STUDY THE ARTS OF WAR, OF LITERATURE, OF RIGHTEOUS-
NESS!
Dale. A movie's fine.
Steve. I FOUGHT THE WARS OF THE THREE KINGDOMS!
Dale. An ordinary movie, let's go.
Steve. I FOUGHT WITH THE FIRST PIONEERS, THE FIRST WARRIORS THAT CHOSE TO FOLLOW THE WHITE GHOSTS TO THIS LAND!
Dale. You can pick okay?
Steve. I WAS THEIR HERO, THEIR LEADER, THEIR FIRE!
Dale. I'll even let him drive, how's that?
Steve. AND THIS LAND IS MINE! IT HAS NO RIGHT TO TREAT ME THIS WAY! [Hwang 1983, 47–48].

A literary technique underscores the characters' occupation of different space: the capitalized font sets the two characters and their performative space apart while the dialogue itself brings them together in the present time. Furthermore, the character Steve, together with his persona in mythology Gwan Gung and his representation of Chinese American history, occupy multiple time as well as space.

Multiple times throughout the play, Grace and Steve transform into their respective mythological personae and shift back to real-life characters in contemporary America. In his conscious effort of incorporating literary references to Fa Mu Lan and Gwan Gung and giving them a theatrical spin, Hwang does not merely draw inspiration from Chinese American mythology. Rather, through acting out these myths on stage the playwright appears to be asking the audience: "what good those myths do us in America" (Kingston viii). In this sense, *FOB* fulfills Hwang's literary mission to write plays that "claim a place for Asian Americans" (Pace D4) and in the process to flesh out Chinatown stereotypes (Weinraub).

The first legendary character Fa Mu Lan has become familiar to a sizeable number of English-speakers thanks largely to Maxine Hong Kingston's acclaimed book, *The Woman Warrior: Memoirs of a Girlhood among Ghosts* and Disney Studio's animated feature films, *Mulan* (1998) and *Mulan II* (2005). By appropriating a textual privilege that previously had been predominantly male, Kingston heralds a new Chinese American tradition, and by extension Asian American literature, that embraces female sensitivity. In his interviews, Hwang repeatedly talks about the influence of Kingston's book on his playwriting. In his conversation with Jeremy Gerard, for example, Hwang states: "I read Maxine's book ... and felt immediately excited by the possibility that you could interweave the hyperrealistic details of contemporary American life with the larger, mythical ghost story in the background" (44+). A decade later in another interview with Bonnie Lyons, he reiterates: "It was reading *Woman Warrior* that made me feel that I could find my own voice. As an Asian-American, she was the first author who spoke in a voice that seemed special, directly related to *me*.... I really credit her with enabling me to believe my own concerns could be made into literature" (241; italics in the original). In *FOB*, myth thus becomes a powerful tool in staging a fluid Chinese American identity. As Tina Chen has suggested, "by considering how impersonation helps us to focus on the shared terrains animating the performance of stereotype *and* of identity, we might usefully consider the ways in which stereotypical performance becomes the common ground upon which Asian Americanness as coalitional identity and political mobilization is performed into possibility" (2005, 64; italics in the original).

The second legendary character Gwan Gung, a historical figure from the Three Kingdoms period (220–280 A.D.), has been and still is a character virtually known by every household in China. Chen Shou's (233–297 A.D.) work of history, *Sanguo zhi* (*The Records of the Three Kingdoms*), includes some biographical information about him. Later his story is further elaborated and popularized by Luo Guanzhong's (ca. 1330–ca. 1400) novel, *Sanguo yanyi* (*The Romance of the Three Kingdoms*). Besides written literature, stories about Gwan Gung also flourish in Chinese theatre, folk tradition, and local worship. In traditional Chinese culture, his character is usually portrayed as the ultimate embodiment of bravery, loyalty, and righteousness. His influence also extends beyond geographical boundaries, having accompanied some immigrants' transpacific journeys to arrive in the United States. In the late nineteenth century, Gwan Gung was considered "the most popular and powerful of several deities honored by Chinese in California, who celebrated his exploits in Cantonese opera productions" (Chu 478). Thus the name Gwan Gung is not unfamiliar to many in Chinese American communities as well as to those in the field of Asian American studies. As Hwang has stated, "with the emergence of the railroads, came regular performances of Cantonese opera, featuring Gwan Gung, the adopted god of Chinese America" (1983, 10). This character has appeared repeatedly in Asian American literature and theatre. Frank Chin, for example, adapts this semi-historical figure in his plays, novels, and essays in his efforts to reconstruct a positive, masculine image of the Chinese American man. Hwang accredits Chin's play, *Gee Pop*, to be a direct literary reference that has inspired and influenced his dramatic creation.[14] After *FOB*, Gwan Gung's character and story have continued to be revived in Chinese American literature: Maxine Hong Kingston's novel, *Tripmaster Monkey: His Fake Book* (1989) Frank Chin's novel, *Donald Duk* (1991) are among such examples.

In *FOB*—through storytelling, dialogues, and other interactions—Steve, Dale, and Grace perform mythic as well as onstage battles. In this sense, this play leads the way for Hwang's career in playwriting in terms of its portrayal of "diametrically opposed characters" (Savran 118). Steve and Grace's theatrical identification with the mythical characters Gwan Gung and Fa Mu Lan is introduced at the beginning of Act I, develops in several dimensions, and runs through the end of the play. Upon their first encounter, Steve claims himself to be Gwan Gung, "god of warriors, writers and prostitutes;" Grace challenges him not with physical prowess but rather with articulation: "Tell me, then. Tell me, if you are Gwan Gung. Tell me of your battles. Of one battle. Of Gwan Gung's favorite battle" (Hwang 1983, 16). The verbalization of Gwan Gung's mythical battle in which he slaughters villagers randomly and massively while wearing a custom-made silk blindfold is juxtaposed with a stage battle in which Grace retrieves the box, a symbolic object in the play, from Steve's hands. Subsequently Grace claims that she "won the battle" and therefore she is the woman "Who Had Defeated Gwan Gung" (Hwang 1983, 17). In both mythical and staged battles, Fa Mu Lan/Grace outshines Gwan Gung/Steve in physical strength and wisdom as well as the power of articulation.

Later the battle, again in the form of articulation, becomes more complicated when Dale joins Steve and Grace to play Group Story. The discursive battle between the characters is performed through their collective storytelling, in which Steve, Dale, and Grace "take on various mythologies and try to find themselves in relation to those mythologies, almost as if the search for identity is so difficult and complex that it is easier to hang your hat on a preestablished identity and try to have that become you or you become that thing" (Lyons 231). Their narrative, in weaving together the myths of Fa Mu Lan and Gwan Gung, gives clarity to their confrontation. Furthermore, it interlaces scattered pieces of Chinese American immigration history.

Intertwined with her combat against Steve/Gwan Gung, Grace also performs battles with her American born cousin Dale, thus highlighting the role of gender in transnational migration and Chinese American identity pursuit. Dale and Grace's first interaction onstage presents a ritual battle in which the woman wins. When Dale arrives at the restaurant, Grace, in her mythical persona of Fa Mu Lan, discovers the remains and ruins of her family and village as a result of Gwan Gung's storming attack. As Dale enters without announcing himself, approaches, and touches her from behind, Grace "reacts by swinging around and knocking him to the ground. Only after he is down does she see his face" (Hwang 1983, 22). Different from Gwan Gung, Grace's impersonation of Fa Mu Lan is not as a goddess but as a girl, "a girl who takes her father's place in battle" and a woman, a "warrior-woman ... and ghost" (Hwang 1983, 19). In the play, Grace tries to accommodate Dale and Steve as well as the two traditions that they represent and in the process becomes a pivot between two men and two cultures. Being positioned between these male characters who cannot seem to agree on anything, Grace witnesses them competing for the box as well as her attention while she ends up making all the decisions for the evening, thus settling the disputes and symbolically winning all the battles.

After dinner at the restaurant, the play presents a battle among the characters. "Grace enters from the kitchen with the box wrapped in Act I. she sits in a chair and goes over the wrapping, her back to Steve. He gets up and begins to go for the box, almost reaching her. She turns around suddenly, though, at which point he drops to the floor and pretends to be looking for something. She then turns back front, and he resumes his attempt" (Hwang 1983, 36). Dale, in his protective gestures to keep Steve's hands off Grace both literally and metaphorically, represents the imperialist sentiment on a different level. To borrow Gayatri Spivak's framework, it is not of white men saving yellow women from yellow men but of yellow men who identify with white men saving yellow women from yellow men (93). These interactions between the three characters in *FOB* as well as the all–Asian American cast illustrate that both Asianness and Americanness are representational and ethnicity is a performance. *FOB* "call[s] attention to the persistent divisions within characters who internalize the impulse toward individual success and repudiate a collective Asianness. The resulting tensions are indicative not so much of a split between Asian and American as of a rupture in a distinctly American system of values" (Lee 1997, 32). Therefore Hwang, in drawing on specific Chinese American sources and allusions without supplementing explanation, poses a challenge to the audience who is not familiar with Chinese American culture. Thus, in his attempt to validate the existence of a previous Asian American literary tradition," Hwang explores two mythological characters and brings them together in Torrance, California through "cross-fertilization" and "fusion of Asian and Western theater" (Hwang 1989–1990, 16).

Although Hwang did not envision a combination of Chinese and American theatrical traditions when he wrote *FOB*, this blending and juxtaposition subsequently become an important aspect in the play's production.[15] In the first staging of *FOB* at Stanford, he resorted to ritualistic movement and triangular placements of the characters in order to stage the mythical battles. In its later productions, Chinese opera becomes an important element to visualize the battle sequence; this newly adopted ingredient of form helps to express and reinforce the content of the play (Cooperman 366). Later, in Joseph Papp's New York production, Hwang worked with director Mako and actor John Lone to incorporate this style of opera into the play. This inclusion of traditional Chinese opera also enables the dream-like battle scenes between Fa Mu Lan and Gwan Gung to be integrated successfully as well as allows both cultures to be staged at the same time (Cooperman 204), thus portraying "a theatrical meeting of the minds" (Cooperman 202). The play has evolved into an invitation to the audience to pay attention to the conflicts between Asianness and Americanness, yet at the same time advocating the possibility of cultural combination. In this sense, *FOB* launches Hwang's continuing efforts to create "new theatrical statements" and to demonstrate onstage how the theatre can bring cultures together (Cooperman 202).

Theater, like music, remains "a highly racialized and racializing field of culture" (Wang 889). Hwang stages the gestures, voices, accents, and faces of Chinese Americans, thus confirming the existence of a community and reassuring that "there is a place called Chinese America" (Kingston vii). In the end, Steve's mythological persona Gwan Gung joins Grace's impersonation of Fa Mu Lan and becomes a warrior: a warrior who travels, tells stories, and is no longer a god. Dale is left alone in the back room to re-examine the words on the blackboard as well as his understanding of *FOB*. To some degree, *FOB* marks the beginning of Hwang's search to locate a new potential vision for Chinese American-ness suspended between the historical stereotypes and the contemporary reality, a literary exploration that he continues in subsequent plays (Moy 123). By the end of Act II, the preconceptions of FOB's and ABC's introduced early on have been dismantled. If *M. Butterfly* unmasks the "Western colonial/imperial politics of violence in the process of colonization on the Other" (Kang 27), *FOB* thus stages a performance of the fluidity of identity through the characters' masking and unmasking in mythic, theatrical, and ritual battles. Hwang's hope that there will come a time when the expression, "ethnic theater," no longer has any meaning (Ross) seems more promising than ever within the "current context of late modernity and globalization [in which] performance is increasingly drawn from intercultural creativity and located in multicultural milieu" (Um 1).[16]

Notes

1. *M. Butterfly* opened on Broadway on March 20, 1988 and became the longest-running nonmusical play on Broadway since Peter Shaffer's *Amadeus* in 1980 (Ester Kim 128). For Hwang's biography, see Street.

2. Lisa Lowe's insightful article, entitled "Heterogeneity, Hybridity, Multiplicity: Marking Asian American Differences," theorizes stratification within the Asian American communities that is based on gender, class, generation, as well as other elements and leads the way in the discussion on Asian American identity politics (24–44). For discussion on hybridity and ethnicity, also see Yao 357–78.

3. The spelling of their names is not consistent. Fa Mu Lan's name also has appeared as Mulan, Hua Mulan, and Fa Mulan in literary works and in the media. Gwan Gung's name is spelled also as Guan Gong and Kwan Gung. This chapter adopts Hwang's spelling in *FOB*.

4. For discussion on Kingston and Chin's usage of Chinese American mythology, see Cheung 1999, 2006; Dong; Elaine Kim 1982, 1990; Solovitch.

5. The other two plays are *The Dance and the Railroad*, which won the 1982 Drama Desk Nomination, the CINE Golden Eagle Award, and was a Pulitzer finalist and *Family Devotion*, also a 1982 Drama Desk Nomination. In 1982 Hwang received a Chinese American Cultural Council Award for his Chinese American trilogy (Pao 202).

6. In his phone interview with Dorinne Kondo in 1993, Hwang explains the common theme of unmasking in his plays as a dramatic representation of the "fluidity of identity," in which different characters transform into other characters or trade identities (214). Later in his interview with Bonnie Lyons in 1999, Hwang reiterates that "all my work in some sense confronts the issue of fluidity of identity" (231).

7. In this chapter, I use the term "Chinese American" in an inclusive way to refer to both immigrants and American born generations—that is, both FOBs and ABCs.

8. For a brief discussion on such figurative distance in plays by American-born playwrights such as *FOB*, Frank Chin's *Year of the Dragon*, and Darrell Lum's *Oranges are Lucky*, see Lee 1998, 52–53. In her article, Lee addresses the problems of immigration and hyphenation in the process of theorizing Asian American theater.

9. Although the play, *Ah Sin*, was not successful at the time, it has historical significance. For a brief introduction and the play, see Williams 39–95.

10. "Gold Mountain," a literal translation of the Cantonese term "Gam Saan," refers to California after the 1848 gold rush. Sometimes it also refers to the United States in general. See Novas and Cao 10–11.

11. I borrow the phrase "strangers from a different shore" from Ronald Takaki. See Takaki's *Strangers from a Different Shore: A History of Asian Americans* (1989).

12. After the Chinese Exclusion Act of 1882, some Chinese immigrants entered the United States as sons or grandsons of U.S. citizens with purchased fraudulent documents if they could memorize details about the new family and passed the immigration interrogation. They are called "paper sons." There are few "paper daughters." See Novas and Cao, 35–36. There are a number of literary works referring to "paper son;" for example, Maxine Hong Kingston's *China Men* (1980), Fae Myenne Ng's *Bone* (1993), Tung Pok Chin's *Paper Son: One Man's Story* (2000).

13. Hwang talks about Shepard's influence on his playwriting in different interviews. For example, in his 1987 interview with David Savran, Hwang specifies how Shepard's juxtaposing reality and myth as well as linking characters with their past and collective history have significant impact on him (120). Hwang also uses non-realistic structure and non-realistic characters in his other plays. For example, for an analysis of the gothic aesthetics in his *The Sound of a Voice* and *The House of Sleeping Beauties*, see Jew 2008, 140–55.

14. Frank Chin's *Gee Pop: A Real Cartoon* was written in 1976. Its production, directed by Rae Creevey, opened on June 23, 1977 ("Gee Pop").

15. Hwang once said "When I first wrote *F.O.B.*, I didn't necessarily have the idea that the battle sequences at the end would be done in stylized Chinese opera fashion. It was something that everybody else who read the script saw fairly clearly, but I didn't know" (qtd. Ross).

16. For a brief overview of ethnic theatre in America, see Shteir.

Bibliography

Chen, Tina. "Betrayed Into Motion: The Seduction of Narrative Desire in *M. Butterfly*." *Hitting Critical Mass: A Journal of Asian American Cultural Criticism* 1.2 (1994): 129–54.

_____. *Double Agency: Acts of Impersonation in Asian American Literature and Culture.* Stanford, CA: Stanford University Press, 2005.

Cheung, King-kok. "The Deployment of Chinese Classics by Frank Chin and Maxine Hong Kingston." *Querying the Genealogy: Comparative and Transnational Studies in Chinese American Literature*. Ed. Jennie Wang. Shanghai: Shanghai yiwen chubanshe, 2006. 217–30.

_____. "The Woman Warrior versus The Chinaman Pacific: Must a Chinese American Critic Choose between Feminism and Heroism?" *Maxine Hong Kingston's* The Woman Warrior: *A Casebook*. Ed. Sau-ling Wong. Oxford and New York: Oxford University Press, 1999. 113–33.

Chin, Frank. *Chickencoop Chinaman and the Year of the Dragon: Two Plays*. Seattle, WA: University of Washington Press, 1981.

_____. "Come All Ye Asian American Writers of the Real and the Fake." *The Big Aiiieeeee! An Anthology of Chinese American and Japanese American Literature*. Eds. Jeffrey Paul Chan, Frank Chin, Lawson Fusao Inada, and Shawn Wong. New York: Meridian, 1991. 1–92.

_____. *Donald Duk*. Minneapolis, MN: Coffee House Press, 1991.

_____. *Gunga Din Highway*. Minneapolis, MN: Coffee House Press, 1994.

Chu, Patricia P. "David Henry Hwang." *The Asian Pacific American Heritage: A Companion to Literature and Arts*. Ed. George J. Leonard. New York and London: Garland Publishing, 1999. 473–80.

Cooperman, Robert. "Across the Boundaries of Cultural Identity: An Interview with David Henry Hwang." *Staging Difference: Cultural Pluralism in American Theatre and Drama*. Ed. Marc Maufort. New York: Peter Lang, 1995. 365–73.

_____. "New Theatrical Statements: Asian Western Mergers in the Early Plays of David Henry Hwang." Maufort 201–13.

Dong, Lan. "Writing Chinese America into Words and Images: Storytelling and Retelling of *The Song of Mu Lan*." *The Lion and the Unicorn* 30.2 (2006): 218–33.

"Gee Pop." The Online Archive of California. California Digital Library. 2006. 8 July 2009 <http://content.cdlib.org/view?docId=tf1489n74f&chunk.id=c02-1.2.7.6.42&brand=oac>.

Gerard, Jeremy. "David Hwang: Riding on the Hyphen." *New York Times* 13 March 1988: 44+.

Gussow, Mel. "Culture Shock in Hwang's 'F.O.B.'" *New York Times*. New York Times. 20 May 1990. 7 July 2009 <http://theater2.nytimes.com/mem/theater/treview.html?res=9C0CE5D91330F933A15756C0A966958260>.

Hwang, David Henry. "Evolving a Multicultural Tradition." *MELUS* 16.3 (1989–1990): 16–19.

_____. *FOB and The House of Sleeping Beauties: Two Plays*. New York: Dramatists Play Services, 1983.

_____. "Foreword: The Myth of Immutable Cultural Identity." *Asian American Drama: 9 Plays from the Multiethnic Landscape*. Ed. Brian Nelson. New York: Applause Theatre Book Publishers, 1997. vii–viii.

Jew, Kimberly M. "Dismantling the Realist Character in Velina Hasu Houston's *Tea* and David Henry Hwang's *FOB*." *Literary Gestures: The Aesthetic in Asian American Writing*. Eds. Rocío G. Davis and Sue-Im Lee. Philadelphia, PA: Temple University Press, 2006. 187–202.

_____. "Gothic Aesthetics of Entanglement and Endangerment in David Henry Hwang's *The Sound of a Voice* and *The House of Sleeping Beauties*." *Asian Gothic: Essays on Literature, Film and Anime*. Ed. Andrew Hock Soon Ng. Jefferson, NC: McFarland Publishing, 2008. 140–55.

Kang, Hyeong-min. "Unmasking the Colonial Politics of Violence: David Henry Hwang's *M. Butterfly*." *Journal of Modern British and American Drama* 18.1 (2005): 23–46.

Kim, Elaine H. *Asian American Literature: An Introduction to the Writings and Their Social Context*. Philadelphia, PA: Temple University Press, 1982.

_____. "'Such Opposite Creatures': Men and Women in Asian American Literature." *Michigan Quarterly Review* 29 (1990): 68–92.

Kim, Esther S. "David Henry Hwang." *Asian American Playwrights: A Bio-Bibliographical Critical Sourcebook*. Ed. Miles Xian Liu. Westport, CT and London: Greenwood Press, 2002. 126–44.

Kingston, Maxine Hong. "Foreword." *FOB and Other Plays*. David Henry Hwang. New York: New American Library-Penguin Books, 1990. vii–ix.

_____. *The Woman Warrior: Memoirs of a Girlhood among Ghosts*. New York: Vintage Books-Random House, 1989.

Kondo, Dorinne. "Interview with David Henry Hwang." *About Face: Performing Race in Fashion and Theater*. New York and London: Routledge, 1997. 211–25.

Lee, Josephine. "Between Immigration and Hyphenation: The Problem of Theorizing

Asian American Theater." *Journal of Dramatic Theory and Criticism* 13.1 (1998): 45–69.

_____. *Performing Asian America: Race and Ethnicity on the Contemporary Stage.* Philadelphia, PA: Temple University Press, 1997.

Lei, Daphne. "Staging the Binary: Asian American Theatre in the Late Twentieth Century." *A Companion to Twentieth-Century American Drama.* Ed. David Krasner. Blackwell Publishing, Blackwell Reference Online. 2006. 7 July 2009 <http://www.blackwellreference.com/subscriber/tocnode?id=g9781405110884_chunk_g978140511088422>.

Lowe, Lisa. "Heterogeneity, Hybridity, Multiplicity: Marking Asian American Differences." *Diaspora: A Journal of Transnational Studies* 1.1 (1991): 24–44.

Lyons, Bonnie. "'Making His Muscles Work for Himself': An Interview with David Henry Hwang." *The Literary Review: An International Journal of Contemporary Writing* 42.2 (1999): 230–44.

Moy, James S. *Marginal Sights: Staging the Chinese in America.* Iowa City, IA: University of Iowa Press, 1993.

Novas, Himilce and Lan Cao. *Everything You Need to Know about Asian-American History.* New York: Plume-Penguin, 2004.

Pace, Eric. "I Write Plays to Claim a Place for Asian Americans." *New York Times* 12 July 1981: D4.

Pao, Angela. "*M. Butterfly* by David Henry Hwang." *A Resource Guide to Asian American Literature.* Eds. Sau-ling Cynthia Wong and Stephen H. Sumida. New York: The Modern Language Association of America, 2001. 200–08.

Ross, Jean W. "Interview." Gale Research. 28 June 1989. 6 July 2009 <http://www.tuvy.com/resource/books/authors/h/david_henry_hwang.htm>.

Savran, David. *In Their Own Words: Contemporary American Playwrights.* New York: Theatre Communications Group, Inc., 1988.

Shteir, Rachel. "Ethnic Theatre in America." *A Companion to Twentieth-Century American Drama.* Ed. David Krasner. Blackwell Publishing, Blackwell Reference Online. 2006. 7 July 2009 <http://www.blackwellreference.com/subscriber/tocnode?id=g9781405110884_chunk_g97814051108846>.

Solovitch, Sara. "Finding a Voice." *The Mercury News.* San Jose Mercury News. 30 June 1991. 8 July 2009 <http://www.sarasolo.com/mn2.html>.

Spivak, Gayatri Chakravori. "Can the Subaltern Speak?" *Colonial Discourse and Post Colonial Theory: A Reader.* Eds. Patrick Willams and Laura Chrisman. New York: Columbia University Press, 1994. 66–111.

Street, Douglas. *David Henry Hwang.* Boise, ID: Boise State University, 1989.

Takaki, Ronald. *Strangers from a Different Shore: A History of Asian Americans.* Boston, MA: Little Brown, 1989.

Um, Hae-kyung, ed. *Diasporas and Interculturalism in Asian Performing Arts: Translating Traditions.* London and New York: RoutledgeCurzon, 2005.

Wang, Grace. "Interlopers in the Realm of High Culture: 'Music Moms' and the Performance of Asian and Asian American Identities." *American Quarterly* 61.4 (2009): 881–903.

Weinraub, Bernard. "Fleshing Out Chinatown Stereotypes." *New York Times.* New York Times. 14 Oct. 2000. 8 July 2009 <http://www.nytimes.com/2001/10/14/theater/theater-fleshing-out-chinatown-stereotypes.html>.

Williams, Dave. *The Chinese Other 1850–1925: An Anthology of Plays.* Lanham, New York, and Oxford: University Press of America, Inc., 1997.

Yao, Steven G. "Taxonomizing Hybridity." *Textual Practice* 17.2 (2003): 357–78.

PART III: MULTINATION, TRANSNATION AND COMMUNITIES

RE-IMAGINING HAPPILY-EVER-AFTER IN BHARATI MUKHERJEE'S *JASMINE*

Amy N. Nishimura

In her essay "Immigration and Diaspora," Shirley Geok-lin Lim argues that the distinction between assimilationist writing and diasporic writing should be examined according to lines of "national identity" (289). Lim underscores Asian America as generally falling into two categories where one either emphasizes immigrant experience or erases historical memory, constructing a loss or what she refers to as cultural amnesia. This is one of the criticisms leveled against Bharati Mukherjee and her novel *Jasmine* (1989), in that it supports the ideology of an immigrant who secures a seemingly happily-ever-after ending. *Jasmine* has been accused by critics including Lim of pandering to a cosmopolitan audience while leaving aspects of cultural memory and diaspora to the periphery. Some might argue that Mukherjee's work plays to an audience that merely celebrates or pities the immigrant experience—binding the immigrant to a polarized rather than complex position. However, such criticism fails to recognize how Mukherjee constructs a range of images that highlight an intertwined and multinational cultural memory representing a global intersection within American society. These images are reflected through complex interpersonal dynamics in an American city landscape and then interrupted and re-interpreted in the Midwest. Embedded throughout *Jasmine* are signifiers suggesting an enmeshed cultural pluralism that the protagonist navigates through constant migration and transformative experiences. Thus, cultural memory is demonstrated not through overt markers but nuances that Jase/Jasmine re-interprets and then re-invents. Consequently, despite a nod to American audiences through a "happily-ever-after" structure, Mukherjee's novel displays how ethnic identity and representation are not fixed. In this light, Jase/Jasmine's journey is both repression and progression, sometimes mirroring an opportunistic representation of America and sometimes deflecting individuation. Also, at one point in the text, the author signifies the era of complex global markers where immigrants are constantly reminded of boundaries and limitations imposed by international and American politics. At the same time, these boundaries are deconstructed within a global marketplace that is constantly re-inventing itself. The closure of the novel is not a simplistic reading of "happily-ever-after" but a pronouncement of an ongoing struggle to identify oneself within a multinational arena.

Citing the problematic structure of an all encompassing happy ending, Lim argues how the novel replicates fairy-tale epics: "assimilation narrative in *Jasmine* reproduces the hegemonic epic of the United States as the nation of limitless opportunity, freedom, and triumphant individualism, repeating a master narrative of individual autonomy, economic competition, and race-assimilation that masks the convergence of the discourse of nationalism with that of racism and sexism" (307). The "limitless opportunity" Lim refers is bound in Jasmine's appearance or exotic beauty; her encounters with Americans are marked by how they perceive her: as someone who is pitied, admired, or cherished. She is pitied by the Vadharas who provide her with food and lodging upon her arrival to America after her husband, Prakash, is killed; she is helped by Kate Gordon, a woman who attempts to help immigrant women; she is then hired by an upper-middle class couple who objectify her and treat her like a daughter; finally, she marries a Midwestern banker who notes her exotic beauty. Indeed, this simplistic rendering of accumulating her experiences echoes sentiments that she is achieving a version of manifest destiny — she continues to move forward, to move west in search of vital independence after she has garnered the help of several Americans.

While Mukherjee notes how Jase/Jazz/Jyoti/Jasmine is coveted for her beauty and her "voice that sounds like a telephone operator," she also renders Americans accountable for how they objectify Jasmine, thus noting how the capitalist structure objectifies immigrants and sometimes reduces them to two-dimensional figures. In this sense, the author constructs a positionality whereby Americans are read as caricatures, while presenting Jasmine with the gift of sight as she observes, and processes the behavior of those around her. On one hand, we can say that she is constructed as an epicenter in which the majority of the action within the novel progresses; however, Mukherjee also presents a multi-dimensional range whereby Jasmine is not merely assimilating and joining the process but defining the parameters independently. Certainly, *Jasmine* embraces, as Lim notes, the tenor of "triumphant individualism" (305) but she can only comprehend her identity through a reflection of others. Thus, is the assertion one of individualism or of entanglement as she attempts to move forward while retaining some of the characteristics bestowed on her multinational identity? The novel also situates the character as someone who notes the trappings, angst, and lack of identity within American institutions that lead not just to a sense of individualism but to a pronouncement of being othered.

Shirley Geok-lin Lim criticizes Mukherjee's text as an erasure of history and draws a comparison to other Asian American writers such as Carlos Bulosan or Maxine Hong Kingston both of whom have been accused of shadowing a form of orientalism and perpetuating an American normalcy. The loss of memory or identity structure is transparent within the novel: the Hindu village girl moves away from her homeland, hardly stopping to resist or question how to integrate her cultural identity; her choices are based on intersecting what she has chosen to forget but is also struggling to retain. Given her movement from a patriarchal society to a hyper-capitalist patriarchal society, even her linear journey is thin; she falls in love with Prakash who renames her Jasmine and reminds her of what she must learn: standard English, the language of empire and business. This choice is not based on a desire for her own autonomy; rather, she learns hegemonic English to please her husband and to gain access to American culture. At this point, her choices are derived and dictated for her so when Prakash calls her Jasmine, this renaming re-invents her into a "city woman" (77). For Jasmine to "shuttle between identities" (77), between Jyoti, her Indian name, and Jasmine, her sweetly perfumed pseudo–American name is a trope for passing between two worlds that have increasingly become intertwined; in this sense, her identity is based on a skilled ability to move lithely among various experiences.

As a young married couple, Prakash and Jyoti are enamored by the travel brochures and the lofty descriptions of America. Mukherjee constructs a prototypical newlywed couple, regardless of national identity; at the same time, she nods to the problematic construction of America as a traveling destination or site where dreams come true. Nestled in travel brochures, the escape mechanism and the promise of security and wealth are hypnotic for both Prakash and Jyoti. The marketing of America as a global stopping point, as a continuum of the 1970s suburban dream world, where everyone can achieve the American dream, is re-set in India. Fetishizing the west, they become situated as immigrants who believe that life in the United States holds great promise and opportunity. Prakash imagines working in America as a middle or upper-class white-collar worker equal to Americans and, in this sense, it is not that he or Jyoti suffer from amnesia but that Mukherjee presents them as believing America is sanitized — rendered clean and impeccable within the global arena. Transferring his material desire to Jyoti, Prakash encourages her to learn as much about America as possible, as though one can comprehend the land in a black and white progression. However, Jasmine comes to accept the patriarchal construct that Prakash imposes on her, she does not question what she is being told to learn, nor does she question her husband's motivations and desires. This shallow pursuit sets the stage for the Americanization of Jasmine as she makes her way west; like many female protagonists, she is unable to define individual feminist criteria for herself.

The character's initial proclamation that she has adopted a Western construct occurs in the home of an upper-middle class couple: "in an apartment on Claremont Avenue across the street from a Barnard College dormitory"

(165). An affluent location, Claremont Avenue is marked by Columbia University and Barnard College, marking Jasmine's geographical surroundings by educational institutions which espouse Western ideology and traditional curriculum. Living in the city and amongst those who attempt to live their liberal ideology, Jasmine is employed by a professor and editor and cozily becomes part of a nuclear family. However, as a "day mummy," her role is conscripted not merely as a laborer or tangential family member; she becomes more of a centerpiece within the family: "Duff was my child; Taylor and Wylie were my parents, my teachers, my family" (165). After rejecting an Indian family in Flushing, New York who attempted to care for her, Jasmine decides to adopt this seemingly utopian family and an erasure occurs along transparent cultural lines, but her feminine identity is not as easily severed from her nationalist identity. While her dispersion of the Indian family stems from the rigid patriarchal control of the father figure, her role in the "American" family is embraced. That is, she believes she is valued within the American structure, the core of democratic values, the family unit in which she is not merely someone to be looked after but someone who actively contributes. However, the reconstruction of her South Asian American identity is built around necessity and commodification, a problematic theme within Asian American literature. How can she assert an actual nationalist identity or sense of autonomy when her identity is layered with even a sub-set of hegemonic mores? On one hand, her presence validates and justifies Taylor and Wylie's privileged role/status in society—they are too busy and successful to raise a child on their own and must hire a "day mummy," something made fashionable especially among New York City's privileged. On the other hand, Jasmine's identity reminds them of their status and the need to categorize her not as other but as an inclusive, convenient member: "I don't know what I'd do without her. Jasmine's a real find. Not like that last one who threw the front-door keys in the incinerator when she walked out on us. Or: "I won't say I'll definitely be at the fund-raiser until I've checked Tuesday night out with my caregiver. Caregiver. The word sang off my tongue. I was a professional, like a schoolteacher or a nurse. I wasn't a maid-servant" (175). The comparison to naming Jasmine and othering the "last one" demonstrates that Jasmine's value is only based on a perceived sense of lack, not actual skill. The title of "caregiver" allows them to believe there is equality within the household and that power is disrupted. However, this superficial guise that Wylie's character underscores in this conversation with her acquaintance becomes apparent as she categorizes Jasmine with the "last one." Believing in the separation from the dichotomy of us versus them, of unthreading the power structure, allows both Jasmine and Wylie to believe that their relationship is built on something valid and lasting. Jasmine also takes note of her living situation and offers a comparison to the Vadhera's: "[u]nlike the Vadheras, they bought useless things, silly things, ugly things—wooden ducks, two wooden Indians, a wood cutout of Carmen Miranda—and arranged them in clusters. Some of them seemed offensive to blacks or women or Red Indians" (174). The role assigned to Jasmine as caregiver does not diminish her ability to assess that the space she occupies is symbolic of emptiness indicative of American consumerism and a national identity beset with insulting images of others. Curiously, Mukherjee positions Taylor and Wylie in the epicenter of cosmopolitan living: they are well-educated and have achieved a white-collar privileged status that many would categorize as sophisticated and stylish. However, the observational commentary that Mukherjee offers through Jasmine places them in the polar opposite because the objects they collect demonstrate an ignorance of cultures and a grotesque display of arranging cultures in "clusters." This collective arranging and re-arranging signals a heteronormative environment where those in the privileged situation attempt to control those who remain on the periphery of society. In this particular situation, Jasmine's ability to recognize such attempts allows her to select her own arrangement in regards to societal constructions of "family." At this point in the novel, Jasmine begins to believe that she has achieved enough power in America so that she may begin to define a sense of independence.

Transformative Beginning/Middle/End

This reading of the character's ability to observe particular contexts and behavior might be a primary reason why the novel has achieved such popularity — a female immigrant seemingly achieves the American dream but she criticizes American citizens during her epic journey and offers parallels to her life and the lives she has encountered in India and America. The audience is able to salute Jasmine's behavior as she, at least on the surface, adopts American sensibilities and assimilates with little to no aggressive behavior. To some extent, this kind of observational reading and editorial by the author allows some Americans to assuage their feelings of guilt or shame that the power structures they abide by contribute to the diasporic living situations likened to that of Jasmine. The first line in the novel reads "lifetimes ago" (3) and mixes folklore, science, and technology, astrology, a satellite dish, along with a fortune teller. The traditional is mired with the modern and Jasmine's various lifetimes begin before she is even born. For her future, as Mukherjee makes clear, is pre-destined as a daughter, as one of several daughters in a culture where girls and women hold no material value, where gender roles are defined. Within the first three pages of the text, her station is established: "[A] girl shouldn't be wandering here by herself," (4) mothers tend to daily chores and Jasmine is told to "join her sisters" (4) who appear happy on a superficial level. An attempt to provide a unique quality to Jasmine is presented through a sage-like quality, a third-eye, which the character uses throughout her multiple lives as a wife, immigrant, laborer, caregiver/day mummy, American wife, American mother, and autonomous woman. Also, within the first three pages of the text an abrupt departure from the present is offered as Mukherjee moves from a young, adolescent girl to a woman of twenty-four. Here, readers are consistently reminded of what Jasmine does not "want to become" (5) which is another body amongst other bodies floating somewhere lifeless in a river, stream, city, or village. In this sense, the author offers a portal to her present situation, living in Baden, Iowa, and connects water, the metaphor for rebirth, as Jasmine smells the putrid decay of her past each time she takes a sip of water in her present, in Iowa. The lines between past, present, and future become fluid and interchangeable and many encounters in America are linked back to India. The identity presented is not fixed or stationary; rather, one can argue that Jasmine's memory is haunted because she cannot forget or refuses to forget, and, at the same time, she refuses to remain paralyzed or stationary. It is not that Jasmine chooses to forget her past for she cannot; she is faced with reconciling her present position with her past and Mukherjee presents this as a process-oriented journey.

Jasmine highlights particular contexts of an Indian woman's immigrant experience; thus, cultural memory is not entirely erased but disrupted momentarily and fused together in obscure moments. I argue that this is essentially one of the reasons why the novel has aspects of cultural memory and fragmentation due to her experiences—from the horrifically violent to the objectified exotic figure — she does not integrate them fully and reflects on the patriarchal structures she inhabits in India and America:

> In Baden, the farmers are afraid to suggest I'm different. They've seen the aerograms I receive, the strange lettering I can decipher. To them, alien knowledge means intelligence. They want to make me familiar. In a pinch, they'll admit that I might look a little different, that I'm a "dark-haired girl" in a naturally blond county. I have a darkish complexion" (In India, I'm "wheatish"), as though I might be Greek from one grandparent. I'm from a generic place, "over there," which might be Ireland, France, or Italy. I'm not a Lutheran, which isn't to say I might not be Presbyterian. About which they're ignorant; farmers are famously silent, and not ashamed [33].

In this passage Mukherjee stresses a multitude of points: first, readers are reminded that Jasmine, as an exotic immigrant, is consistently othered in the Midwest; second, in certain pockets of America, people attempt to make themselves feel comfortable by looking for an odd or not so odd, discernible characteristic that resembles what they look like or cannot name; third, the need for homogeneity is illusory because one's skin color is a false determinant for nationality or religion. Yet, it is this need to classify, to separate and make distinctions that make people in Baden feel comfortable; the classification of others allow Americans to draw an imaginary finger on a map and configure a decipherable code in terms of location and identity. Here, Mukherjee does not fragment but offers a similarity among people in India and people in America. A little further in the novel, Jasmine recalls the difficulty of simply having clean, running water: "I boiled the river water three and four times, when everyone else just let the mud settle before drinking" and a comparison among farmers is offered: "[f]armers there were like we were; they, too, worried about weather, about families sticking together during terrible times, about arranging decent weddings for their children. He said the world would be a saner planet if it were run by farmers instead of by generals and politicians" (45). Quoting someone she admires in her previous community, Masterji, the text demonstrates a clear reverence for her past and an ability to link people and contextualize cultural similarities and differences. Linking both locations to each other indicates the necessity of cultural memory, of a viability that may not be replete with distinct markers but exists nonetheless.

This phase in Jane's life, this middle phase between the east and west, the place of middle–America, offers a curious lens as Mukherjee presents another diasporic character by way of a Vietnamese boy in order to dissect transnational identity in America. Du Thien is Bud and Jane's adopted son, the one person she feels an authentic connection to while residing in Iowa; they watch television together and they share similar sentiments as they view the FBI raid an underground immigrant operation. When Du arrived from Honolulu, HI, he was wearing an "ALOHA Y'ALL T-shirt and a blue-jean jacket [and] was one of the hard-to-place orphans" (14). This character, from his very first superficial physical appearance, intersects the exotic with the exoticized, (since Honolulu is one of the most popular tourist sites in Hawaii and an Aloha shirt signifies a code of dress within the islands) with one of the most American symbols of dress, blue jeans. At the same time, this character embodies and signifies immigrants who are displaced due to war, famine, or various aspects of colonialism; the isolation he and Jane emote in the text is contextualized in Du's behavior. Shutting himself in his room, he opts to fix inanimate objects instead of converse or socialize with his peers and family members. His hesitation to communicate is emphasized by his pronounced and heavy accent and is notably compared to Jane's smooth telephone operator voice. His sense of alienation is further highlighted when Jane encourages him to make some connection with the earth, asking Du to fill a gutted, old, radio tuner with soil so he may plant some corn or beans. Instead of taking an interest in farming and engaging with something other than technological gadgets, his response is frightening: "[M]aybe I'll make a bomb" (157). The contrast between wanting to invent something that destroys versus constructing something that gives life is a loud underpinning for someone who may feel invisible or silenced. As a transnational immigrant in America, a boy like Du is acutely aware of the challenges he faces; this is a point Jane can relate but in a different sense. The utter sense of helplessness Du feels coupled with a desire for violence, makes an impression on Jane, who continues to identify with other immigrants because of her own transformative experiences. The polarization between various selves, as an Indian woman and as someone assimilating to American culture, becomes increasingly complex as the character moves between past and present and back again.

In "Women's Time," Julia Kristeva argues that traditional notions of time are fixed and rigid; they are dependent on western concepts of linear time in which trajectories are maintained according to static positions. She argues for the urgency of "multiplicities" regarding female expression and illuminates on fundamental differences between the sexes outside of normative, hegemonic structures. That is, she asks us to consider how various multiplicities or multifaceted dimensions of how meaning in a feminine dynamic allows western civilization to deconstruct binarisms and to consider how matrilineal time is different from patriarchal mechanisms. In this sense, Jane/Jasmine's decisions are examined not according to assmilationist or diasporic constructions but through a prism demonstrating an individual's journey in defining her unique female self. Kristeva's work provides a window to consider how Mukherjee's novel, as well as other novels, functions with trauma-related experiences or injuries to the psyche and body. If we can argue that one's sense of time (monumental, matriarchal, and patriarchal) operates based on memory production and sensory recall or that it may be repressed, dependent on a woman's process for constructing meaning, then in this type of ideological structure, the point of time as fluid rather than linear would be privileged. Therefore, time is defined as fluid and contradictory to any particular fixed meaning or ideology. In *Jasmine*, Mukherjee constructs time according to lines of trauma and a fragmented identity structure that Jyoti/Jazz/Jane/Jasmine must re-define according not merely to her past but her geographical, physical, and psychological position within an elastic present.

An impression of fluid movement occurs once Jasmine decides to make the trek to America, complete with illegal travel documents but resolute in her independence to complete Prakash's journey. At this point in the text, Mukherjee disrupts normative narrative structure and places the character as an observer of transnational migrations; the entire chapter can be interpreted in a number of ways: as author to audience, as character monologue, as a specific vignette to address cultural memory and immigrant subjectivity, or as an angst ridden widow at a cross-roads represented at an airport. There is no apparent linear movement, just a culmination of various configurations which blend and cloud identity: "But we are refugees and mercenaries and guest workers; you see us sleeping in airport lounges; you watch us unwrapping the last of our native foods, unrolling our prayer rugs, reading our holy books, taking out for the hundredth time an aerogram promising a job or space to sleep, a newspaper in our language, a photo of happier times, a passport, a visa, a laissez-passer" (101). If part of diaspora or transnational literature is defined by how immigrants must write themselves into history and literature because their homelands are destroyed by imperialism and colonialism, chapter fifteen defines Jasmine's place as an immigrant searching for a parcel of land to identify. "What country? What continent?

We pass through wars, through plagues. I am hungry for news, but the discarded papers are in characters or languages I cannot read" (101). These questions contextualize not only the sentiment for an Indian vestige but provides a hallowed airport, a signifier for a disturbing rite of passage for those who have survived wars or plagues and have no country or continent to firmly arrive. At the same time, Mukherjee suggests that the immigrant position is no longer objectified because she is acutely aware of the space she occupies upon entrance into a transnational lounge — a rest stop in the air and clouds but no actual soil or land thus suspending any hope of authentic personage. The text acknowledges the immigrants fate from a diasporic perspective: immigrants are scattered about, looking for a way home, looking backward and forward at the same time, and always dealing with a government system that may or may not recognize them as citizens. Also, the character is again an observer to her own respective situation, and Mukherjee positions her as someone who is standing within the narrative but also as someone witnessing what is taking place around her.

Various signifiers remind readers that many immigrant narrative memories are consistently disrupted or collected in a snapshot, a photo framing a moment "of happier times" (101) and their position in America only brings momentary security. Chapter fifteen begins with a metaphor for flying and national airline carriers which offer a diverse hybrid of people. As the description turns to "native foods, unrolling [of] prayer rugs, reading holy books, [and] taking out for the hundredth time an aerogram promising a job or space to sleep" (100), there is a blurred distinction between a starting or ending point. Where does the displaced rest, ponder, or practice their traditional customs and rituals? This lack of clarity can be read as a lack of knowing where the dominant lines from one continent begin and where the next continent begins— where does one begin to leave one identity behind in order to attempt to build a new one? The chapter continues with references to "the outcasts and deportees, strange pilgrims visiting outlandish shrines, landing at the end of tarmacs" (101). As the immigrant passes through multiple destinations, as she walks through unfamiliar airports, it seems clear she is not simply crossing into a national territory but a terrain that is more cyclical than linear, a space that may welcome immigrants but, at the same time, provide very rigid spaces for their identities to exist. Mukherjee's novel attempts to construct elastic spaces for Jasmine to explore and while this may privilege a more westernized settler-ism, it does not discount her Indian ideology and heritage. The author asserts that there are numerous ways to conceive of Jasmine's identity and Kristeva's work give us pause to consider a different construct:

> [T]he time has perhaps come to emphasize the multiplicity of female expressions and preoccupations so that from the intersection of these differences there might arise, more precisely, less commercially and more truthfully, the real fundamental difference between the two sexes: a difference that feminism has had the enormous merit of rendering painful, that is, productive of surprises and of

symbolic life in a civilization which, outside the stock exchange and wars, is bored to death [1982, 193].

As scholars and critics compare commercial success within parameters of diaspora and assimilation, we may have overlooked multiple variants in terms of the shape and scope of a woman's identity. Within the novel, it appears that Jasmine has very few choices and, at first, her life is constructed for her; she knows she will become Prakash's wife and she looks forward to traveling to America where she will fulfill the expectations he has shaped for her. Once this dream is disassembled and she continues to travel to America alone, her divergent selves cannot coalesce for even her diasporic self has no voice due to the trauma she has suffered. From a Western perspective, her sense of self has never developed or blossomed but her Eastern identity propels her to move forward despite Prakash's death; however, even this decision is made from a place of obligation rather than independence. Jasmine's movements, then, become simultaneous to her training as a female figure, one who must perform and demonstrate obedience in various ways; thus, she is not simply a one-dimensional figure who must embody Indian characteristics, mores, and values. Mukherjee presents Jasmine as someone who begins to recognize her training as a dutiful wife living in a patriarchal construct to someone who is able to construct her own identity.

The quote offered from Julia Kristeva contextualizes symbolic life and the various representations this might entail for various cultures. Deconstructing Asian American female literature should involve considerable variables instead of a polarizing debate which follows a patriarchal methodology and argumentative structure. The work of Julia Kristeva, Hélène Cixous, Luce Irigaray, and King-Kok Cheung has prompted various communities to consider transnational reading from various perspectives. In this sense, Mukherjee's work does not glamorize the life of an Asian American female immigrant; rather, she contextualizes the challenges involved in arriving to a country that has a particular set of privileges that many are not able to experience. For Jasmine life/death become intertwined and a sense of survival ensues; she is introduced to drastic differences and similarities among the two at an early age, witnessing multiple deaths and processing them inform her identity. Ultimately, her attempts to comprehend what death means arrives in fragmented moments, in "monumental time" where she recalls specific moments or conversations. While nothing definitive is mentioned, readers note a detached sense of consciousness as she struggles to build meaning and define her sense of place within America's landscape.

Cultural Memory and Transformation

Jasmine's crossing into America after Prakash's death is met with horrific violence: her first experience on American soil is being raped by a war veteran,

Half-Face. Signifying another life/death transformation, Jasmine is forced to make decisions that figuratively "murder who she was" in order to provide life to someone new, and while a reductionist reading would categorize it as assimilationist, I argue that her rebirth is more of a statement about a woman's ability to fuse an honorary past (a former identity) with a blurred future. The point of blurred or fragmented is emphasized here because the character, as an immigrant, is not a citizen who is able to make declarative or definitive statements about her future. She is unable to set goals according to a heteronormative structure — she cannot rely on family for support because she has none in America; she cannot rely on financial assistance because she is not a citizen; she cannot rely on health care; nor can she discuss or verbalize the violent act she has endured. The character Half-Face represents a portion of America that immigrants are not able to see; they do not recognize the gross inhumanity or the injustice. Instead, they may recognize the glamour represented in travel brochures, brochures that promise safe passage and plentiful opportunity — the brochures that Jasmine and Prakash viewed when planning their happily-ever-after future. The half that remains invisible is what Mukherjee renders as the unimaginable and it is a fraction of reality that many immigrants must face upon entry to America. It is a side that Jasmine's character is forced to face and survive — not necessarily to homogenize herself within the culture — she must provide her own brutal entry within America. At this point in the novel, another transformation/rebirth occurs; after the brutal violation of psyche and body, Jasmine cleanses her body and symbolically dies. At the same time, she is able to recollect her initial mission of honoring her husband's dream of coming to America, and while she does not feel the presence of Lord Yama, a figurative symbol for Indian culture, she does feel a vague sense of obligation for the task she feels compelled to complete. However, she cannot complete her task until she murders her previous identity along with the abject body Half-Face destroyed. As she attempts to remain cognizant and recover in the bathroom stall, she reaches for her knife, slits her tongue, and embodies the goddess Kali, the Indian deity of time and transformation. The cultural reference provides further context for Mukherjee's attempt to tie social/anthropological/political statements to Jasmine's character. As a woman, she has been guided, mistreated, and abused by numerous men in her life; thus, the appearance of a deity and especially of Kali, positions this particular rendering of Jyoti/Jase/Jane/Jasmine as a warrior, ready to defend herself despite lines relating to one's sense of nationalism. By referencing Kali, Mukherjee makes clear the line segmented back to an Indian cultural marker. No matter the destruction she causes, the character resists the patriarchal arc and subsumes her own matriarchal identity. Depicted in various forms, Kali is noted for her fierce nature and striking features such as a dark complexion, multiple limbs, and numerous heads. She is considered all things, names, creatures, and various forms disappear in her presence or being and in some depictions, her numerous heads represent a well of ceaseless knowledge. Her three eyes represent past, present, and future; thus, the portrayal of Jyoti/Jase/Jasmine as a figure who transcends and embodies time simultaneously allows us to gain greater comprehension of the choices the character of Jasmine makes. In this sense, while Mukherjee presents Jasmine as lacking in cultural memory, she also presents a character who embraces feminine and primal characteristics.

After slaying the man who rapes her, Jasmine feels little remorse: "what an infinitesimal thing, is the taking of a human life; for the second time in three months, I was in a room with a slain man, my body bloodied. I was walking death. Death incarnate" (119). The symbolic death of her past and of her ability to reconcile her present is immediate, one of instinct to survive in a location that she once believed would fulfill her dreams. Her rebirth and the reference to Kali can be likened to a commercial aspect of new age deity worshipping — something fascinating for the reader to participate in, finding the object (Jase) an exotic creature able to reinvent herself and murder someone else violently in order to create a new identity. In this interpretation/reading, the "I" or individual is prototypically championed for making a decision that will propel her forward, a primarily American quality/characteristic based on instinct and survival, an entrenched belief stemming from the model minority myth or the ability to "pull oneself up by their bootstraps." However, I argue that this reading is not only limiting but enables a two-dimensional caricature of the novel and character. According to Margaret Noble, Kali is referred to as the "dark mother," she is connected to nature, the earth and sky; she also subsumes the color black, so all signifiers are absorbed by her. In this sense, I argue that Jasmine's ability to discern particular situations and people are, in part, because of her ability "to see," to place past, present, and future into a particular context and note what is peculiarly unnatural to what is seemingly natural. Her ability not to engage in false consciousness is particularly interesting for throughout the novel she tries not to engage in falsehoods. After her transformation, she is able to recognize situations and people for what they are; though she may seem naïve in certain places within the text, she is also portrayed with sharp insight. She notices and observes the behavior of other people and especially of Americans who treat her as a foreigner, as an object.

This connection to the material/physical and meta-spiritual is also connected to the larger cultural context presented through Kali. Mukherjee presents a female warrior who, in the act of murdering a previous identity, chooses not to repress her history and alters her situated object position in a transnational location that mitigates violence and terror. As a woman and exotic object in a materialistic, consumer culture, the abject rituals displayed in the text support the argument of multiplicities and an aspect of suspended or re-constructed time. Mukherjee presents the actions of Jasmine with a strikingly calm demeanor and the character is non-reactive to the sight of blood, to the fact that she has killed another human being. After Jasmine murders Half-Face, she "purifies" (119) herself again and gargles with cold water until the bleeding stops (119). The reference to blood and water serve as tropes demonstrating a choice to heal and transform. Blood serves as a reference to life and death while water functions as a symbolic reference to rebirth or a resurgence of life. The ability to murder not only Half-Face but her former self signifies a re-creation because of the horrific violence her body/psyche has endured. Within the same moment, Mukherjee presents a vignette of memories from the past: "I remembered the hateful police inspector in Jullundhar, his reports to us of fingerprint evidence on the bomb fragments. I'd been impressed, and now I remembered. I went back to the bathroom and wiped the sink and shower taps" (120). If the Hindu goddess represents a transcendental consciousness, in this moment, Jasmine shifts from past to present and aims to clarify or justify her actions. Also within this moment is a need to re-visit previous events of trauma and violence; thus, this allows her to make sense of her own violent actions. The repression that occurs is signified through the compulsive need to wipe clean the "sink and shower taps" (120). In *Unclaimed Experience*, Cathy Caruth positions those who survive horrific trauma as those who "awaken" (90) from witnessing traumatic events. Those who suffer from post-traumatic stress disorder process information from seemingly distorted viewpoints. Subjects may remain within a dream-like state or contort what is taking place on a conscious level because of a wish to remain suspended in time — they do not wish to "wake-up" and awaken to what has occurred. As Jasmine begins to make sense of the violence within her life thus far, her ability to push through past events and meld them with the present suggest a conscious reminder of her sense of survival. The repetitive cycle of memory recall and pausing on specific moments mark the character with an ability to transform in spite of extremely difficult internal and external variables.

Re-Imagining Ever After

Given what the protagonist/heroine/warrior has survived throughout her journey as a young adolescent girl, as an exotic object, and as a female warrior who reclaims her identity, it is fitting yet problematic that Jasmine steps away from her mid-western banker husband, Bud. On the surface, her life with him is plentiful: she has achieved one of the most momentous aspect of the American dream, that of financial security. At the same time, she has also stepped into a family dynamic where her position is one of servitude and objectivity. Mukherjee establishes the "happy ending" syndrome at the beginning of the novel, however, it is with a resigned tone on the part of the protagonist: "Bud wants me to marry him, "officially," he says, before the baby comes. People assume we're married. He's a small-town banker, he's not allowed to do impulsive things. I'm less than half his age, and very foreign. We're the kind who marry. Going for me is this: he wasn't in a wheelchair when we met. I didn't leave him after it happened" (7). Within the first several pages, Mukherjee establishes several things about heteronormativity in America; she situates that the female heroine does not want to subscribe to the institution of marriage. She also positions Jasmine as a woman who comprehends how the society she lives in judges or views her on a daily basis because she is much younger than Bud and appears "foreign." The latter comes with a host of positionalities which involve assuming Jasmine into a submissive position and renders her silenced into an American environment which privileges a verbal aggressiveness over a restrained silence. In King-Kok Cheung's *Articulate Silences*, the author negotiates how various modes of communication, whether it be through body language, touch, or other mechanisms, convey patterns of articulate meaning which should be valued but are not, especially in Western society. Her insightful study of various Asian-American texts and poetics help highlight what Mukherjee and other novels aim to do: subvert the Eurocentric attitudes regarding verbal play and silence (23). Although Jasmine's character is often reduced to an object position, Mukherjee repeatedly conveys an active sense of agency that may not always be heard on a loud trajectory but is recognized. Jasmine's insight into her domestic situation is characterized as someone who does not merely want to follow suit with the seemingly superficial nature of domestic bliss. It is those around her, and especially other Americans who have suited her to perform certain roles. From the moment Mrs. Ripplemeyer (Bud's mother) meets her, she is positioned as someone with little to no feminist beliefs:

> Bud says that when Mother called him and told him that she was sending over a starving Indian to save he'd pictured a stick-legged, potbellied, veiled dark woman like the ones he'd seen fleeing wars, floods, and famines on television. He says, I saw you walk in and I felt my life was just opening to me. Like a door had just been opened. There you were in my bank, and I couldn't believe it. It felt as if I were a child again, back in the Saturday-afternoon movies. You were glamour, something unattainable. And you were standing there with my mother [199].

In this sense, Mukherjee offers the stereotypical label of the ignorant American who knows little to nothing about countries outside of the United States. Not only does he believe the insidious images propagated by the media but he only imagines what is undesirable until he witnesses the image up-close. Perhaps the most disturbing aspect of this passage is the red-blooded American male who works in one of the most imperialistic professions and he is being handed a prospective bride by his mother. It is an indirect reference of not just taking care of one's son but the disturbing cycle of thinking that one can obtain whatever one wants and all at the hands of one's mother. It epitomizes the patriarchal structure Jasmine knows she has walked into; thus, she compares Baden, Iowa with the little village she was raised. Baden is the middle-point of America, half-way between the east and the west and captures the absolute mundane environment Jasmine floats in and bears. She compares farmers in Iowa to farmers in her hometown; whether this indicates a simple lifestyle ill-fitting for her nature or her ability to recognize her life with Bud will remain stagnant, her decision is fittingly complex. When she says she does not leave him after he is placed in a wheel-chair, she notes that she has fulfilled her obligation to this man who has offered her financial security in exchange for a nurse-maid. She has fulfilled notions of filial piety in both worlds, to both patriarchal structures and believes she can move forward on her own terms.

Had she remained with a husband who is practically incapacitated and raised a child with him, Jasmine's fate would resemble a 1950s suburban ennui where there is little room for a woman's self-development. Thus, at the close of the novel, as Jasmine steps in front of Taylor, readers are presented with a complex image of a woman who decides to leave her husband for another man and essentially decides to raise her child with someone else; her assertion in stepping ahead of Taylor is an obvious pronouncement that she intends to lead an alternative lifestyle; in opposition to the beginning of the novel, Jase/Jyoti/Jane/Jasmine has shifted her object position and the text suggests that she will continue to construct her own identity; albeit, in a complex American paradigm that might subjugate her Indian identity. For those unfamiliar with the historical and cultural context of Asian Americans in the United States, they may only understand the cosmopolitan lens that Lim points out:

> Mukherjee's novel Jasmine reformulates the American romance, depicting the development of an autonomous subject who enters the new world and successfully negotiates the dangers posed by the instability of capital (Jasmine's Midwestern banker-lover is paralyzed by an aggrieved debtor-farmer's bullet; her young neighbor, under the stress of banking loans and reinvestment, hangs himself) to a happily-ever-after conclusion with her true love, a university professor, and his affectionate daughter [303].

As Jasmine becomes increasingly successful, her character perpetuates the model minority myth: she is able to overcome adversity despite her lack of American English speaking skills and despite a lack of education. Lim claims the ending of the novel demonstrates a euphoria whereby the female protagonist has achieved a resolution, a concretized conclusion; however, when we examine the position of *Jasmine*, it seems her journey has only begun. As she steps forward, ahead of Taylor, she claims a position that is not subservient and assumes an air that signals an independent authority. That Taylor has arrived on her doorstep at the close of the story may conclude that they will live together but none of the other complicated markers are mentioned: they will raise a child that is not his own, how will she work toward a financial and independent state as a woman in America or will she subsume another suburban housewife personality? Jasmine is heralded as a survivor who endured harsh cruelty and can be used as a token minority success story or as an example of someone with a diverse background who was able to assimilate successfully. It is the latter which remains problematic because in order to attain a sense of "normality" or comfort in this society, most immigrants must move toward a negotiated sense of material complacency. As it is suggested throughout the text, Jasmine must move forward so that a re-emergence can occur for herself as an immigrant woman living in America. In *Woman, Native, Other*, Trinh Minh-ha argues that women must re-write their bodies and re-write them for ourselves because, in a historical and cultural context, they have been written for us. She argues,

> "Women must write through their bodies," Must not let themselves be driven away from their bodies. Must thoroughly rethink the body to re-appropriate femininity. Must not however exalt the body, not favor any of its parts formerly forbidden. Must perceive it in its integrity. Must and must-nots, their absolution and power. When armors and defense mechanisms are removed, when new awareness of life is brought into previously deadened areas of the body, women begin to experience writing/the world differently [Trinh 36].

If women's writing attempts to blur the distinctions that a patriarchal system has forced on society, Mukherjee's novel is one attempt to provide a female protagonist with power. *Jasmine* disrupts the hierarchical imposition that women must choose between an either/or dichotomy and Mukherjee unravels the happily-ever-after ending because the emphasis is about choice, a woman's choice. The focus on Taylor as the savior or hero is a misreading of the text because while Jasmine is happy to see him, we cannot know how she feels about stepping out into the unknown — another journey where she may or may not be content with her decision. Given how her body has been transported, shipped, brutalized, conditioned, and re-routed numerous times by men and women in the novel, that it ends with a step forward, away from Taylor, signifies that she will continue to define her own experiences regardless of who is standing beside her.

Bibliography

Caruth, Cathy. *Unclaimed Experience: Trauma, Narrative, and History*. Baltimore, MD: Johns Hopkins University Press, 1996.
Cheung, King-Kok. *Articulate Silences: Hisaye Yamamoto, Maxine Hong Kingston, Joy Kogawa*. Ithaca, NY: Cornell University Press, 1993.
Kristeva, Julia. *Powers of Horror: An Essay on Abjection*. New York: Columbia University Press, 1982.
_____. "Women's Time." *The Kristeva Reader*. Ed. Tori Moi. New York: Columbia University Press, 1986. 108–34.
Lim, Shirley Geok-lin. "Immigration and Diaspora." *An Interethnic Companion To Asian American Literature*. Ed. King-Kok Cheung. Cambridge and New York: Cambridge University Press, 1997. 289–309.
Mukherjee, Bharati. *Jasmine*. New York: Grove Press, 1989.
Noble, Margaret Elizabeth. *Kali The Mother*. Charleston, SC: Forgotten Books, 2008.
Trinh, Minh-ha T. *Woman, Native, Other*. Indianapolis: Indiana University Press, 1989.

Adopting a Different Posture and Relocating One's Roots
The Trung Legend in Vietnamese American Narratives

Tina Lynn Powell

Transnationalism — the method of moving across national borders and operating in more than one national space — is currently a mode of scholarship used to interrogate identity formation in immigrant populations. In many ways, transnationalism is about cultural negotiations and "crossing borders" in diasporic populations; as people arrive in new national spaces, as my title suggests, they must decide how to maintain ties to "home" through language, tradition, cultural practices, and national narratives while adopting certain cultural markers of the new home. According to Geoffrey Kain, this negotiation is a result of the migration process that challenges self-perception and therefore demands "some degree of self-redefintion" (1). While recent studies on transnationalism tend to focus on first generation immigrant groups, it is particularly useful in interrogating how refugee groups such as Vietnamese Americans negotiate loss by adopting a transnational stance.

Vietnamese Americans form a distinct part of the fabric of Asian American and American experiences. Their movement from Viet Nam[1] to the United States occurred as part of a mass exodus that resulted directly from the collapse of the Republic of Viet Nam (RVN).[2] This exodus separates their experience from many other immigrant and ethnic groups. Their experiences and identity are intricately tied to United States foreign policy. There is a sense that they will never be able to go "home" and the literature deals extensively with "death and other irreconcilable losses and long[ing] always for peace" (Truong 219).

Vietnamese American literature is a recent addition to Asian American and American literature. While the form varies from fictionalized memoirs[3] to scant short fiction and to poetry, the first published Vietnamese American narratives—written by refugees who were adults at the fall of Saigon—primarily retell experiences of war, escape, and sometimes resettlement. For instance, Jade Ngoc Quang Huynh's memoir, *South Wind Changing* (1994), focus almost exclusively on the Vietnam War, re-education camps, and the flight from Viet Nam with a short concluding chapter on resettlement. Little critical attention has been paid to these memoirs beyond their historical importance. In the mid– to late–1990s, works by writers who were children at the fall of Saigon were published; writers like Bich Minh Nguyen, Lan Cao, Dao Strom, and lê thi diem thúy, focused more on resettlement in the United States than the war itself and often came back to visit Viet Nam physically or symbolically.

As the thematic focus of the texts has shifted, so has the critical discourse about Vietnamese American literature. At first, critical discourse in texts like Al Santoli's *To Bear Any Burden* (1985) and James Freeman's *Hearts of Sorrow* (1989), which are primarily collections of Vietnamese American oral narratives of the war, interrogates the ideological battles between communism and capitalism and the counternarratives of the Vietnam War implicit in Vietnamese American narratives. Santoli and Freeman, as Monique Truong argues, tend to reinforce the polemic of America as defenders of democracy and Southeast Asians as victims of Communism while also reflecting an imbalance of power as American collaborators assert authorial and editorial control over refugee narratives. With the publication of Renny Christopher's *The Viet Nam War/The American War* (1995), critics began to look at identity formation in narratives of resettlement. In her seminal study on the Vietnam War canon, Christopher argues that "Vietnamese exile writers' representations [of the war(s), the refugee experience] are focused on cultural negotiations, on the process of becoming bicultural ... becoming 'American' [while insisting] on remaining Vietnamese at the same time" (30). To do this, writers often negotiate representations of the past in terms of the war(s) and "the unfinished business (social, familial, political) that their flight as refugees forced them to leave behind" (Christopher 36). The past and the "unfinished business" that the past represents are the ties that continue to root Vietnamese Americans in Viet Nam. In trying to maintain those ties with their "homeland," Vietnamese American writers often incorporate nostalgic descriptions of Viet Nam and place emphasis on cultural practices or stories in order to form their transnational identity.

One way this identity formation occurs is with the negotiation between the Vietnamese heroic past and narratives of flight and resettlement. This chapter focuses on the invocation of the legend of the Trung sisters in Le Ly Hayslip's *When Heaven and Earth Changed Places* (1989), Dao Strom's *Grass Roof, Tin Roof* (2003), and Lan Cao's *Monkey Bridge* (1997) as specific examples that trace and narrate individual Vietnamese American experiences and contestations over subjectivity through history, culture, and self-representation. The female protagonists in each narrative claim themselves as embodiments of the Trung sisters (or Phung Thi Chinh for Hayslip), "women warriors" in Hayslip's and

Strom's words, as a discursive strategy to control their identity formation. Hayslip evokes a cultural connection to the Trung sisters and an ancestral lineage to the Trung sisters' loyal soldier, Phung Thi Chinh, as a way to indict the brutalities of war and punctuate the trauma of her dispossession. Strom uses the Trung sisters as symbols of cultural authority that grant narrative power. Both Hayslip's and Strom's usage of the legend subverts the mythologizing of the war and asserts the protagonists' subjectivity. Lan Cao's work, on the other hand, relies on the mythologizing of culture to map the struggles of Mai, her young protagonist, to try to form a transnational, bicultural identity. As "women warriors," these protagonists are able to assert a posture that is rooted in Viet Nam while negotiating life in the United States. Asserting this posture emphasizes the loss that entails "crossing borders."

While Hayslip, Strom, and Cao's texts do not explicate extensively on the Trung legend, a brief rendering of the legend and the methods of appropriating it are necessary for contextualization. Viet Nam has a long history of "women warriors," several of whom have become immortalized in Vietnamese legend. The Trung sisters, Trung Trac and Trung Nhi, who are collectively called Hai Ba Trung, are revered in Vietnamese culture and national history as the first liberators of Viet Nam from the oppressive Chinese. Historically, the Trung rebellion was prompted by a change in Chinese policy towards Viet Nam. As Keith Weller Taylor notes, this new Chinese policy in the first century A.D. focused on two things: development of an "agrarian economy as a stable source of tax revenue" and the establishment of "a patriarchal society" that benefited Chinese rule (36). These changes incited the Vietnamese Lac lords (local officials of title)[4] and they increasingly tested Chinese authority. Su Ting, one of the Chinese local officials, specifically focused on "restraining" Thi Sach, one of the Lac lords. Thi Sach was married to Trung Trac and as the legend goes, Su Ting murdered Thi Sach, put his body on display, and raped Trung Trac (Fraser 237). In order to avenge Thi Sach's death, Trung Trac and her sister Trung Nhi, both trained in weaponry and the art of warfare, assembled a large army. On the battlefield, Trung Trac spoke these words:

> Foremost, I will avenge my country,
> Second, I will restore the Hung lineage,
> Third, I will avenge the death of my husband,
> Lastly, I vow that these goals will be accomplished [qtd. in Tran and Nguyen].

With her sister and several other women leading her armies, Trung Trac was able to drive the Chinese back. Phung Thi Chinh is one of Hai Ba Trung's "women warriors." Phung Thi Chinh was loyal to the Trung sisters; she led the central flank and although late in her pregnancy, she jumped into battle (Tran and Nguyen). She gave birth on the battlefield, strapped her baby to her back, and continued to fight (Bois). The Trung sisters and their army drove the Chinese out of Viet Nam in 39 A.D. Upon claiming independence for Viet Nam,

Trung Trac attempted to remove the very policies that had incited the uprising; she got rid of tribute taxes and the patriarchal Chinese values ("Biography"). Hai Ba Trung ruled as sister queens until 42 A.D. when they were defeated by the Chinese. Rather than being captured, the two sisters committed suicide by jumping into a river and drowning (Fraser 237). Phung Thi Chinh and her child followed (Bois).

The legend of their sacrifice for family and culture, as eventually retold through poetry,[5] differs greatly from the historical record.[6] As Antonia Fraser argues, the legend subverts history because "a Warrior Queen — or female ruler — has often provided the focus for what a country afterwards perceived to have been its golden age ... [she is] a rallying point for the chivalric feelings of her nation" (9). As Taylor notes, the Trung sisters' legend was inscribed to fit the needs of an emerging national identity that countered the Chinese imperial authority. As early as the thirteenth century, poets used their story to establish a pre–Chinese royal lineage. At the same time, the emphasis on their gender and their "[violation of] normative patterns" shamed men who did not take up arms against China (Pelley 179). Later, the legend was used to emphasize romantic love, ideal womanhood, patriotism, and Confucian values like filial piety.

At the beginning of the twentieth century, Viet Nam was a colony of France and anti-colonial scholars re-appropriated the Trung legend for their anti-colonial struggle. Most notably, in 1913, Phan Boi Chau used the Trung sisters in an oral drama that re-envisioned the Chinese and Trungs as colonial and anti-colonial archetypes. David G. Marr points out that Phan's main purpose was to "focus on the role of Vietnamese women in the forthcoming anti-colonial struggle" against the French (153); Phan's usage inferred that sacrifice was necessary to serve one's country (Turley 794). Therefore, the sisters' filial duty was interpreted as merely a catalyst that "[energized] her preexistent love of country and her desire to expel the foreign invader" (Marr 153). Like Phan Boi Chau's appropriation, the use of the Trung sisters myth helped intellectuals develop a "Vietnamese national soul" based on the "spirit of resistance to foreign aggression," which placed Viet Nam in a "fundamentally defensive posture" (Pelley 142, 145). After the French were expelled in 1954, this "national essence" of resistance helped to externalize conflict to sublimate internal strife during attempts to reunify the two halves of Viet Nam (Pelley 145).

The mythic Trung sisters were evoked again during the Vietnam War so that "twentieth-century Vietnamese who struggled against American aggression shared the eminence of first-century heroes who had resisted the Chinese" (Pelley 145).[7] Their importance to soldiers fighting "foreign aggressors" was such that soldiers "would carry pictures of the Trung sisters as a source of inspiration to fight for freedom" (Tran and Nguyen). In 1975, archaeologist Pham Huy Thang attributed the reunification of Viet Nam to the Trung sisters and the courage they stirred in the Vietnamese people (Tran and Nguyen). Hai Ba Trung's importance, despite political, religious, or socioeconomic divisions, is such that when Saigon was renamed Ho Chi Minh City and its streets renamed after Vietnamese patriots, the street honoring the Trung sisters was the only one not renamed (Cao 124).

The Trung sisters' legend is one of the few cultural narratives that transcend political affiliations. Their importance as symbols of Viet Nam — filial duty, protection of "homeland," cultural allegiance, patriotism — and its nostalgic past resound in the struggle of refugees to form an identity that negotiates loss of home with life in the United States. Le Ly Hayslip, in her memoir *When Heaven and Earth Changed Places*, invokes the Trung sisters. In trying to act as a bridge between Americans and Vietnamese, Hayslip offers herself as representative of all Vietnamese peasants and their experience through her embodiment of the Trung sisters myth.

Hayslip tells the story of her youth; Le Ly is a young peasant girl who experiences the French-Indochina War on its periphery, becomes a member of the Viet Cong as a teenager, moves to Saigon to be a domestic servant, and marries an American civilian and immigrates to the United States. Interwoven with this narrative is Hayslip's return to Viet Nam in 1986, fifteen years later. The aim of her book, as proclaimed in her prologue, is for reconciliation with Americans. She wants Americans to make peace with all that Vietnam signifies and hopes to provide a tool to help the reader understand the Vietnamese civilians for whom the war was fought (Nguyen 109).[8] In order to do this, she claims to be a representative of all Vietnamese civilians and embodies Vietnamese cultural heritage.

Hayslip's prologue begins with her individual experience and ends with a collective voice. She offers herself as representative of Vietnamese civilians caught between the larger forces of politics, class struggle, and ideology and equates herself with the American GIs who went to war "because your country demanded it" (xv). In so doing, she promotes reconciliation between Viet Nam and America. She writes: "I was a peasant girl in Ky La.... My father taught me to love god, my family, our traditions, and the people we could not see: our ancestors" (ix). When she discusses her active role as a supporter of the Viet Cong, Hayslip drops the first person pronoun and introduces a binary of us versus them. The "us" she uses to speak with her family eventually refers to all Vietnamese civilians manipulated by the Viet Cong, "them." With this binary, Hayslip rejects the "us" in the Viet Cong's speeches. They state: "the independence of *our* fatherland and the freedom of *our* people. *Our* greatest right is ... to determine *our* own future as a state," and Hayslip reinscribes the "our" with implied "thems"—"Communist freedom," "Communist happiness" (xii; italics added). Finally, when Hayslip begins to shift from discussing her experience to the experience of American GIs, she links the "we" of Vietnamese civilians with the "you" of American GIs. Statements like "we slept as little as you did" textually join Vietnamese experience with American experience (xv).

Hayslip's narrative focuses on the physical, emotional, mental, and sexual trauma that the French-Moroccan soldiers, Republic of Viet Nam soldiers, Viet

Cong cadres, her employers, Americans, and the war itself have inflicted on Le Ly. Her experience as a Vietnamese civilian allows her status of an "emblematic victim," which is "the way in which the victimized body politic manifests itself in American discourse...[;] the fact that one of the oppressed speaks is taken to mean that the oppressed in general have spoken" (Nguyen 112). Viet Thanh Nguyen argues that Hayslip's narrative has two faces of the victimized body politics: one for the American audience that presents the victimized body as the exploited Vietnamese, and the other for the Vietnamese audience that transforms the victimized body into a heroine (Kieu from *The Tale of Kieu*) from Vietnamese national history. Nguyen argues that this strategy undermines possible perceptions of Hayslip "as a whore and traitor" (110). In Nguyen's reading, Hayslip's appropriation of a Vietnamese heroine positions Le Ly as "the ideal woman who retains her spiritual virtue in the face of overwhelming circumstances that deprive her of her 'chastity'" (110). Nguyen's analysis stems strictly from the parallels of Hayslip's life to the poem *The Tale of Kieu* that portrays a young woman, Kieu, who is tricked into prostitution. Although her chastity is lost, a different chastity—"the spiritual one of submissive duty"—is intact. Kieu marries but her marriage is platonic; she fulfills her filial duty and the marriage is blessed with ideal love rather than physical love. Most importantly, *The Tale of Kieu* is read as symbolic of "the nation's purity through the notion of female chastity" (Nguyen 121).

While the parallels to Kieu mark Hayslip's spiritual virtue, Hayslip's use of the Trung sisters and Phung Thi Chinh marks her victimhood through cultural lineage and punctuates the trauma of dispossession. Hayslip's memoir carefully maps her connection to the Trung sisters and Phung Thi Chinh. In her prologue, she specifically refers to the Trung sisters as a significant part of Viet Nam's national "essence." Hayslip writes: "our ancestors called us to war. Our myths and legends called us to war. Uncle Ho's cadre called us to war. Even President Diem called us to fight" (xiv). In this list, culture and Confucian teachings of filial piety and duty give way to political machinations. While Hayslip uses this reference to the Trung sisters as a way to expiate American guilt, this usage is not sustained in the narrative. Rather, her narrative maps the way in which the Viet Cong and RVN used the Trung sisters to manipulate civilians. Madame Ngo Dinh Nhu, the first lady of South Viet Nam (1955–1963), suggested alluding to heroes like the Trung sisters to appeal to local children and young women in order to create "defense brigades" of "women warriors" to "repel the Viet Cong terrorists" (33–34). The Viet Cong also used the Trung sisters to rally young women to their cause; they also encouraged Le Ly and others to commit suicide if in danger of being captured. Le Ly was told that by dying in battle, she would "be immortalized as [a hero]" (46). Looking back on her experience, Hayslip peppers her memoir with criticisms of these tactics of manipulation. These criticisms reinforce Le Ly as the representative victim and allude to the abuse of Vietnamese cultural heritage.

Rather than molding herself as a Trung sister, Hayslip uses the figure of Phung Thi Chinh. Le Ly's father tells her that Phung Thi Chinh is her ancestor. This genetic tie emphasizes filial duty to family and land. Le Ly is told that a woman warrior "live[s] in peace and tend[s] the shrine of [her] ancestors" (32–33) but also stands "her ground against the enemy" (44). Le Ly sees her mother as a woman warrior and learns certain traits from her. While working on the family's land, "[she] copied [her] mother's stance in the muddy water, planting [her] feet like a woman warrior.... Being a woman warrior was harder than [she] expected" (11–12). Hayslip links peasant work to the physicality of women warriors. While there is a larger argument of economic oppression by the Vietnamese upper-class and colonial/neo-colonial French and American systems in this scene, which Christopher takes up in her analysis of Hayslip's book (70–86), Hayslip is explicitly "planting" the cultural and familial heritage of the Trung legend firmly in the land. Her embodiment of a woman warrior partially requires a physical tie to her homeland. The values that women warriors embody are what Le Ly defines her selfhood with. She speaks from the authority of a shared cultural heritage as well as through her victimized body.

As a teenager, Le Ly is easily manipulated by the Viet Cong because they re-inscribe filial duty with revolutionary actions. The responsibilities of filial duty change from tending the ancestor's shrine and family's land to avenging family and protecting the farm by killing the enemy (Hayslip 32). As a Viet Cong lookout, Le Ly is caught and tortured by Republican soldiers several times. When the Viet Cong suspect that she is no longer loyal, she is targeted for execution, violently raped, and left for death. As the Viet Cong cadres she had befriended beat her, she reminds us of her familial connection to Phung Thi Chinh and that death will keep her from fulfilling her filial obligations. Hayslip shows the trauma inflicted to her body and in the process presents her attackers as other. Loi, the first cadre to rape her, transforms into something "grotesque and distorted, scarcely human ... [a] twisted soul" (93). While Le Ly notes that the rape was not sanctioned by the Viet Cong, there is a sense of their complicity because Loi and Mau, her other attacker, will not be punished. Through this "othering," Hayslip clearly separates herself and those she represents from the Viet Cong.

For Le Ly, the rape is the most traumatic abuse because losing her virginity she feels she is robbed of having her own family. Le Ly laments: "my whole life now seemed burdened with time: time I would not spend with a husband for whom I had been ruined; time free of happy children that I would never bear" (94–95). This is contrasted with the occasion of Le Ly reaching puberty, a "step towards fulfilling my destiny as a Phung Thi Chin [sic] — a woman and woman warrior who would, with her womb now as well as spirit, link [her] ancestors to the generations that would follow" (103). Hayslip compounds the trauma of her rape with the burden of a lost heritage; her ancestors have lost a line of people to tend their shrine, she will have no one to tend her shrine, and Viet Nam has lost a genetic link to its cultural heritage.

Her victimized body is not only representative of the Vietnamese people, but also a physical representation of the damage done to Vietnamese culture, Confucian values, family ties, the national "soul," and all women warriors. Like Le Ly, these will retain their spiritual virtue but not in the hands of the Viet Cong or the RVN or in Viet Nam. Le Ly must leave Viet Nam and carry on those values in the United States; however, geographic displacement bars her from tending the shrine of her ancestors or her land. Le Ly's father's mantra and her mother's feminine strength in the land are severed; to live in peace means she cannot embody her cultural heritage, she cannot be a "woman warrior," which only highlights her dispossession.

Like Hayslip, Dao Strom also uses the Trung sisters to emphasize the dispossession of "crossing borders." Strom's *Grass Roof, Tin Roof* is a collection of interconnected short stories that revolve around one Vietnamese American family. The first lengthy short story, titled "Papier," focuses on the matriarch of this family, Tran, and her career in Saigon. Tran, who wants to be a writer, appropriates an American war classic, *Gone with the Wind*, as a Vietnamese romance set against the French-Indochina War. Tran writes her *Gone with the Wind* in serialized form for a local newspaper and takes the pen name Trung Trinh, alluding to the Trung sisters. As a woman warrior, Tran seeks for power over her present to create her own story amidst political upheaval, sexual manipulation, and restrictive gender roles.

A young, unmarried woman with an illegitimate son trying to make a living in Saigon, Tran sees herself lacking subjectivity. Tran is desperate to assert some authority over her own life and to foresee an unchangeable future. She finds herself confined by gender roles in Viet Nam and manipulated by the various factions in Viet Nam, all of which create a present she cannot control and injure her ability to "know." She resents how Vietnamese men treat women; her father is a philanderer, "as so many Vietnamese men were" (25); her first lover abandons her when she becomes pregnant (7); and her last Vietnamese lover Giang, who is also a philanderer, uses Tran to publish his "subversive" material. Tran sees her mother as "a victim of submission" (25) and refuses to submit in the same way. To reject the gender roles that deny her subjectivity, she refuses to feel ashamed when her son points out that other women are calling her a "half-woman" (26) or when Muoi, her maid, disapproves of her relationships with men, her illegitimate son, and her disinterest in getting married (30–31). This control over authority of one's perception spills into larger conflicts over who controls knowledge in the Vietnam War. Tran investigates a report of a massacre of children by Republican soldiers and hopes to document some evidence before the various factions spin the situation to support their agendas. She and the other reporters witness the torching of a nearby village and construct their own truth that details corruption of government and military officials, whereas the official report, the one recognized as "truth," is that the village was a Viet Cong stronghold (22, 21).

One method that Tran attempts to assert control over her own present is through language. When Tran becomes involved with a French media correspondent, Gabriel, she is able to assert some control over him, something she could not do with a Vietnamese lover. For instance, while teaching him Vietnamese words, she tells him the word for the palm of a hand is the word for the foot's arch. Such games make her "realize how arbitrary and tenuous the association between an object and its linguistic representation could be.... Language, she saw, was a thing that relied on faith" (6). This game is replayed during her revision of *Gone with the Wind*. Phuong-Li, the Scarlett O'Hara of the novel, delights in remembering childish games, specifically assigning nicknames without giving meaning, because "they gave her a sense of importance, of secret control" (14). Like Phuong-Li, Tran constructs her subjectivity through control of language and through storytelling.

Tran's attraction to Margaret Mitchell's *Gone with the Wind* is significant to her sense of history, possibility, and female power. To her, the novel is "a grand story with many events and an inconclusive ending, and it left her with an ache in her brain and heart, a feeling akin to wanting ... the ending would always be inconclusive — and this was why the story worked as well as it did; this was why it was affecting and rending and lingering" (2). Tran sees *Gone with the Wind* as a representation of ideals; it illustrates societal decorum, ideal womanhood, and masculine heroism. She decides to rewrite the novel; she takes the themes, romance, and heroism of the novel and supplants it against the backdrop of the French-Indochina War:

> Instead of Atlanta at the crumbling of the Southern Confederacy, it would be the northern port town of Haiphong at the climax of French rule. The heroine would be from a rice farm in a small northern village, and her family devout French-influenced Catholics. The family would be forced to flee south at the advance of Viet Minh, and the story would follow that passage, which would bring the heroine to Haiphong [10].

To Tran, romance and heroism are tools to escape the pervasiveness and reality of the Vietnam War. Heroism is cathartic and Saigon in 1969 needs catharsis; to Tran, "a sense of hopelessness and consternation pervaded the streets" and the fervor of everyday life "seemed now volatile and dangerously indifferent" (3). Giang, owner of the newspaper she writes for, tells her that "I am starting to think the only reprieve we will ever get from this war is when we are able to create" (11). To Giang, a romantic tale that parallels the recent past of Viet Nam is a necessary escape but also a valuable tool of authority. Tran sees her story as cathartic, not just for Viet Nam but for her as well. She takes the pen name Trung Trinh with little thought to its importance.

As Tran's version of *Gone with the Wind* continues and her life becomes more entangled in reactionary politics, Tran is able to narrate her own life through her writing and express her feelings about betrayal, loss, and fear. She literally tells her own story and is able to narrate the past, present, and possible future. By using *Gone with the Wind*, Tran also places the French-Indochina War and its aftermath, the Vietnam War, into an American war classic. But this parallel cannot be sustained; the tendency of Mitchell's novel to subvert the brutalities of war and ideological conflicts to romantic analogies of the American spirit does not work. The story transforms from mirroring a world of "horses and hoop dresses and colored silks, of idle, well-educated, well-mannered women ... [and of] tall, handsome, white-skinned men in waistcoats" (15) to highlighting its fiction. Appropriating Mitchell's novel helps expose the reality of the war around her. As the war encroaches further on Saigon and into Tran's life, she realizes that Viet Nam is "too visceral and incongruent next to the polished drama of the America in her mind. Even her imagined version of Vietnam ... was humid and overcrowded and raw.... There were no equivalents [in Viet Nam] to the panoramic views of rolling green hills outside windows of estate houses.... Even the war here was not so noble and deeply felt a calamity as it seemed to be there. Here the war was bogged down by the clearly unromantic facts" (15). Romanticizing only hides the reality and her story becomes more violent and more appropriate for the historical setting. As she becomes more involved in Giang's politics, she realizes "sentiments, false hopes, the old *yens* of her former romanticism, could no longer sway her ... [although] her new skepticism threatened to desensitize her to the actual issues, she could not fathom going back. Her previous position seemed now unconnected and vulnerable and embarrassingly innocent" (23). Her story takes on political overtones that mirror Giang's politics; she denounces all sides of the conflict. Although she has become Giang's pawn, both politically and sexually, she realizes that status affords her a certain amount of freedom. Her pen name takes on significance; she is called "master of the woman's style of attack" (23). Like the Trung legend in the twentieth century, Tran's romanticization of war takes on political meaning that previously had not been there. Her pen name actually gives Tran some power; people credit her for things she did not do based purely on the character her name implied (23). She becomes a cultural authority.

However, in the end, like the Trung sisters, Tran is merely a pawn for political maneuverings and power plays by Giang and the other reporters. Giang abandons her and denies their illegitimate daughter, Tran's second child; the RVN accuses her of subversion; the Viet Cong rapidly encroach on Saigon, leading to an increase of suicide in Saigon, lynchings in the countryside, and frequent photographs of corpses and mass graves in the newspapers (34). As Saigon loses control over its destiny, Tran loses all control over her life. Her marriage to an American is arranged to get her out of Viet Nam. The story ends with her husband, Hus, holding power over Tran through the English language. In a moment that echoes Tran's language game with Gabriel, Tran tries to explain her suffering to Hus. However, she replaces the "u" with an "a." This small mistake makes Hus think she is writing "saffron" instead of "suffering." Tran is frustrated trying to make Hus understand her; eventually, she submits to his authority. He finally understands her error and begins to teach her the difference between the vowels. Tran's subjectivity, like her home, is lost. The shift in language demanded of refugees underscores Tran's inability, as a Vietnamese American, to narrate her own present and future, a power that the affiliation to the Trung legend granted her. Tran's method of creating her own reality and controlling her past and present is stripped from her.

Like Hayslip's and Strom's texts, Lan Cao's *Monkey Bridge* traces the refugee experience from Viet Nam to America. Cao's novel is shaped by dual perspectives of Mai, a young Vietnamese American who left Viet Nam two months before Saigon's fall, and her mother Thanh, a woman who tries to hide her family's past from Mai. Thanh's story is grounded in the past; her journal unravels the lies of her family and slowly reveals the truth. Mai's story is grounded in her present; as she struggles to find a place in America, she tries to reclaim her past and navigate perceptions of Viet Nam and Vietnamese Americans. Cao's novel illustrates the conflicting nature of reclamations of the past and the reality of the present in diasporic identity formation. The novel weaves Thanh's story with Mai's formation of her identity as a Vietnamese American. Mai's struggle to create this identity is a result of the instability of her status as Vietnamese American. She cannot construct a narrative of her past and present and America rejects her claims to "Vietnamese-ness" and America. Thanh underscores Mai's struggle in describing her as "so lost between worlds" (53).

Part of Mai's struggle is in her uncertainty about her legal status—"Resident Alien." In one episode, Mai and her best friend, Bobbie, decide they need to track down Thanh's father, Baba Quan, in Viet Nam and bring him to the United States because Thanh's mental, emotional, and physical suffering is due to Baba Quan's absence. However, because of the embargo of Viet Nam, Mai cannot make contact with him from the United States. Bobbie and Mai decide to cross into Canada to track down Baba Quan; however, Mai is so fearful of losing her American residency status that she will not cross the border, despite the callings of filial duty. Mai tries to ground her decision in Vietnamese history and Trung mythology—"[Viet Nam] had ... primarily a history of defending, not crossing boundaries" (29)—but the Canadian border is uncrossable because without American citizenship, Mai risks the claim on her new home.

Mai's sense of instability is illustrated by her narrative. Michelle Satterlee describes these moments of instability as narrative dissociation, a narrative strategy that represents "psychological dissociation" caused by trauma. For Satterlee, these moments "[capture] the distortion of identity and reality produced by trauma" and reflect the "struggle over how to remember origins as well as how to articulate a diasporic identity and cultivate a sense of place in the adopted nation" (144). At times Mai slips between Viet Nam and America, transporting the reader through time and space. For instance, the plot begins with Mai visiting Thanh in Arlington Hospital after her stroke. The novel starts in Viet Nam. The Saigon military hospital barrages Mai with the sensory evidence of the horrors of war; she smells blood, feels stillness, sees the swaths of white, "the color of mourning ... for ghosts, bones, and funerals" and hears gunshots hitting the hospital walls (1). Mai then slips into Arlington Hospital several years later, which is starkly different from the Saigon military hospital she remembers. This slippage illustrates Mai's inability to escape the narrative of the Vietnam War; her feeling of instability is brought on by her refugee experience and her lack of agency over narratives of Viet Nam and America. Therefore, Mai's representations of Viet Nam fall into a binary: the brutal war, which she cannot control, and the idyllic, mythic homeland, which is her way of "repositioning" the past.

As the novel opens, it is clear that Mai is traumatized not only by the refugee experience but also by the war itself. Mai is plagued by images of the carnage of war; she takes No-Doz to avoid going to sleep because she does not want to relive the brutal memories of the Vietnam War. Mai describes several instances that revolve around the Saigon military hospital that opens the novel, where she met Uncle Michael, a wounded soldier with a bloody and scarred face (72). When the novel opens, Mai remembers witnessing a wounded man with a grenade embedded in his abdomen blow up (1). Mai has no control over how she remembers the war and it impedes her mythic past, destabilizing her attempts to narrate her present.

Unlike memories of the war, the mythic homeland is a form of remembering the past that a refugee can control. Claire Stocks argues that the move to America and the refugee's ability to rewrite identity and history allows Thanh to "[contain] the Vietnamese" through mythologizing to "[deny] Mai access to her family history" (83). Stocks' argument primarily refers to Thanh's presentation of Baba Quan, her father, as a mythologized figure. Baba Quan is presented as a man who adheres to Confucian values, uses folklore to guide his decisions, and appears "on a gray wisp of mist" to lead Uncle Michael and his unit through a treacherous minefield (111). Stocks argues that this mythologizing of Baba Quan is Thanh's attempt at hiding the truth that Baba Quan is not Thanh's father but rather the murderer of Thanh's father and a Viet Cong agent in order to control family history for Mai. As Stocks argues, "the unconscious knowledge transmitted through generations is, in this sense, also the memory of a certain national history that Mai never directly experienced.... The several traumas that Thanh has suffered are linked not only to her own family but to a wider sense of cultural loss that constitutes an unavoidable part of Vietnamese memory and Mai's inheritance" (99). Mai embraces this myth and participates in continuing the mythologizing of Baba Quan and extends it to other people in her past.

As Cao's use of the Trung sisters illustrates, that authority is undermined by America's reclamation and appropriation of what Viet Nam (the country and the war synonymously) signifies. Stocks reads the cultural myths of Viet Nam as illustrating "the inescapability of the Vietnamese past in the formation of refugee identity" (100). Mai wants to ground her identity in the mythic past and its intimate connection with the land and Vietnamese culture, which is illustrated by her invocation of the Trung sisters. Mai begins the Trung legend by noting that her parents taught her it. This small but significant point grounds the story as part of Mai's cultural heritage, something "handed down" by her forebears. As Mai begins to tell the story, she transforms herself into Trung Trac and tells the narrative through first-person perspective (118–23). Mai's use of "I" is not just a child's game; it signifies her sense of self as vested in the cultural heritage and the mythic past that the Trung myth represents.

But the use of Vietnamese heroines is not just about the significance or "inspiration" (Cowart 157) of Vietnamese history in identity formation. Since Cao contextualizes this retelling into Mai's college interview at Mount Holyoke, the interview itself is important in reading the use of the legend. For Mai, college is a way "to flee from a phantom world that could no longer offer comfort or sanctuary" (32); this phantom world is Thanh's representation of Viet Nam and its prostration to karma and ancestor worship. Although part of that "phantom world," the Trung sister legend also provides a strategy to navigate and adapt to America. Mai's purpose in retelling the Trung sisters' myth is to cull a strategy for the "battlefield" that is the college interview. There, Mai asserts Vietnamese cultural heritage to adapt to American life. She writes: "I would enter the realm that had delivered Vietnam into a history of brilliant battlefield maneuvers that I could imitate to win over the interview" (118). These "brilliant maneuvers," Mai concludes, are to guard against and hide her weak spots. However, the college interviewer, Amy Layton, immediately undermines Mai's strategy and reclaims America's authority to speak of Viet Nam.

Amy opens the interview by renaming Mai; she calls her Mai Nguyen, reversing the order of her family name and given name (125). She then asks if Mai is from Viet Nam, a question that "always numbed [Mai]" (126). The question reminds Mai of Americans who feel compelled to identify the physical and emotional losses caused by the country, such as "the school-bus driver who informed me the first day we met that her husband had done door-to-door combat in the streets of Hue in 1968. 'My husband lost both his legs over there,' the woman had said, and I hadn't known what to say in response" (126). Her lack of response echoes several instances in the novel when Mai is faced with a narrative that differs from her own. For instance, Mai encounters an unquestioned racist depiction in the American media of a Vietnamese American family suspected of eating an elderly neighbor's dog. This particular instance refers to a larger discussion of American racism towards Asian Americans compounded with American hostility to the specter of the Vietnam War. Mai's silence is a result of "the dominant [culture's efforts] to prevent any voicing of the minority experience" and she "[articulates]—question[s], report[s], expose[s]—the silences imposed on [herself] and [her people] ... in the form of ... historical or political invisibility" (Cheung 1993, 3–4). There is a clash over who has authority to narrate Viet Nam throughout the novel, and these moments highlight one of several instances when Mai loses authority to narrate Viet Nam to America's authority.

Mai responds to Amy's opening question with "Yes. I came in 1975" (126). Amy does not let Mai claim America as her own; she insists on reminding Mai of her "alien" status, asking "Were you there until 1975?" followed by "So you were there the whole time the war was going on?" (126). Amy's repetition of the year 1975 forces Mai and the reader to refer back to Mai's description of leaving Saigon for the United States in 1975 and the public dissolution of South Viet Nam and American involvement in Southeast Asia on April 30, 1975. Both of these events punctuate Mai's sense of loss and dispossession. When Mai leaves Saigon on a Pan Am flight, she watches Viet Nam disappear through her airplane window. As the land grows smaller, "the fear of separation I suddenly understood ... to be a fear as primordial as death" (97). Separation from the things that form identity, in this case from land, family, culture, and language, is equated with death. A few months later, sitting in Uncle Michael's living room in Connecticut, Mai watches the fall of Saigon on television. Mai precedes her description of the spectacle with "I saw my future unfold on television.... I witnessed my own untranslatable world unfold to Americans half a globe away" (97–98). Mai and Uncle Michael watch in horror as the last U.S. helicopter, burdened with the weight of desperate Vietnamese clinging to it, leaves the Saigon embassy against a backdrop of tin-roofed houses, smoke from nearby bombings, and thundering tanks. In this moment, Mai realizes that she will never return to Viet Nam; the news report is a visual moment of trauma that marks Mai forever as dispossessed. Mai tells us:

> Of course, I had been watching all this, along with Uncle Michael and Aunt Mary, and like the rest of America, in the safety of our living room. I saw how Farmington, Connecticut, and just about every city in the United States had wanted the tragedy to end. It was as if all of America were holding its breath, waiting for a diseased body, ravaged and fatigued, and now all too demanding, to let go. Death must be nudged, hurried, if only it could be [98].

It is also in this moment that Mai realizes she has lost her agency to narrate and claim Viet Nam. When she slips into "the ancient frontier of dreams," she sees the helicopter again and the pressing mass of Vietnamese hoping to gain entry into the U.S. embassy (99). The American media continue to show the evacuation of the U.S. embassy so that the history of Vietnam could "[continue] to be dissected and remodeled by a slew of commentators and experts after April 1975" (42). The American narrative of Viet Nam, which "meant war, antipathies" (42), displaces Mai's narrative of family, myth and home.

The struggle over who has authority to claim Viet Nam and America continues throughout Mai's interview. When Amy asks her about "the war," Mai wants to undermine Amy's authority by pointing out that America's war was only one in a series of wars and that Amy's identification of "the war" is more about "the American rite of passage and the American experience gone wrong" than it is about the Vietnamese, including Mai (126). Amy prods Mai about her life in Viet Nam by asking about family and where Mai lived. When Saigon comes into the conversation, Mai desperately wants to confront Amy's preconceived notions of Saigon being "all about rocket fires and body bags" (128) by giving her a description of Mai's house and showing Saigon through her eyes as she rides in the family's Citroen with her parents and goes to the sky market with her mother. Mai wants "to reveal something palpable, something that would make the country crack open so she could see the tender, vital, and, most important, mundane parts" (127–28). However, like her realization of America's appropriation of the narrative of Viet Nam, Mai realizes that "the Vietnam delivered to America had truly passed beyond reclamation. It was no longer mine to explain" (128). Instead, as the conflicts between mythic imaginings and remembrances of the war demonstrate, Viet Nam is replaced by America's Vietnam, which is strictly told through American history, racism, the media, and Hollywood. Though Uncle Michael confirms for Mai that films like *The Deer Hunter* are wildly inaccurate (100), Hollywood's versions nonetheless dominate American perceptions of Viet Nam. In the end, the Trung sisters' strategy of guarding the weak points doesn't work; Amy finds and exposes each of Mai's weak points. So the Trung sisters' strategy transforms into one of evasion; Mai not only won't confront Amy's pre-conceived notions, but she cannot confront them (129).

The interview ends with Amy bringing attention to Mai's "foreign-ness" again. Amy states: "You speak English very well. You sound just like an American.... I never would've guessed ... otherwise" (130). This strips Mai of her self-perception in at least two ways. First, Amy targets Mai's source of pride—her excellence at English, which Mai sees as her "real tongue" (37) and second, Amy positions Mai as other. In fact, during the entire interview, Layton's questions and responses to Mai reinforce Mai's status as other. As Liam Corley argues, the use of English by Asian Americans, even a native speaker of English, continuously marks Asian Americans as foreign, which injures their ability to claim English as their language and therefore, America as their home. Corley builds his argument from Lisa Lowe, who argues that U.S. national memory always refers to Asian American as an immigrant, "the foreigner-within" (qtd. in Corley 57). Mai even echoes Lowe's idea; she calls herself "an outsider with insider information" (Cao 41). Amy's interrogation of Mai reflects orientalist attitudes of America towards Vietnamese Americans, and the conflict between "Self and Other, subjectivity and objectivity, [and] of the power structure inherent in such a dichotomy" (Ma 17).

Amy reminds Mai that she cannot claim authority over Viet Nam and that she has no claim on American-ness; in addition, Mai's reliance on her Vietnamese heritage, represented by the Trung sisters, leads to anemic results. Mai cannot form her own identity; it becomes dictated by Americans. Instead of a woman who can tap into a rich cultural heritage and who can claim her past and present, Mai is reduced to merely a refugee; she is constantly reminded of her position as a "resident alien," not a citizen, and Americans perceive her as part of "a ragtag accumulation of unwanted, an awkward reminder of a war the whole country was trying to forget" (15). While the values that Mai culls from the Trung sisters do little to help her navigate the Vietnamese American experience, their legend does teach her something. The Trung sisters did not pursue the Chinese into China; they stayed in Viet Nam. The story reminds her that she should never have crossed a border; to cross boundaries, to leave home, is unsettling and disrupts a sense of self. This message of the Trung legend is yet another reminder that "made [her] know in no uncertain terms that [Mai and Thanh] would not be returning to the familiarity of [their] former lives…. [Sustaining] a new identity … had to do with being able to adopt a different posture, to reach deep enough into the folds of the earth and relocate one's roots and bend one's body in a new direction" (39). As Mai's narrative shows, this is an impossible task.

The importance of the land, a "rootedness" of self to culture and family history, to what Satterlee identifies as "ethnic identity," is a site of struggle for Le Ly Hayslip, Dao Strom, and Lan Cao. The "crossing of borders," the disruption of place, plays a pivotal role in diasporic identity and the invocation of the Trung legend illustrates each author's concern over identity formation, subjectivity, and the dispossession of the refugee experience. Although each protagonist eventually has some resolution to their struggles—Le Ly has children, marries, and returns to Viet Nam to reconcile with her past; Tran finds a balance between her self-perception as a strong woman and refugee; Mai is admitted to Mount Holyoke—the Trung legend is a tool that underscores the women's struggle to control their own past and present and therefore, their own subjectivity as refugees.

Notes

1. I follow Renny Christopher's spelling of Viet Nam as a way of distinguishing between the country (Viet Nam) and the war (Vietnam) even though the texts cited in this essay do not adhere to this semantic difference.

2. Ronald Takaki points out that in 1964 only 603 Vietnamese lived in the United States. In 1975, there were 130,000. In 1985, there were 643,200 (448–54). For a more detailed discussion of the resettlement of Vietnamese refugees, see Takaki's *Strangers form a Different Shore*, Paul Rutledge's *The Vietnamese Experience in America*, Sucheng Chan's *The Vietnamese American 1.5 Generation*, Min Zhou and Carl L. Bankston's *Growing Up American: How Vietnamese Children Adapt to Life in the United States*, and Hien Duc Do's *The Vietnamese Americans*.

3. For example, Tran Van Dinh's *Blue Dragon, White Tiger* (1983) is considered a novel but is heavily autobiographical.

4. Lac refers to the earliest recorded name for the Vietnamese people. Lac lords were

local rulers who were loyal to the king and enjoyed wealth and prestige (Taylor 13). For more information about the Lac lords, Hung kings, and early history of Viet Nam, see Keith Weller Taylor's *The Birth of Vietnam*.

5. For more on the texts that the Trung legend is based on, see Taylor's *The Birth of Vietnam*. Taylor consulted Chinese historical writings, Vietnamese historical writings, and Vietnamese poetry for his research.

6. For more on the historical record, again see Taylor's *The Birth of Vietnam*. His work carefully marks the places where the legend diverges from history.

7. For further discussion of the use of Vietnamese history and myth in the formation of a Vietnamese national history that disentangled itself from French colonial and Chinese imperial representations of Viet Nam, see Patricia M. Pelley's *Postcolonial Vietnam*.

8. Unsurprisingly, Christopher notes that Hayslip's book is one of the few narratives from a non-white, male perspective that is taught as part of the canon of Vietnam War literature.

Bibliography

Bacholle-Bošković, Michèle. "The Exiled Woman's Burden: Father Figures in Lan Cao's and Linda Lê's Works." *Sites: The Journal of Twentieth Century Contemporary French Studies* 6.2 (2002): 267–81.
"Biography: The Trung Sisters." *Women in World History*. 2005. 2 May 2009 <http://www.womeninworldhistory.com/heroine10.html>.
Bois, Danuta. "The Trung Sisters." *Distinguished Women of Past and Present*. 5 May 2009 <http://www.distinguishedwomen.com/biographies/trung.html>.
Cao, Lan. *Monkey Bridge*. New York: Penguin, 1997.
Chan, Sucheng. *The Vietnamese American 1.5 Generation*. Philadelphia, PA: Temple University Press, 2006.
Cheung, King-kok. *Articulate Silences: Hisaye Yamamoto, Maxine Hong Kingston, Joy Kogawa*. Ithaca, NY: Cornell University Press, 1993.
_____, ed. *An Interethnic Companion to Asian American Literature*. Cambridge and New York: Cambridge University Press, 1997.
Christopher, Renny. *The Viet Nam War/The American War*. Amherst, MA: University of Massachusetts Press, 1995.
Corley, Liam. "Just Another Ethnic Pol": Literary Citizenship in Chang-Rae Lee's Native Speaker." Lim et al 55–74.
Cowart, David. *Trailing Clouds: Immigrant Fiction in Contemporary America*. Ithaca, NY: Cornell University Press, 2006.
Dinh, Tran Van. *Blue Dragon White Tiger: A Tet Story*. Philadelphia, PA: TriAm Press Inc., 1983.
Do, Hien Duc. *The Vietnamese Americans*. Westport, CT: Greenwood Press, 1999.
Fraser, Antonia. *The Warrior Queens*. New York: Alfred A. Knopf, 1989.
Freeman, James. *Hearts of Sorrow: Vietnamese-American Lives*. Stanford, CA: Stanford University Press, 1989.
Hayslip, Le Ly. *When Heaven and Earth Changed Places*. New York: Penguin, 1990.
Huynh, Jade Ngoc Quang. *South Wind Changing*. Saint Paul, MN: Graywolf Press, 2000.
Janette, Michele. "Guerilla Irony in Lan Cao's *Monkey Bridge*." *Contemporary Literature* 42.1 (2001): 50–77.
Kain, Geoffrey. *Ideas of Home: Literature of Asian Migration*. East Lansing, MI: Michigan State University Press, 1997.

Kim, Elaine H. *Asian American Literature:An Introduction to the Writings and their Social Context*. Philadelphia, PA: Temple University Press, 1982.
Koshy, Susan. "The Fiction of Asian American Literature." *The Yale Journal of Criticism* 9.2 (1996): 315–46.
Lim, Shirley Geok-lin, John Blair Gamber, Stephen Hong Sohn, and Gina Valentino, eds. *Transnational Asian American Literatures: Sites and Transits*. Philadelphia, PA: Temple University Press, 2006.
Ma, Sheing-Mei. *Immigrant Subjectivities in Asian American and Asian Diaspora Literatures*. Albany, NY: State University of New York Press, 1998.
Marr, David G. *Vietnamese Anticolonialism 1185–1925*. Los Angeles, CA: University of California Press, 1971.
Nguyen, Viet Thanh. *Race and Resistance*. Oxford and New York: Oxford University Press, 2002.
Pelley, Patricia M. *Postcolonial Vietnam: New Histories of the National Past*. Durham, NC: Duke University Press, 2002.
Rutledge, Paul. *The Vietnamese Experience in America*. Bloomington, IN: Indiana University Press, 1992.
Santoli, Al. *To Bear Any Burden*. Bloomington, IN: Indiana University Press, 1999.
Satterlee, Michelle. "How Memory Haunts: The Impact of Trauma on Vietnamese Immigrant Identity in Lan Cao's *Monkey Bridge*." *Studies in the Humanities* 31.2 (2004): 138–62.
Stocks, Claire. "Bridging the Gaps: Inescapably History in Lan Cao's *Monkey Bridge*." *Studies in the Literary Imagination* 37.1 (2004): 83–100.
Strom, Dao. *Grass Roof, Tin Roof*. Boston, MA: Mariner Books, 2003.
Takaki, Ronald. *Strangers from a Different Shore*. Boston, MA: Little, Brown, 1998.
Taylor, Keith Weller. *The Birth of Vietnam*. Los Angeles, CA: University of California Press, 1983.
Tran, Tuyet A., and Chu V. Nguyen. "Trung Trac and Trung Nhi." *Viettouch*. 5 May 2009. <http://www.viettouch.com/trungsis/>.
Truong, Monique T.D. "Vietnamese American Literature." In Cheung, King-kok. *Articulate Silences: Hisaye Yamamoto, Maxine Hong Kingston, Joy Kogawa*. Ithaca, NY: Cornell University Press, 1993. 219–46.
Turley, William S. "Women in the Communist Revolution in Vietnam." *Asian Survey* 12.9 (1972): 793–805.
Zhou, Min, and Carl L. Bankston. *Growing Up American: How Vietnamese Children Adapt to Life in the United States*. New York: Russell Sage Foundation, 1999.

The Nicole Subic Rape Case and the *Chingada* in the Philippine Imaginary

Danicar Mariano

After 9/11, due to "training exercises" meant to quell Muslim insurgent forces in the south, U.S. military presence in the Philippines has steadily increased. With increased militarization comes tourism and thereby "military prostitution," a term Cynthia Enloe coined to allude to the flourishing sex industries in regions where U.S. troops are stationed. In 1985, the U.S. military had become the second largest employer in the Philippines, hiring over 40,000 Filipinos (Moon 33). "Hospitality" jobs comprised the majority. Indeed, until the Nicole Subic Trial against U.S. marines, bases and prostitution go unnoticed as part of the normal scheme of things, that is, until a woman cries out "rape" in public. As Cynthia Enloe explains,

> Except when the bases raise questions about international strategic doctrine or blatant infringements of national sovereignty, they seem to fade into the backdrop of ordinary life. This sort of nationalist approach to American bases—or any foreign military bases—makes women invisible except occasionally as symbols.... If the fit between local and foreign men and local and foreign women breaks down, the base may lose its protective cover. It may become the target of nationalist resentment that could subvert the very structure of a military alliance [66].

In the Philippines, the controversial 2005 Nicole Subic rape case deeply troubled the Philippine-American military alliance. Much of the discourse before and during the trial revolved around whether rape could ever happen in a place like Subic where there are so many willing and available Filipina prostitutes. Subic was the largest U.S. military base in the Pacific since World War II until the U.S. bases were voted out in the late 1990s. For a woman, it was as if going to Subic and participating in its nightlife automatically transformed her into a sex worker who by her very nature could not be raped. The highly publicized Nicole Subic rape case pegged twenty-two-year-old "Nicole" against

Lance Corporal Daniel Smith and three other marines. It became an allegory for Philippine nationalists to demand accountability from the country's former colonizer, the U.S. In a bar in Subic, a drunken Nicole was picked up by Smith in a van. She was raped while three or four of his fellow marines allegedly cheered him on. At dawn, witnesses recounted how they saw two U.S. marines carrying Nicole by her hands and feet "like a pig," unloading her from the van unto the side of the road: unconscious, half-naked, condom still stuck to her underwear. The image stuck in the minds of many Filipinos and soon feminists, nationalists, columnists, and politicians were rallying around Nicole, calling for the abolition of the U.S.-Philippine Visiting Forces Agreement (VFA) that gives American soldiers special rights while they are training in the Philippines. The accused was tried and after an agonizing year convicted and sentenced to forty years in jail, but to the ire of many activists, he was eventually whisked away from Philippine custody into the hands of the U.S. embassy, never to be seen again. Several years later, Nicole, after the harrowing trial and having her real name exposed by the media, submitted an affidavit in March 2009 that basically recanted everything that she stood for during the trial and trumpeted the opposing side's rhetoric that the sexual intercourse must have been consensual because she was drunk. Nicole's lawyer, as well as other Filipino intellectuals and activists, suspect foul play and sense that a deal has been struck with the U.S., especially since the affidavit came out shortly after Obama's private phone call to President Arroyo, renewing the U.S. commitment to its "partnership" with the Philippines. Nicole is now living in the U.S., which, according to her mother, has always been her dream even before the rape trial. Intellectuals and feminists are disappointed with Nicole's acquiescence to what they see as an obvious buckling to pressure from the U.S., the Philippine government, and VFA supporters. But some of them also understand it is the lack of government support that compelled it since, even after repeated calls to the Philippine government for justice and to have Smith sent to a Philippine jail, Nicole's pleas fell on deaf ears.

This chapter contextualizes the Nicole Subic rape case through militarization, immigration, and sovereignty woes afflicting the sexualized and feminized Philippine nation by looking at the image of the Filipina as a marker of the nation's morality and modernity. The chapter will also address the U.S.-Philippine Visiting Forces Agreement and what impact the rape case has on it. In the Philippines, where "racism and sexism" is seen as the fulcrum of national sovereignty (Santos in Moon 34), the Subic rape case is one of the political issues on which feminism and nationalist rhetoric have agreed and converged. Feminist activists and nationalists, though often with diverging views in the Philippines, came together to rally for the abolition of the VFA. Both factions saw U.S. military bases as a common enemy and espoused the belief that the government's encouragement of the continuing stay of the bases for tourism and for industry is responsible for condoning the widespread prostitution of Filipinas and is tantamount to selling the sovereignty of the nation itself. This view has a historical precedent stretching back as far as the U.S. colonization of the islands in 1989. According to Cynthia Enloe, "prostitution especially in militarized zones has become an issue defined in terms of nationalist anger and nationalist hopes" (86). Central to the issue of the Philippines' sovereignty that the Subic rape case highlights is the U.S.—Philippine Visiting Forces Agreement. VFA, as many detractors define it, gives U.S. soldiers immunity from the Philippine law. The rape case put the VFA to the test and brought out its ramifications. Because of the case, the clamor among Filipino politicians and activists residing in the Philippines is louder than ever to re-examine and repeal the VFA. Because of this and the Iraq-Afghanistan war, Filipino Americans in the U.S. also grow more conscious and disdainful of how their tax dollars are being used to militarize regions that do not necessarily welcome it.

Although rape cases against U.S. military personnel have erupted before in other countries, this chapter will articulate what makes the Philippine controversy unique compared to cases happened in other Asian countries. To highlight similarities between the Philippine culture and Latin American countries that also have been colonized by Spain, this chapter brings in the transnational archetype of the *chingada*. Latin America developed the concept of the *chingada*, a Spanish term for "a woman ripped open," to refer to the passive woman "who asks for it," a category traditional Catholicism fosters for women who do not live up to its virginal ideals. This analog helps demonstrate the split that haunts Filipino identity as well as the dichotomy that positions the rape-complainant Nicole either as a nationalist heroine or as a whore that gives the country a bad name. The framework of the *chingada* will highlight not only the Philippines' long colonial history under Spain and the U.S. and how it has impacted the country's ideals and values, but also the role that Catholicism plays in perpetuating discourses about women who are rape victims in the Filipino mentality. In the section that delves into why Filipinos break identification with Nicole, this analog of the *chingada* helps explain Filipino men's propensity to chastise and police Filipina women. It also explains their disgust at what they perceive as Filipina women's betrayal of their country.

Octavio Paz's landmark essay, "The Sons of La Malinche," describes the *chingada* as a woman who suffers from violence:

> She in passive, inert, open, in contrast to the active, aggressive and closed person who inflicts it. The *chingon* is the macho, the male, he rips open the *chingada*, the female, who is pure passivity, defenseless against the exterior world. The relationship between them is violent, and it is determined by the cynical power of the first and the impotence of the second. The idea of violence rules darkly over all meanings of the word, and the dialectic of the "closed" and the "open" thus fulfills itself with an almost ferocious precision [77].

Latin American theorists argue that the *mestizo* class is spawned by La Malinche, the ultimate *chingada* who embodies passivity, treachery, and the call for violence against her sex. La Malinche was believed to be an Aztec princess who was cast away as a slave, only to later become the mistress and translator of Cortez, the Spanish leader for the Mexican expedition. La Malinche is therefore seen as instrumental to the colonization of Latin America and thus, a traitor. In fact, it is the myth of La Malinche that forged and crystallized the concept of the *chingada.*

In "The Sons of La Malinche," Octavio Paz articulates his take on mimicry and hybridity, with the "almost-but-not-white existence" of Mexicans serving as the source of their rejection, anger, and machismo. Paz's postcolonial interpretation of La Malinche's tale is psychoanalytic as well. The sons of La Malinche are the *hijos de puta* who blame their mother for their inability to belong and for their burden of solitude where they could neither claim allegiance to the dominant race of their father, nor the conquered race of their mother. *Mestizos* project their hatred of their absent or unknown father towards their "sexually willing and covetous" mother, while simultaneously trying to usurp the power of their father's race.[1]

Paz's discourse on La Malinche is his explanation for the racialized and nationalistic tone that patriarchy has often taken on in Latin American countries where nationalists have vilified La Malinche as a whore. Moreover, the stigma attached to being the daughter of the La Malinche justified why Latino men can claim superiority over women since: "the male *mestizo* carries the sign of victory for having fought against the conqueror, while the female is blamed for the downfall of the native culture because she established an alliance with the conqueror and betrayed her people" (Stein 132). La Malinche exemplifies the Mexican woman who deserves violence for being open to the culture and influence of colonizers.

In juxtaposing La Malinche and Nicole, I compare old and new myths that frame the Latin American as well as Filipino understandings of rape and violence against women that also articulate their gendered and sexualized view of interracial dynamics. Both the Philippines and Mexico have a troubled history with the U.S. and both have been colonized and Christianized by Spain for centuries. By looking at blog posting of news articles and editorials on the Nicole Subic rape case together with the commentaries and blog discussions it has spurred among activists, Filipino Americans, and the Filipino general public from 2005 to 2008, this study examines public discourses around the controversial trial. Analyzing the forums and discussions found on weblogs and websites that were put up by Filipino feminists, (Nicole Information Bureau's "Nicole Subic Rape Case Site"), Filipino Americans (the blogs of "Philippine Commentary" and "Composed Gentleman"), as well as Filipino general readers (*The Philippine Daily Inquirer* and *Pinoy Spy Reporter*, a local tabloid), this chapter has collected both formal and informal online discourses about Nicole. The comments are from Filipinos living in and outside of the Philippines. I believe blogs and other online commentaries, precisely because they are raw and mostly un-moderated, articulate the Filipino public's diverse and often unconscious beliefs about rape and U.S.-Philippine relationships. Due to greater anonymity and freedom online, the Internet relieves Filipinos from their usual politeness, encouraging them to be more honest and direct about their views.

Blogs by Filipinos living in the Philippines and America as well as Americans with Filipino wives have time and again questioned the credibility of Nicole and her supporters based on the well-ingrained notion that deep down, Filipinos really love America and really want to be with Americans. Given so much admiration for America, they reason, it is incredulous that such hatred for Americans could exist side by side with it. For them, Nicole's case is not about a woman searching for justice for a crime committed against her, but an act of vengeance against the U.S.

The Nicole Subic Rape Case

In Japan, Korea, and the Philippines, U.S.-foreign relations have been ruptured by controversial rape cases against U.S. service men that highlight issues of sovereignty and the legitimacy of U.S. military presence.[2] Unlike the 1991 Korean rape case and 1995 Japanese rape case against U.S. military which had the majority of the country standing by the victims, Nicole, was heavily stigmatized by her fellow countrymen and women, as if it was her integrity that was on trial. Half the public discourses on the rape case revolved around whether Nicole was a prostitute, trying to prove to many that she could not possibly have been raped. Although Japanese and Koreans also discriminate against their fellow women who sleep with foreigners, the stigma comes from a "highly racialist conscience" as well as a perceived racial homogeneity; that is, the "fallen women" are accused of contaminating the purity of their race.[3] In the Philippines, where the *mestizo* or hybrid race dominates and where the American dream prevails, the source of discrimination against raped and prostituted women who "covet" American men are different.

Analyzing the fantasy behind the U.S.-Philippine colonial relationship and its highly gendered and sexualized undertones, Neferti Tadiar has argued that, when given a chance, many Filipina women would like to marry Americans. She argues that if America projects the Philippines as its feminine ideal, mutually the Philippines sees the U.S. as its masculine ideal:

> [R]elations between the Philippines and America operate according to a fantasy of heteronormative relations between masculine and feminine ideals that has become dominant in economically advanced nations—a sexual masquerade in which the Philippines serves the U.S. feminine ideal, servicing its power the way Philippine prostitutes service U.S. military men, symbols of U.S. national (masculine) strength.... Hence "American" in turn becomes the Philippines' masculine ideal, determining the shape of the desire expressed by this "bar waitress" who might speak for the Philippines as well: "Sure I would like to marry an

American! I want to help my family. If I marry a Filipino, it will be the same; but if I marry an American, maybe it will be better" [47–48].

This mentality abounds, not just among hostesses or bar girls, but among well-educated Filipina women as well. In an exit survey that looked at Filipina women married to Australian men, Filipina wives were found to have the highest educational attainment compared to most other racial groups (Brown 2008). Online discourses about Nicole argue against the validity of the case based on the premise that it is the Filipina's dream to marry an American — or any white man, for that matter. Many claim that Nicole is just suing Smith for rape because she wants more money from him or as vengeance for his refusal to take her seriously and marry her. Behind this belief is the assumption that it is every Filipina's dream to have a green card. As some Filipino American blog commentators have argued, the presence of so many illegal immigrants in America proves the existence and commonality of such a dream.[4] Operating on this assumption, Nicole's own government-assigned prosecution team allegedly negotiated an unsolicited settlement for Nicole amidst the trial. The settlement promised Nicole and her sister permanent residency in the U.S., her mother and other relatives multiple entry U.S. visas, as well as financial compensation. When Nicole's family, feeling offended, rejected this offer and asked the entire prosecution side to be replaced, the prosecution side defended itself by saying "they were only looking out for Nicole, since she said in a TV interview that, after all this, she just wanted to go to a faraway place where no one knew her and thought that maybe the settlement would be the perfect solution." Still, there were accusations that Nicole was just pushing through with the rape case for a green card and for the money ensued. Regardless, Nicole forged on with the case until the judge finally found Smith guilty of rape.

In March 2009, however, several years after she had won the case, Nicole released an affidavit that contradicted her earlier testimony and echoed the defense logic of consensual sex with Smith, leaving her critics feeling more righteous than ever in their self-fulfilling prophecy that Nicole is nothing but a "selfish liar" willing to trouble crucial links with the U.S. for nothing more than media attention and a "free pass to the U.S." (Kritz 2009).

Conflicting Allegiances: Why Filipinos Fail to Identify with Nicole?

Apart from the belief that Filipinas just want money or marriage from Americans, a well-established colonial aesthetics makes Nicole's case hard to believe in the eyes of many Filipinos. Nick Tiongson, who studied colonial aesthetics in Philippine drama and films, argues how this deeply ingrained standard that "white is beautiful" has been damaging to the country. He laments that plays and films during and after the colonial era portray protagonists as *mestizo* or *mestizuhin*, while native-looking actors could only play either the *kontrabida* (antagonist) or the comedian (Tiongson 1977).

Exasperated, Filipino male bloggers question how the Subic rape case can be taken seriously when other women are out there, swooning over how handsome Smith is, claiming they would be fine if they were in Nicole's place. In a rather vicious albeit typical comment posted in a *Pinoy Spy Reporter* forum, a Filipina tells Nicole to be ashamed of her lie because she could not have possibly been raped, due to her being "ugly" and Smith being *gwapo* or "good-looking."

> Ey Nicole, you should feel ashamed. You know the truth, you know it in your conscience. You are ugly and smith is handsome.... Yuck!! Your [sic] just running after money and you just want to be popular that's why you did that.... Your [sic] not satisfied in one guy, shame on you Nicole...
>
> You are arrogant, you think people will take pity on you, give you scholarship, a job, a house and lot. You really have a thick hide.... And you insinuate you want to start a new life in another country so they would give this to you.... It is just because you couldn't catch a Yankee, that's why you're hysterical right now.... What were you doing in Subic, anyway, Yankee hunting???[5]

Other female bloggers also echo this view, wondering why Smith would ever settle for Nicole when he, as an American, could have any other *Pinay*. Another commentator angrily explained on the same forum: "Leftists are just using her [to discredit Americans], can somebody post her pics? Ugly eh?" In the blog quote above, the Filipina also accuses Nicole that "she can't get enough of one guy" or more precisely, she cannot get enough of American GIs, which is why she was "GI-hunting" in Subic. This is also the slant of the defense team in the trial. "Why was she drinking if she wasn't inviting rape?" commentators asked. "What was she doing there in the bar, if she was engaged to another?" Nicole and her boyfriend met through a little canteen in Zamboanga that Nicole's family owns and that caters to U.S. soldiers. Nicole helps out in the store. Nicole broke into tears when asked how her family treated U.S. soldiers who were the main patrons of their canteen. "We don't treat them like outsiders, we show them that they are family, we value them so they don't feel homesick."[6] The fact that Nicole had a GI boyfriend both before and during the rape trial was also used to support the defense argument that first of all, "she is not a virgin, therefore she cannot be raped," and secondly, that she has "opened" herself up to an American before and therefore she will certainly do so again. This strange bias has many culturally specific assumptions: it assumes that a woman is poor or of questionable morals if she lives around the U.S. bases because she is out to get the GI's money. If she wants the GI's money, then she will probably use any means to get it, including sex work and lying about rape. Hence, Nicole's trial is only seen as an extension of Nicole's family's business, a way to further extract money from U.S. soldiers. As a comment by "manofwar" from the *Pinoy Spy* blog forum states, "'Nicole' is a known prostitute in Zamboanga city. She has another 'boyfriend' who also happens to be a U.S. Marine who is now based in Okinawa, Japan. The reason they're keeping pictures of her from the press is because she will undoubtedly be recognized by quite a few 'boyfriends' of hers who send her money from time to time whenever she writes them letters pleading for monetary support."

Many self-declared nationalists also broke solidarity with Nicole, failing to see the issue within the larger context of U.S. colonization of the Philippines, seeing it instead as merely a bad diplomatic move on the Philippines' part and something that further stains the reputation of Filipinas in the international realm. "I just hope that the world remembers that, unlike Nicole, there are still decent Filipino women out there," a female blogger remarks on the *Pinoy Spy* forum. This comment implies the class or cultural divide that separates Nicole and prostitutes, on the one hand, and "proper" women, on the other hand. In the Philippines, colonial mentality, which breaks down any empathy one may feel for a fellow Filipina, ensures that being from the province or being dark or coming from a poor or lower middle class family can all serve as categories to qualify a person as an "other"—the whore or the woman who asks for it. Similarly, the myth of La Malinche as the *chingada* is one that serves to reinforce self-loathing among women, illustrating how patriarchy breaks down female identification and with it any source of solidarity one may feel for a fellow country mate.

In "Rehabilitating the Tarnished Image of the Filipina," a self-published essay by Robyn Magalit Rodriguez, the Filipino American laments that the Nicole fight is futile despite the activism that fuels it, because regardless, Google ads would still display how Filipinas are for sale. Rodriguez, who decries the sad lot of Filipino sovereignty, proposes the policing of women and their sexuality as the solution:

> If Filipinos want to get serious about rehabilitating the image of the Filipina in the eyes of the world, then it should be done, not by meting-out 40-year jail sentences to young soldiers like Daniel Smith, *but by getting to the root of the problem* and closing down places like the Neptune bar where *predatory women* seek out unsuspecting foreigners; by shutting down all those massage parlors and Karaoke TV bars that are really just brothels in disguise; by taking offline all those mail-order-bride websites full of photos of Filipinas who are willing to marry any man sight-unseen.... *It is high time we reconstruct the Filipina image, and if we have to be tough on the men, we have to be just as tough on the women* ["Rehabilitating the Tarnished Image of the Filipina"; italics added].

As exemplified by Rodriguez' comment, women's bodies become the site where the moral crisis of the nation are waged (Rinaldo 2008). The policing and disciplining of "predatory Filipinas," their bodies, identities, and practices, is his proposed solution to the problems of the nation. Similarly, Latin American theorist Cherrie Moraga explains how women of color have always known that sexuality holds the key to a woman's essence and identity. She asserts that "patriarchal religions—whether brought to us by the colonizers cross and gun or emerging from our own people have always known this. Why else would the female body be so associated with sin and disobedience?" (Moraga 132). In many cultures, women have always served as receptacles of tradition as well as markers of modernization. Hence, because women are seen as symbols of community identity, it is no surprise that moral debates in the public sphere focus on them as well. Particularly in times of crisis or social change, society tends to focus on women's behaviors and women's bodies. In the Philippines, this clamor for the policing of women's behavior and sexuality is legitimized by religion.

Religion and the *Chingada*

In order to better understand the origin and pervasiveness of the *chingada* archetype in Mexico and the Philippines, we must understand Catholicism as well. Similar to Mexico, Spanish-dominated Philippines has a long-standing Catholic tradition, practiced by over 90% of the country's population. La Malinche, the Mexican Eve, is deeply ingrained in the Catholic imagination because of its contrast to the cult of *Marianismo*, the elevation of the silent suffering female martyr. Sacrifice is central to the idea of *Marianismo*. This is why, similar to the rhetoric that black women should not complain about being raped by black men because it exposes black men to "the tyranny of an all male white justice system" (Bourke), many Filipinos reason that Nicole should not complain about Smith, because it further emasculates and castrates the Philippine nation. Her cry of rape therefore makes her selfish and incapable of sacrificing for the greater cause. Without U.S. military fortification, her critics argue, the country would degrade into anarchy, powerless against Muslim terrorist and communist insurgents.

One need not look far or outside the Nicole Subic rape case to see how Catholicism plays an important role in crafting and embedding the image of the *chingada* in the Philippine collective consciousness. Within the highly publicized rape case itself, Catholic discourses were used to gain sympathy from the Filipino people—sometimes for Nicole's side, as in the argument that she could not be a prostitute because she came from Ateneo de Davao, a reputable Jesuit University, but more often to argue for the guilt of the "seductress" and the innocence of the accused.

According to feminist theologian, Carol Adams, Catholicism creates dominant and subordinate hierarchies that often condones violence against women and turns a blind eye to rape. Catholicism, moreover, teaches that violence against women is just a family matter, all the while valuing social cohesion, sacrifice and forgiveness of the accused (Adams 68–73). The dynamics cited by Adams are certainly at work in Philippine Catholicism. In a sly move, the defense called on Fr. Reuter, an icon of the People Power Revolution and a U.S.

expat who has lived in the Philippines for several years, to serve as the U.S.'s public face in the rape case. At over eighty years old, the aging priest acted as the "spiritual adviser" of Smith and the other U.S. marines. Even though he did not witness the events that transpired during the night of the rape, nor did he know Nicole or Smith before the case, his testimony as spiritual adviser was heard in court. He refuted the rape claims of Nicole, saying that she, as the older woman, had to be the one who seduced Smith, all the while vouching for the innocence of Smith. "They are nice guys, clean cut guys, especially one who has it in the neck, Danny Smith," Fr. Reuter said, at once conjuring Catholicism's stance on the forgiveness towards the "repentant" rapist as well as its diversion of blame towards the woman as seductress (Mydans).

In line with this, Adams dissects how, within Catholicism: "[t]he clergy identify with abuser, especially if he is a church member. Thus, the tendency is to see the violence as an aberration rather than as a chronic problem. This protects the offender. Often the church believes in the abuser's contriteness, and thus emphasizes forgiveness, especially when there is any sign of remorse. Abusers can manipulate religious language in their own interest. Remorse is confused with acceptance" (67). During the rape trial, Fr. Reuter also supposedly sent out a "prayer brigade" via email for Smith and the other marines on trial. When the guilty verdict of Judge Benjamin Pozon came out in December 2006, the priest called it an "unjust" decision that was brought about by heightened emotions. The young marines were tried by publicity, he said, earning the ire of leftists and several women's groups.

Many Filipinos saw race as a factor that played an important role in Fr. Reuter taking side with the accused. Indeed, when asked why he agreed to take part in the controversial trial, he said "I deal with Filipinos 99% of the time, now I'm asked by an American. Am I going to say no?" (Mydans). Having once been a prisoner in a Japanese prison camp, he also admitted that he would never forget the pride and triumph he felt when the U.S. "saved" the Philippines from the Japanese: "That's when I knew what it was to have a country," he said. "That's when I made up my mind that I would never change my [U.S.] citizenship" (Mydans).

Feminists have questioned Fr. Reuter's motives and source of allegiance. Evalyn Ursua, Nicole's lawyer, remarked: "I feel pity for Father Reuter, who has been such a respected priest in the country for so long.... I think he is allowing his position to be used as a propaganda ploy to deodorize the accused. And for that reason alone I have lost all respect for him. Obviously his nationality is a paramount factor of his being on that side" (Nicole Information Bureau). Some Filipino feminists criticize Fr. Reuter's rhetoric, deconstructing it in the tradition of Catholicism: "I'm glad Fr. Reuter did not live to see Jesus' time, because if he saw Mary giving birth out of wedlock, he would have called Mary a seductress," Melba explained. Melba, commenting on a *Herald Tribune* article on Fr. Reuter's role in the case as reposted by the Nicole Information Bureau, deconstructs the power of religious hierarchies manifested in their authority to regulate women's bodies, which are often devalued in relation to their functions as signs of men's status (Bayes and Tohidi 46). Melba observes how no one would dare contest a priest and even if they themselves are the abusers, they would never be held accountable because of their esteemed position in the Philippine society. Hence, this deeply embedded respect for priests could also translate into irrational respect for other figures of authority and men in uniforms, for instance: U.S. marines.[7]

Malinche as a Whore, Nicole as a Hero

Sympathy for Smith is pervasive among Filipinos; some of them even having "text brigades" or hotline numbers for supporting him. Nicole, on the other hand, has also found an uncommon ally among Filipino leftists and nationalists. In fact, Nicole's detractors accuse her of riding the hype brought on by noisy nationalist and feminist groups who are only "using her" for their cause. Nicole's critics also blame the nationalists and feminists for supporting Nicole and egging her on, thereby making the issue bigger than it actually is. Nonetheless, whereas Malinche is deemed a traitor by Latin American nationalists, Nicole is seen as a heroine by Filipino nationalists. As this chapter mentioned above, the Nicole Subic rape case is one of the issues on which feminist and nationalist rhetorics have agreed and converged. This is striking because ever since the U.S. occupation of the Philippines, nationalists accused feminist suffragists of taking attention away from the greater issue of independence and the two have not always seen eye to eye. Nationalist communists saw feminist preoccupations with the personal and the domestic as frivolous and petty bourgeois (Santos 2003). Both factions, however, saw U.S. military bases as a common enemy and espoused the belief that the government mandated or condoned prostitution of Filipinas is tantamount to giving away the nation's sovereignty.

Ever since the U.S. bases were voted out of the Philippines in 1991, Washington has aggressively lobbied for the passage of the VFA, which allows the U.S. "continued 'access rights' to the Philippines under the provision of training exercises" (Tadiar 66). According to the Nicole Information Bureau, "the VFA does not set the number of American troops to be designated in the Philippines within a period of time. It may reach hundreds or thousands of American soldiers." In fact, according to Nicole's testimony, "a permanent American camp is now even being built inside the southcom camp in Zamboanga City" (Nicole Information Bureau). The Executive Director of the Coalition of Anti-Trafficking against Women described how "prostitution and rape of Filipino women and children increased once again after the signing of the VFA in 1998." Since 1999, she said, the number of women in prostitution had risen once more to roughly 8,000 in three years' time (Nicole Information Bureau).

The Nicole Information Bureau also points out that the power imbalance is quite large in the VFA. Whereas it is a scandal for a U.S. military marine to be tried by a Philippine justice system for a crime committed on its soil, Filipino soldiers visiting the U.S., on the other hand, will fully be in the "jurisdiction of American court and laws, especially if there are any violations involved." They emphasize that "the only notable privilege given to [Filipino soldiers in the VFA] is the entitlement to shop PX goods at military commissaries" (Nicole Information Bureau).

The Philippine government's open willingness to ratify the VFA is manifested through President Gloria Macapagal Arroyo's eagerness to increase militarization in the Muslim south. Because of her openness to militarization, President Arroyo herself has been called a whore by her detractors. Hence, the Filipino public also sees President Arroyo as another *chingada* for allowing the Philippines to be "penetrated" by U.S. forces once again. The U.S. threatened that it would "pull out" from the training exercises if the Nicole Subic rape case continued. This is compounded by the Philippine government's fear of emasculation and castration since it knows it would not be able to defend itself without the aid from the U.S. A considerable number of Filipinos agree with the view that because of inept, corrupt leadership, the Philippines cannot stand on its own feet. After Nicole recanted her statement in 2009, in fact, protest against the VFA was curtailed or pushed into the backseat because Philippine newspapers and the media immediately followed up with the dispute over Spratley Island, which represents the growing threat of neighboring China on the Philippine sovereignty and territory and demonstrates why the Philippines needs U.S. protection. Suspiciously, when the Subic rape case was just about to receive attention again, newspapers suddenly had the long standing Spratley Island dispute back in the headlines, as if to remind the public of the importance of maintaining the Philippines' connection with the U.S.

Many Filipinos and Filipino Americans were also upset about the rape case and the hypocritical and ungrateful stance it represented, arguing that the U.S. does valuable, magnanimous work in the country and that without it, communism, terrorism, and anarchy would reign in the Philippines. Hence, not only is feminization of the Philippines at work during the trial, but infantilism also plays a role. This is reminiscent of the strategy employed during the U.S. occupation wherein images of U.S. military soldiers were only shown together with Filipino babies or children, illustrating their relationship to their "little brown brothers."

Nicole's mother expressed extreme disappointment at President Arroyo and the government's continuous patronage and defense of the VFA during and after the rape case. When Smith was whisked away from the custody of the Philippines and smuggled to the U.S. embassy, a devastated Nicole remarked: "The Philippine Government will not and cannot protect us. The American government is better, because it protects it citizens, even if they are criminals"

(Nicole Information Bureau). This echoes the betrayal that La Malinche feels towards her native mother who abandoned her and who could not protect her.

The *Chingada* in the Philippine Imaginary

With the Philippines exemplifying the sexualized feminization of Southeast Asia, making it a veritable "multinational brothel," the Nicole Subic rape case that took place in none other than the U.S.'s largest naval and air base in the Pacific. By analyzing both formal as well as informal discourses on this case espoused by the Philippine Government, Filipino Americans, Filipino feminists, nationalists, and the general public, this chapter argues that Octavio Paz' psychoanalytic and postcolonial take on La Malinche as the archetypal *chingada* could apply to Nicole as well. Through investigating how and why Filipinos fail to identify with Nicole, the discussion above explores possible psychoanalytic explanations of the Filipino public's continuing colonial aesthetics and reasoning. For most Filipinos, Filipina *chingadas* who prey on "unsuspecting foreign men" serve to justify why women's bodies should be regulated and policed in order to redeem the tarnished reputation of the country. Articulating the place of the *chingada* in international diplomacy, this chapter takes a close look at the postcolonial trauma of the nation, analyzing rape myths as it coincides with the dark side of Philippine assimilation into the global sphere.

As a subordinate group exposed to multiple oppressors, it is believed that it is up to women of color to maintain the status quo of gender relations not only between themselves and their countrymen, but also between themselves and foreign men. In the particular case of military prostitution in the Philippines, women become an unacknowledged backdrop of everyday life until a woman cries out "rape." Fostering this blindness is a feudal and hierarchical Catholicism that pervades the country. As represented by Fr. Reuter, the clergy often turns a blind eye to rape, taking side of the accused and portraying the woman as the temptress. This echoes the idea of La Malinche as the Mexican Eve, an icon of betrayal that Latin American nationalists blame. Curiously, though, Nicole's image is seen as representative of both feminist and nationalist struggle and her trial puts the U.S.-Philippine VFA to the test. Most struggles of the powerless against superpowers are losing battles. Nonetheless, the public saw the Nicole Subic rape case against the world's superpower as symbolic of the state of the Philippine sovereignty.

Notes

1. We could say that, in today's society, the new sons of La Malinche also take the form of the Amerasian "souvenir" babies that are rejected both by their fathers' and mothers' societies (Diokno in Moon, 34). Over half of these American babies grow up

to serve American pedophiles or are resold to be trafficked, with the half African American-half Filipinos, having no paternal racial superiority, fetching a much lower price.

2. In the highly publicized rape trial in Okinawa, Admiral Richard Macke, commander of U.S. military operations in the Pacific, was forced to take an early retirement after publicly stating that, instead of renting a car on the night of the rape, they should have hired a prostitute. In late 1995, the rape of a twelve-year-old girl in Okinawa by three U.S. marines proved to be the last straw for Okinawans who have long been displeased by U.S. military presence on their island. In March 1996, the three marines were convicted in an Okinawan court (Bevacqua 162). The trial resulted in a loss of "admiration and respect for the U.S. and was replaced by a gradual erosion of public support for U.S.-Japan alliance, and a growing antipathy towards the U.S." (Moon 32). In Korea, the murder and rape of a prostitute in 1991 angered many Koreans who stood in solidarity with the victim and believed that the crime manifested "what the U.S. really thinks of Koreans," inciting calls for the U.S. military to leave (33).

3. Katherine Moon further elaborates on why prostitutes who service GIs are seen as the "lowest of the low" in Korean society: "The fact that they have mingled flesh and blood with foreigners (yangnom) in a society that has been racially and culturally homogenous for thousands of years makes them pariahs, a disgrace to themselves and their people, Korean by birth but no longer Korean in body and spirit" (Moon 34).

4. Filipinos comprise the third largest racial group in the U.S., next to Chinese and Mexicans.

5. All translation of blog and article comments in this article is mine, unless otherwise noted.

6. See "Nicole Tells Her Story" by Jhong De La Cruz, posted on July 6, 2006.

7. Moreover, many Filipinos who respect the court decision to convict Smith do so out of reverence to the one who was presiding over the trial, Judge Pozon. Pozon is presented as a kind father and an authority figure, representative of the male justice system that otherwise mostly reject women's claims of rape.

Bibliography

Adams, Carol. "I Just Raped My Wife, What Are You Going to Do about It Pastor?" *Transforming a Rape Culture*. Eds. Emilie Buchwald, Pamela Fletcher, and Martha Roth. Washington, DC: Milkweed Editions, 2004. 59–86.
Ang See, Teresita. "Like Thieves in the Night." *Subic Rape Case*. 27 Oct. 2008 <http://subicrapecase.wordpress.com/2007/01/11/like-thieves-in-the night/>.
Bacobo, Dean Jorge. "Rina Jimenez David on Patriotic Prostitution and Sovereign Rape." *Philippine Commentary by Dean Jorge Bacobo*. 10 Dec. 2008 <http://philippinecommentary.blogspot.com/2007/03/rina-jimenez-david-on-patriotic_11.html>
_____. "Subic Rape Case: Nicole's Surprised Reaction to Being Outed on Live TV." 10 Dec. 2008 <http://philippinecommentary.blogspot.com/2006/12/subic-rape-case-nicoles surprised.html>.
Bayes, Jane, and Nayereh Tohidi, eds. *Globalization, Gender, and Religion: the Politics of Women's Rights in Catholic and Muslim Contexts*. New York: Palgrave, 2001.
Bevacqua, Maria. *Rape on the Public Agenda: Feminism and the Politics of Sexual Assault*. Lebanon, NH: Northeastern University Press, University Press of New England, 2000.
Bourke, Joanna. *Rape: Sex, Violence, History*. Washington, DC: Shoemaker & Hoard, 2007.
Brown, Anthony. "Myths Contribute to Violence Against Filipina Women." 10 Dec. 2008 <http://www.greenleft.org.au/1994/148/9446>.

Caagusan, Flor, ed. *Halfway Through the Circle: The Lives of 8 Filipino Survivors of Prostitution and Trafficking*. 2nd ed. Quezon City, Philippines: Women's Education, Development, Productivity and Research Organization (WEDPRO), 2000.

"The Composed Gentleman." 30 Mar. 2009 <http://salaswildthoughts.blogspot.com/>.

Contreras, Volt and Tarra Quismundo. "Defense Drift: 'Nicole' Wanted More Sex." *Philippine Daily Inquirer* 16 Jun. 2006. 19 Mar. 2009 <http://www.pinoyspy.com/2006/12/04/subic-rape-case-us-marine-daniel-smith-found-guilty-in-nicole-rape/>

Cypess, Sandra Messinger. *La Malinche in Mexican Literature: From History to Myth*. Austin, TX: University of Texas Press, 1991.

"Deconstructing Nicole." *Philippine Daily Inquirer*. 19 Mar. 2009 <http://opinion.inquirer.net/inquireropinion/editorial/view/20090320-195108/Deconstructing-Nicole>.

Depasubil, William. "Nuns: No to Reversal of 'Nicole' Ruling." *Manila Times*. 25 July 2008. 20 Dec. 2008 <http://www.yehey.com/news/Article.aspx?id=220805>.

Enloe, Cynthia. *Bananas, Beaches and Bases: Making Feminist Sense of International Politics*. Berkeley, CA: University of California Press, 2000.

Feminist Peace Network. 2006. "Analysis of the Subic Bay Rape Verdicts." 10 Dec. 2008 <http://www.feministpeacenetwork.org/2006/12/05/analysis-of-the-subic-bay-rape-verdicts>.

Franco, Jean. "La Malinche: From Gift to Sexual Contract." *Critical Passions: Selected Passions*. Eds. Jean Franco, Mary Louise Pratt, and Kathleen Newman. Durham and London: Duke University Press, 1999. 66–83.

Kritz, Benjamin. *Right Crime Maybe But Wrong Victim*. 20 Mar. 2009 <http://filipinovoices.com/right-crime-maybe-but-wrong-victim>.

Kwiatkowski, Lynn and Lois A. West. "Feminist Struggles for Feminist Nationalism in the Philippines." *Feminist Nationalism*. Ed. Lois A. West. London and New York: Routledge, 1997. 147–69.

Moon, Katherine. *Sex among allies: Military Prostitution in U.S. Korea Relations*. New York: Columbia University Press, 1997.

Mydans, Seth. "Priest Backs Marines, Angering Filipinos." *International Herald Tribune*. 2006. 20 Mar. 2009 <www.nytimes.com/2006/09/03/... /03iht-priest.2679540.html>

"Nicole: I still have faith in God." 2006. *The Philippine Star*. 20 Dec. 2008 <http://www.newsflash.org/2004/02/hl/hl104953.htm>.

Nicole Information Bureau. "The Subic Rape Case in Relation to the Visiting Forces Agreement." 20 Dec. 2008 <http://subicrapecase.wordpress.com/the-subic-rape-case-in-relation-to-the-visiting-forces-agreement/>.

Paz, Octavio. "The Sons of La Malinche." *The Labyrinth of Solitude*. New York: Grove Press, 1961. 65–88

The Pinoy Spy Reporter. "Subic Rape Case: U.S. Marine Daniel Smith Dound Guilty in Nicole Rape." 10 Dec 2008 <http://www.pinoyspy.com/2006/12/04/subic-rape-case-us-marine-daniel-smith-found-guilty-in-nicole-rape/>.

Quismundo, Tarra. "Nicole's mom hits Arroyo for siding with U.S." 25 Dec. 2006. *Philippine Daily Inquirer*. 12 Feb 2010 <http://forum.gov.ph/thread.asp?rootID=144412&catID=9>.

"Rehabilitating the Tarnished Image of the Filipina." 2007. 10 Nov. 2008 <http://robynmagalitrodriguez.blogspot.com/2007/02/rehabilitating-tarnished-image-of.html>.

Rinaldo, Rachel. "Engendering Morality: Women, Islam and the Nation State in Indonesia." International Conference on Religion in Southeast Asian Politics: Resistance, Negotiation and Transcendence. Institute of Southeast Asian Studies, Singapore. 11 Dec. 2008.

Rodriguez, Robyn Magalit. "Arroyo Welcomes Resumption of Balikatan Exercises."

2007. 10 Nov. 2008 <http://robynmagalitrodriguez.blogspot.com/2007/02/arroyo-welcomes-resumption-of-balikatan.html>.
_____. "Rehabilitating the Tarnished Image of the Filipina." 2007. 10 Nov. 2008 <http://robynmagalitrodriguez.blogspot.com/2007/02/rehabilitating-tarnished-image-of.html>.
Santos, Aida F. Personal Interview. 12 Oct. 2003.
_____. *Violence against Women in Times of War and Peace.* Manila: University of the Philippines, University Center for Women's Studies, 2001.
Stein, Laura Guzman. "The Politics of Implementing Women's Rights in Catholic Countries of Latin America." Bayes and Tohidi 127–56.
"Sworn Statement." *Philippine Daily Inquirer.* 19 Mar. 2009 <http://newsinfo.inquirer.net/inquirerheadlines/nation/view/20090318-194694/SWORN-STATEMENT>.
Tadiar, Neferti. *Fantasy Production: Sexual Economies and Other Philippine Consequences for the New World Order.* Quezon City, the Philippines: Ateneo de Manila University, 2004.
Tiongson, Nicanor. "Four Values in Filipino Drama and Film." *Rediscovery.* Eds. Cynthia Nograles Lumbera, and Teresita Maceda. Quezon City, the Philippines: Ateneo de Manila University, 1977. 198–211.
Tolentino, Rolando B. *National/Transnational: Subject Formation and Media on the Philippines.* Quezon City, the Philippines: Ateneo De Manila University Press, 2001.
Vox. "The U.S. Military and Rape." 10 Nov. 2008 <http://voxexmachina.wordpress.com/2008/01/26/the-us-military-and-rape/>

Part IV: (Un)Spoken Subjects, Cross-Cultural Heroines and Media

LOST IN TRANSLATION
American Critical Audience and the Transnational Chinese Swordswoman[1]

Catherine Gomes

Crouching Tiger, Hidden Dragon, Hero, and *House of Flying Daggers* are significant films as they broke American box office records when they were released. However, for many American film critics, it is the figure of the Chinese swordswoman who stands out the most.[2] In *Crouching Tiger*, the Chinese swordswoman takes the form of three characters: the young, talented, and morally confused Jen Yu (Zhang Ziyi), the veteran *Wudan* swordswoman Yu Hsui Lien (Michelle Yeoh), and the elderly and bitter character Jade Fox (Cheng Pei-pei).[3] *Wudan*, as Ang Lee explains, is a form of martial arts that signifies inner strength (2000, 134). In *Hero*, the Chinese swordswoman figure is characterized by the heroic yet vengeful Flying Snow (Maggie Cheung) and the apprentice/servant Moon (Zhang Ziyi). The Chinese swordswoman is represented in *House of Flying Daggers* by Mei (Zhang Ziyi), a member of a rebel group called House of Flying Daggers, who goes undercover as a blind dancer in a brothel.

Surveying film responses provides insight into the codes that the American critical audience utilizes when translating texts that are transnational and in this case, gendered as well. The Chinese swordswoman is transnational as the films she appears in are transnational. Although they are Mandarin Chinese films shot in China and utilize Chinese history to fuel their narratives, *Crouching Tiger, Hero,* and *House of Flying Daggers* are not strictly products of Chinese cinema. Instead they are transnational pan–Asian/Hollywood productions that have become successful international blockbuster films. For example, *Crouching Tiger* boasts producers from China (China Film Co-Production Company, Asia Union Films and United China Vision), the U.S. (Columbia Pictures Film Production Asia, Good Machine International and Japanese-owned Sony Pictures Classics), Hong Kong (EDKO Film International), and Taiwan (Zoom Hunt

International Productions). Director Ang Lee is Taiwanese; one of the film's scriptwriters—James Schamus—is American. The cast is made up of transnational Chinese actors: Chow Yun Fat from Hong Kong, Michelle Yeoh from Malaysia, Zhang Ziyi from mainland China, and Chang Chen being Taiwanese American. Likewise, both *Hero* and *House of Flying Daggers* have transnational Chinese casts even though the production companies are from mainland China and Hong Kong. In *Hero*, Jet Li and Zhang Ziyi are China-born and Tony Leung Chiu-Wai and Maggie Cheung are from Hong Kong. *House of Flying Daggers* casts Zhang Ziyi from China, Andy Lau from Hong Kong, and Takeshi Kaneshiro who is a Taiwanese national—half Taiwanese and half Japanese. Such areas of filmmaking and casting inevitably leave a transnational imprint on the figure of the Chinese swordswoman and the way she is viewed by popular presses and film commentators.

A study such as this indicates the challenges film reviewers face when confronted with the complexities and fluidity of cultural representation brought about by transnational products. This analysis of American popular and critical film reviews of the Chinese swordswoman suggests that she is not read from an Asian centered or an Asian specific lens that understands her as metaphors for the community she represents, but from a fabricated structure that struggles to make sense of the physical strength of the gendered "foreign" woman. This imaginative structure features localized knowledge of Hollywood conventions on strong, beautiful women with a yearning to make allegorical links to contemporary China. Sometimes "forgetting" that the Chinese female fighter is a transnational figure, American critics cling to the familiar in their decoding of the Chinese swordswoman, thus revealing the difficulties they encounter when engaging with texts that present nuanced representations of transnational Chinese communities such as Chinese diaspora in America. These critics, in other words, read the Chinese swordswoman from an Orientalist lens where the Chinese woman is positioned as powerless in the historical East-West relationship. Postcolonial theorist Edward Said notes that Orientalism takes place when the West interprets the East on the West's own terms. In other words, Chinese American culture and people are interpreted within American notions of what it thinks and envisions Chinese America to be. This envisioning is often romanticized where the beauty of Chinese culture, geography, and people are emphasized.

Chinese America is a transnational Chinese community because its members share a common ethnic and cultural heritage. The bi- and multi-cultural identities of diasporic Chinese have been touched by non–Chinese influences. These non–Chinese influences can emerge from the host nation or surface out of modernity and globalization. Aihwah Ong and Donald Nonini, for example, note that ethnic Chinese who have migrated to North America contribute significantly to their host nation in terms of society, culture, economy, and landscape. Their work illustrates the challenges faced by the Chinese in North

America to maintain cultural identity through remembering practice, performance of rituals, among others. The result is a rich, diverse, and evolving entity. Reading the Chinese swordswoman within the context of Chinese America as a transnational community indicates certain attempts to understanding Chinese American issues and concerns. Such sentiments reveal maturity and evolution in racial and ethnic relations in multicultural America. The ethnic Chinese are a populous community in multicultural America and have become one of the most visible ethnic communities in America through birth and recent immigration trends. Many American-born Chinese can trace their ethnic lineage back to the 1840s when numerous émigrés from China entered America as cheap laborers working on railroad construction and in the gold mines. Since then ethnic Chinese from China and elsewhere have been attracted to America for a variety of economic, social, and political reasons.[4] Permanent and temporary migrants from China, together with American-born Chinese, have become integral members of American society, involving themselves in such diverse areas as local community, business, academia, entertainment, and politics.[5] Technology has also assisted in bringing transnational Chinese productions—particularly those from Hong Kong—into American households through the VHS in the 1980s and more recently, through new media outlets such as DVDs, online communication, and broadcast sharing tools.[6]

Through an investigation of the film criticism from the general public as well as scholars on the swordswomen characters from *Crouching Tiger, Hero,* and *House of Flying Daggers*, this chapter suggests that American film reviewers miss the opportunity to utilize the transnational Chinese swordswoman as an effective tool to read Chinese America. Instead of recognizing the links between this transnational Chinese figure and Chinese America, reviewers often choose to decode her within familiar and conventional frameworks of gender and nationality. While such familiar structures are helpful in aiding the general audience to recognize and possibly identify with these physically strong women and therefore raising the popularity and accessibility of these Chinese female fighters, they do not push the boundaries that allow nuanced interpretations of transnationalism.

The Chinese Swordswoman as Narrative Device and Problematic Hero

Some popular reviews read the Chinese swordswoman as an object of romance for narrative and plot purposes. Carla Meyer observes that *House of Flying Daggers* is primarily a romance between Mei and Jin who are "the prettiest pair ever to grace the Tang dynasty" (E(5)). A.O. Scott comments online that while revolutionary intrigue dominates the beginning of the film, the narrative is soon reduced to a love triangle between Mei, Jin, and Leo. Likewise in *Hero*,

Flying Snow's tragic romance with Broken Sword is often the subject of film critics' discussion. The title of Richard Corliss' online review of *Hero*, "In the Mood for Swordplay," alludes to Wong Kar-wai's film of romance, *In the Mood for Love* and signifies his impressions of romantic heroism in this martial arts epic. Maggie Cheung (Flying Snow) and Tony Leung Chiu-Wai (Broken Sword) also played star-crossed lovers in *In the Mood for Love*. In his review, Corliss states that *Hero* is a film that demonstrates "the ways love may find its fulfilment only in death."

One possible reason for film critics to pinpoint romance as a central theme in *House of Flying Daggers* is the film's target audience. It is believed that director Zhang Yimou intended the film to be consumed by Western audiences (Tong 7(B)). For that purpose, he probably inject Western-style narratives of romance into his films to make them palatable to Western audiences. The romances between Mei and Jin and between Flying Snow and Broken Sword have similar Western-style Romeo and Juliet tragically fatal endings. Romance is used as a thematic device. The romance between Mei and Jin, for instance, is navigated by placing self-happiness before self-sacrifice for community. In Chinese-language martial arts films, particularly those with production links to the Hong Kong film industry prior to the 1997 British handover to China, displays of lost love, personal sacrifice, and the maintenance of ideology for community benefit are generic and unyielding themes. Romance in Hong Kong martial arts films was used to support these ideas.

While some critics read the transnational Chinese swordswoman as a narrative device for plot development, others who write for both popular and scholarly publications recognize her as a much more complex character. Considering her a problematic hero due to her anti-heroic behavior many critics propose that she complicates and challenges the common understanding of female heroism and feminism within Western frameworks. Almost exclusively referring to *Crouching Tiger*, critics find Jen Yu and Jade Fox particularly fascinating because they challenge patriarchal power and authority. Stephanie Zacharek observes that Jen Yu is "never completely readable;" her character "strings" audiences along; and this ambiguity is "one of the movie's pleasures." This questioning of Jen Yu as a problematic hero is echoed by Stephen Short who wonders if Jen Yu is a "fearless heroine or ferocious killer" (166). While film commentators and reviewers raise the question of Jen Yu's heroic qualities, they tend to agree that she is a female hero even though a problematic one. Writing about Jade Fox, film commentators note she is perhaps the most fascinating yet problematic female character in the film as she is both a hero and a femme fatale. Gary Morris states: "[w]ith her hefty figure, ravaged face, and palpable desperation as she feels Jen Yu slipping away from her grasp," Jade Fox gives *Crouching Tiger* "an unexpected poignancy and power." On the other hand, Matthew Levie, suggests that Jade Fox is dangerous because her ambition is subversive. Jade Fox transgresses the feminine-masculine divide with her ambition to learn the secret manual of *Wudan*, the martial arts text that is denied access to women in the film.

Jade Fox's subversion makes her problematic and a femme fatale. After all, the femme fatale's strength and power come from questioning and challenging the patriarchal establishment. Often, the femme fatale is similar to the female hero in terms of their ambition, strength, and cunning. The difference between the femme fatale and the female hero is the femme fatale's lack of adherence to the values of the dominant culture and society of which she is a part. Often this culture and society is shaped by masculine values. The femme fatale thus questions and challenges the dominant culture and society by hurting the male hero through the process of undermining his power and authority rather than supporting him as the female hero would do (Fries 71–72).

It is useful to view Jen Yu and Jade Fox through a lens that highlights the dominant ideologies of powerful women present in Hollywood films. Hollywood's physically strong women are allegories for issues such as feminism and the difficult state of gender relations in contemporary society (Inness 160–76; Tasker 3–25; Buttsworth 185–99; Crosby 153–78). The Hollywood heroine thus becomes representative of the ambivalent position women have in Western society. Film reviewers' readings of strong female characters in films such as *Crouching Tiger*, for instance, are linked to their knowledge of strong women in Hollywood. Hollywood has iconized the warrior woman characters from the 1980s to the 2000s, for example: Alien-fighting Ripley (Sigourney Weaver), *Terminator: Judgment Day*'s Sarah Connor (Linda Hamilton), Xena (Lucy Lawless), Buffy (Sarah Michelle Gellar), Lara Croft (Angelina Jolie), and *The Powerpuff Girls*' Blossom (Cathy Cavadini), Bubbles (Tara Strong), and Buttercup (Elizabeth Daily). These characters have ignited varied discussions among American film critics and scholars in film studies and gender studies on their cultural representation. On one level, these characters are independent and strong, hence allowing for feminist readings. On another level, however, these individuals are also portrayed as vulnerable, requiring the assistance of men for emotional and physical support.

The Chinese swordswoman is neither American nor Chinese but transnational. Ken-fang Lee argues convincingly that the Chinese swordswomen Jen Yu and Jade Fox are allegories for the changing gender dynamics within the global transnational Chinese community (281–95). Reading Jen Yu and Jade Fox as femme fatales, Lee suggests that their behaviour questions and challenges patriarchal notions of dominance and power by their independence and by following their ambitions. Jade Fox, for example, is a powerful woman because she "has her own will and wants to enjoy her freedom" (Ken-fang Lee 290). Lee's readings of power through resistance indicate the inevitable changing of gender dynamics in transnational Chinese communities. Rather than being a scorned woman, Jade Fox becomes a character that "empowers and inspires women" (Ken-fang Lee 290).

Transnational Chinese Films

The Chinese film industry no longer produces solely Chinese productions but also transnational films in collaboration with other Asian cinemas and Hollywood. These transnational collaborations affect all aspects of financial and creative input into these films. For example, while *Crouching Tiger* was shot in China, it was produced by production companies in Hollywood, China, and Japan. The film was edited in both China and the United States; the orchestra music was recorded and produced in Shanghai (Sunshine 144). Likewise, its crew is also transnational: Director Any Lee is Taiwanese-born and Hollywood-based; Action Choreographer Yuen Woo-ping is from Hong Kong and has worked on Hollywood blockbusters including *The Matrix*; Cinematographer Peter Pau is from Hong Kong and has worked extensively with Hong Kong filmmakers John Woo and Tsui Hark; American-born Chinese singer CoCo Lee sings the title song "A Love Before Time" composed by Chinese national Tan Dun and written by Jorge Calandrelli and James Schamus (Sunshine 144). Ang Lee also brought his long-time film collaborator James Schamus, an American who has worked with him as screenwriter for many of his previous productions (Schamus 130).[7] While *Crouching Tiger* may well be one of the largest joint productions in the history of cinema, *Hero* is also significant for its transnational connections. For example, American distributor Miramax screened the film in the U.S., the United Kingdom, Africa, and Australia while Alliance Atlantis Communications distributed the film in Canada. The film has an international production and editing crew who originally are from China, Hong Kong, America, and Australia; the cast of *Hero* was made up of diaspora Chinese who have appeared in films outside China.[8]

Similarly, *House of Flying Daggers* is a film that is not solely a product of China. Instead, it is a made-in-China film where the production companies are from China (Beijing New Film Picture Company and Zhang Yimou Studios) and Hong Kong (Elite Group Enterprises), the film was distributed globally by major Hollywood studios such as United International Pictures and Warner Brothers as well as by Japan's Sony Pictures Classics. In addition, the costumes in *House of Flying Daggers* were designed by Japanese designer Wada Emi who has worked on Hong Kong martial arts swordplay productions, *Bride With White Hair* and *The Storm Riders* ("Emi Wada"). The composer, Shigeru Umebayashi, is also Japanese ("Shigeru Umebayashi"). Like Wada, he has worked on non–Japanese productions such as Hong Kong auteur Wong Kar-wai's *2046*. Like *Hero* and *Crouching Tiger*, the cast members of *House of Flying Daggers* are eclectically international.

A major reason that contributes to these films' popularity outside of China is that they are made within the paradigm of Hollywood blockbusters—visually spectacular big-budget films. *Crouching Tiger*, for example, has a budget of $15 million while *Hero* and *House of Flying Daggers* costS$31 million and $20 million respectively (Leung 42; Fuchs). While *House of Flying Daggers* may not have done well in American cinemas ($11 million), the high budgets for *Crouching Tiger* and *Hero* paid off significantly, as *Crouching Tiger* earned $150 million in total U.S. box office and video takings while *Hero* earned $55.6 million from the U.S. box office and video rentals. *Crouching Tiger* was in the top ten in American cinemas for fifteen weeks. *Hero* was likewise successful, being the first Chinese language film to hold the number one position in American theatres. It held this position for the first two weeks after its release in the United States. *House of Flying Daggers* was the least successful of the three films with its highest ranking at the box office being fifteenth ("Box Office and Rental History for *Crouching Tiger, Hidden Dragon*"; "Box Office and Rental History for *Hero*"; "Box Office and Rental History for *House of Flying Daggers*").

The makers of *Crouching Tiger*, *Hero*, and *House of Flying Daggers* readily admit that they had Western audiences in mind when they made these films (Schamus 130). However, while *Crouching Tiger*'s filmmakers acknowledge that narrative was a fundamental tool that attracted audiences, Zhang Yimou's credibility and reputation in the Europe, America, and Australia is based on his visually enticing cinematography. *Judou* and *Raise the Red Lantern*, for example, are films that put Zhang Yimou on the international cinematic map as producing visually beautiful films. Hence when *Hero* and *House of Flying Daggers* were released, Western "art house" audiences were expecting the visual feasts they had grown used to in Zhang Yimou's earlier films. Moreover, general audiences were also equally anticipating consuming *Hero* and *House of Flying Daggers* in the theatres because of their experience with *Crouching Tiger* (Chan 57).

The Chinese swordswoman is obviously a transnational product due to her pan–Asian and American (Hollywood) influences. However, instead of decoding her from a complex transnational Chinese framework that implicates Chinese America, many American viewers and film critics only recognize her from Hollywood-tinted lenses, particularly commenting on her role as Western-derived narrative device or problematic heroine within a Hollywood ideological gender-society framework. How do American critics analyze (or fail to analyze) the actresses who play these swordswomen? What are the implications of these reviews on Chinese America? To answer these questions it is necessary to look at two of the most noted Chinese swordswoman actresses in the American popular press: Zhang Ziyi and Maggie Cheung.

Sexualizing the Chinese Actresses: Zhang Ziyi and Maggie Cheung

American film reviews frequently sexualize the Chinese swordswoman through the actresses who play her, often emphasizing glamour, beauty, and sensuality. Discussions on the glamorous Chinese actress—together with discussions on her as a problematic heroine — rely on existing Hollywood frameworks. Charles Taylor, for example, describes Maggie Cheung's performance in *Hero* as comparable with the legendary stars of the silent film era. He observes that Cheung exudes "a poetry and mystery that's Garboesque" as even "her eyes are capable of transmitting hauteur, disdain, wounded eroticism and unutterable sadness." Similarly, Manohla Dargis finds Zhang Ziyi's performance in *House of Daggers* to be reminiscent of classical Hollywood glamour (1(2)). Dargis states: "There are images of Ms. Zhang in *Flying Daggers* ... [w]ith her alabaster skin and dark pooling eyes, her body adorned in rich brocades, and bathing alfresco while discreetly veiled by green woodland; Ms. Zhang doesn't just look bewitchingly lovely; she looks like an MGM pinup (1(2))."[9]

American reviewers draw parallels between the films and Hollywood. An anonymous article published by the *UPI NewsTrack* entitled "Chinese Filmmakers Embrace Glamour" claims that *Hero* and *House of Flying Daggers* are evidence of a return to classical Hollywood glamour. This classical Hollywood glamour, according to Dargis, ceased with the end of the studio system in the 1950s and the death of glamorous film actress Marilyn Monroe in 1962. The *UPI NewsTrack* article observes that the "current crop of Chinese filmmakers has gone back 60 years to create a generation of Classical Hollywood-style glamour films." Dargis also observes that "[t]he era of lustrous screen sirens lives on, thousands of miles from Hollywood" (1(2)). Dargis states:

> These days no one does glamour better than Chinese filmmakers. In American film, where violence invariably trumps sex, glamour tends to surface in period stories like *L.A. Confidential*, where the director Curtis Hanson explored the distance between gleaming false fronts and hard-boiled reality. David Lynch wields glamour to similar if more disturbing effect in films like *Mulholland Drive*, while Steven Soderbergh likes to put an old-studio polish on bagatelles like *Ocean's Twelve*. Meanwhile, in the major Chinese cinemas — those of China, Hong Kong and, to an extent, Taiwan — glamour is serious business. Much as it was in Classical Hollywood, glamour in contemporary Chinese film is a device, a disguise and a luminous end in itself [1(2)].

Dargis explains that her understanding of Hollywood glamour is based on glamour photography during the classical Hollywood period. She observes that glamour photographers "created the shimmering images that sold the stars and their movies to the public" at the time (1(2)). Dargis clarifies that it was through glamour photography that Hollywood film stars were immortalized as icons of glamour. Dargis observes that the rise of the Chinese screen goddess is due to Chinese filmmakers being able to recreate the Hollywood glamour of the 1930s and 1940s (1(2)). However, other cross-cultural film critics who describe Maggie Cheung and Zhang Ziyi as embodiments of classical Hollywood glamour do so by eroticizing these Chinese actresses.

While some American critics choose to look at glamour, others concentrate on the sensuality and beauty of the actresses — particular linking physical power with sexuality. For example, Jami Bernard of *New York Daily News* and James Berardinelli of *Reelviews* both write that Zhang Ziyi is as seductive as she is physically powerful. Bernard observes that although Zhang Ziyi as Mei in *House of Flying Daggers* is "meltingly beautiful," she is also "quick on her feet" and "downright ambidextrous." Bernard implies that Mei's beauty hides her martial arts skills, an ability that mystifies and clouds the judgment of the male authorities. Bernard argues that Mei's ambidextrousness mirrors that of Zhang Ziyi herself, whose allure lies in her "seeming delicacy" hiding "a roundhouse kick that could knock out a mule." Berardinelli notes that Zhang Ziyi is "more than just a pretty face" as she "captures the arrogance and vulnerability of Mei perfectly." Zhang Ziyi, Berardinelli explains, can be "sexy and seductive one moment" but "deadly the next." Claudia Puig points out that swordplay heightens Zhang Ziyi's sexuality. She observes that while Zhang Ziyi may have played a "strong-willed and courageous young warrior" in *Crouching Tiger*, she has "an even more powerful and luminous presence" in *House of Flying Daggers*, in which she easily shifts from "bewitching and elaborate dance" to "masterful sword fighting."

While these critics do not explore Zhang Ziyi's sexuality beyond the obvious, others provide more nuanced and informed readings linking the Chinese swordswoman to China. Such readings choose to examine Zhang Ziyi's sexuality as a metaphor of the changing culture in contemporary China.[10] Writing for *The New York Times*, Jean Tong observes that *House of Flying Daggers* "may be the first large scale Chinese movie to assert a frank, liberated approach to sex" (7(B)). She theorizes that while the film's sexual scenes, such as a drunken Jin (Takeshi Kaneshiro) tearing Mei's (Zhang Ziyi) dress in the brothel, may be playful and innocuous by Western standards; yet they reflect the sexual revolution among young Chinese (7(B)). Chinese sociologist Xiaozheng Zhou notes that Chinese youths between the ages of fourteen and twenty are now having their first sexual experience at the age of 17.4 years, while those between twenty-one and thirty were doing so at the age of 21.9 years (10(Asia)). Zhou states that the sexual revolution amongst Chinese youths is due to the "opening up of Chinese society and early arrival of puberty in the young" (10(Asia)). Wendy Larson observes that sexuality in Chinese-language cinema is not as playful as it is in Western cinema. Rather, sexuality is "an expression of revolutionary passion, or it's linked to loyalty to your tradition or your martial arts group" (qtd. in Tong 7(B)).

American film reviews and criticism on Zhang Ziyi and Maggie Cheung as illuminating a glamorous Hollywood past or as objects that blend physical power with beauty and sensuality have multiple implications. Such writing applies Hollywood structures to interpreting the actresses who play Chinese swordswomen. Like their film characters, these actors have transnational cultural locations. These reviews also reveal that both the actresses and the films are placed in China-centered rather than transnational Chinese position. In other words, reviewers acknowledge only the Mainland Chinese link rather than the transnational Chinese dimension which extends beyond the geographical borderlines of China to Hong Kong and Chinese diasporic communities in America. Hong Kong cinema, after all, has a visible tradition of featuring physically strong and powerful female figures.

Female Warriors and Transnational Community

The transnational Chinese woman is connected to the figure of the female fighter in Hong Kong cinema that has a symbolic relationship with its people. Cinema captures the essence of the people in Hong Kong and the female fighter plays an important role in these productions that can be traced back to the 1920s. In the 1960s and 1970s the female fighter represented stability as Hong Kong faced cultural change; often she was portrayed as the upholder of tradition in a society in flux due to industrial growth. In the 1980s and 1990s, the female fighter was an ambivalent character who signified stability as well as confusion. She connotated stability because she was a familiar figure in Hong Kong cinema; she was also adopting unusual characteristics such as gender confusion. Such confusion became a signifier for people's fear of uncertainty, a result of the prospect of being handed over from British capitalist rule to communist Chinese government.

One of the first Chinese films featuring a female fighter was released in 1925. *Heroine Feifei* was a Shanghai-made film that displayed a female protagonist engaged in martial artistry (Arons 27; Ho 40). *Heroine Feifei* was made by Runje Shaw, one of the founders of Tianyi Film Company which later became the Shaw Brothers Studio, the largest production company of Hong Kong films. Hong Kong films featuring strong female figures, particularly female knights-errant such as *The Swordswoman of Huangjiang*, were soon to follow. It was between the 1920s and the 1930s, argues Zhen Zhang, that martial arts films featuring the swordswoman manifested "the cultural ambivalence toward 'science' and 'democracy' propagated by the May Fourth ideology," capturing "the popular imagination of the time." The "power" of the swordswoman, Zhang suggests, became a signifier of this cultural ambivalence in the post–May Fourth Movement.[11] Female protagonists were thus integral to the films and functioned as emblems of wider socio-cultural dynamics.

Such a tradition continues and evolves in the 1960s when female figures played important roles in the swordplay Hong Kong films. Although swordswomen are warriors, they are portrayed either as femme fatales or as subordinate and secondary to men, particularly in the 1960s and early 1970s (Koo 30–32). The femme fatales challenged men and patriarchal control (Koo 30–32). These women, who were demonized in 1960s films such as *One-Armed Swordsman* and *The Magic Snowflake Sword*, were eventually killed. The ideal swordswomen in swordplay films in this era were aware that the harmony of society could only be maintained through their subordination to the Chinese patriarchy (Koo 30–32). These women, like those in *The Deaf Mute Heroine*, were portrayed as heroic through sacrifice. They were often rewarded with marriage to the heroic male character after attempting to sacrifice their own lives for the greater good of the hero or their village (Koo 32).

This theme of female subordination is evident in films by King Hu, the legendary Hong Kong filmmaker who championed and promoted strong and skillful swordswomen protagonists. The first film to feature the swordswoman in a leading role was *Come Drink with Me* (Logan 153–54). In this film, the protagonist, Golden Swallow, was played by Cheng Pei-pei in her first leading film role.[11] Golden Swallow is an emissary, soldier, and daughter of the local governor. She has arrived in a village to negotiate her kidnapped brother's release from a group of bandits led by Jade Faced Tiger (Hung Lieh-chen). While Golden Swallow's exceptional skill is displayed in a tense scene at an inn and a spectacular fight sequence at the bandit's headquarters, the character's strength is undermined by the presence of the masculine hero, Drunken Knight (Yueh Hua). Drunken Knight is not only her guardian angel but he is also the heroic figure in the second half of the film. Drunken Knight takes over the role of protagonist in *Come Drink with Me* when Golden Swallow is weakened and wounded after her battle with the bandits at the temple. Throughout this part of the film, she is nursed back to health by Drunken Knight, acts as a foil to his skill, and is repeatedly saved by him. In the final battle with the bandits and evil Abbot Liao Kung (Yang Chih-Ching), it is Drunken Knight who rescues a nearly defeated Golden Swallow because he is the only person who is skillful enough to defeat Liao Kung.[12] The character of Golden Swallow thus is portrayed with ambivalence and inconsistence. Such an image exposes the patriarchal politics of Confucian society where the male is the dominant figure in the community.

Poshek Fu provides an explanation for the ambivalent way the swordswoman was portrayed in the Hong Kong films in the 1960s. He states that at the time Hong Kong was facing upheavals due to the economic boom. The economic boom created a high demand for labor, which could only be met by youths and women leaving the domestic space and entering the labor market. Women thus became independent because they were no longer financially dependent on their husbands or fathers. By doing so they slowly broke away from the Confucian gender hierarchy. Because the swordplay films are generally analogical references to real world concerns, the portrayal of swordswomen, particularly in the 1960s and early 1970s swordplay films, most likely reflected the transformations of Hong Kong society (Fu 71–89). Fu's opinion echoes the view of David Harvey, a postmodern theorist, who, drawing on work by Georg Simmel, argues that a society draws on tradition (religion, cultural ideology) in order to provide stability in an unstable situation created by economic change due to modernity (171).

The most significant swordplay film produced in the 1960s was *The Black Rose*; it set the tone for the contemporary Chinese swordswoman. *The Black Rose* prompted a plethora of films featuring female Robin Hood figures within the format of Hollywood's "James Bond" films. These films came to be commonly known as "Jane Bond" films. Hong Kong-based film critic Sam Ho notes that "nowhere in the history of Chinese film, and arguably world cinema, are fighting women more dominant than in the Jane Bond films of Hong Kong" (40). The dominance of these fighting women goes beyond their ability to win the battles or to outwit their enemies. Rather, films like *The Black Rose* are allegorical discussions of globalization and modernity in Hong Kong society.

The Black Rose was one of the first films within the martial arts tradition to marry "Cantonese film's acrobatic swordswoman" with the stoic or subdued and somber police inspector (Ho 40). In other words, there is a blending of both chivalric swordplay and contemporary kung fu traditions in the film. *The Black Rose* followed the "James Bond" format in employing spectacular displays of technology in the form of everyday gadgets—lipstick guns, death-ray watches, ultra-violet shades—as well as the special effects that enabled them to work (Ho 43). *The Black Rose* and its other Jane Bond successors of the 1960s also portrayed their protagonists as "modern" women who not only enjoyed Go-Go dancing and lived in opulent excess, but also possessed "good" traditional Chinese family values (Ho 42–45).

Ideologically, the Jane Bonds reflected the financial independence Hong Kong women were encountering as they entered the workforce during the colony's economic boom (Fu 74). *The Black Rose*'s female protagonists, played by Josephine Siao and Chen Po-chu, for example, represented the "new" Hong Kong woman (Ho 40–46). These actors were cast in similar roles, as the young and beautiful Jane Bond spies whose opulent and decadent lifestyles intertwined with their ability to uphold justice.[13] These roles were important because they became allegories not only of Hong Kong women but also of Hong Kong society as a whole, blending modernity with traditional Chinese culture. Ho observes that these characters emphasized family values, as "the fighting woman must eventually return to her rightful position in the family" (Ho 45). Like the swordplay heroine, the Jane Bond character also became a site of tension between modernity and cultural tradition.

In his research on the Jane Bond phenomenon, Ho describes Hong Kong as a metaphor for Chinese modernity. He speculates that, in turn, the Jane Bond films reflected the colony's rapidly emerging modernity (Ho 45). This was shown in the technological gadgets the female protagonists used and the glamorous lifestyles they led. In 1992, filmmaker Jeffrey Lau made *The Black Rose* contemporary in the parody sequel *92 Legendary La Rose Noire*. The significance of this sequel was that it was a pastiche of Hong Kong's historical and commercial modernity in the 1960s. This was alluded to through the references to *The Black Rose* seen on the television screen in the film. However, the key to understanding the rationale behind Jane Bond becoming a site for cultural discussion on modernity lies in Gayle Rubin's speculation that women are mobile. In her essay "The Traffic in Women: Notes on the 'Political Economy' of Sex," Rubin puts forth the argument that women as objects of exchange are allowed by the patriarchy to be more flexible and circulate more freely (157–210). She explains that as units of exchange in marriage, women have traditionally been allowed by the patriarchy to circulate in established groups such as families, clans, communities, nations, and races. Postmodernity and feminism, however, have reduced the significance of patriarchal institutions such as marriage and given women the opportunity to enhance their mobility by venturing beyond home. Precisely because of her ability to be mobile, Jane Bond is able to provide a popular and believable site for discussion on the changing countenance of Hong Kong society's relationship with modernity. This "mobility" provided Jane Bond with the capability to navigate through these changes. Since the Chinese female fighter, through the swordswoman, was already a familiar and prominent character in Hong Kong cinema, Jane Bond became a significant cultural icon of Hong Kong's encounter with modernity.

Come Drink with Me and *The Black Rose* not only reflected Hong Kong's modernity but also set the standards for future martial arts films featuring female fighters. Hong Kong cinema featuring female fighters in the 1980s was comprised of contemporary kung fu films that most notably featured women as law enforcement officers (Teo 102). In the 1980s, films such as *Yes Madam* and *The Inspector Wears Skirts* saw intrepid female fighters battling corruption and drug lords.[14] These policewomen's quest for justice was reflective of the real concerns that Hong Kong faced during this period, as corruption was rife in the Hong Kong police force and the triads were powerful criminal organizations, ironically with links to the local film industry (Passmore). Such films later influenced television programs such as *Armed Reaction*, a Hong Kong Television Broadcasts Limited production which traced the lives of female police officers in Hong Kong.

Modernity is also discussed in female fighter films of the 1990s. This period was more inclined towards spy films on a global scale. Of particular interest were films such as *Project S* whose plot involved terrorist activities and *Black Cat*, an Asian version of Luc Besson's *Nikita* (Logan 171). The spy films can be considered successors of the 1960s Jane Bond films with a more sophisticated commentary on Hong Kong's modernity. These films not only used stylish gadgets, but they were also set in overseas locations similar to Jackie Chan and John Woo films. Hence these films became commentaries on Hong Kong as a transnational space.

In the 1980s and early 1990s, films featuring the swordswoman once again became prominent. The main allegorical theme of the swordplay revival was concerned with the 1997 handover of Hong Kong to China. Films such as *Moon Warriors, New Dragon Gate Inn, Bride with White Hair,* and *Wing Chun* featured strong, independent swordswomen who were equally or more skilled than their male contemporaries. However, these female fighters were not portrayed as independent. Instead, they sought the approval of their male contemporaries through love. In *Moon Warriors*, swordswomen Hsien (Maggie Cheung) and Yuet (Anita Mui) are rivals because they are both in love with the male hero Fei (Andy Lau). In *New Dragon Gate Inn*, the rebel swordswoman Yao Mo-yan (Brigitte Lin) drowns her sorrows in alcohol when her lover Chow Wai-on (Tony Ka-Fai Leung) marries the flirtatious inn owner Jade King (Maggie Cheung). In *Bride with White Hair*, assassin Lian Nichang (Brigitte Lin) turns violent, revengeful, and emotionally self-destructive when she learns that her lover Zhou Yihang (Leslie Cheung) betrayed her trust. Likewise in *Wing Chun*, heroine Yim Wing-chun (Michelle Yeoh) pines for her lost love Leung Pok-to (Donnie Yuen). While these fighting females were portrayed as physically strong, they were also conventionalized as feminine (Arons 28). The generic concept of Hong Kong cinema's female fighter during this period was double-edged as she was caught in the "Deadly China Doll Syndrome," where the Hong Kong female fighter is "powerful but delicate" (Hunt 120). A possible explanation for this ambivalence can be derived from Rey Chow's theorization that women in Chinese society are often located as upholders of tradition (86). As Hong Kong experienced great angst and fear during the 1997 handover due to the anticipation of the greatest political, social, and cultural change, the swordswoman provides a form of stability.

In his groundbreaking work, prolific filmmaker Tsui Hark created a new form of swordswoman that represented the confusion of an impending 1997 handover: the gender-bending swordswoman. The transgendered swordswoman was epitomized by Tsui Hark's muse at the time, Taiwanese-born and Hong Kong-based actress Brigitte Lin. Lin's most famous portrayal of the transgendered swordswoman is Asia the Invincible in Tsui Hark's *East is Red* (1992). Asia the Invincible was not only sexually and morally ambivalent, but she is also a highly skilled, yet extremely violent, swordswoman. It was this sexual and moral ambivalence that Hong Kong people could relate to as an allegory of their own ambivalence about "returning" to China (Bordwell 10). While China was the ancestral home of Hong Kong, it now has a communist government, thus an antithesis of Hong Kong. Communism also contradicted the economic policies of Hong Kong, which for one hundred and fifty years had been governed by the capitalist British (Fu 71–6).

While the analysis of American film reviews of the Chinese swordswoman seem dire in their recognition of transnational themes focusing on Chinese America, hope springs in the ever growing number of popular press critics who posses informed and scholarly knowledge of cinemas other than Hollywood. Leading international expert in film studies David Bordwell is an exemplary film commentator who writes for scholarly publications as well as for the general audience. Bordwell writes prolifically about Chinese-language cinema, particularly

Hong Kong cinema. It is with expectation and anticipation that a more complex framework incorporating the various tenets connected to transnational Chinese productions will be constructed. Doing so will provide more nuanced observations on transnational communities such as Chinese America when decoding multifaceted pan–Asian/Hollywood films.

Notes

1. Parts of this chapter were previously published as "'The Era of Lusteous Screen Sirens Lives on, Thousands of Miles from Hollywood': The Cross-Cultural Reception of Chinese Martial Arts Cinema's Sword Wielding Actresses" in *Reception: Texts, Readers, Audiences, History* 1 (Fall 2008): 82–86. They are reprinted here with permission.
2. Some of these film critics are members of popular venues such as *The New York Times* and *The San Francisco Chronicle* while others wrote for specialist cinema forums such as *Salon.Com* and *Bright Lights Film Journal*.
3. In the Mandarin version of *Crouching Tiger*, Zhang Ziyi's character is called Jiao Long while in the English-dubbed version of the film, her character is known as Jen Yu.
4. The U.S. has a history of engaging in different ways with Chinese cultures and ethnic Chinese. While American encounters with Chinese culture and people have increased ever since China opened its doors to the global community with much gusto since the 1990s, their acquaintance with Chinese culture is rooted far earlier in the twentieth century through U.S. involvement in economic, political, militaristic, and tourist ventures in other parts of Asia and elsewhere.
5. Temporary migrants are those who enter a country, amongst other things, for work or study.
6. Hong Kong films have long been considered transnational productions. For example, its martial arts genre borrows heavily from early Hollywood silent cinema and from Japanese postwar samurai films.
7. Chinese novelist Wang Du Lu wrote socialist realist dramas and martial arts novels. *Crouching Tiger* is based on the fourth novel in his martial arts pentalogy *Crane/Iron/He-Tie Pentalogy* (Schamus 130).
8. *In the Mood for Love* won Leung the best actor award at the 2000 International Film Festival at Cannes. Cheung is also well known for doing projects outside Hong Kong. She appears as herself in French director Olivier Assayas' French-English film *Irma Vep* and as a Chinese doctor in the 1999 French film *Augustin: King of Kung Fu*. Later she appeared in another critically acclaimed Assayas film entitled *Clean* where she plays a drug addict recovering from addiction. Her role won her the best actress award at Cannes in 2004.
9. Metro-Goldwyn-Meyer (MGM) is a major Hollywood studio that was well known as a producer of glamorous stars during the classical Hollywood period.
10. The legacy of the powerful Chinese woman warrior as signifier of cultural uncertainty and ambivalence is precisely what was to follow in later films in the martial arts genre.
11. Cheng Pei-pei also stars in other notable martial arts films such as *Golden Swallow/Hsia Yu-yen* and *The Lady Hermit/Zhong Kui Niang Zi*, reprising her warrior role in *Crouching Tiger* as the villainous Jade Fox.
12. David Bordwell notes a similar theme in a Zhang Che's film *Golden Swallow* (25). While this film featured Cheng again in the lead role, the narrative featured the tragic hero Silver Roc rather than its eponymous heroine.

13. Other Jane Bond films include *Diamond Robbery/Zhuanshi Da Jien* and *Lady Bond/ Nü Shashou* (*The Lady Professional*). For a more comprehensive list, see Ho 45.

14. One of the lead actresses in *Yes Madam* was Caucasian actress and martial arts expert Cynthia Rothrock. Hong Kong martial arts cinema, especially in the 1980s, featured Caucasian actresses such as Cynthia Rothrock and Sophia Crawford in warrior women roles (Tasker 24–26).

Bibliography

Armed Reaction/Tor Cheung See Jei. Television Broadcasts Ltd., 1998.
Arons, Wendy. "If Her Stunning Beauty Doesn't Bring You to Your Knees, Her Deadly Drop Kick Will: Violent Women in the Hong Kong Kung Fu Film." *Reel Knockouts: Violent Women in the Movies*. Eds. Martha McCaughey and Neal King. Austin, TX: University Of Texas Press, 2001. 27–51.
Assayas, Olivier, dir. *Irma Vep*. Zeitgeist Films, 1996.
Berardinelli, James. "*House of Flying Daggers*." *Reelviews*. 2004. 15 December 2009 <http://www.reelviews.net/movies/h/house_flying.html>.
Bernard, Jami. "Daggers Make a Great Stab at 'Greatness.'" *New York Daily News*. 3 December 2004. 13 December 2009 <http://www.nydailynews.com/archives/entertainment/2004/12/03/2004-12-03__daggers__makes_a_stab_at_gr.html>.
Besson, Luc, dir. *Nikita/La Femme Nikita*. Roadshow Entertainment, 1990.
Bordwell, David. *Planet Hong Kong: Popular Cinema and the Art of Entertainment*. Cambridge, MA: Harvard University Press, 2000.
"Box Office and Rental History for *Crouching Tiger, Hidden Dragon*." *Rotten Tomatoes*. 15 December 2009 <http://www.rottentomatoes.com/m/crouching_tiger_hidden_dragon/numbers.php>.
"Box Office and Rental History for *Hero*." *Rotten Tomatoes*. 15 December 2009 <http://www.rottentomatoes.com/m/hero/numbers.php>.
"Box Office and Rental History for *House of Flying Daggers*." Rotten Tomatoes. 15 December 2009 <http://www.rottentomatoes.com/m/house_of_flying_daggers/numbers.php>.
Buttsworth, Sara. "'Bite Me': Buffy and the Penetration of the Gendered Warrior-Hero." *Continuum: Journal of Media and Cultural Studies* 16.2 (2002): 185–99.
Chan, Evans. "Zhang Yimou's *Hero*: The Temptations of Fascism." *Film International* 2.2 (2004): 14–23.
Chan, Felicia. "*Crouching Tiger, Hidden Dragon*: Cultural Migrancy and Translatability." *Chinese Films in Focus: 25 New Takes*. Ed. Chris Berry. London: British Film Institute Publishing, 2004. 56–64.
Chan, Jackie, dir. *The Inspector Wears Skirts/Ba Wong Fa*. Pony Canyon, 1988.
Chen, Lipin, dir. *The Magic Snowflake Sword/Xuehua Shenjian*. Magic Crane, 1964.
"Chinese Having Sex at a Young Age." *The Straits Times* 4 July 2005: 10 (Asia).
Chow, Rey. *Women and Chinese Modernity: The Politics of Reading between West and East*. Minnesota, MN: University of Minnesota Press, 1991.
"Company Credits for *Wo Hu Cang Long*." *IMDB: The Internet Movie Database*. 15 December 2009 <http://www.imdb.com/title/tt0190332/>.
"Company Credits for *Ying Xiong*." *IMDB: The Internet Movie Database*. 15 December 2009 <http://www.imdb.com/title/tt0299977/companycredits/>.
Corliss, Richard. "In the Mood for Swordplay." *Time*. 23 December 2002. 15 December 2009 <http://www.time.com/time/magazine/article/0,9171,400044,00.html>.

_____. "Martial Masterpiece." Crouching Tiger, Hidden Dragon: *Portrait of the Ang Lee Film*. Ed. Linda Sunshine. New York: Newmarket Press, 2000. 8–13.
Crosby, Sarah. "The Cruellest Season: Female Heroes Snapped into Sacrificial Heroines." *Action Chicks: New Images of Tough Women in Popular Culture*. Ed. Sherrie A. Inness. New York: Palgrave Macmillan. 2004. 153–78.
Dargis, Manohla. "Glamour's New Orientation: The Era of Lustrous Screen Sirens Lives on Thousands of Miles from Hollywood." *The New York Times* 5 December 2005: 1(2).
"Emi Wada." *IMDB: The Internet Movie Database*. 15 December 2009 <http://www.imdb.com/name/nm0905253/>.
"*Flying Daggers* Tops Chinese 2004 Box Office." *China Daily*. 23 December 2004. 15 December 2009 <http://www.chinadaily.com.cn/english/doc/2004-12/23/content_402756.htm>.
Fontaine, Anne, dir. *Augustin: King of Kung Fu/Augustin. Roi Du Kung-fu*. Pathé, 1999.
Fries, Maureen. "Female Heroes, Heroines, and Counter-heroes: Images of Women in Arthurian Tradition." *Arthurian Women*. Ed. Thelma S. Fenster. New York: Garland Publishing Inc., 1996. 59–77.
Fu, Poshek. "The 1960s: Modernity, Youth Culture, and Hong Kong Cantonese Cinema." *The Cinema of Hong Kong: History, Arts, Identity*. Eds. Poshek Fu and David Desser. Cambridge: Cambridge University Press, 2000. 71–89.
Fuchs, Cynthia. "*Hero*." *PopMatters Media, Inc*. 27 August 2004. 15 December 2009 <www.popmatters.com/film/reviews/h/hero-20042.shtml>.
Gomes, Catherine. "Crouching Women, Hidden Order: Confucianism's Treatment of Gender in Ang Lee's *Crouching Tiger, Hidden Dragon*." *Limina: Journal of Historical and Cultural Studies* 11. University of Melbourne. 2005. 15 December 2009 <www.limina.arts.uwa.edu.au/__data/page/90432/gomes.pdf>.
_____. "'The Era of Lustrous Screen Sirens Lives On, Thousands Of Miles From Hollywood': The Cross-Cultural Reception Of Chinese Martial Arts Cinema's Sword-wielding Actresses." *Reception: Texts, Readers, Audiences, History* 1 (2008). 15 December 2009 <http://www.english.udel.edu/RSSsite/Gomes.pdf>.
_____. "*Wu xia pian* and the Asian Woman Warrior." *Traffic* 7 (2005): 95–108.
Harvey, David. *The Condition of Postmodernity: An Enquiry into the Origins of Cultural Change*. Cambridge: Blackwell, 1990.
Ho, Meng-Hwa, dir. *The Lady Hermit/Zhong Kui Niang Zi*. Shaw Brothers, 1971.
Ho, Sam. "Licensed to Kick Men: The Jane Bond Films." *The Restless Breed: Cantonese Stars of the Sixties*. Hong Kong: The 20th Hong Kong International Film Festival, 1996. 40–46.
Hu, King, dir. *Come Drink With Me/Da Zui Xia*. Shaw Brothers, 1966.
Hung, Sammo, dir. *Moon Warriors/Zhan Zhen Chuan Shuo*. Hong Kong Legends, 1993.
Hunt, Leon. *Kung Fu Cult Masters: From Bruce Lee to Crouching Tiger*. London: Wallflower Press, 2003.
Inness, Sherrie A. *Tough Girls: Women Warriors and Wonder Women in Popular Culture*. Philadelphia, PA: University of Pennsylvania Press, 1999.
Keung, Lau Wai, dir. *The Storm Riders/Fung Wan: Hung Ba Tin Ha*. Golden Harvest Company Ltd., 1998.
Koo, Siu-fung. "Philosophy and Tradition in the Swordplay Film." *A Study of the Hong Kong Swordplay Film (1945–1980)*. Ed. Lau Shing-hon. Hong Kong: The 5th Hong Kong International Film Festival, 1996. 25–46.
Lau, Jeffrey, dir. *92 Legendary La Rose Noire/92 Hak Mooi Gwai Dui Hak Mooi Gwai*. Hoventin Films Production, 1992.

Law, Kar and Frank Bren. *Hong Kong Cinema: A Cross-Cultural View.* Lanham, MD: The Scarecrow Press, 2004.
Lee, Ang, dir. *Crouching Tiger, Hidden Dragon/Wo Hu Cang Long.* Sony Pictures Classics, 2000.
_____. *Eat Drink Man Woman/Yim Shi Nan Nü.* The Samuel Goldwyn Company, 1994.
_____. *The Ice Storm.* 20th Century–Fox, 1997.
_____. "The *Wuxua* According to Ang Lee." Crouching Tiger, Hidden Dragon*: Portrait of the Ang Lee Film.* Ed. Linda Sunshine. New York: Newmarket Press. 2000. 134.
Lee, Ken-fang. "Far Away, So Close: Cultural Translation in Ang Lee's *Crouching Tiger. Hidden Dragon.*" *Inter-Asia Cultural Studies* 4.2 (2003): 281–95.
Lee, Raymond, dir. *New Dragon Gate Inn/Xin Long Men Ke Zhan.* Mei Ah Entertainment, 1992.
Leung, William. "Crouching Sensibility, Hidden Sense." *Film Criticism* 26.1 (2001): 42–57.
Levie, Matthew. "*Crouching Tiger, Hidden Dragon*: Ang Lee — Third-Stage Feminist." *Bright Lights Film Journal.* July 2001. 15 December 2009 <http://www.brightlightsfilm.com/33/crouchingtiger.html>.
Logan, Bey. *Hong Kong Action Cinema.* New York: The Overlook Press, 1995.
Matsu, Akinori, and Chin Hung Kuei, dir. *Lady Bond/ Nü Shashou. Lady Bond/ Nü Shashou.* Shaw Brothers, 1971.
Meyer, Carla. "House of Flying Daggers." *San Francisco Chronicle* 17 December 2004: E (5).
Morris, Gary. "Beautiful Beast: Ang Lee's *Crouching Tiger, Hidden Dragon.*" *Bright Lights Film Journal.* 31 January 2001. 15 December 2009 <http://www.brightlightsfilm.com/31/crouchingtiger.html>.
Ong, Aihwa, and Donald Nonini. *Ungrounded Empires: The Cultural Politics of Modern Chinese Transnationalism.* New York: Routledge, 1997.
Ong, Aihwa. *Flexible Citizenship: The Cultural Logics of Transnationality.* Durham and London: Duke University Press, 2000.
Passmore, Sarah. "Triads and Film." *BBC World Service.* 15 December 2009 <http://www.bbc.co.uk/worldservice/specials/163_wag_globalcrime/page4.shtml>.
Puig, Claudia. "*Flying Daggers*: A Dream Brought to Life." *USA Today.* 12 February 2004. 15 December 2009 <http://www.usatoday.com/life/movies/reviews/2004-12-02-flying-daggers_x.htm>.
Rubin, Gayle. "The Traffic in Women: Notes on the 'Political Economy' of Sex." *Toward an Anthropology of Women.* Ed. Rayna R. Reiter. New York: Monthly Review Press, 1975. 157–210.
Ryans, Tony. "The Sword as Obstacle." *A Study of the Hong Kong Swordplay Film (1945–1980).* Ed. Lau Shing-hon. Hong Kong: The 5th Hong Kong International Film Festival, 1996. 155–58.
Said, Edward W. *Orientalism.* New York: Pantheon Books, 1978.
Schamus, James. "Co-Writing the Screenplay." Crouching Tiger, Hidden Dragon*: Portrait of the Ang Lee Film.* Ed. Linda Sunshine. New York: Newmarket Press, 2000. 130.
Scott, A.O. "Silk Brocade Soaked in Blood and Passion." *The New York Times.* 9 October 2004. 15 December 2009 <http://movies2.nytimes.com/2004/10/09/movies/09hous.html?ex=1146196800&eN=6af861a9a74a4b87&ei=5070>.
Shaw, Runje, dir. *Heroine Feifei/Nüxia Feifei.* Tianyi Film Company, 1925.
"Shigeru Umebayashi." *IMDB: The Internet Movie Database.* 15 December 2009 <http://www.imdb.com/name/nm0880839/>.
Short, Stephen. "Year of the Tiger: High Art Meets High Spirits in a Rapturously Romantic Epic that Really Kicks Butt." *Time Magazine* 156.23 (2000): 166.

Simmel, Georg. *The Philosophy of Money.* London: Routledge, 1978.
Sunshine, Linda, ed. Crouching Tiger, Hidden Dragon: *Portrait of the Ang Lee Film.* New York: Newmarket Press, 2000.
Tasker, Yvonne. *Spectacular Bodies: Gender, Genre and the Action Cinema.* London: Routledge, 1993.
Taylor, Charles. "*Hero.*" Salon.Com. 27 August 2004. 15 December 2009 <http://dir.salon.com/story/ent/movies/review/2004/08/27/hero/index.html>.
Teo, Stephen. *Hong Kong Cinema: The Extra Dimensions.* London: British Film Institute, 1997.
Tong, Jean. "*House of Flying Daggers.*" *New York Times* 27 November 2004: 7(B).
UPI NewsTrack. "Chinese Filmmakers Embrace Glamour." *UPI.com.* 6 December 2004. 15 December 2009 <http://www.upi.com/Entertainment_News/2004/12/06/Chinese-filmmakers-embrace-glamour/UPI-77501102355593/>.
Wachowski, Andy and Larry Wachowski, dir. *The Matrix.* Warner Brothers, 1999.
Wong, Kar-wai, dir. *In the Mood for Love/Fa Yeung Nin Wa.* USA Films, 2000.
_____, dir. *2046.* 20th Century–Fox, 2004.
Wu, Ma, dir. *The Deaf Mute Heroine/Long E Jian.* Golden Harvest Company Ltd., 1971.
Yu, Ronny, dir. *Bride with White Hair/Bai Fa Mo Nü Zhuan.* Century Pacific, 1993.
Yuen, Chor, dir. *The Black Rose/ Hei Meigui Yu Hei Meigui.* Melek Films, 1965.
_____, dir. *Diamond Robbery/Zhuanshi Da Jien.* Kong Nge, 1967.
_____, dir. *Yes Madam/Huang Gu Shi Jie.* Hong Kong Legends, 1985.
Yuen, Woo-ping, dir. *Wing Chun/Yong Chun.* Century Pacific, 1994.
Zacharek, Stephanie. "Crouching Tiger, Hidden Dragon." Salon.Com. 8 December 2000. Salon Media Group, Inc. 25 April 2006 <http://Dir.salon.com/story/ent/movies/review/2000/12/08/crouching_tiger/index.xml>.
Zhang, Che, dir. *Golden Swallow/Hsia Yu-yen.* Shaw Brothers, 1968.
Zhang, Yimou, dir. *Hero/Ying Xiong.* Beijing New Pictures Company, 2002.
_____. *House of Flying Daggers/Shi Mian Mai Fu.* EDKO Film International, 2004.
Zhang, Zhen. "Abstract for Embodiment of Excess? The Proliferation of the 'Martial Arts' Film and the Image of the Female Knight-Errant in Shanghai Cinema. 1920s–1930s." China and Inner Asia Annual Meeting of the Association for Asian Studies. Washington. D.C. 26–29 March 1998. Presentation. 15 December 2009 <http://www.aasianst.org/absts/1998abst/china/c190.htm>.

PHOOLAN DEVI
The Primordial Tradition of the Bandit Queen
J. Sunita Peacock

Through the medium of film, globalization can be literally viewed on the screen as it shows the growth of capitalism, marketing, and consumption, especially in Asian countries. In particular, India and China experienced globalization as both countries began expanding economically and socially to become powerhouses in the global enterprise in the 1990s. If one examines the films of China in the 1990s, one sees a decided shift from the "national" dramas that showed the growth of modernity, nation-building, anti-imperialism, anti-feudalism, and new gender identities flourish on the screen to cinemas that show "an unprecedented process of internationalization" and "a system of market mechanization" (Lu 9). In the Chinese American context one sees films like Wayne Wang's *Eat a Bowl of Tea* (1989) and the effect of the Chinese Exclusion Act on Chinese immigrants (Lu 19). Similarly, films like *The Joy Luck Club* (1993) reveal cultural conflicts of Chinese American women. Despite the transnational movement in Chinese films, the recent cinematic discourses seem to return to the symbolic victimization of the female repeatedly. In many cases, even if the female is liberated, it comes with a process of "gender erasure" (Lu 21). Zhang Yimou's films are such examples that address not only gender erasure but also "dysfunctional sexuality, impotency, concubinage and emasculation," all seemingly veiled allegories of the nation (Lu 23).

Similarly, Indian cinema that began in the early nineteenth-century and coincided with the nationalist movement in India shifted from anti-imperialist in nature to a neorealist form of urban and rural themes in the early part of the twentieth century. Notably, film director Satyajit Ray has made films that show the atrocities faced by women, especially widows, and have won many international awards. It is important to note, though, the visible division between popular Indian cinema and the neorealist Indian cinema. Artistic film directors, such as Satyajit Ray directed films that show to the world a different

India from what has been portrayed in the popular Bollywood genre of musicals usually shot in exotic European locations. Interestingly, the transnationalism of Indian cinema seems more apparent in popular films as stories about conflicted identities of Indians living abroad clash with Indian values from time to time. Shekar Kapoor's film, *The Bandit Queen* (1994) reflects the growth of the Indian nation, the question of gender in the lives of Indian women, the effects of class, caste, history, politics, and social revival in the lives of Indian women as the country moved from being a national to an international phenomenon in the global marketplace through the story of the warrior, bandit queen Phoolan Devi. The similarity between the subject of *The Bandit Queen* and the subject of several films in transnational Chinese cinema lies in the gender erasure of females, the victimization of women, and the effects of class, national, and political agendas coinciding with the identities of women in their struggle for a voice in their nation. This is where discourses about gender, power, nationalism, and transnationalism come together. This chapter will address Phoolan Devi's life and through this case study examine how Indian women's lives have been affected and in most cases victimized because of the interplay of gender, caste, and religion.

Besides Shekar Kapoor's raw and heart-wrenching film, *The Bandit Queen*, this chapter also examines other sources regarding the life experience of Phoolan Devi. Aside from her biography available in English, *The Bandit Queen of India: An Indian Woman's Amazing Journey from Peasant to International Legend* (2006), co-authored by Phoolan Devi, Marie-Therese Cuny, and Paul Rambali, most of the information about Phoolan Devi emerges from newspaper and news magazine articles published when Phoolan Devi was causing havoc in her rampage together with the group of bandits under her command and when she was captured by the Indian police. Shekar Kapoor's film summarizes her entire life succinctly and serves as one of the primary sources in understanding the dynamics of Phoolan's brief stint as the warrior queen of modern India. Ultimately, Phoolan's life serves as a backdrop in the understanding of caste, class, gender, religion, politics, and history of India through the culture's treatment of women based on the roles that they are expected to play because of the social categories embedded in Indian society. This chapter further highlights how the female warrior in India is riddled with the arrows of traditions, caste, class, religion, economics, and political agendas as she battles her way through the multi-faceted layers of Indian society.

The story of the Bandit Queen is a popular and bloody one set in the late twentieth century with all the trappings of the legend of a warrior queen only meant for tales told by a fireside. Nonetheless, it is not a legend but a true story about a young woman who "endured a life of rape and abuse after being sold into marriage at the age of eleven."[1] As an adult, Phoolan Devi meted out revenge against her male perpetrators who had ravaged her both mentally and physically when she was a tender young girl. She joined a group of bandits or dacoits as they are termed in India and created terror, going on a brutal rampage in many villages in the Northern Indian state of Uttar Pradesh. After she was jailed for her misdeeds by the Indian police, from her jail cell she became a champion for women, for the untouchable caste of India to which she belonged, and for minorities throughout the country who have been and still are being negated by the society at large.

Three very important aspects of Indian society—caste, religion (Hinduism), and the dichotomous role of the Indian goddess that is violent and demure at once—have strong impact on the perceived roles of the Indian woman who is both closeted and revealed at the behest of her national and colonial masters in pre- and post-independent India. When Phoolan Devi finally surrendered to the Indian police, after all charges were dropped against her men, she remained in jail for eleven years. During her imprisonment, Phoolan became famous. Journalists began to interview her; people started to write and translate her life story. The film, *The Bandit Queen*, draws from her biography, which is written from her perspective and by and large remains true to *her story*, a neologism coined in the 1960s in feminist discourse referring to history written from a feminist perspective.

Phoolan Devi was born in 1963 in Gorha Ka Purwa, in Uttar Pradesh, North India to a low caste family known as Mallah. This particular caste was so low that it "was even beneath the Brahmanical order" of the four castes: Brahmin, Kshatriya, Vaishya, and Sudra (Devi, Cuny, and Rambali Intro ix). Since her childhood, Phoolan had to suffer not only because of the caste (untouchable) that she belonged to, but also because of her gender. In a country where having daughters was considered a curse, especially in rural areas, Phoolan was the second of four daughters. Her parents were poor and her father owned only an acre of land. At the age of eleven, Phoolan was married off to a thirty-year-old widower for a cow, which would be of more use and value to the family than a daughter. Because of the abusive treatment from her husband and his family, Phoolan returned to her own family and was treated as an outcast in her village. Yet she was not afraid and fought in court on behalf of her father when his land was taken away from him. During the process she was incarcerated, raped, and beaten by the village police. When she returned home from jail, she was sold to a band of dacoits by her cousin Maiyadin, against whom she was fighting for her father's stolen land. The dacoits' leader, Babu Gujar, raped and ill-treated Phoolan, an adolescent at the time, in front of his men. One of his fellow dacoits, Vikram Mallah, who belonged to the same low caste as Phoolan, tired of Gujar's relentless cruelty to Phoolan and finally shot him after watching him rape and beat Phoolan over a period of several days. Vikram then made himself the leader of the dacoits and appointed Phoolan as second in command. "He taught her how to use a gun, how to run all night along the banks of the Yamuna river without leaving footprints, how to escape police— how to survive un-beholden to anyone. Phoolan took the lessons to heart"

(Devi, Cuny, and Rambali Intro x). Soon Phoolan transformed into the Bandit Queen who helped the poor and oppressed by looting and killing the upper caste men, especially an upper caste group called the Thakurs who had severely raped and punished her when she was a girl. Phoolan was feared in the region because she was a woman of the lowest caste and was making chaos in the lives of the upper caste men and helping the underprivileged in and around the state of Uttar Pradesh. Fear was also rooted in "Indian national politics where, ever since Gandhi took up the cause of the untouchable castes of India, there had been a fear among the nation's ruling castes" of the power of the untouchables of the country (Devi Cuny, and Rambali Intro xi). Thus Phoolan was "relentlessly hunted" till she finally "agreed to surrender in exchange for a promise from the Home Minister, or governor, of the state of Uttar Pradesh that all charges against her and her gang be dropped" (Devi, Cuny, and Rambali Intro xi). Phoolan was then jailed at the age of twenty-one and languished in prison for eleven years.

In February 1994, Phoolan was released by the orders of the new Home Minister, Malayam Singh Yadav who belonged to a low caste as well. All charges against her were dropped. The minister then made her part of his ruling Samajawadi Party and encouraged her to stand for Parliament: "In a democracy in which 85 percent of voters are low-caste and illiterate, the Bandit Queen had a powerful appeal" (Devi, Cuny, and Rambali Intro xi). Phoolan's release is connected with the Minister's political agenda. Yadav wanted to strengthen his party and represent the voice of the illiterate who previously did not have a voice. Phoolan served the Samajawadi Party well and soon became a member of the Parliament, always fighting for the cause of women and the lower castes in the rural areas of Uttar Pradesh. However, the upper-caste Thakur men never forgot their "brothers" who were killed by Phoolan and her gang of dacoits. On July 25, 2001, thirty-eight-year-old Phoolan was assassinated near her residence by a young man named Sher Singh Rana who was probably hired by the Thakur men to carry out such a mission, although the Thakurs denied any association with the assassin or the incident (Devi, Cuny, and Rambali Intro xiii).

In examining the lives of Indian women throughout history, we have to consider the complex roles they have played. Several reasons contribute to such complexity. the traditional Indian culture is rooted in the texts of Hinduism and is influenced by other political powers in history, including Greeks, Persians, and Anglo-European. These and other elements bring about a conglomeration of issues that further complicate the role of women in Indian society. Gender, caste, religion, slavery, as well as nationalistic and political ideals have affected the women in the past and continue to play significant roles in shaping Indian women's lives in the twentieth-and twenty-first centuries. Devi's life is able to encapsulate the cultural, social, historical, and political aspects of India because of her gender, caste, and career, all of which help formulate her unique character.

The Minority Subject: Female Body, Sexuality, and Caste

Phoolan Devi's metaphorical visibility/invisibility, caste, and gender all contribute to her minority status. Homi Bhabha's definition of the minority subject in his essay, "Cultures In-Between," can be used to describe people who belong to a class on the fringes of the caste-ridden society of India.[2] Bhabha notes: "The inscription of the minority subject somewhere between the too visible and not visible enough ... is beyond logical demonstration, and it requires that the discriminated subject even in the process of reconstitution, be located in a present moment that is temporarily disjunctive and effectively ambivalent" (56). We see this visibility and the lack of visibility that Phoolan Devi faces throughout her life as she battles the barriers of her caste in her quest for justice and recognition in daily life. When she was married, one of her duties as a wife was to draw water from the village well for her husband's family. Because she belonged to a low caste, she had to wait for the upper caste women to draw water from a particular side of the well into their gleaming copper pots before she could draw water with her clay pot. On her way back to her husband's house, young boys around her age threw stones and harsh words at her and broke her pot, simply because of her low caste. On her return, Phoolan's mother-in-law reprimanded her. She responded: "Well, if the pot were made of copper, it wouldn't have been broken." Phoolan does not back down and demands visibility. She is severely punished and raped by her husband for her bold outspokenness. Phoolan can be compared to "the discriminated subject/community" who occupies for a brief moment "a contemporary period that is historically untimely, forever belated" (Frantz Fanon qtd. in Bhabha 57). As Fanon notes in *Black Skin, White Masks*, this belatedness is because there will "always be a white world between you and us" (qtd. in Bhabha 57). In Phoolan's case there is always a clear line setting her apart from the world of the male and the upper caste. Although Fanon is referring to race, caste in India functions in similar ways in terms of dividing people into different social groups with differing privileges or lack thereof.

The geography of "disjunctive borderlines" followed Phoolan Devi throughout her life. Even when she was in a powerful situation where she as the Bandit Queen and led the dacoits to several villages in India where they plundered, looted, and killed, she still occupied, "a hybrid space of negotiation where power is unequal but its articulation may be equivocal" (Bhabha 58). This hybridity stems from the fact that she is a woman from a minority community of bandits and low caste. As Phoolan roared through the village brandishing her weapon and commandeering her men to loot and kill all the people with money, she told women and children that they were safe. In one instance, Phoolan broke the glass of a jewelry store and pulled out a trinket and handed it to a young girl on the street and told her that this trinket had become the young girl's wedding trousseau. This gesture suggests her hybrid agency and showed how her voice and gesture articulated "a dialectic that does not seek cultural supremacy or sovereignty" (Bhabha 58). Hybrid voices, such as Phoolan's, seek to "deploy the partial culture from which it emerges to construct visions of community and versions of historic memory" (Bhabha 58). The memory that Phoolan tried to create for young girls and women was that of independence. Phoolan creates a cultural identity for herself, her community of bandits, and the disenfranchised minority group through her banditry. Her life as a bandit depicted in Shekar Kapoor's film follows the Robin Hood pattern of helping the poor through the spoils of the rich. Furthermore, she is also able to "memorialize lost time, and to reclaim lost territories" because her career as a bandit shows how minority groups can, albeit briefly, be victorious, but because of its brevity her victories become "ambivalent" (Bhabha 59).

In his discussion on the minority or subaltern subject, Lawrence Grossberg notes: "The subaltern represents an inherent ambiguity or instability at the centre of any formation of language (or identity) which constantly undermines the language's power to define a unified stable identity" (90; parenthese in the original). According to Grossberg, because of a lack of a stable identity "the subaltern is defined only by its internal negation of the colonizer" (91). The idea of the subaltern parallels the notion of hybridity because a lack of stability can point to a lack of a legitimate space in society, which in turn moves the subaltern or hybrid away from the center to the border. As a subaltern Phoolan frequently remained in the borderlands as she physically hid in the hills with the bandits and only made sporadic incursions into society when she carried out attacks. Because of her geographic abode as a bandit, Phoolan symbolically lived on the borders of Indian society as a low caste woman and a bandit and could not have knowledge, tradition, or history. She came "under attack by society" in the form of the law, the upper caste men, and her tradition as a woman of her caste because she ignored the heterogeneity of power and reduced it to "discourses of representation and [ignored] its material realities" (Grossberg 92).

In her book, *Rich and Strange: Gender History Modernism*, Marianne DeKoven examines the modernist texts after World War I and notes how texts written by men and women have "mutually exclusive paradigms" (21). In her analysis of female theorists, such as Luce Irigaray, DeKoven notes how female sexuality is relegated to "undefinability, invisibility" (28). In Plotonius' texts, women are shown as being "liquid" and without form (DeKoven 32). In Phoolan Devi's case, her invisibility is symbolized by the woman's body, which is used as the nation's text by men but brutalized when occupying it, rendering it invisible and without rights. The nationalists fighting against imperialism in India between 1930 and 1947 looked at the Indian woman as the holder of the nation's culture thus disallowing her to be in the forefront of the nation's struggle against its colonizers. The "Bhadramahila" or respectable woman had to stay home and retain the nation's culture and tradition. She had to remain invisible in the independent movement. She did not have the rights that men enjoyed, such as their involvement in the freedom struggle. The definition of one's rights is tied to one's gender. In post-independence India, the woman was still relegated to the domestic space as seen in the life of Phoolan Devi before she became a bandit. Phoolan was poor and belonged to a low caste and because of her poverty and caste, she was bartered off in marriage because her father could not feed her and the rest of his family. 80% of the women in India still reside in villages now and many of them still face similar issues. In one instance, before becoming the Bandit Queen, Phoolan was forced to parade naked in the village in front of the men because she defied her position as a meek woman. She was regarded as being defiant because she had left her abusive husband and returned to her village. She had also fought for her father who had lost his land. To punish her disobedience, fourteen upper caste men raped her and then branded her as a whore and put her on public display. This incident demonstrates how the female body is often identified in terms of its reproductive organs and thus the erasure of its totality and individuality makes it apparent that female sexuality and morality are not private entities but appropriated within public discourses as we see in the violation of Phoolan's body and her public display in front of the entire village emphasizing visibility of shame. This can be paralleled to modernist texts/modern nations/capitalist institutions and their role in securing men through the scarring of the woman's body/text/cultural institutions (i.e., caste, class, and marriage).

The sexuality of the female body continues to serve as a metaphor through Phoolan's vulnerability and the vulnerability of underrepresented Indian women in general. According to the annals of Indian history, some religious texts have been translated into the decline of the social status of women. This decline began around 200 B.C.E. when the Code of Manu began taking shape. Before then there was equality between men and women. Women's secondary social standing still has a strong foothold in India in the twentieth century. In Phoolan's case she was doubly disfranchised because of her caste and gender. In the ancient Code of Manu, "women and sudras were regarded as life-long slaves from birth to death, with slavery inborn in them" (Liddle and Joshi 65). Even in the twentieth century this ancient code gave both upper caste and lower caste men full power over Phoolan as reflected in the fact that she was both raped by both the upper caste Brahmin men and the lower caste bandit leader. One should also note that upper caste women, though not mentioned in Phoolan's biography or in the film, *The Bandit Queen*, may suffer in the hands of male perpetrators because of their gender. Phoolan's brief respite came when Vikram killed his leader and took his place. From Vikram Phoolan learned the art of banditry and later she gained respect from other bandits as she and Vikram became co-leaders in banditry. In her both biography and the film, one notices, though, a lack of legitimacy of a woman unless she is associated with a man (Phoolan was the only female in the group). Phoolan did not gain legitimacy unless she was with Vikram, her lover. Being a woman and belonging to a low caste made Phoolan doubly impure. The caste system in India also put the burden of the double impurity of women from the lower caste on their men who could not control their women: "This idea reinforced the caste divisions, for if the lower castes behaved like the Brahmins, the distinctions would dissolve. So, the gender division reinforced the caste division, and the gender ideology legitimated not only the structure of patriarchy but also the organization of caste" (Liddle and Joshi 69).

Caste was first introduced to India by the Aryans in their ancient texts, the Vedas (1500 B.C.). With the caste system came the patriarchal joint family system and "women became the property of men in the same way as the field belonged to the men of the family" (Liddle and Joshi 62). Caste divides the population into four major groups: the Brahmin (priestly) at the top, followed by the Kshatriya (warrior caste), and then the Vaishya (traders and artisans) and Sudras (laborers and untouchables). Caste has had a particular impact on women in India since 700 B.C. until now; women's "sexual purity is linked with the purity of caste, and women are seen as points of entrance or 'gateways' to the caste system, since the main threat to purity of the group comes from female sexuality, it becomes vital to guard it" (Liddle and Joshi 60). In the life of the Bandit Queen, the reader sees the idea of women being the property of men when Phoolan was married at a young age to a much older widower. Because of her sex, she was perceived as a burden to her family and therefore was quickly traded to her husband so that her father could support the rest of the family from the meager amount of money he made tending to his small piece of land. In order to make a living, he had to get rid of a piece of property, his daughter. Her family also followed the ancient Hindu laws from the Smritis (law books) that "advocated marriage before puberty for girls" (Liddle and Joshi 63). Phoolan was eleven years old when she married. In the Smritis, the Code of Manu notes that women should never be independent and a woman is always under the rule of the man (father, husband, or son) because her nature is inherently evil. An important rule we see in Phoolan Devi's life is that "women remain chaste only as long as they are not in a deserted place and do not get the chance to be acquainted with any man, and that women do not hesitate to transgress morals because they are of an adulterous nature" (Liddle and Joshi 63). In the first half of the film, *The Bandit Queen*, Phoolan is attacked by the young upper caste men (Thakurs) of the village and they always tease and accost her when she is by herself in a deserted place. Later when she is raped by the upper caste Brahmin men of her village, she is told repeatedly that it is because of her adulterous nature and that her penchant for roaming in deserted areas asked for sexual favors from the men.

We see the definition of women being adulterous even in the two ancient Indian epics, the *Ramayana* and the *Mahabharata*. In both texts, the two most important women characters, Sita and Gandhara, respectively follow the Code of Manu when they refer to themselves as "pativrata" or husband worshippers. In the *Ramayana*, Sita has to prove to her husband, Rama, that she was not seduced by her abductor, Ravana, by fire so that she is not rejected by her husband. Gandhara blindfolds herself for life when she discovers on her wedding night that her husband was blind (Liddle and Joshi 64). Unlike Sita and Gandhara, Phoolan did not respect her husband and did not obey her mother-in-law, which leads to her husband raping her before she reached puberty while her mother-in-law approving it by silence. The sexual assault Phoolan experienced repeatedly is an important metaphor that suggests how the body of woman warrior is mapped relentlessly because of the nation's foray into it due to the patriarchal nature of Indian history, politics, and culture.

Hinduism and the Contradictory Nature of the Mother Goddess

As noted above, caste is closely intertwined with Hinduism, which brings the reader to the complex role of women as goddess and warrior in the Hindu tradition. In her article, "Gender Complementarity and Gender Hierarchy in Purānic Accounts of Creation" Tracy Pintchman notes: "Vedic cosmogonies portray the 'varnas,' the broad classes comprising Indian society on which caste divisions are based, as being created 'in the beginning' in conjunction with the creation of all other things, beings, and worlds; hence the division of people into 'varnas' is represented as aboriginal, as hard-wired into the essence of reality, as the 'way things are because they were created that way" (257). She goes further to explain that "religions have always depended on myths of origins to validate the dictates of particular human beings living in particular historical eras;" "both Vedic and Hindu religions bestowed such cosmogonic legitimations on the social system they advocated and instituted such ideas in India" (Pintchman 257). Because these texts were written by men of the upper Brahmin caste, they gave themselves the highest position and made the point of not including themselves as the authors of the "varnas" but by "portraying the Vedic texts as authorless, eternal and embodying absolute truth" (Pintchman 258). In Brahmanical scriptures, "high-caste males are usually privileged over their subordinates who comprise both low-caste individuals and females." In the ancient Brahmanical law book, the Laws of Manu, for example, "both women and sudras (the lowest of the four castes) are often portrayed as inherently inferior beings and are excluded, at least theoretically from studying the Vedas reciting the Vedas and performing sacrifices" (Pintchman 258). Pintchman notes:

> Both caste and gender tend to function socially in similar ways. Like caste, gender plays an important role in structuring social hierarchy in contemporary Indian culture, and both caste and gender have been invoked to legitimate inequitable distributions of wealth and power, differences, in status, discrepancies

in rights, divisions of labor, and hierarchical notions of inherent worth.... The original difference of male and female is the key to order; the caste hierarchy can go, but the gender hierarchy is natural and necessary [259].

In ancient Hindu or Brahmanical scriptures (also known as Puranas), the male god is seen as holding "creative power principle" (Pintchman 265). On the other hand, the power of the goddess or "sakti" is embedded within the male god or creator. When creation occurs, the female "sakti" becomes "prakrit" and separates itself from the male power. With this separation comes the "gendered view of cosmogony" (Pintchman 265). Furthermore, if one were to examine creation in sexual terms one notes the insemination of the male god's "virya" into the female goddess. According to Pintchman, when this "agitative" moment occurs, "mahat" or intellect is born (266). Therefore, despite both genders' participation in the creative process, it is the male who is seen as initiating the process: the "virya" of the male is inserted into the womb. Even though the female helps with the survival of "vaikrata creations," in Hindu scriptures the dominance of the male over the female abounds (Pintchman 275).

There is another complex theory in the ancient Hindu scriptures dealing with androgyny, which could be used to describe Phoolan Devi's role as the bandit queen, yet not being considered strong despite her masculine status in her role as a bandit. In the film, *The Bandit Queen*, Phoolan Devi is shown wearing male fatigues and tying a bandana around her head, giving her a masculine sexual appearance. This image resembles male figures in Hindu scriptures that are described as being pregnant. But when it comes to the woman or goddess she does not suddenly find herself "endowed with a phallus," nor is she able to produce children by herself. "Thus, femaleness is portrayed as a power (sakti) of the male with no autonomous ontological status" (Pintchman 275). This proves that despite Phoolan's masculine appearance, she ultimately has to rely on men to fight for her rights. All the traditional roles of women contributed to Phoolan's suffering till one of the male bandits took pity on her and saved her and made her a bandit queen.

There is always a dichotomy when it comes to the role of the Indian woman as noted in the dichotomous role of the Indian goddess. As Gyatri Spivak has discussed in her article, "The Rani of Sirmur: An Essay in Reading Archives," the dichotomous role of the Indian goddess deseminates into the dichotomous role of Indian women in general. Spivak states that although it has been argued that the Indian woman has been silenced in "the colonial archive," pursued in the courts for absconding from brutal or unacceptable husbands, pursued by the courts for killing their spouses, however using the same legal structures to redress their grievances and assert their rights, rebellious Indian women have left their mark on the colonial archive" (247). We see this in Phoolan's rebellion nurtured by the women of the past and internalized in her blood without her realizing it. Throughout Indian history and culture on the one hand women contested divorce as early as in the 1880s; yet on the other hand women also had a long history of engaging with purdah (forms of seclusion) and the practices of sati (widow burning) in a "uniformly common" manner (Spivak 247). At any rate, such complex roles of women in Indian culture hearken to the complexity of the female goddess in Hindu scriptures.

The legendary Hindu sage Manu called himself the descendant of the creator Brahman who asked him to explain the sacred Hindu laws, which Manu recorded in the law books known as Smritis. Manu's laws then became the rules and laws of Hindu culture beginning from 200–300 B.C.E. (Bühler xii). Despite Manu's low opinion of women, the Brahmin priests who were in charge of religious texts allowed mother goddesses to enter the pantheon of gods. According to Liddle and Joshi, "the goddess Lakshmi is benevolent because her controlled sexuality bestows legitimate heirs for the maintenance of caste wealth and retains family property within the caste. Kali is malevolent because her uncontrolled passion is liable to introduce impure blood into the caste and to dissipate caste wealth, making a mockery of patrilineal inheritance and the accumulation of property, and thereby destroying the caste system itself" (68). Furthermore, Liddle and Joshi state:

> It is intriguing to consider that Brahmin priests, holding Manu's opinion of women, yet allowing the introduction of matriarchal goddesses into the pantheon. The mother goddess was associated with magic, sexual orgies, and blood sacrifice, representing the miracle of birth, the creation of life through sexuality, and menstruation as a symbol of fertility. To the Brahmin, childbirth, sexuality and menstruation were all sources of pollution, yet this polluting matriarchal culture was absorbed into the pure patriarchal religious ritual in the form of mother worship [68].

When it comes to examining the identity of the Indian goddess, it is fairly ambiguous. In Hindu religion and mythology, the female goddess cannot be reduced to an identifiable being because by doing so one does not grasp her "real nature" (Michaels 224). So in examining the traits of many goddesses in India who all emerge from the "female cosmic energy (sakti) of the male god Siva," one notes multiple manifestations of this energy into various goddesses and multiple manifestations of traits within a single goddess. Yet another example of the dichotomous or complex identity of the goddess is in the description of the goddess Saraswati. She appears in ancient Hindu texts as an "embodiment of science and art" and pale complexioned. She also appears as a "Dark or Blue Saraswati" who is less peaceful than her fairer counterpart. Saraswati not only appears in Hindu texts, but Buddhist and Indian folk religions. Thus the Indian goddess can absorb "contradictions, because she basically has infinitely many identities and does not need any boundaries. In sharp contrast to Western ideas of identity, the goddess, especially, reflects that belief in the power of the primary, preverbal, preconscious experiences of reality" (Michaels 226). In Indian society, dichotomy is noted in the role of a woman in the household. The wife is seen as the property of her husband and "publicly, the wife represses any manifestation of sexual desire, which would be considered detrimental to an old ideal of fidelity, as embodied (for men) by Sita, the wife of the god Rama, who courageously resisted all lascivious advances of the demon Ravana" (Michaels 127). On the other hand, there is an Indian saying — "A wife who is modest and shy will always be hungry" (Michaels 128).

According to Brahmanic-Sanskritic doctrine:

> On the one hand, women must compensate for their congenital impurity; on the other hand, in the minds of many men, women also constitute a special force and power, the dynamic part of the cosmos, life-giving energy. There is so much of this divine force (sakti) that, as Indian men occasionally say, they don't need any ritual. They frequently call their wives, "my government" or "my goddess." Because women have this sakti, they can be deified healers, strong politicians such as Indira Gandhi (India's first woman Prime Minister) or brave gang leaders such as Phoolan Devi [Michaels 130].

The goddesses reflect the complex images of women in India: on the one hand we see this in the marriage between Vishnu (one of the important male gods in the Hindu pantheon) and his subordinate, obedient goddess Lakshmi, who is always portrayed physically smaller than her male counterpart in iconography; on the other hand, in Hinduism there is the erotic, nearly equal love between the male god Krishna and his female lover Radha as well as the goddess Kali who has her husband Shiva lying at her feet. But generally speaking "in Brahmanic ritualistic religiosity, usually the first type of image predominates; in devotionalism, the second; and in heroism the third" (Michaels 131).

This idea of the warrior goddess as seen in the traits of Kali and Durga are noted in Phoolan's life when she ran away from her marriage because she was abused. As an adult, she returned to torture and kill her husband after she became a bandit. Phoolan was treated as an equal by her lover and partner Vikram Mallah who rescued her from his merciless leader Babu Gujar. To some degree, Phoolan's and Vikram's relationship embodied the erotic love of Radha and Krishna.

Toward the end of her young life, Phoolan is hailed as the goddess or "Devi" of the oppressed and women as she plunders the lives of the rich and helps the poor and disenfranchised. Despite her having been raped and ravaged by men of different castes, we see this warrior woman's body becoming a metaphor for the nation of India and its history. A country that is referred to as "Bharatmata" or Mother India in Sanskrit is violated by outside forces from the Aryans, Persians, Greeks, to the British colonizers. Through the metaphorical body of the bandit queen, we see Phoolan being subsumed by the metaphor of the nation, which brings her back to her subaltern and hybrid status. Furthermore, according to Neluka Silva, "the woman's body then becomes the embodiment of the nation and can function in one of two ways—"either as 'pure' (and synonymously maternal) body, spiritual, inviolable, and intact or as bruised, ravaged, raped, and violated by invaders" (212).

Slavery and the Bhadramahila Concept

Slavery has been an integral part of Indian history throughout the centuries. Even before British colonial rule, the buying and selling of slaves was popular in India by the various groups that colonized the country before the British. According to Indrani Chatterjee, during the time of the Delhi Sultanate and the Mughals the slaves were referred to as "chelas."[2] The Marathas, a warrior clan in India, referred to enslaved women as "daughters of the state" or rajbeti (18). Slavery continued during European colonization where the selling of females and children was popular between one European family and another. Records have been found during the French stay in Pondicherry (Chatterjee 179).[3] Chatterjee also sees the life of slaves as "kinlessness" because although the slaves were assimilated with the host "family" or "society" there was always a sense of "powerlessness" and "impoverishment." Similarly in the twentieth century and during Phoolan Devi's lifetime, she was treated as a slave and branded with such labels as wife, prostitute, and lower caste adulterous being. As in eighteen-century India, there was no separate division between the "state" and the "family." There was a non-market transaction of slaves because parents sold their children during difficult times—famines, floods, and other crises (Chatterjee 22).

The idea of "gift giving" is common in Indian history when the landowners or zamindars offered their daughters to English collectors because the Englishmen took care of their businesses (Chatterjee 23). Kings would give their daughters as gifts to the Brahmin priests to reward them for performing certain important rituals for the kings (Chatterjee 24). This idea of "gift giving" continues in the twentieth century. Phoolan was passed from one man to another since childhood. This is comparable to "testamentary transactions" of slaves in Indian history when upon the death of a slave holder the slave was passed from "one holder to another" (Chatterjee 24).

The label of the *Bhadramahila* or "respectable woman" was popularized during the nationalist movement in Bengal during the nineteenth century. Many Bengali activists, such as Rammohun Roy, Bankim Chandra Chattopadhayay, and Buhdev Mukhopadhayay, supported the idea of Indian women receiving an education in the schools that were set up for them by the English missionaries and colonial masters. But as Partha Chatterjee and Dipesh Chakarbarty note in their respective works, the woman still had to be "respectable" or a *bhadramahila*. She could not wear western clothes, smoke and drink, or talk to men. She was the holder of her home culture and therefore had to retain it by remaining in the shadows. Thus colonial thinking (the ideas of the imperial masters were similar to the ideas of patriarchy in India) was well in place in colonized India. The books written by male activists such as Rammohun Roy and Bankim Chandra told stories of widows who had a "spiritual" love for their families and so served them even after their husbands' deaths. And even if they fell in love with other men, it was pure. The imperialist/colonialist idea stands in conjunction with the Vedas and "pativrata" or submission to the husbands/men and women in the ancient scriptures are told to care for the auspiciousness of the house as men do for the purity and prestige of the paternal line. Women are supposed to practice divine worship in many forms both at home and in the temple, and this is still true in countless homes in India in the rural as well as urban areas.

In Phoolan's case she is not respectable because she rebels against being a wife, and thus she is treated like a slave, a commodity, a whore. Her low caste also marks her unreliable. The concept of *bhadramahila* further parallels the virtues of the Hindu/Indian woman from the past. In Hinduism the word "respectability" is used often. In the Code of Manu, the woman is relegated to a list of virtues that she has to possess and a way in which she has to conduct herself outside the home despite all outside distractions. The definition of home for the Indian nationalist was similar. The home paralleled country and the values of the country which had to be preserved by the women. Bengali patriarchy and the concept of *bhadramahila* were also similar to European enlightenment. Chakarbarty notes the latter idea in the writings of Rammohun Roy who shows, "the sense of compassion and reason gleaned from Europe, which helped the Indian woman in her public sphere (wrote against widow burning and allowing widows to remarry 1856 Act), but her private side could not be delineated" (124). In such writings one never heard the widow's side of the argument. Thus the Bengali male, in keeping with the European idea of Enlightenment, follows David Hume's and Adam Smith's theories of objectivity and universality of human nature instead of its "subjectivity" and "interiority" (Chakarbarty 129). We see this duality in the thinking of Indian males, ancient Indian scriptures (Vedas), and Hinduism. Despite the fact that Indian women were given the chance to vote around 1917, which predates European women gaining voting rights, the women of India were still debarred from "sexual equality" in personal law; that is, the law of inheritance, inter-caste marriage, and divorce. The nationalists wanted the women to have suffrage because they needed the numbers to "undermine Britain's position of power" (Liddle and Joshi 36). But when it came to personal law and the revision of the Hindu Code, this "threatened their own privileges as men in the family" (Liddle and Joshi 36). Even after independence, Indian women both in the educated and uneducated classes were underrepresented in the implementation of personal equality among men and women. The female body is associated with "community origins." So women are "positioned as 'place' in the pure space of 'home' in which tradition is preserved from outside contamination" (Liddle and Joshi 95) bringing the *bhadramahila* concept to the full circle.

In conclusion, the broken body of Phoolan Devi who is murdered for political reasons reflects that her victories were short lived. For a brief moment in history Phoolan Devi was able to help women and the lower caste by being a

Robin Hood type of figure rebelling against the rules of caste, class, patriarchy, and religious ideals of her time. Unfortunately, she was not allowed to retain her warrior woman status for long. Nonetheless, she has made more than a dent in the lives of women living in rural India who still regard her as a goddess of the disenfranchised despite her early demise. *Herstory* will live both orally and literally in the annals of India history and society.

Notes

1. All unidentified quotations in this chapter come from the 1996 film, *The Bandit Queen*.
2. The lowest or untouchable castes in India are given several names, such as Dalits, Harijans, Mallahs, among others. Phoolan Devi belonged to the Mallah group.
3. The Delhi Sultanate was between the tenth and twelfth centuries. The Mughals of Persian descent, whose first ruler was Babur, ruled between the twelfth and seventeenth centuries and was defeated by European colonialism.
4. Pondicherry was a French settlement through which the British allowed the French to keep even after the British defeated them in the early 1800s when the East India Company established itself as the governing body of India.

Bibliography

Angol, Padma. *Women's Agency and Resistance in Colonial India*. London: Ashgate Publishing, 2006.
Bhabha, Homi K. "Cultures In-Between." *Questions of Cultural Identity*. Eds. Stuart Hall and Paul Du Gay. London: Sage Publications, 1996. 53–66.
Bühler, G. *The Laws of Manu: Translated with Extracts From Seven Commentaries*. Delhi: Motilal Banarsidass, 1971.
Chakarbarty, Dipesh. *Provincializing Europe: Postcolonial Thought and Historical Difference*. Princeton, NJ: Princeton University Press, 2000.
Chatterjee, Indrani. *Gender Slavery and Law in Colonial India*. New Delhi and Oxford: Oxford University Press, 1999.
Chatterjee, Partha. "Colonialism, Nationalism and Colonialized Women: the Contest in India." *American Ethnologist* 16 (1989): 622–33.
DeKoven, Marianne. *Rich and Strange: Gender, History, Modernism*. Princeton, NJ: Princeton University Press, 1991.
Devi, Phoolan, Marie-Therese Cuny and Paul Rambali. *The Bandit Queen of India: An Indian Woman's Amazing Journey from Peasant to International Legend*. Guilford, CT: Lyons Press, 2006.
Grossberg, Lawrence. "Is That All There Is?" *Questions of Cultural Identity*. Eds. Stuart Hall and Paul Du Gay. London: Sage Publications, 1996. 87–107.
Kapoor, Shekar, dir. *The Bandit Queen*. Channel Four Films, 1994.
Liddle, Joanna, and Rama Joshi. *Daughters of Independence: Gender, Class, and Caste in India*. London: Zed Books, 1986.
Lu, Hsiao-peng Sheldon. *Transnational Chinese Cinema: Identity, Nationhood, Gender*. Honolulu, HI: University of Hawaii Press, 1997.

Michaels, Axel. *Hinduism: Past and Present.* Trans. Barbara Harshav. Princeton, NJ: Princeton University Press, 2004.
Pintchman, Tracy. "Gender Complementarity and Gender Hierarchy in Puranic Accounts of Creation." *Journal of the American Academy of Religion* 66.2 (1998): 257–82.
Silva, Neluka. *The Gendered Nation: Contemporary Writings from South Asia.* New Delhi: Sage, 2004.
Spivak, Gyatri. "The Rani of Sirmur: An Essay in Reading Archives." *History and Theory* 24 (1985): 247–72.

Translating Mother's Tongue(s) and Traveling Bodies
Palimpsest and Diaspora in Maxine Hong Kingston's The Woman Warrior
Pei-Ju Wu

In the essay collection on cultural mobility, Stephen Greenblatt mentions the urgency to rethink "the fate of culture in an age of global mobility" (1). Transnational flows of ideas, theories of hybridity, diaspora, and migration bring scholars to question the transformation of culture from one location to another. This chapter focuses on the reconstruction of the matrilineal text/body, particularly the two major tactics of palimpsest and diaspora,[1] which Maxine Hong Kingston[2] reveals in *The Woman Warrior: Memoirs of a Girlhood among Ghosts* (1976). In order to understand the matrilineal textual bodies that the first-person narrator Maxine endeavors to construct, this chapter suggests that a transnational perspective is useful to examine the "traveling awareness." In Maxine's case, her narrative position is neither simply Chinese nor American because she is voicing multiple subjects. When rewriting or remembering the past, Maxine's narrative positions are divided into a series of complicated, almost indecipherable signs of power. To understand Maxine's narrative positions while her writing consciousness traveling through the stories of her matrilineal past, we will engage with such issues as inequalities, racism, colonization, patriarchal sexual repression, and class differences through unpacking her retrospective narrative. Many scholars, such as Inderpal Grewal, Caren Kaplan, Rey Chow, Chandra Talpade Mohanty, have discussed these elements in relation to the current developments of transnational feminism.

In *An Introduction to Women's Studies: Gender in a Transnational World*, Inderpal Grewal and Caren Kaplan propose a transnational approach to women's studies. They deliberately require new methods that would move across national boundaries with "interdisciplinary perspective" (xxii). Moreover, they use the term "transnational" to emphasize "new forms of international alliances and networks across national boundaries that are enabled by new media and technologies as well as contemporary political, economic, and cultural movements" (Grewal and Kaplan xxii). Grewal and Kaplan attempt to work across differences in cultures, requesting a holistic understanding of women's studies. As Kaplan elaborates in "The Politics of Location as Transnational Feminist Critical Practice," it is through "affiliation" that we can best identify "the grounds for historically specific differences and similarities between women in diverse and asymmetrical relations" (139). Chandra Talpade Mohanty's proposal of "feminism without borders" indicates another heightened awareness that is useful in interpreting the circulation of matrilineal bodies in Maxine's stories. Mohanty claims that instead of "borderless" feminism, her conception of "feminism without borders" acknowledges the "fault lines, conflicts, differences, fears, and containment that borders represent" (2). Mohanty wants to draw attention to "the tension between the simultaneous plurality and narrowness of borders and the emancipator potential of crossing through, with, and over these borders in our every lives" (2). These arguments provide a rich metaphor of spatial and historical displacements that is useful in understanding *The Woman Warrior*. Without the traveling awareness and the acknowledgement of her unwillingness to be silenced, Maxine's memoirs would only be read as a girl's imagination instead of a request for understanding and translation.

The translatability of culture decides its mobility. In *The Woman Warrior*, Maxine's sorrow and her repetitive effort in reimagining the matrilineal texts represent her struggles with how to establish Chinese American awareness within the American culture. For Maxine, neither Asian nor American culture provide translatable milieu for her growing-up experiences. Rey Chow reminds us: "through women's experience of social subordination, to the barbarism and mutilation that go on in other spheres of know production" (120). While analyzing the politics and pedagogy of Asian literatures in North America, Chow pinpoints the "split" of Asian identities that has been rooted in the knowledge of the history of Asian immigrants: "The concern with identity as such, of course, is not only about the personal self; however, problematizing the self does become a major theoretical development through which modern Asian texts depart from trajectories of the classics" (140). Intrigued by the tradition of "my mother talking-story," Maxine in *The Woman Warrior* deliberately narrates the forbidden secrecy, which has been silenced by patriarchal social norms. These norms have been deliberately represented by various female characters' life stories in different episodes. The revealing of "no name woman's" story releases the "linguistic admonition" (Huntley 87), of which the thou-shalt-not-tell taboo stipulates the desire to disclose stories. In other words, Chow's comment of an emerging critical means of gauging modern Asian experience in "multiplicity" stands as an legitimate one (140). However, in reading *The Woman Warrior*, not only do we have to read beyond transnational woman writers' interdisciplinary scope, we also need to take into account the inclusive as well as exclusive scope of identity that Chow has inquired and the discontinued Asian "identities" due to a split in the grand paradigms of the classical understanding of ancestry and the Asian immigrants' diasporic deprivation (140).

Like six pieces of dominos, the chapters in *The Woman Warrior* push forward one after another to build up the seemingly broken continuity. Yet, the final line of the concluding chapter, "It translated well," accumulated such a thrust that connects these stories, mythical or fictional, to enable a reconstruction of a woman writer's selfhood. To be more specific, this thrust comes from the "translation," a way that Horace Gregory has mentioned in his introduction to William Carlos Williams' *In the American Grain* and that a good writer has the power to translate fact into fabulae: "The truth of events as a cautious historian may come to know it and the meaning of that same truth to a people who have converted it into a common heritage demand a living, active synthesis. This is as true today as it always was, and the fabulae of American history, youthful and knowingly familiar as they may seem to some of us, are no exceptions to the rule" (xi). The imaginative power with which Kingston tells and retells her family story, therefore, is the narrative tactic that enables the protagonist to become a well-rounded character in search of her identity. The identity embodies multiple selves that have died but have been recollected in the lost myth and memory.[3] The verbalization of her matrilineal texts in remembering of her mother and aunts creates an instrumental self which gives birth to the music of sorrowful womanhood. Paradoxically, the rewriting of these stories—writing on top of the matrilineal texts—represents circular cycles of rebirth and death that fulfill the role of a mother. The reproduction of previous matrilineal bodies/texts, what I called "palimpsest," are the composition, translation, and transformation of memories and Maxine's understandings of the past.

Retelling the Maternal Past, Shaping Multiple Identities

The palimpsest form of narrations is a way of projecting Maxine's retrospective gazes into her-stories. Trinh T. Minh-ha has mentioned that only through writing bodies women can "rethink the body to re-appropriate femininity" (36). Taking the re-appropriation as a way of rethinking and rewriting the maternal past, the act of retelling the past is one way Maxine liberates her "selves" from repressed pain and sorrow, which does not necessarily belong to her as a person but as a descendant of her foremothers.[4] The story of her no name aunt, the woman warrior Fa Mu Lan, her mother Brave Orchid's shamanistic power in fighting the sitting ghost during her study to become a doctor, her aunt Moon Orchid, a stereotypical Chinese woman and her later insanity, and Ts'ai Yen and her diasporic song-singing, all in all, are lengthy preludes that Maxine "edited" and "released" into her own story. Many critics have pointed out that being first American-born generation Maxine is challenged to reinvent stories of her own while facing the "pain and anxiety" of being devoured into the meta-adventures of her foremothers (DeShazer 41). Thus, the final sentence of *The Woman Warrior*, "It translated well," has a special connotation, which ends the endless regenerations of all the painful or silenced talk-stories. In *Woman, Native, Other*, Trinh T. Minh-ha describes woman's writing using terms like "organic writing," "nurturing-writing" (*nour-ricriture*)" which draws its "corporeal fluidity from images of water (38). Indeed, Maxine's stories gain their lives through the reincarnations of her mothers' stories, the blood, the tears, and female bodies. Meanwhile, the sentence "It translated well" switches the flow of the storyline and connects backward to the opening chapter "No Name Woman," in which a circular scheme exists. The authorial stamp that Maxine claims to end her foremothers' talk-stories in a song and the translated sound of her diasporic sadness request her readers to retrace her heritage: "Here is a story my mother told me, not when I was young, but recently, when I told her I also talk story. The beginning is hers, the ending, mine" (106). There is no ending to this book because memories had been thrown back into the space of ancient China, a space filled with Barbarian Reed Pipe, a memoir that ends at not even semiotic representation or linguistic contemplation but mere sounds of the pipe.

If writing is an act of "self-assertion, self-revelation, and self-preservation" as Amy Ling defines, why would Maxine Hong Kingston return her storytelling journey back to such a hollow space (219)? Within such hollow space, there exists explosive power that the narrative keeps connecting back to the beginning into something that projects the coming of a later development. It is the *möbius* flow of the narrative fluidity and the air flush that inspire this chapter. I contend that it is precisely the ceaseless mother-daughter connection that seduces Kingston to create her womanhood and selfhood. However, the mother-daughter relationship does not only refer to the narrow definition of blood relationship. The translation expresses the atavistic complexity of the general "foremothers" inside or outside of the family. The mothers and daughters have not only blood relationship but also the metaphysical transcended connection, which can mythically, sympathetically, or fictionally related and strengthen the tie in between.

Tracing back to her heritage creates the sad image of Maxine as a spirit in a ghost land, except that now she becomes the ghost among the rest of the Americans. The other land living experiences takes a double-edge in referring to both the long lost China in Maxine's lexicon and the de-familiarized America that she can hardly return. In America, she speaks a language that people cannot fully comprehend, as that of Ts'ai Yen's "high and clear" voice (109). Her sadness is further worsened in her expression of a cut frenum, a mouth that will not express herself fluently in Chinese or Cantonese. Sarcastically, it has the counter-effect that Maxine's mother wished it to have. It was a great maternal expectation for her to "speak languages that are completely different from one another" and "to pronounce anything" (164). Even if so, the incomprehensible, though impenetrable and indecipherable, has successfully "trans-lated" her desire in ending the story the way that turned out to be unintelligible. This translation carries both the denotative unspeakable quality of the trauma of Chinese women within the patrilineal society and the connotative delay of vocalizing their sorrow through musical notes. The interpolated her-story would never sound alike the straightforward his-story; nevertheless, it is the diasporic power and the constantly rewriting of the forbidden maternal text, which transfers those talk-stories into written texts. Moreover, these "forever wandering" texts are not fixed and do not withhold an unchangeable rigidity; they may sound like Chinese, but "the barbarians understood their sadness and anger" (169).

The sorrow of diaspora echoes to what Kingston mentioned in a video produced by Modern Educational Video Network, in which she emphasizes the importance of multicultural environment in San Francisco and her education in Berkeley. Her retreat to Hawaii during the vehemently anti–Vietnam war protests, her travel to China under the sponsorship of the American Writer association with Toni Morrison and several renowned American poets and writers, and her son, a hybrid American who works as a Hawaii cruise musician, seem to conclusively established the realistic twentieth-century version of "A Song for a Barbarian Reed Pipe." In *The Woman Warrior*, the tactic that Kingston adopts is what Catherine Lappas mentioned as the "third culture" that cross-culturally mixes reality and myth (58). The alter-culture issue I shall address further other places in the future. Here, I wish to focus on the exercises of the renewal and the infuriating strength of the storytelling, which allows Maxine's stories to reach the "mythical construction" (Lappas 58).

This power of renewal is frequently seen in women's autobiographical writing. According to Sidonie Smith, "twentieth century autobiographical narrative often become absorbingly contestatory and unabashedly 'fictional' as the autobiographer asks the reader to follow her in order to see something new, to see the same thing anew" (44). The "No Name Woman" story is told not to inform but to understand who her mother is and how her mother retells the story. Maxine tells her readers:

> If I want to learn what clothes my aunt wore, whether flashy or ordinary, I would have to begin, "Remember Father's drowned-in-the-well sister?" I cannot ask that. My mother has told me once and for all the *useful* parts. She will add nothing unless powered by *Necessity*, a riverbank that guides her life. She plants vegetable gardens rather than lawns; she carries the odd-shaped tomatoes home from the fields and eats food left for the gods [6; Italics added].

"Useful" and "necessity" are the value that Brave Orchid lives in. Maxine tries to understand what might have happened in her aunt's life and she reasons to structure the unsaid part of her aunt's life: "Adultery is extravagance.... To be a woman, to have a daughter in starvation time was a waste enough. My aunt could not have been the lone romantic who gave up everything for sex. Women in the old China did not choose. Some man had commanded her to lie with him and be his secret evil" (6). Maxine's questions and conjectures of the "truth" of her aunt's unlawful pregnancy conjures the horror, sour-and-sweet sadness, and fragility of being a woman in a Chinese society: "She always did as she was told" and "[But] women at sex hazarded birth and hence lifetimes. The fear did not stop but permeated everywhere" (6, 7). At this point, the story interjects her mother's storytelling. Maxine begins to narrate the potential versions of her aunt's life. Tracing back to her aunt, she explains how Chinese society networks strangers justly into sibling during those days of poverty through dowries or family bonds. The harsh accusation, "[A]dultery, perhaps only a mistake during good times, became a crime when the village needed food" highlights the iron-fact of how women or being women in that scenario is alienated and isolated as inhuman (13).

On the one hand, the refreshing but astonishing way that Kingston narrates the "child-birth" and suicide scene shows high-voltage of humanity and motherly love:

> At its birth the two of them had felt the same raw pain of separation, a wound that only the family pressing tight could close. A child with no descent line would not soften her life but only trail after her, ghost-like, begging her to give it purpose...
> Full of milk, the little ghost slept. When it awoke, she hardened her breasts against the milk that crying loosens. Toward morning she picked up the baby and walked to the well.
> Carrying the baby to the well show loving. Otherwise abandon it. Turn its face into the mud. Mothers who love their children take them along. It was probably a girl; there is some hope of forgiveness for boys [15].

On the other hand, it shows the pathetic ugliness of a malfunctioning patriarchal society. The Catharsis climaxes when both the terror and beauty explode, but Kingston does not stop there. She grabs the drill and stabs through her established paper-thin story. Kingston had Maxine admits her crime of participating in the constitution of this hypocritical paternal order. Her silence is complicitous. The story could have ended there with sadness and self-condemnation; however, Maxine moves on, offering more contemporary and enhanced thoughts upon her family and her aunt during the Mao-period China. The social-communism disrupts the concept of consanguinity as an inclusive relationship among people.

Since Mao's ideology focused on soldiers and workers, it omits the tradition of the lineal ancestry. Thanks to this discontinuity of marriage-recruited family, the no name aunt remains now the outcast ghost who "remains forever hungry" (16). The haunting is no longer the terror toward the unknown member of the family, for Maxine, it is rather the unforgiving water-ghost aunt with her young baby outside of the family tradition that scares her. Even Maxine is not sure if her aunt means her well. Though Maxine's paper is "not origamied into houses and clothes," it is "pages of paper" devoted to her, to accommodate her story of the contempt and the conspicuous female body.

In her essay "This Sex Which is Not One," Luce Irigaray proposes the notion of contiguity, which was embedded in female voice. Irigaray draws our attention to "the multiplicity of that female desire and female language" (253). Kingston's palimpsest weaving of her-stories reverberates coincidently with Luce Irigaray assertion:

> Woman always remains several, but she is kept from dispersion because the other is already within her and is autoerotically familiar to her. Which is not to say that she appropriates the other for herself, that she reduces it to her own property. Ownership and property are doubtless quite foreign to the feminine. At least sexually. But not *nearness*. Nearness so pronounced that it makes all discrimination of identity, and thus all forms of property, impossible. Woman derives pleasure from what is *so near that she cannot have it, nor have herself*. She herself enters into a ceaseless exchange of herself with the other without any possibility of identifying either [254; italics in the original].

The multiple exchanges of herself and her mothers' stories within the patriarchal triangle encourage the narratives to indulge in entering selves. In *The Woman Warrior*, the narratives initiate this voracity so that the narration continues to weave diversity. This stripe of five prose episodes in *The Woman Warrior* touches upon one another with Maxine's ceaseless voice behind all the stories. According to Irigaray, as long as woman dares to say something concerning herself, she constantly "steps ever so slightly aside from herself with a murmur, an exclamation, a whisper, a sentence left unfinished.... When she returns, it is to set off again from elsewhere" (253). The spirit of mumbling from the other point of view, of always engaging in weaving stories that combines pleasure and pain, of breaking up the exact meaning to come to the multiple she-selves, and of extolling each stories to another beginning, in short, are the female energy of motherly sentiments that elevate and extend Kingston's story to so many different perspectives and to have been taught, analyzed, and critiqued by different ethnical readerships and disciplines (Huntley 13–14, 75).

Moreover, the fact that Kingston is an American-born Chinese writer gives her a unique niche in addressing such communions of multiple identities.[5] Because there are multiple narrators talking their stories, the palimpsest marks are everywhere in the text. For example, in the beginning of "Shaman" episode, Maxine opens her mother's story this way: "Once in a long while, four times so far for me, my mother brings out the metal tube that holds her medical diploma" (57). This constantly repetition of physical contact with objects is a key connection, networking memories of her mother which restore and reboot the programming of the stories.

Palimpsest as Translated Memories

Rebuilding the memories to remember the past, for Maxine, becomes a task that has to include sensual depictions. Maxine's storytelling invites visuality of sensual depictions. As Shu-mei Shih mentions in her *Visuality and Identity*, "contemporary identities are much more nuanced, fragmented, and multiple. It is increasingly the case that linguistic and cultural boundaries do not coincide with national boundaries" (20). Maxine's delineation of her diasporic selves in foreign lands is historically rooted in her immigrant identity as an in-between character. Considering the stories as a textual body, Maxine's narrative selves are multiple and each has to be perceived through different layers of senses. Scent is one of the most obsessive and mesmerizing feature of being. In the description of her mother's diploma in the metal tube with the ideograph "joy" in abstract, Kingston's writing demonstrates the visual simplicity of how the tactics of palimpsest broadens the notion of memory: "When I open it, the smell of China flies out, a thousand-year-old bat flying heavy-headed out of the Chinese caverns where bats are as white as dust, a smell that comes from long ago, far back in the brain. Crates from Caton, Hong Kong, Singapore, and Taiwan have that smell too, only stronger because they are more recently come from the Chinese" (57). This reuniting the regional smells and the odors of the past are imprints that the narratives can possibly bear the weight and fragmentation of genetic, ethnic, and even sinophone identities. Not only do we have textual depictions of smells, there are also images of "chrysanthemum," "breast," and visual delineations of her parents in motionless portraits (59). However, these portraits are brought back alive. According to Seyla Benhabib, "the narration is also a project of recollection and retrieval. We can only retrieve more or less, retell more or less, those memories ingrained upon the body, those somatic impressions of touch, tone, and odor that have defined our early being-in-the-world" (230). Benhabib discusses the narrative formation from psychoanalytical viewpoint, addressing the working of unconsciousness during the process of narrating memories. In Maxine's stories, the difference lies in the contrast between father and mother. Her father owns so many snapshots while her mother has none but the one graduate photo with her classmates. This image of mother among her comrades and father alone in the picture taken while he was studying places men and women in a segregated time and space—when men sailed to another country alone while his woman stays in China with no one but her fellow female friends.

The palimpsest exist everywhere, it brings back the memories of the physical mother while simultaneously establishing the mystique of female knowledge without commenting on the social system. In her mother's case, it was fortunate to mingle among the girls rather than reposed back at home and ended up like her no name aunt: "Free from families, my mother would live for two years without servitude. She would not have to run errands for my father's tyrant mother with the bound feet or thread needles for the old ladies, but neither would there be slaves and nieces to wait on her. Now she would get hot water only if she bribed the concierge. When I went away to school my mother said, "Give the concierge oranges" (62). This passage pinpoints that Maxine is not only re-producing what had happened to her mother and what would have had happened if her mother didn't go for the medical school; meanwhile, there is the transition of motherly heritage at the end of the description. Maxine tells how her mother built up a reputation for being brilliant and how she allows other students to take a "glimpse" at her paper. For Maxine's mother, memorizing medical information from books is not the gist. The mystique is not words but "clues in actual diagnosis" (Kingston 64). Brave Orchid does not worry about her paper begin plagiarized because she emphasizes on the tradition of sharing and also her understanding of medical knowledge as one that is not a doctor's egotistic establishment:

"Did you ever try to stop them from copying your paper?"
"Of course not. They only needed to pick up a word or two, and they could remember the rest. That's not copying. You get a lot more clues in actual diagnosis. Patients talk endlessly about their ailments. I'd feel their pulses knocking away under my very fingertips— so much clearer than the paperdolls in the textbooks. I'd chant the symptoms, and those few words would start a whole chapter of cures tumbling out. Most people don't have the kind of brains that can do that." She pointed at the photograph of the thirty-seven graduates. "One hundred and twelve students began the course at the same time I did." [64].

The mentality of a taste of the past allows more rooms for rethinking the original of herself. She is the daughter of a mother who shares tea, "the act of humility," with everyone around her. In comparison to her father's ability in reciting whole poems, Brave Orchid's meekness leads to the conclusion that she might not have the "right kind of brains," thus, she did secretly studying. Her philosophy is that "the sweat of hard work is not to be displayed. It is much more graceful to appear favored by the gods" (64). Maxine's retelling of her mother's story through unveiling her mother's thoughts and the disclosing the ontological differences between herself and her mother; thus, the differences guide her to her own being.

The name-calling exercises in the Chinese tradition reveals the private space in which women inhabit a place with second or multiple names. Before Brave Orchid enters the room to investigate the ghost, she paused at the door and said to her friend: "'[If] I am very afraid when you find me, don't forget to tweak my ears. Call my name and tell me how to get home.' She told them her personal name" (68). In a discussion of the narrative constitution of the self, Benhabib uses Charles Taylors' *Sources of the Self* in relating to the dialogical contingency of the metaphor of the "webs of interlocution" (224–25). It is impossible to be a self while there is no relation with a group of conversation partners. In Chinese tradition, married women would only be addressed as their husband's wife. Most of the female acquaintances do not know each other's names. Personal names are exchanged only among intimate private circles. Brave Orchid's deliberate reminder of calling out her name tells how she can regain herself through chanting. This is a process which we can adopt Charles Taylor's "webs of interlocution" (36) to understand Brave Orchid's being able to return to her body. Furthermore, In "Sexual Difference and Collective Identities," Seyla Benhabib also uses the Heideggerian sense of *Geworfenheit* when discussing the constitution of self, she says: "[To] be and to become a self is to insert oneself into webs of interlocution: it is to know how to answer when one is addressed; in turn, it is learning how to address others" (225). With a connotation of Heidegger's sense of *Geworfenheit* and Taylor's argument about self-constitution, it is pivotal to say that the name-calling awakening of Brave Orchid from the ghostland back to her human being is a process of returning to her id-entity. Without her name, she cannot return and recognize her body. That is why the chanting and storytelling are important and have been constantly repeated to her daughter.

Similar to this narrative tactics in formulating self, Alicia Partnoy, the Argentina poetess, says, "I talked and talked, telling everybody my story. In a sense this is what I have been doing since I went into exile. I have been talking about what happened to me in the framework of what happened to the whole country, to the whole continent. That's the way to make people understand" (195). Alicia Partnoy realizes in her exile that she has to search for political surveillance to dwell in America away from political persecutions. Staying in her second homeland, she cannot change back her pure Argentina identity and origin. In exile, the only way to heal and understand her is to continuing the process of naming herself. To release her stories to her surroundings, Brave Orchid will return from her exile into the unknown back to her body and her story.

Here, my emphasis is the importance of the family spirit expressed by the name-calling ceremony. The fact that there is a community as her support, indeed, breaks the limits of being possessed by the ghost under the limits of master and slave. Once the intimacy of the name-calling is performed through the interlocution of a group of female friends, Brave Orchid will return from the isolated prison return back to a household that includes multiple, complex perspectives and voices that argues and contests each other; hence, she would become alive again (Benhabib 229). The speech that Brave Orchid delivers while encountering the ghost is a successful talking tactics that defunct the name of the ghost:

> "I do not give in," she said. "There is no pain you can inflict that I cannot endure. You're wrong if you think I'm afraid of you. You're no mystery to me. I've heard of you Sitting Ghosts before. Yes, people have lived to tell about you. You kill babies, you cowards. You have no power over a strong woman. You are no more dangerous than a nesting cat. My dog sits on my feet more heavily than

you can. You think this is suffering? I can make my ears ring louder by taking aspirin. Are these all the tricks you have, Ghost? Sitting and ringing? That's nothing. A Broom Ghost can do better. You cannot even assume an interesting shape. Merely a boulder. A hairy butt boulder. You must not be a ghost at all. Of course. There are no such things as ghosts" [70].

The homecoming chanting, like translations of the family histories, writes out a train of the location of herself: "Return, daughter of New Society Village, Kwangtung Province. Your brother and sisters call you. Your friends call you. We need you. Return to us. Return to us at the To Keung School. There's work to do. Come back. Doctor Brave Orchid, be unafraid. Be unafraid. You are safe now in the To Keung School. All is safe. Return" (71–72). The multiple echoing of self-understanding and returning from the haunted-land consistently bring back the thickness of palimpsest.

To specify Kingston's rewriting of selves from others, I would like to raise an extreme example to juxtapose aside it the difference of young male understanding. In the beginning of James Joyce's *A Portrait of the Artist as a Young Man*, Stephen Dedalus try to understand himself while reading a book of geography. Instead of becoming himself among his peers, Stephen writes out, alone and quietly, a hierarchical graph of himself in order to picture himself in the universe:

Stephen Dedalus
Class of Elements
Clongowes Wood College
Sallins
County Kildare
Ireland
Europe
The World
The Universe [15].

The zooming-out self-declaration does not help him to understand himself. There is no one around him. On the opposite of the page, there are four lines verses: "Stephen Dedalus is my name,/ Ireland is my nation./ Clongowes is my dwellingplace/ And heaven my expectation" (16). For Stephen, if verse were read backwards, there is no poetry. However, Brave Orchid's girl friends' chanting, forward or backward, will still be effective in calling her lost mind back to her body. While establishing himself as an individual in the universe, Stephen couldn't stop pondering on one question: "What was after the universe? Nothing" (16). On the contrary, the chanting recalling Brave Orchid back to herself begins from "Come home," and ends at "Return." Unlike Stephen, Brave Orchid does not have to labor to throw himself into the gigantic space alone. Brave Orchid returns, in Maxine's memorial description, to the "Abundant comfort in long restoring waves" (72). Returning to her community, Brave Orchid's soul "returned fully to her and nestled happily inside her skin, for this moment not traveling in the past where her children were nor to America to be with my father. She was back among many people. She rested after battle. She left friends watch out for her" (72). I am not saying that Stephen Dedalus' contemplation as a singular projection whereas Maxine's self-understanding of her mother and aunt's stories, based on such returning tactics repetitively, returns to the beginning. The sisters went through a smoke ceremony into the Ghost room; after the ceremony ends, they found a piece of wood dripping with blood. Together they burned the wood (75). Readers will never know how they look like when "they laughed at the smell of the corpse exhumed for its bones" (75); nevertheless, the smell reconnects to the beginning of the story, resuscitates the communal Chinese smell, the smell with "joy." The mother-daughter relationships, in the later part when Maxine begins her own story after her mother come to join her father, becomes a translated story full of motherly love, teaching, cooking, and memories in the real ghostly America.

This palimpsest tactics brings Kingston to the platform of ethnic autobiographic writing. Her memoirs are not only documents of individual identity and life, like that of the fictional Stephen Dedalus, they are also written works of an translator who has reached her own specific ethnic self-recognition, using "memory to trace their collective development as a people" (Hernandez 41). Adapting the example of Anzaldúa, Jennifer Browdy de Hernandez mentioned about the non–Western oral tradition and the various ritualistic acts that inscribes the ethnic autobiography, she proposes, "the individual identity is subordinate to the collective identity, and this emphasis appears in their autobiographies, which fuse the Western autobiographical 'I' with the ethnic 'we'" (42). Immigrated to American, the prodigal daughter Maxine keeps reminding her mother the fact that they are now a different breed: "We belong to the planet now, Mama. Does it make sense to you that if we're no longer attached to one piece of land, we belong to the planet? Wherever we happen to be standing, why, that spot belongs to us as much as any other spot." Can we spend the fare money on furniture and cars? Will American flowers smell good now?" (107). Throughout her talk-story, we have the sense that Brave Orchid had struggled with her ethnic identity and the living standard of America: "This is terrible ghost country, where a human being works her life away," she said, "Even the ghosts work, no time for acrobatics. I have not stopped working since the day the ship landed. I was on my feet the moment the babies were out. In China I never even had to hang up my own clothes. I shouldn't have left, but your father couldn't have supported you without me. I'm the one with the big muscles" (104). Her self-understanding contains images of the migration birds[6], the images of the wings attached to her big muscles, and the protecting wing attached to her hands around her babies. The powerful working mother with big muscles embodies the collective human memories from the occidental Paleolithic mother goddess enshrined in figurines to Inanna of Sumer, Isis of Egypt, Aphrodite of Greece, the Joan of Arc, the goddess of Columbus, the status of

Liberty to the oriental goddess of Nu Wa, the goddess of the creativity, the West Queen Mother, and Lei Zu, to name just a few among thousands.

On the one hand, I want to emphasize the thickness of this enriched mirroring to the past, the palimpsest tradition of the constant migration from self to self, from nation to nation, from body to another; on the other hand, I want not to overlook the attenuating tendency of migration embedded in the text, that is, from mother to daughter, from China in the past to Chinese American at the present, from once upon the time to nowadays. The thinness of Maxine's own story lies in the fictional aspect of her memoirs which attains the flexibility of translating from the known to the unknown, from fragmented to the collective memories, and from the sights and scenes to mere sounds.

Diasporic Sorrow: Homeless Women

The migrated Brave Orchid passes from a point of refusal to a certain degree of acknowledgement of her new life. The struggling also causes the thinness of the palimpsest to attain the elasticity:

> "I don't want to go back anyway," she said. "I've gotten used to eating. And the Communists are much too mischievous. You should see the ones I meet in the fields. They bring sacks under their clothes to steal grapes and tomatoes from the growers. They come with trucks on Sundays. And they're killing each other in San Francisco. One of the old man caught his visitor, another old fellow, stealing his bantam; the owner spotted its black feet sticking out of his guest's sweater.... They're [the new immigrants] Chinese, and Chinese are mischievous. No, I'm too old to keep up with them. They'd be too clever for me. I've lost my cunning, having grown accustomed to food, you see. There's only one thing that I really want anymore. I want you here, not wandering like a ghost from Romany. I want every one of you living here together. When you're all home, all six of you with your children and husbands and wives, there are twenty or thirty people in this house. Then I'm happy. And your father is happy." [107–08].

However, Maxine will not stay with her parents and her mother compromises with that decision. She is no longer the "little dog" who needs the pseudonym in prevention from god's curse or jealousy. She will not behave abide by the ancient Chinese rules. Both her and her mother spent much time in American; both of them born in dragon years and Maxine is "practically a first daughter of a first daughter," the eldest dragon of her dragon mom. The diaspora senses of fear and loss demonstrate well in the different opinions between her mother and herself. Her mother does not want her to speak Chinese with the "Garbage Ghost" because she worries that once the "White Ghost" learns how to speak Chinese, they lives will be endangered. Her mother warns her: "You mustn't talk in front of them again. Someday, very soon, we're going home, where there are Han people everywhere. We'll buy furniture then, real tables and chairs. You children will smell flowers for the first time" (98). Her mother's nostalgia toward the 'China in her memory, the place where she and her husband were originally from has changed. Maxine grows up and becomes more and more "scientific" that she does not feel the same way as her parents does. She has oscillating feelings, both fear and curiosity, toward this land her mother called "home"; she imagines her situation in China as a girl maggot who has to witness all the insensible and incomprehensible social myth, she says in fear, "[In] China my parents would sell my sisters and me. My father would marry two or three more wives, who would spatter cooking oil on our bare toes and lie that we were crying for naughtiness. They would give food to their own children and rocks to us. I did not want to go where their ghosts took shapes nothing like our own" (99). R. Radhakrishnan had discussed this issue of both home country and the adopted country of residence become "ghostly locations" in terms of the "depoliticization" of both venues (123). The lost of rooted authenticity, of habitually return to a point when one has to ask where is their motherland, eventually, lead to the result of this diasporanic sense of hollowness.

Nonetheless, this diasporic hollowness is also a full whole in Kingston's writing — the feminine writing which resembles to the monthly lunar changes, from new to full moon. In resisting the mere sorrow, the palimpsest tactic does not necessarily fall to the sadness of self-pity. To the end of her own story which imbricates from her foremothers' stories, Maxine has a story ends her way. The barbarians, though cannot speak Ts'ai Yen's Chinese words, "understood their sadness and anger. Sometimes, they thought they could catch barbarian phrases about forever wandering" (209). The sense of returning to the embrace of an alien community transgresses the seemly impossible boundaries between words and music. The theme of identity cannot be decided in traditional linear writing:

> Personal identity is the ever fragile achievement of needy and dependent creatures whose capacity to develop a coherent life-story out of the multiple, competing, and often irreconcilable voices and perspectives of childhood must be cherished and protected. Furthering one's capacity for autonomous agency is only possible within a solidaristic community that sustains one's identity through listening to one and allowing one to listen to others with respect within the many webs of interlocution that constitute our lives [Benhabib 230].

The Chinese American identity is not a fixed, established, or a priori term. The ad-hoc-ness of the identity construction is what Stuart Hall called the "becoming" (236). Lisa Lowe interprets this process of the birth of cultural identity in terms of a "spectrum of positions" which I find it relative to my previous arguments of the "beginningness," "reincarnation," "migration," "palimpsest," and "circulation," Lowe comments, "at one end, the desire for a cultural identity represented by a fixed profile of traits and, at the other, challenges to the notion of singularity and conceptions of *race* as the material *locus* of differences, intersections, and incommensurability" (136; italics in the original). This thrust of palimpsest writing is a stable progress which accommodates various practices that can be "partly inherited, partly modified, as well as partly invented" (Lowe 136).

Looking at the reworking of Maxine's stories, we discover that the maternal bodies have been either deleted from family history, obligated to put on male garments, relinquished professional aspiration as a medical doctor, turned delirious or merely seen as a reproductive machine for giving Han descendants. The contrast between a Han and an American shows a problematic political argument contextualized within the narrative. Regardless of Han or Chinese American heritage, the maternal bodies travel from one "place" to another, but they can hardly be replaced within the order of the Fathers as an equal subject. In Chinese tradition, this incapacity to be properly acknowledged within the patrilineal order relegates the women in Maxine's stories to a fringe post. Similarly, the Chinese American is deemed as the lower-class laborer, doing laundry or mining. The inherited matrilineal understandings of her past, for Maxine, reveal the potential for traveling in between two statuses: reworking her Chinese-ness while reinventing her selfhood into a transformed Chinese American.

In the ending note, Maxine introduces Ts'ai Yen's "Eighteen Stanzas for a Barbarian Reed Pipe." Her attempt to reconstruct the Chinese American maternal text/body is a retro of an earlier story. The re-articulation of the past and the reweaving of the sounds in the past into the present representations of pages dedicate to the endless construction of Maxine's ethnic identity. Remembering the past is a way she adds another tune into her names. The palimpsest tactics calligraphies Maxine Hong Kingston's name and memories of her past, and mixes her-stories into a jade dish full of reflections. The mirroring of a self-image through the past reflection is never going to reach an illuminating level of clarity. Nevertheless, the music embodies the subversive power, yet, the concluding line "it translated well" does not translate. Instead, the three-word sentence requires more effort to connect Chinese and American understanding of the maternal past. Moreover, the inscription of thou-shall-not-tell urges the birth of a nonentity, a ghost within her textual body. Maxine has arrived at the painful retelling of the past but the hyphenated Chinese-American subjectivity as a woman, like the song of everlasting music, remains a "-", instead of a signifier. As the story has been thrown into sound at the end, the hyphenation remains a scar that segregates multiple identities.

Notes

1. The matrilineality is considered one of the important characteristics of Chinese American literature. Sau-ling C. Wong has listed several fictionalized biographies with such matrilineal component (51).
2. In this chapter, I will follow Paul Outka's reference in calling the author Kingston and the protagonist as "Maxine" (448).
3. According to Sidonie Smith's extensive study on the truth and identity out of mythical construction, she uses Goria Anzaldúa, Cherrié Moraga, and Hélène Cixous' proclama-

tions to demonstrate the transformation and mystique figuration of women's polylogical selves within different cultures. See Smith's article, "Construing Truth in Lying Mouths: Truthtelling in Women's Autobiography."

4. Many memoirs have reflected such quality, such as George Eliot, James Joyce, and Wordsworth's poems. Proust's novel deals directly with the memories of the dead. A.S. Byatt commented that such tie in between memories and the dead connects not only the memories of the dead, "both the immediately dead and remembered, and long-dead whose memories construed the culture we live in and change in our turn" (51).

5. Amy Ling points out special traits that American-born Chinese writers share, that is, because of the growing up experiences of always imbibing the customs of two cultures, of being raised up as a "racial minority," they are conscious of their identity. See Ling 220.

6. This is a lyric sang by Libana. "There's a river of birds in migration/ a nation of women with wings." The song is collected in *A Circle Is Cast* sang by Oregon Women's Land Community in celebrating the spirit of community.

Bibliography

Anzaldúa, Glora. *Borderlands/La Frontera: The New Mestiza*. San Francisco, CA: Spinsters/aunt lute, 1987.
Benhabib, Seyla. "Sexual Difference and Collective Identities: The New Constellation." *Virtual Gender: Fantasies of Subjectivity and Embodiment*. Eds. Mary Ann O'Farrell and Lynn Vallone. Ann Arbor, MI: Michigan University Press, 1999. 217–43.
Benstock, Shari. "The Female Self Engendered: Autobiographical Writing and Theories of Selfhood." *Women and Autobiography*. Eds. Martine Watson Brownley and Allison B. Kimmich. Wilmington, DE: Scholarly Resources Inc., 1999. 3–13.
Braziel, Jana Evans, and Anita Mannur. "Nation, Migration, Globalization: Points of Contention in Diaspora Studies." *Theorizing Diaspora*. Eds. Jana Evans Braziel and Anita Mannur. Oxford: Blackwell, 2003. 1–22.
Byatt, A. S. "Memory and the Making of Fiction." *Memory*. Eds. Patricia Fara and Karalyn Patterson. Cambridge: Cambridge University Press, 1998. 47–72.
Chow, Rey. "Against the Lures of Diaspora: Minority Discourse, Chinese Women, and Intellectual Hegemony." *Writing Diaspora: Tactics of Intervention in Contemporary Cultural Studies*. Bloomington and Indianapolis, IN: Indiana University Press, 1993. 99–119.
DeShazer, Mary K. "A Whole New Psychic Geography": Women Poets and Creative Identity." *Inspiring Women: Reimagining the Muse*. New York: Pergamon, 1986. 1–44.
Greenblatt, Stephen. "Cultural Mobility: An Introduction." *Cultural Mobility: A Manifesto*. Eds. Stephen Greenblatt, Ines G. Županov, Reinhard Meyer-Kalkus, Heike Paul, Pál Nyíri, and Friederike Pannewick. Cambridge and New York: Cambridge University Press, 2010. 1–23.
Gregory, Horace. "Introduction" in William Carlos Williams' *In the American Grain*. New York: New Directions, 1956. ix–xx.
Grewal, Inderpal and Caren Kaplan, eds. *An Introduction to Women's Studies: Gender in a Transnational World*. Boston, McGraw-Hill Higher Education, 2006.
_____. *Scattered Hegemonies: Postmodernity and Transnational Feminist Practices*. Minneapolis, MN: University of Minnesota Press, 1994.
Hall, Stuart. "Cultural Identity and Diaspora." *Theorizing Diaspora*. Eds. Jana Evans Braziel and Anita Mannur. Oxford: Blackwell, 2003. 233–46.
_____. "From 'Routes' to Roots." *A Place in the World*. Eds. Doreen Massey and Pat Jess. New York and Oxford: Oxford University Press, 1995. 206–07.

Hernanez, Jennifer Browdy De. "The Plural Self: The politicization of Memory and Form in Three American Ethnic Autobiographies." *Memory and Cultural Politics: New Approaches to American Ethnic Literature.* Eds. Amritjit Singh, Joseph T. Skerrett, Jr., Robert E. Hogan. Boston, MA: Northeastern University Press, 1996. 41–59.

Hunt, Linda. "'I Could Not Figure Out What Was My Village': Gender vs. Ethnicity in Maxine Hong Kingston's *The Woman Warrior*." *MELUS* 12.3 (1985): 5–12.

Huntley, E.D. "The Woman Warrior: Memoirs of a Girlhood among Ghosts." *Maxine Hong Kingston: A Critical Companion.* Westport, CT: Greenwood, 2001. 75–114.

Irigaray, Luce. "This Sex Which Is Not One." *Writing on the Body: Female Embodiment and Feminist Theory.* Eds. Katie Conboy, Nadia Medina, and Sarah Stanbury. New York: Columbia University Press, 1997. 248–56.

Joyce, James. *A Portrait of the Artist as a Young Man.* 1916. Ed. Chester G. Anderson. New York: Viking Press, 1968.

Kaplan, Caren. "The Politics of Location as Transnational Feminist Critical Practice." *An Introduction to Women's Studies: Gender in a Transnational World.* Eds. Grewal and Kaplan. Boston: McGraw Hill Higher Education, 2006. 137–52.

_____. "Resisting Autobiography: Out-Law Genres and Transnational Feminist Subjects." *De/Colonizing the Subject: The Politics of Gender in Women's Autobiography.* Eds. Sidonie Smith and Julia Watson. Minneapolis, MN: University of Minnesota Press, 1992. 115–38.

Kingston, Maxine Hong. *The Woman Warrior—Memoirs of a Girlhood Among Ghosts.* New York: Vintage, 1989.

Lappas, Catherine. "'The way I heard it was...': Myth, Memory, and Autobiography in *Storyteller* and *The Woman Warrior*." *CEA Critic* 57.1 (1994): 57–67.

Ling, Amy. "Chinese American Woman Writers: The Tradition behind Maxine Hong Kingston." *Redefining American Literary History.* Eds. A. La Vonne Brown Ruoff and Jerry W. Ward, Jr. New York: MLA, 1990. 219–36.

Lowe, Lisa. "Heterogeneity, Hybridity, Multiplicity: Marking Asian-American Differences." Braziel and Mannur 132–55.

Minh-ha, Trinh T. *Woman, Native, Other: Writing Postcoloniality and Feminism.* Bloomington and Indianapolis, IN: Indiana University Press, 1989.

Mohanty, Chandra Talpade. *Feminism Without Borders: Decolonizing Theory, Practicing Solidarity.* Durham, NC: Duke University Press, 2003.

Outka, Paul. "Publish or Perish: Food, Hunger, and Self-Construction in Maxine Hong Kingston's *The Woman Warrior*." *Contemporary Literature* 38.3 (1997): 447–82.

Partnoy, Alicia. "They Cut Off My Voice, So I Grew Two Voices." *Women in Exile.* Ed. Mahnaz Afkhami. Charlottesville, VA: University Press of Virginia, 1994. 100–09.

Radhakrishnan, R. "Ethnicity in an Age of Diaspora." Braziel and Mannur 119–55.

Shih, Shu-mei. *Visuality and Identity: Sinophone Articulations across the Pacific.* Berkeley, CA: University of California Press, 2007.

Simmons, Diane. *Maxine Hong Kinston.* New York: Twayne, 1999.

Smith, Sidonie. "Construing Truth in Lying Mouths: Truthtelling in Women's Autobiography." *Women and Autobiography.* Eds. Maritine Watson Brownley and Allison B. Kimmich. Wilmington, DE: Scholarly Resources, 1999. 33–52.

_____. "Virtually Modern Amelia: Mobility, Flight, and the Discontents of Identity." *Virtual Gender: Fantasies of Subjectivity and Embodiment.* Eds. Mary Ann O'Farrell and Lynne Valone. Ann Arbor, MI: University of Michigan Press, 1999. 11–36.

Taylor, Charles. *Sources of The Self.* Cambridge, MA: Harvard University Press, 1989.

Wong, Sau-Ling C. *An Interethnic Companion to Asian American Literature.* Cambridge: Cambridge University Press, 1997.

About the Contributors

Lan Dong is the author of *Reading Amy Tan* (Greenwood, 2009), *Mulan's Legend and Legacy in China and the United States* (Temple University Press, forthcoming), and a number of articles and book chapters on Asian American literature, children's literature, and popular culture. She is currently editing a critical collection on teaching graphic narratives. She holds a Ph.D. in comparative literature and is assistant professor of English at the University of Illinois–Springfield where she teaches Asian American literature, world literature, and global culture.

Catherine Gomes is a lecturer in the School of Media and Communication at RMIT University in Melbourne, Australia where she specializes in Asian media and culture. She has published widely in the areas of gender and ethnicity in Chinese cinema, cross-cultural reception of transnational Chinese films, and memory and transnationalism in Singapore. She is currently working on the Singapore experience in Australia, a book project based on her doctoral thesis and an edited book collection on homelands.

Nancy Kang is a faculty fellow in the humanities at Syracuse University, affiliated with the Department of English and the Transnational Asian/Asian American Studies Program. She specializes in American ethnic literature, particularly African American, Asian American, and Native American prose of the nineteenth and twentieth century. Her work has appeared in such journals as *African American Review* and *Essays on Canadian Writing*.

Karen An-hwei Lee is the author of *Ardor* (Tupelo Press, 2008), *In Medias Res* (Sarabande Books, 2004), and *God's One Hundred Promises* (Swan Scythe Press, 2002). She holds an M.F.A. from Brown University and a Ph.D. in British and American literature from the University of California at Berkeley. The recipient of a National Endowment for the Arts Grant and a poet and literary critic, she chairs the English Department at a faith-based college in southern California.

Danicar Mariano holds an M.A. in literary and cultural studies from the Ateneo de Manila University. She also has an M.A. in Asia Pacific studies from the University of San Francisco. In 2007-2008, she received the Yuchengco Graduate Fellowship from the Center of the Pacific Rim. She has published in *Antithesis* journal and has worked as writer-researcher for a book project entitled *People's Communications* *for Development* at the International Development Research Center and Isis International Manila. She is a member of Women, Education, Development and Productivity Research Organization (WEDPRO). Her research interests include gender and sexuality as well as trafficking and prostitution.

Amy N. Nishimura is an assistant professor at the University of Hawai'i at West Oahu. She teaches courses on rhetoric and composition, Asian American literature, and multicultural literature. Her research interests include diaspora studies, feminist literary theory, and globalization. Her current research is on the women internees in Hawai'i during World War II with a particular focus on the Honolulu and Sand Island camps on the island of Oahu.

J. Sunita Peacock, associate professor of English, received her Ph.D. from Southern Illinois University in 1996. She currently teaches world and Eastern literatures at Slippery Rock University in Pennsylvania. She has published in such refereed journals as *Commonwealth Novel in English*, *Pakistani Women's Journal*, *International Journal of the Humanities*, and *South Asian Review* and in an anthology, *Violence and the Body: Race, Gender and the State* (Indiana University Press, 2003).

Tina Lynn Powell is a Ph.D. candidate in American literature at Fordham University in the Bronx, New York. Her dissertation is on Vietnamese American narratives and American tropes and motifs. She received her M.A. from Florida State University and her B.A. from Lehigh University.

Cathy J. Schlund-Vials is an assistant professor of English and Asian American studies at the University of Connecticut at Storrs where she is associate director of the Asian American Studies Institute. Her research interests include refugee cultural production, critical race theory, and contemporary literary studies. Her first book, *Modeling Citizenship: Jewish and Asian American Writing* (Temple University Press, forthcoming) focuses on the interplay between naturalization, immigration policy, and immigrant writing. She is currently completing another book, *Resistive Memory: Cambodia American Memory Work and Genocide Remembrance* (University of Minnesota Press, forthcoming).

Silvia Schultermandl is an assistant professor of American studies at the University of Graz, Austria where she teaches courses on American literature and cultural studies. She has published widely on contemporary American literature including ethnic American literature, canonicity, and 9/11. She is the author of *Transnational Matrilineage: Mother-Daughter Relationships in Asian American Literature* (LIT Verlag, 2009). Together with Erin Kenny (Drury University), she is the co-editor of LIT Verlag's book series "Contributions to Transnational Feminism."

Marie-Therese C. Sulit is an assistant professor of English at Mount Saint Mary College. She has contributed book chapters on contemporary women writers of the Philippine diaspora to *Pinay Power: Theorizing the Filipina/American Experience* (2005) and *National, Communal and Personal Voices in Asian America and the Asian Diaspora* (2005). She also has published on the role of service-learning in literature courses in the journal *Pedagogy* (2007) and the anthology *Community-Based Learning and Literary Matters* (2007).

Pei-Ju Wu is an assistant professor at Huafan University in Taiwan. She received her Ph.D. from the University of Southern Carolina in 2009. As a former Fulbright scholar, she specializes in identity discourses, cosmopolitanism, and travel in twentieth-century novels. Her current project is a book tentatively entitled *Cosmopolitan Identity: Toward a Literary Theory of Migration and Cultural Imagination*.

INDEX

Abe, Shinzo 21
abuse 2, 26, 32, 34, 35, 38, 39, 41, 74, 75, 77, 79, 139, 140, 188; *see also* domestic violence
Ackerman, Robert Alan 104
Adams, Carol 160–61
agency 4, 12, 17, 18, 19, 21, 34, 69, 74, 131, 145, 147, 192; female 4, 9, 19, 63–64, 65
agents 17, 18, 107, 145
Ah Sin 107, 115n9
Ahn Chang-ho, Yu Gwan-sun 64, 77, 80n1
Akutagawa, Ryunosuke 42n2
alienation 3, 14, 41, 53, 93, 124
aliens 3, 27, 30, 34, 38, 39, 43n11, 107, 147, 149, 172, 216
alternative kinships 28
ambiguity 3, 31, 56, 171, 192
America Is in the Heart 33
American Dream 20–21, 120, 122, 130, 156
American Town 23n10
Americanization 52, 53
amnesia 64, 73, 75, 79, 118, 120
Anderson, Benedict 82, 100n16
Angkor Wat 3, 46, 47, 48, 53, 60n4, 61n8
Anzaldúa, Gloria 30, 100n10, 214, 217n3
appropriations 2, 10, 13, 15, 19, 20, 21, 22n3, 89, 137, 139, 145, 148, 205
Articulate Silences: Hisaye Yamamoto, Maxine Hong Kingston, Joy Kogawa 131
Asian North American 2, 3, 26, 29, 34, 35, 38
Asianness 30, 113
assassin 181, 190
assassination 68
assimilation 29, 34, 54, 55, 67, 89, 119, 127, 164
Australia 83, 84, 85, 92, 97, 99n2, 99n3, 173, 174
authenticity 11, 12, 15, 21, 62n14, 216
autobiography 32, 58, 61n8, 97, 214

babaylan 4, 82, 87, 88, 89, 91, 92–95, 97, 98, 100n6, 100n7, 100n14; *see also catalonon*
Bandit Queen 6, 187, 188, 190, 191, 193, 194, 196; *see also* Phoolan Devi
The Bandit Queen (film) 6, 188, 189, 193, 194, 196, 201n1
The Bandit Queen of India: An Indian Woman's Amazing Journey from Peasant to International Legend 6, 188
Bankston, Carl L. 149n2
Barthes, Roland 15
beauty 5, 48, 119, 169, 174, 175, 176, 208
Benhabib, Seyla 210, 212
Bhabha, Homi 91, 100n13, 191
Bildungsroman 3, 11, 22n3, 26, 51, 52
biography 6, 66, 114, 188, 189, 193
birth 33, 63, 65, 66, 74, 106, 136, 170, 205, 216, 217
The Birth of Vietnam 150n4, 150n5, 150n6
birthmark 20
birthmother 11, 18
The Black Rose (film) 179–80
Black Skin, White Masks 191
Blue Dragon, White Tiger 149n3
Bobis, Merlinda 4, 82–102
The Body in Pain 68, 70
Bone 115n12
A Book of Her Own 92
Bordwell, David 181, 182n12
Brewer, Carolyn 88–89, 100n6
Buddhism 53
Bu-ja, Choi Lee 74, 80n5
Bulosan, Carlos 33, 119

Cambodian American 3, 46–62
Cao, Lan 5, 135, 156, 144–49; *see also Monkey Bridge*
Carbó, Nick 88, 89, 90, 91
Caruth, Cathy 130
caste 6, 188, 189, 190, 191–95, 197, 198, 200, 201; *see also* untouchable

catalonan 4, 82, 87, 88, 89, 91, 92–95, 97, 98, 100n6, 100n7; *see also* babaylan
Catholicism 87, 88, 100n18, 154, 160, 161, 164; Catholic church 89
Cha, Theresa 3, 4, 63–81; *see also Dictée*
Challenges to the Inner Room 92
Chan, Jackie 180
Chan, Sucheng 149n2
Chandler, David 47, 50, 60n1
Chau, Phan Boi 137
Chen, Tina 22n1, 107, 111
Cheng Pei Pei 168, 178, 182n11
Cheung, King-kok 28, 29, 33, 127, 131
Cheung, Maggie 168, 169, 171, 174–77, 181
Chhang, Youk 46, 48, 51, 59, 60, 62n15
childhood 26, 31, 32, 36, 189, 199
Chin, Frank 40, 104, 111, 114n8, 115n14
Chin, Mikyung 78
Chin, Tung Pok 115n12
China Men 115n12
Chinese American 6, 34, 36, 104–13, 169, 170, 187, 204, 215, 217, 217n1; identities 4, 104, 109, 111, 112, 216; mythology 4, 110, 114n4, 114n7; women 13, 22n6, 187
Chinese Exclusion Act 107, 115n12, 187
Chinese swordswomen 6, 168, 169, 170, 171, 172, 174, 176, 179, 181
chingada 5, 154, 155, 159, 160, 163, 164
Chinh, Phung Thi 135, 136, 137, 139, 140
Chow, Rey 6, 181, 203, 204
Christ 40, 68, 70; *see also* Christianity
Christianity 64, 100n18; *see also* Christ
Christopher, Renny 135, 140, 149n1, 150n8
citizenship 42n7, 49, 50, 53, 60, 144
Cixous, Hélène 127, 217n1
CLIO HISTORY 65–66, 68, 70, 71
Code of Manu 193–94, 200
Cold War 51
colonialism 11, 30, 88, 124, 125, 201n3; *see also* colonization
colonization 61n8, 89, 104, 114, 154, 155, 159, 199, 203; *see also* colonialism
Come Drink with Me (film) 178, 180
comfort camps 17, 20
Comfort Woman 2, 9, 10, 12, 14, 15, 16–18, 22n1, 22n3; *see also* Keller, Nora Okja
comfort women 16, 17, 21, 80n5, 18
coming-of-age 3, 50, 51, 52
commodification 16, 121
community 2, 4, 10, 11, 12, 36, 64, 74, 84, 88, 89, 96, 100n14, 100n17, 106, 109, 113, 124, 160, 169, 170, 171, 172, 177, 178, 182n4, 191, 192, 212, 213, 216, 218n6
Confucian family 34
Contentious Traditions: The Debate on Sati in Colonial India 79
Corliss, Richard 171

Crouching Tiger, Hidden Dragon 6, 168, 170, 172, 173, 174, 176, 182n3, 182n7, 182n11; *see also* Lee, Ang
Cruz, Jhong De La 165n6
Cuny, Marie-Therese 188

Dalit 201n2
Davis, Rocío G. 6, 22n2
decolonization 22n3, 91, 93, 97, 98
defiance 18
deities 41, 111, 128, 129
DeKoven, Marianne 192
Deleuze, Gilles 85, 93, 100n15
Democratic Kampuchea (Cambodia) 47, 48, 49, 50, 56, 57, 61n4, 61n5
destiny 119, 143
diaspora 28, 91, 100n20, 118, 125, 127, 203, 207, 215; Asian 1, 2, 3, 7; Chinese 169, 173; Philippine 92, 98, 99
Dictée 3, 63, 65–73, 75, 76; *see also* Cha, Theresa
Dinh, Tran Van 149n3
Disney 53, 110
Do, Hien Duc 149n2
domestic violence 2, 26; *see also* abuse
Donald Duk 111
Double Agency: Acts of Impersonation in Asian American Literature and Culture 22n1
dragon king 50
dragon princesses 3, 46, 50, 52, 53, 60
Duch (Kaing Guev Eak) 47, 61n5

Eat a Bowl of Tea (film) 187
Ebhiara, May 54
Edwards, Louise 80n4
Enloe, Cynthia 152, 154
epic 27, 33, 50, 72, 78, 85, 119, 122, 171, 194
ethnicity 1, 2, 22n2, 113, 114n2
Ezell, Margaret 42n1

Fa Mu Lan 4, 38, 42n3, 104, 105, 110, 111, 112, 113, 114n3, 205; *see also* Mulan
Fanon, Frantz 191
Farewell to Manzanar 27
femininity 12, 80n4
feminist funerals 3, 64–65, 70, 71, 73, 74, 79, 80n5
femme fatale 171, 172, 177
fetishism 86, 90, 91, 92
Fifth Chinese Daughter 26
filial piety 5, 16, 65, 67, 74, 132, 137, 139
filiality 33
First They Killed My Father: A Daughter of Cambodia Remembers 49, 55, 56, 62n14; *see also* Ung, Luong

fixity 103
fluidity 6, 42n1, 114, 169, 206
FOB (Fresh Off the Boat) 105, 106, 107, 108, 114
FOB 4, 104, 105, 107, 109, 110, 111, 113, 114; see also Hwang, David Henry
folklore 4, 27, 83, 122, 145; folktales 12, 22n7
Fox Girl 10, 11, 12, 15, 16, 18–19, 20, 21
Fox Girl 2, 9, 10, 11, 12, 18–19, 22n3; see also Keller, Nora Okja
freedom fighter 4, 67
Freeman, Carla 21
Freeman, James 135

Gee, Pop 104, 111, 115n14
gender 2, 6, 10, 19, 22n2, 29, 30, 42n4, 51, 52, 64, 65, 74, 76, 77, 78, 80n4, 106, 112, 114n2, 122, 137, 141, 164, 170, 172, 177, 178, 187, 188, 189, 190, 193, 194, 196; crossing 32; politics 4, 87–90, 104; and sexuality 1, 2
genocide 46, 47, 48, 49, 55, 57, 58, 59, 61n4, 61n5, 61n6, 62n13
gestation 33, 41
globalization 1, 10, 18, 21, 92, 169, 179, 187
Goellnicht, Donald C. 29
Gold Mountain 108–09, 115n10
Gone with the Wind 141–43
Gotanda, Philip Kan 91
Goto, Hiromi 2, 3, 26–38, 41, 42n1, 42n2
Grass Roof, Tin Roof 5, 135, 141; see also Strom, Dao
Greenblatt, Stephen 203
Gregory, Horace 205
Grewal, Inderpal 6, 203, 204
Growing up American: How Vietnamese Children Adapt to Life in the U.S. 149n2
Guattari, Félix 93, 100n15
Gwan Gung 4, 104, 105, 110–13, 114n3

Haewon, Kim 64, 75, 80n1
hagiographies 68
Hall, Stuart 216
Han, Jongwoo 78
hapa 9, 10
Harris, Lisa 41, 42n1
Harte, Bret 107
Harvey, David 178
Hawai'i 124, 207
Hayslip, Le Ly 5, 135, 136, 138–41, 144, 150n8; see also *When Heaven and Earth Changed Places*
healers 4, 37, 92
Hearts of Sorrow 135
hegemony 30, 68, 100n9

Hero (film) 6, 168, 169, 170, 171 173–75
heroes 33, 36, 38, 71, 72, 133, 137, 139, 162, 170, 172, 178, 181, 182n12
Heroine Feifei (film) 177
heroines 5, 42n3, 50, 59, 66, 130, 131, 139, 146, 154, 162, 172, 174, 175, 179, 181, 182n12
heroism 27, 42n3, 50, 59, 60, 65, 142, 171
Hinduism 189, 190, 195, 198, 200
Hippolyta 42n3
histories 2, 5, 6, 18, 29, 37, 49, 71, 72, 79, 95, 111, 115, 119, 125, 129, 135, 150n6, 173, 189, 204; American 21, 148, 182n4; Cambodian 47, 48, 50, 60n4, 61n5; Chinese 6, 13, 168; Chinese American 104, 105, 108, 109, 110, 112; family 6, 7, 16, 145, 149, 150n4, 217; Indian 188, 190, 192, 193, 195–98, 199, 200, 201; Korean 2, 4, 10, 11, 16, 17, 65–67, 74–75, 80n2; Philippine 4, 83, 87, 89, 92, 94, 98, 99, 154, 155; Vietnamese 5, 136, 137, 139, 142, 145, 146, 147, 150n7
Hollywood 148, 168, 169, 172, 173, 174, 175, 176, 179, 181, 182, 182n6, 182n9
homeland 40, 120, 125, 135, 138, 140, 145, 212
Hong, Terry 9, 10
House of Flying Daggers 6, 168, 169, 170, 171, 173–76
The House of Sleeping Beauties 115n13
Houston, James 27
Houston, Jeanne Wakatsuki 27
Huggan, Graham 85, 86, 87, 90, 91, 99n4, 99n5
human rights 47, 49
Huynh, Jade Ngoc Quang 135
Hwang, David Henry 4, 103; and *FOB* 104–17; and *M. Butterfly* 91, 103–04
Hwang, Keum-ja 17
hybridity 4, 42n6, 95, 104, 114n2, 155, 191, 192, 203
hybridization 2, 10

Imagining the Nation in Four Philippine Novels 99n1
immigrants 1, 2, 5, 20, 26, 27, 28, 29, 30, 34, 39, 43n11, 105, 106, 107, 108, 111, 114n7, 118, 119, 120, 124, 125, 126, 128, 134, 148, 157; Asian 33, 35, 36, 204, 205; Chinese 105, 108, 109, 115n12, 187; newcomers 4, 104, 106; women 21, 122, 123, 127, 133, 210
immigration 5, 10, 18, 21, 22n1, 105, 107, 108, 112, 114n8, 115n12, 153, 170
imperialism 4, 29, 70, 88, 92, 103, 104, 125, 192
impersonation 22n1, 109, 113

In the American Grain 205
Indian goddess 6, 189, 196, 197
An Introduction to Women's Studies: Gender in a Transnational World 203
Irigaray, Luce 127, 192, 209
Issei 31

Jane Bond 179–80, 183n13
Japanese Canadian 2, 26, 29
Jasmine 4, 5, 118–33; see also Muhkerjee, Bharati
Joan of Arc 42n3, 63, 67, 73, 80n3, 214
The Joy Luck Club (film) 187
Joyce, James 213, 218n4
Judou 174

Kain, Geoffrey 134
Kantada ng Babing Mandirang Daragang Magayon 85
Kaplan, Caren 6, 203, 204
Kapoor, Shekar 6, 188, 192
kappa 3, 27, 29, 30, 31, 32, 33, 34, 36, 37, 39, 40, 41, 42n2
The Kappa Child 2, 3, 26–45; see also Goto, Hiromi
Keller, Nora Okja 2, 9–25; see also *Comfort Woman*; *Fox Girl*
Khmer Rouge 46, 47, 48, 49, 50, 51, 52, 53, 55, 56, 57, 58, 60, 60n2, 61n5, 61n6, 61n7, 61n9, 61n10, 62n12, 62n13
the Killing Field 49, 52, 54, 57
Kim, Elaine H. 65, 80n2
Kingston, Maxine Hong 6–7, 12–13, 28, 40, 80n4, 104, 110, 111, 114n4, 115n12, 120, 203–19; see also *The Woman Warrior*
The Kissing (The White Turtle) 83
Kondo, Dorinne 114n6
Koppelman, Susan 37
Korean American 42n3, 77, 78, 79; Korean War 18; women 9, 10, 67, 79
Korean Independence Movement 4, 63, 65, 70, 75, 77, 78
Korteweg, Anna 78
Kristeva, Julia 5, 125–27

La Malinche 154–55, 159, 160, 164; see also Mexican Eve
Lac lords 136, 149n4
Lam, Mai 47
Lappas, Catherine 207
Lau, Andy 169, 181
Ledgerwood, Judy 54
Lee, Ang 168, 169, 173
Lee, Coco 173
Lee, Erika 82
Lee, Jong Kun 23n9

Lee, Ken-fang 172
Lee, Sung-Ae 11, 15
Lee, Young-Oak 9
legacies 11, 16, 17, 21, 48, 55, 61n9, 182n10
legends 5, 11, 12, 13, 15, 17, 18, 21, 22n7, 50, 135, 136, 137, 138, 139, 140, 143, 144, 146, 149, 150n5, 188
Leung, Tony Chiu-Wai 169, 171, 182n8
Lew, Walter 3, 65, 71
Lim, Shirley Geok-lin 5, 118–19
Ling, Amy 206, 218n5
Ling, L. H. M. 78
Literary Gestures: Aesthetics in a Multicultural Age 22n2
Little House on the Prairie 32
Lone, John 113
Lorde, Audre 100n9
Lowe, Lisa 28, 67, 69, 114n2, 148, 216
Lucky Child: A Daughter of Cambodia Reunites with the Sister She Left Behind 3, 46–62; see also Ung, Luong
Ludwig, Sämi 6
Lum, Darrell 114n8
Lyons, Bonnie 110, 114n6

M. Butterfly 91, 103–04, 114, 114n1
Madame Ngo Dinh Nhu 139
Madsen, Deborah L. 23n10
Mahabharata 194
La Malinche 154–55, 159, 160, 164; see also Mexican Eve
Mananzan, Mary Sr. 87, 92, 96, 97, 98, 100n18, 100n19
Mani, Lata 79
marginalization 21, 63, 76, 80
Mariano, L. Joyce 100n17
marketplace 4, 82, 83, 97, 119, 188
Marr, David G. 137
martial arts 6, 168, 171, 172, 173, 176, 177, 179, 180, 182n6, 182n7, 182n10, 182n11, 183n14
Martinez-Sicat, Maria Teresa 99n1
martyrdom 64, 68, 75; see also martyrs
martyrs 3, 63, 67, 68, 69, 70, 72, 74, 75, 79, 160; see also martyrdom
masculinity 33
media 2, 6, 51, 57, 61n7, 64, 73, 114n3, 131, 142, 146, 147, 148, 153, 157, 163, 170, 204
memorialization 48, 59, 60
memory 12, 14, 17, 47, 52, 56, 57, 59, 61n6, 65, 72, 77, 120, 145, 148, 192, 205, 210; cultural 5, 118, 123, 124, 125, 127–30; historical 73, 118
mestizo 154, 155, 156, 158
Mexican Eve 160, 164; see also La Malinche
Meyer, Carla 170

militarism 11; *see also* militarization
militarization 5, 152, 153, 163; *see also* militarism
military brothel 12; *see also* military prostitution
military prostitution 152, 164; *see also* military brothel; prostitution
missionary 21, 63, 66, 71, 73
mobility 21, 28, 180, 203, 204
modernity 5, 92, 153, 169, 178, 179–80, 187
Mohanty, Chandra Talpade 6, 203, 204
Monkey Bridge 5, 135, 144, 149; *see also* Cao, Lan
Monroe, Marilyn 175
monstrosity 34, 39
monumentalization 48, 59, 60
Moon, Katherine 165n3
Moon, Seungsook 78, 80n6
Moraga, Cherrié 159, 217n3
morality 5, 153, 193
Morris, Gary 171
Morrison, Toni 207
Mortland, Carol 54
mother-daughter relationships 14, 206, 214
Mukherjee, Bharati 4–5, 118–33; *see also Jasmine*
Mulan 64, 80n4, 114n3; *see also* Fa Mu Lan
Mulan 110
Mulan II 110
multiplicity 4, 10, 42n1, 103, 104, 109, 204
mythologies 4, 9, 13, 21, 42n9, 71, 89, 104, 110, 114n4, 144, 197; *see also* myths
myths 2, 4, 9, 10, 22n7, 23n9, 28, 42n9, 70, 71, 72, 108, 110, 111, 112, 115n13, 129, 132, 155, 159, 164, 195, 205, 207, 216; Cambodian 49–50; Japanese 3, 29–33; Korean 2, 9–20, 80; Philippine 87–88, 89, 93, 94; Vietnamese 137–38, 145, 146, 147, 150n7; *see also* mythologies

Najmi, Samina 22n3
nation-building 3, 48, 52, 187
nation-state 1, 48, 49, 52, 59, 61n8, 96
nationalism 29, 60, 63, 66, 67, 68, 71, 73, 75, 80n5, 129, 188
necessity 92, 93, 121, 124, 207
New Economy 21
Ng, Fae Myenne 115n12
Nguyen, Bich Minh 135
Nguyen, Viet Thanh 139
9/11 152
Nisei 38
Noble, Margaret 129
nuclear family 35, 121

obituary 16
Okasan 27, 32, 36, 37, 38, 43n11
Oranges Are Lucky 114n8
Orientalism 22n2, 109, 120, 169
otherness 43n11, 92

palimpsest 75, 203, 205, 209, 210, 213–17
panethnicity 42n6, 100n12
Paper Son: One Man's Story 115n12
paper sons 108, 109, 115n12
Papp, Joseph 104, 113
Partnoy, Alicia 212
patriarchy 11, 12, 28, 38, 155, 159, 178, 180, 199, 200, 201
patriotism 5, 67, 77, 137, 138
passivity 32, 154
Pau, Peter 173
Paz, Octavio 154, 155, 164
Pearson, Wendy 28, 43n11
Pelley, Patricia M. 150n7
performances 2, 15, 17, 61n5, 84, 93, 94, 104, 113, 114, 170, 175
Persephone 71, 72, 73
Phoolan Devi 6, 187–202; *see also* Bandit Queen
Pol Pot 47, 51, 61n6, 62n13
politics of location 2, 9
A Portrait of the Artist as a Young Man 213
positionality 87, 119
Postcolonial Vietnam 150n7
postcolonialism 86, 99n4
Princess Pari 10, 15, 16, 17, 18, 20, 21
prostitution 23n10, 93, 139, 152, 153, 162, 164; *see also* military prostitution

race 1, 2, 30, 43, 41, 119, 155, 156, 161, 180, 191
Radhakrishnan, R. 216
Raise the Red Lantern 174
Raiskin, Judith 30
Ramayana 194–95
Rambali, Paul 188
rape 5, 127, 129, 136, 140, 152–67, 189–90, 191, 193, 194, 198
Rashomon 42n2
Ray, Raka 78
Ray, Satyajit 187
rebirth 123, 128, 129, 130
reconciliation 3, 48, 49, 50, 54, 58, 59, 61n5, 138
The Records of the Three Kingdoms 111
redeparture 67, 72
representations 2, 4, 6, 10, 11, 15, 16, 22n5, 64, 65, 66, 67, 68, 69, 70, 71, 73, 75, 76, 77, 78, 79, 91, 110, 114n6, 118, 127, 135,

141, 142, 145, 146, 150n7, 169, 172, 206, 217; media 2, 6; theatrical 104, 107
the Republic of Viet Nam (RVN) 134, 139, 141, 143
Reuter, Fr. 160–61, 164
revisions 4, 13, 63, 64, 68, 70, 71, 73, 79, 142, 200
Rich and Strange: Gender, History, Modernism 192
Ricoeur, Paul 14
rituals 16, 64, 71, 73, 100n11, 126, 129, 170, 199
romance 83, 85, 141, 142, 170, 171
The Romance of the Three Kingdoms 111
Rothrock, Cynthia 183n14
Rutledge, Paul 149n2

Sach, Thi 136
Saja 16
San Juan, E. Jr. 33, 91, 100n12
Santa Ana, Jeffrey J. 2
Santoli, Al 135
Savran, David 115n13
Scarry, Elaine 68, 70
Schamus, James 169, 173
Schiller, Nina Glick 1
selfhood 3, 26, 49, 50, 52, 55, 56, 59, 140, 205, 206, 217
self-sacrifice 4, 63, 64, 68, 70, 74, 77, 79, 171
sex industry 11, 18, 20, 21, 23n8, 23n10; sex slaves 17, 18; sex workers 10, 11, 20, 21, 23n10, 74, 80n5, 93, 152; *see also* prostitution
sexism 13, 103, 119, 153
sexual labor 16, 19, 20, 21
sexual oppression 17, 20, 21
sexuality 1, 2, 30, 31, 159, 160, 176, 191–94, 197
shamanism 2, 9, 10, 22n1; shamans 2, 9, 10, 82, 87, 88
Shibusawa, Naoko 82
Shih, Shu-mei 210
Simmel, Georg 178
slavery 22n1, 23n8, 190, 199
Smith, Sidonie 207, 217n3
The Sound of a Voice 115n13
Sources of the Self 211
South Asian American 121
South Wind Changing 135
sovereignty 5, 50, 153–54, 156, 159, 162, 163, 164
spirituality 4, 87–92, 100n11
Spong, John Shelby 100n18
storytelling 2, 9, 12, 14, 15, 17, 79, 84, 111, 112, 142, 208, 209, 210, 212
Strangers from a Different Shore: A History of Asian Americans 115n11

Strobel, Leny Mendoza 92, 96, 98
Strom, Dao 5, 135–36, 141, 144, 149
subjectivity 2, 10, 13, 51, 63, 67, 70, 100n9, 100n12, 103, 125, 135, 136, 141, 142, 144, 149, 217
subversion 19, 66, 80n4, 143, 172
Suedfeld, Peter 68
survival 11, 17, 18, 31, 60, 64, 70, 89; immigrant 2, 26, 48, 127, 129, 130, 196
swordswomen 6, 168, 169–72, 174, 176, 178–81

Tadiar, Neferti 156
Takaki, Ronald 115n11, 149n2
The Tale of Kieu 139
talk-stories 206, 207, 214
Tan Dun 173
Taylor, Charles 175, 211, 212
Taylor, Keith Weller 136, 150n4
Thang, Pham Huy 137
Third World 3, 20, 28, 96
thúy, lê thi diem 135
Tilley, Maureen 68–70, 79
Tiongson, Nick 157
To Bear Any Burden 135
torture 4, 47, 63–70, 74–77, 89, 198
transformations 1, 36, 42n6, 64, 65, 77, 78, 106, 127–30, 178, 203, 205, 218n3
translation 46, 61n11, 71, 75, 84, 85, 86, 87, 90, 95, 97, 115n10, 165n5, 204, 205, 206, 207, 213
transnational Chinese cinema 188
transnational feminism 1, 6, 7, 203
transnationalism 1, 3, 5, 28, 29, 30, 42n4, 104, 134, 170, 188; transnationality 105
trauma 14, 26 27, 32, 34, 48, 52, 59, 62n9, 125, 127, 130, 136, 138, 139, 140, 144, 145, 147, 164, 207
tribes 27, 94
Trinh, Minh-ha T. 67, 69, 133, 205, 206
Tripmaster Monkey: His Fake Book 111
Trung sisters (Tung Trac, Trung Nhi, Hai Ba Trung) 5, 134–51
Ts'ai Yen 205, 206, 216, 217
Tsui Hark 173, 181
Tuol Sleng 2, 46–48, 60n3, 60n4, 61n5
Twain, Mark 107
Ty, Eleanor 29

U.N./Cambodian Khmer Rouge Tribunal (Extraordinary Chambers in the Courts of Cambodia) 47
Unclaimed Experience 130
Ung, Loung 3, 46–62
untouchable 189, 190, 194, 201n2; *see also* caste
Ursua, Evalyn 161

validity 14, 21, 33, 157
verdict 14, 161
victims 3, 21, 41, 47, 48, 61n5, 61n5, 61n9, 70, 74, 80n5, 106, 135, 139, 154, 156, 165n2; victimhood 38, 59, 139; victimization 21, 187, 188
Viet Cong 138–41, 143, 145
The Viet Nam War/The American War 135
Vietnam War 5, 51, 135, 147, 141, 142, 143, 145, 146, 150n8, 207
Vietnamese American 5, 134, 135, 141, 144, 146, 148, 149
The Vietnamese American 1.5 Generation 149n2
The Vietnamese Americans 149n2
The Vietnamese Experience in America 149n2
visionary 4, 92
Visiting Forces Agreement (VFA) 153–54, 162–64
Visuality and Identity 210
voyeurism 48

Wang, Wayne 187
warlord 94
warrior women 3, 5, 27, 30, 38, 41, 172, 183n14, 198, 201
When Heaven and Earth Changed Places 5, 135, 138–41; *see also* Hayslip, Le Ly
Wilder, Laura Ingalls 32

Williams, William Carlos 205
Woman, Native, Other 133, 206
The Woman Warrior: Memoirs of a Girlhood among Ghosts 6, 40, 80n4, 104, 110, 203–19
womanhood 3, 5, 11, 52, 137, 142, 205, 206
Women in the Trees: U.S. Women's Short Stories about Bettering and Resistance 37–38
The Women's News (Korea) 64, 74, 75, 77, 80n5
Wong, Jade Snow 26
Wong, Kar-wai 171, 173
Wong, Sau-ling C. 2, 7n1, 22n6, 217n1
Woo, John 173, 181
World War I 192
World War II 21, 152
worship 2, 3, 111, 129, 146, 200
wudan 168, 172

Yankee Dawg You Die 91
Year of the Dragon 114n8
Yeoh, Michelle 168, 169, 181
Yu, Guan Soon 3–4, 63–81
Yuen, Woo-ping 173

Zhang, Yimou 171, 173, 174, 187
Zhang, Ziyi 168, 169, 174–77, 182n3
Zhou, Min 149n2
Zia, Helen 34

www.ingramcontent.com/pod-product-compliance
Ingram Content Group UK Ltd.
Pitfield, Milton Keynes, MK11 3LW, UK
UKHW041946140426
5217IPUK00014B/675